THE LIBRARY
RY'S COLLEGE OF MARYLAND
RY'S CITY, MARYLAND 20686

DATA BASE MANAGEMENT

IFIP Working Conference on
Data Base Management
Cargèse, Corsica, France, 1-5 April, 1974

organized by
IFIP Technical Committee 2, Programming
International Federation for Information Processing

Program Committee
J. R. Abrial,   J. C. Boussard,   G. Bracchi,   E. F. Codd,   C. Date,   D. Jardine,
J. W. Klimbie, K. L. Koffeman, B. Langefors, G. M. Nijssen (Chairman),
M. E. Senko,   T. B. Steel Jr.,   H. J. Schneider,   W. M. Turski

1974

NORTH-HOLLAND PUBLISHING COMPANY – AMSTERDAM • LONDON
AMERICAN ELSEVIER PUBLISHING COMPANY, INC. – NEW YORK

DATA BASE MANAGEMENT

Proceedings of the
IFIP Working Conference on
Data Base Management

edited by

J. W. KLIMBIE
ISA-Philips Nederland B.V.

and

K. L. KOFFEMAN
Corporate ISA Department
N.V. Philips' Gloeilampenfabrieken,
Eindhoven, The Netherlands

1974

NORTH-HOLLAND PUBLISHING COMPANY – AMSTERDAM • LONDON
AMERICAN ELSEVIER PUBLISHING COMPANY, INC. – NEW YORK

© IFIP, 1974

All Rights Reserved. No part of this publication may be reproduced, stored in a
retrieval system, or transmitted, in any form or by any means, electronic, mechanical,
photocopying, recording or otherwise, without the prior permission of the copyright
owner.

Library of Congress Catalog Card number: 74-81831
North-Holland ISBN: 0 7204 2809 2
American Elsevier ISBN: 0 444 10704 5

Published by:
NORTH-HOLLAND PUBLISHING COMPANY — AMSTERDAM
NORTH-HOLLAND PUBLISHING COMPANY, LTD. — LONDON

Distributors for the U.S.A. and Canada:
American Elsevier Publishing Company, Inc.
52 Vanderbilt Avenue
New York, N.Y. 10017

PRINTED IN THE NETHERLANDS

CONTENTS

Contents

"One must never ask more of information
than it is capable of giving"
(freely adapted from Napoleon Bonaparte
born in Ajaccio, Corsica 1769)

Editor's Preface

Near the tiny town of Cargèse on the scented Island of Corsica in the
"Institute d'Etudes Scientifiques de Cargèse", the first IFIP TC-2 working
conference on data base management systems was held.

Over 60 participants from 12 countries were assembled from April 1-5 to
report to each other on the state of the art, to exchange ideas and to argue
about the different views.

The beauty of Corsica, the rural environment and the quietness of the
inhabitants contrasted very heavily with the cost-awareness and the
efficient scientific way of thinking of the participants. One became aware of
this conflict very soon, especially when the sun was shining brightly over the
sea.

Yet the working conference was very fruitful for everybody, and many new
initiatives have arisen from it.

In April 1973, on behalf of IFIP TC-2, a program committee was formed.
The P.C. requested over 50 persons to send papers for this working conference.
Many papers and abstracts were received, and evaluated on quality of content,
readability and relevance. On that basis papers were rejected, were accepted
for presentation only, or were accepted for both publication and presentation.

The papers included in this book are arranged according to the sequence of
presentation. Following each paper is a summary of the relevant discussion.
For each session a secretary was appointed (mostly P.C. members) to produce
this summary.
The summary was checked by the participants of that discussion.
The editors are indeed very obliged to the session secretaries for performing
their task so diligently. (The editors recommend this procedure for subsequent
working conferences, instead of trying to type out inaudible tape recordings).

The conference was organized perfectly by the local arrangements committee,
chaired by Professor BOUSSARD, Université de Nice. Our very active secretary
was Marie France HANSELER, Université de Paris.

The French universities provided their beautifully situated conference building
and made both time and enthusiasm of its employees available for technical
assistance:

Mme. ZONNEKEIN, M. FRASSON, M. GRATTAROLA, M. PARTOUCHE.

As editors of these proceedings we would like to express our gratitude to:

Ineke VAN DER HOEF, who, in practice, acted as Program Committee secretary
                 during the preparations of the Conference.

and to our secretaries and typists in Cargèse:

Margaret FONTAINE, Brigitte GELY, Isabelle GRAND-DUFFAY, Lynn ROBINSON.

Knowledge in the field of database management is evolving very fast:
a state-of-the-art report is therefore very bounded in time, so in the
opinion of the editors, such a report must be published as soon as possible.
In some cases typografical quality (different letter types e.g.) was
sacrified to achieve the aim of an early publication.

                                                    J.W.Klimbie

                                                    K.L.Koffeman

Data Base Management, J. W. Klimbie and K. L. Koffeman, (eds.)
©North-Holland Publishing Company (1974)

DATA SEMANTICS

J.R. ABRIAL
Laboratoire d'Informatique
Université Scientifique et Médicale de Grenoble, France

Foreword

It is the author's opinion that in all the "Generalized Data Base Management Systems" [2] the so called "logical" definition and manipulation of data are still influenced (sometimes unconsciously) by the "physical" storage and retrieval mechanisms currently available on computer systems.

This situation has been very well emphasized by E.F. CODD [3] who has developed a relational model for describing and utilizing "large shared Data Banks". The Basis of his model is the (mathematical) n-ary relation.

At the same time, several people, working in the Artificial Intelligence area, discovered that after the realization of several ad hoc systems [4] for describing "facts and events" there was a very strong need for a general formalism for "semantic information processing". C. HEWWIT [1] was one of the first among these people. The Basis of all these formalisms ([1] , [6] , [13]) is the notion of pattern, pattern matching and the pattern matching procedure invocation method (rather than claiming what to do one proposes only a "goal" that can be eventually achieved by different methods).

The present paper comes out of the large confluence of these three streams.

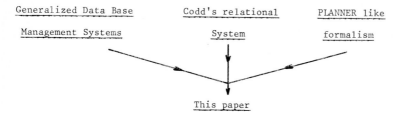

There is of course a difficulty when a person has been influenced too much by different sources : the people belonging to them will claim that this person did not understand what they were doing and that the net result is a kind of a "pot pourri" They are probably right ...!

The paper comprises six main sections. After a rather philosophical introduction (section 1), we describe informally (section 2) the general model for defining Data Base Semantics ; a complete example (section 3) is then developed before entering a rather tiring "formal" description (section 4). We then give some comments about a physical implementation (section 5) and terminate as usually with some "further investigations" (section 6).

Hint for the reader : if you are looking for a definition of the term "semantics", stop reading because there is no such definition in this paper.

1. INTRODUCTION

1.1. The Data Base as the model of a certain reality

The goal of this paper is to study the semantics of Data Bases.

We shall define a Data Base as the _model_ of an evolving physical world. The state of the model, at a given instant, represents the _knowledge_ it has acquired from this world. This knowledge may be grossly defined at different levels which are the following :

a) Elementary facts as for example :

John Taylor was born in New-York on November the first 1973.
The car whose number is 9611-TB-38 is a yellow car.
Socrates was a human being.

b) Simple rules as for example :

All men have, by necessity, at a given time, a marital status which may be one of the following : widower, married, single or divorced.
Every man has necessarily two parents of whom he is the child.
A car has (if any) only one owner which may be a person or an organization. Conversely a person or an organization may have zero, one or several cars.
A person has sometimes a spouse (and only one) and if x is the spouse of y then y is the spouse of x.

c) Some more elaborated rules as for example :

The sex of a person (as well as his birthdate) is not subject to any change.
If x is the spouse of y then the marital status of x and y is "married".
A single person who marries may not be single again in the future.
A person may not be, at a given time, in two different places.

d) Rules allowing one to deduce (or to compute) facts from others as for example :

The profit that one can make out of a product is the difference between the selling price and the buying price of the product.

Notice the use we have made of the words "necessarily" and "may". The knowledge of the model is always described by necessity and possibility : this has of course a strong connection with time.

On the other hand, the model is not the reality : it only has partial knowledge of it. When the model does not know a fact or a law about reality this does not mean that this fact or law does not exist ; this has a very important consequence which is the following : when the model has exactly the same knowledge of two objects this does not mean that they are the same object. Therefore when an object is entering the "perception field" of the model it must identify itself as a new object or an already known object. An easy way to do it is to give to any object a name which identifies it without ambiguity as for example a social security number for a person or a number for a car. Unfortunately it is not always possible (as an example, suppose we want to give to the model information about a letter) and this would require, in any case, an identification procedure which is outside the model.

For these reasons we prefer to give the model the responsibility of naming the objects by some internal mechanism (probably random) provided it is given externally the knowledge that an object is new for it. This, of course, does not exclude the possibility of an object having an externally given name (a synonym).

In order to describe precisely a physical object we need some measurement and therefore the notion of number : integer and real numbers will be necessary, but for some particular measure we will need also (for example) the concept of complex

numbers. Because some facts about objects need to be dated we will need also a time
measurement given (for example) by the (month, day, year) of an event.

Are these things (integers, complex numbers, dates) physical objects like the ones
we were speaking about before (cars, persons) ? It is meaningful to say that the
number "3" is a new object for the model, or that the complex number "4+5i" is
leaving the "perception field" of the model ? This makes the difference between
<u>concrete objects</u> entering and leaving the perception field of the model and
<u>abstract objects</u> whose "existence" is given once and for all. The description of an
object inside the model will be given by the <u>connections</u> it has with other objects
(abstract or concrete).

<u>Example</u> :

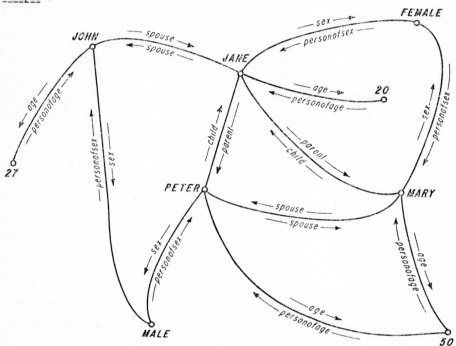

Each connection is labelled with the name of the two <u>access functions</u> which may be
eventually multivalued.

In the example above, we have the following :

        personofsex (MALE) = {JOHN, PETER}
        personofsex (FEMALE) = {JANE, MARY }
        age (JOHN) = {27 }
        personofage (50) = {PETER, MARY}
        child (PETER) = {JANE}
        parent (JANE) = {PETER, MARY}
        etc ..

The various objects of the above Data Base may be intuitively organized into different categories :

> JOHN, JANE, PETER, MARY are persons
> 27, 50, 20 are numbers
> MALE, FEMALE are sex.

Therefore we are able to abstract the structure of this example into the following:

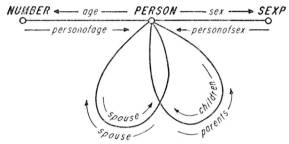

This structure can be further abstracted into the following :

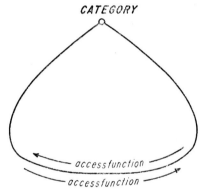

The brief description we have made so far seems to be convenient for describing a world of simple physical objects whose definition can be given by bidirectional connections (or binary relations). But, is it possible to use the same method when the connection itself requires some information ?

Example :

> PETER was invited by PAUL and JANE to PARIS on JULY the 15th of 1973
> JACK sold to HENRY a FORD CAR for 2000 $
> PROJECT P-130 ordered from supplier JOHN, 3 parts whose number is N-4250.

Here, n-ary relations seem to be more appropriate than binary relations. But we can still describe these facts in terms of connections by building three new categories i.e. invitation, purchase, and order and the following structures :

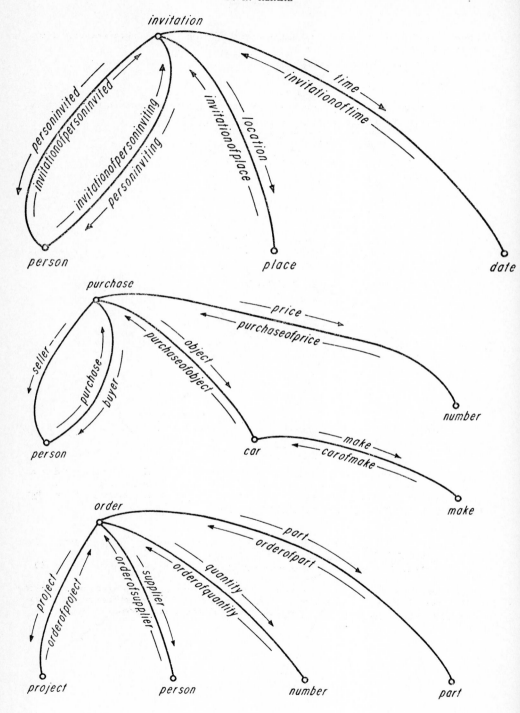

An example of such structures for the cases given above is the following :

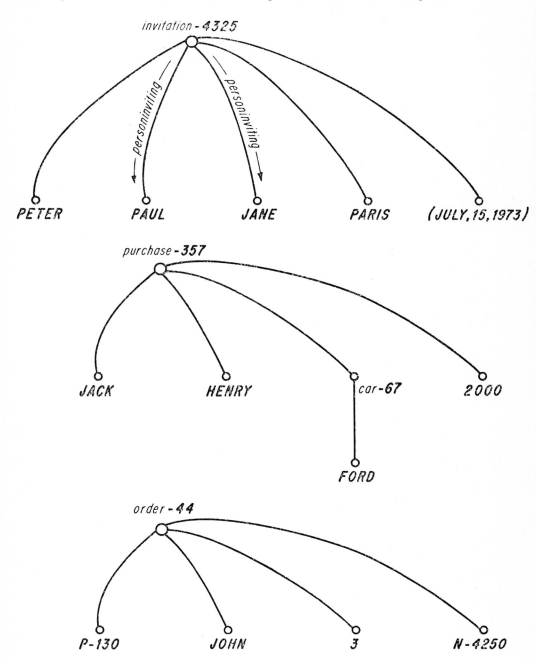

Notice that the names
    invitation-4325
    purchase-357
    order-44
    car-67
are purely internal names.

Notice also that the access functions personinviting is multivalued :
    personinviting (invitation-4325) = {PAUL, JANE}

At the risk of being considered a criminal, one can notice at once the difference
between this presentation and Codd's relational system [3] !...

We consider this more primitive level of description (binary relations and access
functions) to be more adequate for defining the semantics of a Data Base. In fact
we shall see in the next sections how this can be done by giving the properties of
the access functions (essentially their minimum and maximum cardinality) and also
how they can be partly or entirely described by programs when it is necessary
(validity, consistency, redundancy).

1.2. A Data Base, what for ?

Thanks to this model which a human being may interrogate, he is able to get information in an easier manner than by a direct inquiry in the real world.

But if the only usage of the model would have been this one, one could doubt its
real interest. In fact, the human being would like to extract information from the
model in order to modify the reality. Now, if the model has a sufficient knowledge
of the general laws of the reality it is possible to be able to deduce the consequences of a hypothetical modification of the real world, thereby helping the
human being to take decisions.

This requires that the model M be able to generate another model M' whose difference with M are some hypotheses : M' is the imagination of M. M' may also generate a
new model M", etc ..

1.3. How is the model able to give answers to some questions ?

As we have seen in section 1.1., the model acquires its knowledge from the real
world not only as elementary propositions but also from more elaborate rules. The
first question answering mechanism is therefore the one of giving back all the information it knows "by heart".

A second mechanism is to deduce (or compute) an answer from other facts thanks to
some ad hoc deduction rules (programs).

A third one is to store previously deduced information as if it had been entered
directly from the external world. This raises of course a difficult consistency
problem. This third mechanism is performed by "memofunctions" in POP-2 [5] .

As an example of these three mechanisms think of the way a human being gives an
answer to the three following questions :

    1 + 2 ?   by heart
    35 + 67 ?   by deduction (computation)
    35 + 67 ?   by memorizing the previous answer.

In fact these three mechanisms are organized as a hierarchy similar to a memory
hierarchy in a computer system :

First, see if you know the answer by heart, in case of failure try to deduce it by some appropriate rule (program) and in case of success keep the result for a while in case of a future identical question.

And in a virtual memory when looking for a virtual page :

first, look to see if the page is in central core memory (or eventually partly in the cache memory) if not, get it from the drum and in case of failure get it from the disk. When a page stays in central core memory, keep it there, according to a "replacement algorithm".

1.4. What are the characteristics which we may require from the model ?

a) To be able to evolve.

b) To be efficient.

Notice that these qualities are usually contradictory.

c) To be able to check (partially of course) the consistency of the information it acquires.

d) That the way of interrogating it, is independent of mechanism it uses to get the answer. This quality could be called "semantic data independence".

e) That it is capable of describing itself. This quality is somehow an indication of its generality. Notice that it is not only a "theoretical game" but could be also very useful in helping human beings to modify the model by asking for information about its own behavior.

In fact, it is this self description of the model that we are going to look at in the next sections.

2. INFORMAL DESCRIPTION OF THE MODEL

2.1. Categories

To give the model the knowledge that there now exists a new category we may use the operator "cat". To give an external name to a new category let's write for example :

person = cat

This new category has of course also an internal name given automatically by the model. To "create" a new object let us use the operator "generate" followed by the name of a category. For example :

generate person

If we want to give an external name while creating a new object one may use as above the symbol "=". For example :

john = generate person

"john", of course, cannot be the external name of another object. In this case we have a failure. Notice that the operator cat is equivalent to the expression :

generate category

where "category" is the external name of a certain category in the self description of the model (notice the metalinguistic difficulty).

Sometimes it is not necessary to give a newly created object a name but only a nickname : an identifier that may be reused later on for another object. Let's use in that case the symbol " ← ".

For example :

     x ← <u>generate</u> person

If, when evaluating that statement, x was already the nickname of another object, then we have no failure but a change in x's assignment.

When we wish to remove an object from the "perception field" of the model then we use the operator "kill". For example :

     "<u>kill</u> john" or "<u>kill</u> x"

2.2. Binary relations

As we have explained in section 1.1. a binary relation defines an <u>atomic link</u> between pairs of objects belonging to certain categories. While defining a relation one is giving names to the two access functions as well as the minimum and maximum cardinals of the sets they describe.

In section 1.1. we defined a structure with the following schema :

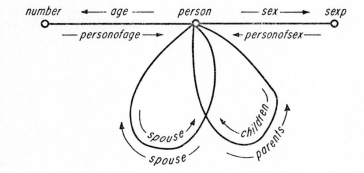

The formal description is the following :

    r1 = <u>rel</u>(person, sexp, sex = <u>afn</u> (1,1), personofsex = <u>afn</u> (0,∞))

    r2 = <u>rel</u>(person, number, age = <u>afn</u> (1,1), personofage = <u>afn</u> (0,∞))

    r3 = <u>rel</u>(person, person, spouse = <u>afn</u> (0,1), spouse)

    r4 = <u>rel</u>(person, person, parents = <u>afn</u> (2,2), children = <u>afn</u> (0,∞))

"<u>rel</u>" and "<u>afn</u>" are (like "<u>cat</u>") operators creating new relations and access functions.

While defining an access function one gives informations about its cardinality. For example in the above definition :

    a person has exactly one sex, one age and two parents, zero or one spouse, or any number of children (including zero).

While defining a relation one gives the categories involved, and one defines the two access functions (inverses of each other). Notice that the relation "r3" is symetric.

Mathematically speaking, an access function is a function which maps one category <u>into</u> the powerset of another (the set of all subsets).

If we define the following relation :

$$rel(C1,C2,f_{12} = afn(-,-),f_{21} = afn(-,-))$$

then we have

$$domain(f_{12}) = C1$$
$$range(f_{12}) \subseteq P(C2) \qquad (P \text{ is the usual symbol for } \underline{powersetof})$$
$$domain(f_{21}) = C2$$
$$range(f_{21}) \subseteq P(C1)$$
$$\text{and } \underline{inv}(f_{12}) = f_{21}$$
$$\underline{inv}(f_{21}) = f_{12}$$

Thanks to this operator "$\underline{inv}$", one need give an external name to only one access function.

When the maximum cardinal of an access function is 1 then it is a function (in the mathematical meaning of this word) and we have the following :

a) $\underline{rel}(C1,C2,f = \underline{afn}(-,1),afn(-,-)$

is equivalent to :

f is a function whose domain is C1 and range is C2

b) $\underline{rel}(C1,C2,f = \underline{afn}(1,1),\underline{afn}(0,\infty))$

is equivalent to :

f is a function from C1 into C2

c) $\underline{rel}(C1,C2,f = \underline{afn}(1,1),\underline{afn}(1,\infty))$

is equivalent to :

f is a function from C1 onto C2

d) $\underline{rel}(C1,C2,f = \underline{afn}(1,1),\underline{afn}(0,1))$

is equivalent to :

f maps C1 into C2

e) $\underline{rel}(C1,C2,f = \underline{afn}(1,1),\underline{afn}(1,1))$

is equivalent to :

f maps C1 onto C2

These mathematical definitions are taken from [9].

One very often encounters the case b) "in nature". It is the usual relation between an object and one of its properties.

<u>Example</u> :

$$\underline{rel}(person, sexp, sex = \underline{afn}(1,1), \underline{afn}(0,\infty))$$

The case d) is also very frequent for the relation between an object and a property identifying it unambiguously.

<u>Example</u> :

$$\underline{rel}(person, ss\#, socialsecuritynumber = \underline{afn}(1,1), \underline{afn}(0,1))$$

In case d) and e), "$\underline{inv}$(f)" is the (mathematical) inverse function of f.

Before closing this section let us give a special notation for the case where one of the two categories involved in a "$\underline{rel}$" has only one element. We then have a $\underline{unary}$ rather than a binary relation (or property). Let us use the operator "$\underline{prp}$" for this special case.

$\underline{Example}$:

> $\underline{prp}$(person, french(0,∞))

2.3. $\underline{Giving\ the\ model\ informations\ about\ relations\ or\ properties}$

To inform the model that, $\underline{from\ now\ on}$, a specific relation exists between two objects, we use the operator "$: \ni$".

$\underline{Example}$:

> parent(x) $:\ni$ y

means that, if x and y are names (or nicknames) of persons, y is a parent of x and equivalently, x is a child of y :

> child(y) $:\ni$ x

When using a "$\underline{prp}$" one writes for example :

> french $:\ni$ x

Formally :

> "f(x) $:\ni$ y" is equivalent to "$\underline{inv}$(f)(y) $:\ni$ x"

While interpreting such a statement the models checks :
> . if x and y belong to the correct categories
> . if the new proposed connection is allowed due to the maximum cardinality constraints.

If these conditions are negative, then the model refuses the statement with a $\underline{failure}$. Conversely, to inform the model that a specific relation does not hold $\underline{any\ more}$ between two objects, one use the operator "$:\not\ni$". For example :

> "spouse(x) $:\not\ni$ y" which is equivalent in this case to "spouse(y) $:\not\ni$ x".

Formally :

> "f(x) $:\not\ni$ y" is equivalent to "$\underline{inv}$(f)(y) $:\not\ni$ x"

While interpreting such a statement the models checks :
> . if x and y belong to the correct categories.

But the model does not require that the minimum cardinality constraints are observed because it accepts the possibility of a $\underline{lack\ of\ information}$.

When the maximum cardinal of an access function is equal to 1, one may use the operator " ← " as a short form for "$:\not\ni$" followed by "$:\ni$".

$\underline{Example}$:

> "sex(x) ← masculine" is equivalent to

> "sex(x) $:\not\ni$ sex(x)" followed by "sex(x) $:\ni$ masculine"

It is important to notice that in the notation "f(x) $:\ni$ y", "f(x)" does not mean any evaluation of the function "f" applied to "x". In fact, a more rigourous notation would have been :

> $:\ni$ (f,x,y)

We are using the notation "f(x : ∋ y" rather than the notation ": ∋ (f,x,y)" only because the first one is more readable though less correct. Now, x and y could very well be replaced by any access function whose maximum cardinal is 1.

Example :

    Suppose we want to inform the model that the sex of the spouse of person x is the same as the sex of the person y. This could be written as :

    : ∋ (sex, spouse(x), sex(y)).

    Or going back to the previous notation we get :

    sex(spouse(x)) : ∋ sex(y).

It is important to notice that the role of the underlined parenthesis is not at all the same as the one played by the other.

We hope that the reader is no longer surprised by the notation :

    sex(x) : ∌ sex(x) which is equivalent to : ∌ (sex,x,sex(x)).

Before closing this section let us make an important remark about the external name of an object and the possible relation between an object and an identifier.

Suppose the following definition :

    person = cat

    rel(person, identifier, name = afn(1,1), afn(0,1))

It is important to notice that the statement :

    john = generate person

and the two statements :

    x ← generate person

    name(x) ← jack

are not at the same linguistic level. In the first case "john" is a synonym of the internal name created by the model while evaluating "generate person". In the second case "jack" is just an identifier such that the evaluation of "inv(name)(jack)" returns the internal name of the newly created person. In the first case the statement :

    "sex(john) ← masculine"

is meaningful while in the second case :

    "sex(jack) ← masculine"

is meaningless ; one has to write :

    "sex(inv(name)(jack)) ← masculine"

or better if we define :

    personofname ≡ inv(name)

then

    sex(personofname(jack)) ← masculine

All of these notions are very well defined in languages such as ALGOL 68 [7].

2.4. Getting information from the model

Evaluating an access function is simply done by writing the name of the access function followed by the name (or nickname) of an object belonging to its domain.

Example :

        parent(x)

gives, as a result, the two persons who are the parents of the person x. In fact, "parent(x)" is short hand for :

        for y ← parent(x)
            resume(y)
            up 1
        end

which is also short hand for the more precise notation (all these notations will be explained in section 2.8.2. and 2.8.4.) :

        p ← open(parent(x))
        do y ← get(p)
            if failure then down 1
                       else resume(y)
                            up 1
                       end
        end
        close(p)

The difference between "nothing" and "unknown"

Suppose we inform the model defined at the beginning of section 2.2. that :

        sex(x) :∌ sex(x)

        spouse(x) :∌ spouse(x)

If now we want to evaluate "sex(x)" and "spouse(x)" we get different results :

        "sex(x)" is unknown because the definition of "sex" was the following
        "r1 = rel(person, sexp, sex = afn(1,1),afn(0,∞))" and "spouse(x)" is
        nothing because the definition of "spouse" was the following :
        "r3 = rel(person, person, spouse = afn(0,1),spouse).

If we want to inform the model that x is married to an unknown person we have to write :

        spouse(x) :∋ unknown

It makes a difference to know that x is either married (to somebody, but it is not known to whom) or to know that x has no spouse at all !

2.5. Getting logical information from the model

Another way to get information from the model is to give it a conjecture (a condition) whose solution could be "true", "false" or "unknown". The first kind of conjecture we can make is about the category of an object. For this we use the operator "is".

Example :

        x is person

        masculine is sexp

The second kind of conjecture is about the relation between two objects. For this we use the operator "∈" (belongs).

Example :

        x $\in$ parent(y)

this conjecture is the same as :

        y $\in$ child(x)

Equality

Equality always means <u>identity of internal names</u>. The conjecture :

        x = john

is true if, for example, "x" is the nickname of an object whose internal name and
"john" are synonyms.

When an access function has a maximum cardinal equal to 1, one may also use the
"=" symbol rather than the "$\in$" symbol.

Example :

        "y = spouse(x)" is equivalent to y $\in$ spouse(x).

We have here an example where the conjecture may have an "<u>unknown</u>" result when
"spouse(x)" is "<u>unknown</u>". One can also test directly for special cases. Example :

        spouse(x) = <u>unknown</u>

        spouse(x) = <u>nothing</u>

We suppose, of course, that for some categories (like numbers) there exist special
logical operators (like $>,<,\leq,\geq$).

Elementary conjectures can be negated by "$\neg$" (not) and connected by "$\wedge$" (and)
and "$\vee$" (or). A generalization of the "$\wedge$" and "$\vee$" operators for the elements of
a set is given by the two quantifiers "$\forall$" (for all) and "$\exists$" (there exists).

Example :

        suppose we want to ask the model if all children of a person x are male.
        We write the following :

        $\forall$y $\leftarrow$ child(x)(sex(y) = masculine)

        If we want to ask the model if at least one child of person x (if any) is
        a male, we write :

        $\exists$y $\leftarrow$ child(x)(sex(y) = masculine)

Notice that, when using "$\exists$y", there is the <u>side effect</u> of assigning the variable
"y" when the conjecture is true.

We may have nested expressions such as :

        $\exists$y $\leftarrow$ child(x) ($\exists$z $\leftarrow$ child(y) (sex(z) = masculine))

2.6. Operations with access functions

We introduce here the classical set operations of union "$\cup$", intersection "$\cap$"
and complement "C". Only the last one requires some explanation : the complement of
an access function defines the <u>set difference</u> between the range of the access function and its subset that this access function describes.

Example :

        <u>rel</u>(person, person, parent = <u>afn</u>(2,2),child = <u>afn</u>(0,∞))

"C child (x)" defines all the persons who are not children of person x;
"child(x) $\cap$ inv(sex)(masculine)" defines the sons of person x.

Notice that a conjecture like

$\exists\, y \leftarrow$ child(x)(sex(y) = masculine)

can now be written in a more symmetric way by

$\neg$(child(x) $\cap$ personofsex(masculine) = nothing) or by

$\exists\, y \leftarrow$ (child(x) $\cap$ personofsex(masculine)).

2.7. Extending the basic semantics

What we have done so far in describing a model is :

. defining categories with the operator "cat" and generating or killing objects with the operator "generate" or "kill" (section 2.1.)

. defining relations, access functions and their properties with the operators "rel" and "afn" (section 2.2.) and updating or erasing connections between two objects with the operators " $\ni$ " or " $\not\ni$ " (section 2.3.).

. asking questions (to the model) by accessing access functions (section 2.4.) or by testing some conditions with the operators "is", " $\in$ ", the usual logical operators and the quantifiers " $\forall$ " and " $\exists$ " (section 2.5.).

We have seen also how the application of these operators may sometimes lead to a failure, (these cases of failure belong to the implicit semantics of the operators) and how the application of these operators may sometimes lead to some implicit side effects :

Example :

" f(x) : $\ni$ y" has a side effect which is "inv(f)(y) : $\ni$ x"

Extending the semantics of these operators is done by specifying special cases of failure or special side effects when applying the operators to some particular parameters. For doing so, we define seven relations between the categories "category" or "access functions" and a new category called "program". These relations are the followings :

rel(category, program, generator = afn(0,1), afn(0,∞))

rel(category, program, killer = afn(0,1), afn(0,∞))

rel(category, program, recognizer = afn(0,1), afn(0,∞))

rel(access-function, program, updater = afn(0,1), afn(0,∞))

rel(access-function, program, eraser = afn(0,1), afn(0,∞))

rel(access-function, program, accessor = afn(0,1), afn(0,∞))

rel(access-function, program, tester = afn(0,1), afn(0,∞))

The category "program" will be defined in the section 2.7.3. Let us say for the moment that a program may be evaluated. When there exists a connection between a category or an access function and a program through one of these seven built-in access functions, this program is automatically evaluated when applying the corresponding operator.

The correspondance is the following :

```
double = prog(x,y)
if ¬(x is node ∧ y is node) then failure end
value(y) ← 2 * value(x)
p ← open(descendant(y))
q ← open(descendant(x))
do value (get(p)) ← 2 * value (get(q))
      if failure then down 1 else up 1 end
end
close(p)
close(q)
```

It is interesting to notice that in this program the roles played by the processes "p" and "q" are symmetric and therefore that it could have been obtained also
from a transformation of a "for" loop on "descendant(y)".

2.9. Examples : definition of the classic mathematical semantics for binary relations

As examples of semantics extension we are going to define now the basic mathematical properties of binary relations namely reflexivity, irreflexivity, asymmetry,
antisymmetry and transitivity.

2.9.1. Reflexivity

Mathematically $R(x,y)$ is reflexive if $\forall x\, R(x,x)$ holds.
This gives :

```
rel(C1,C1,f12 = afn(1,∞), f21 = afn(1,∞))
accessor(f12) ← prog(x)
      resume(x)
      for y ← std(x)
          if y ≠ x then resume(y) end
          up 1
      end
```

2.9.2. Irreflexivity

$R(x,y)$ is irreflexive if : $\forall x\, \neg R(x,x)$ holds. This gives :

```
rel(C1,C1,f12 = afn(0,∞), f21 = afn(0,∞))
updater(f12) ← prog(x,y)
      if x = y then failure end
      std(x,y)
```

2.9.3. Asymmetry

R(x,y) is asymmetric if $\forall x \, \forall y$ $(R(x,y) \supset \neg R(y,x))$ holds. This gives :

<u>rel</u>(C1,C1,f12 = afn(0,∞), f21 = <u>afn</u>(0,∞))

<u>updater</u>(f12) ← <u>prog</u>(x,y)

  <u>if</u> x ∈ f12(y) <u>then</u> <u>failure</u> <u>end</u>

  <u>std</u>(x,y)

2.9.4. Antisymmetry

R(x,y) is antisymmetric if : $\forall x \, \forall y$ $((R(x,y) \wedge R(y,x)) \supset (x=y))$ holds. This gives :

<u>rel</u>(C1,C1,f12 = <u>afn</u>(0,∞), f21 = <u>afn</u>(0,∞))

<u>updater</u>(f12) ← prog(x,y)

  <u>if</u> (x∈ f12(y) $\wedge$ ¬(x=y)) <u>then</u> <u>failure</u> <u>end</u>

  <u>std</u>(x,y)

2.9.5. Transitivity

R(x,y) is transitive if : $\forall x \, \forall y \, \forall z$ $((R(x,y) \wedge R(y,z) \supset R(x,z))$ holds.
For expressing the semantics it is convenient to define a general program for computing the transitive closure of an access function. In this program we are going to use some names which have not yet been defined. They will be in section 4.

```
closure 1  = prog(f,x,s)
    if ¬(f is access-function∧ x is domain (f)
       ∧domain(f) = range(f)∧ s is access-function
       ∧domain(f) = domain(x)) then failure end
    for y ← f(x)
       if¬ (y ∈ s) then s :∋ y
                         resume(y)
                         for z ← closure 1 (f,y,s)
                            resume(z)
                            up 1
                         end
                    end
       up 1
    end
```

The set "s" is used to avoid infinite loops when the graph corresponding to the relation has cycles.

We can now define the program "<u>closure 2</u>" by :

```
closure 2  = prog(f,x)
    if ¬(f is acces function∧ x is domain(f) ∧domain(f) = range(f))
         then failure end
    prp(domain(f), seen = afn(0,∞))
    for y ← closure 1(f,x,seen)
       resume(y)
       up 1
    end
```

Finally a transitive relation is defined by :

$\underline{rel}(C1,C1,f = \underline{afn}(0,\infty), \underline{afn}(0,\infty))$

    $\underline{accessor}(f) \leftarrow \underline{prog}(x)$

        $\underline{for}\ y \leftarrow closure2\ (\underline{std},x)$

            $\underline{resume}(y)$

            $\underline{up}\ 1$

      $\underline{end}$

In section 4 we will need a reflexive closure program whose definition is :

    $closure = \underline{prog}(f,x)$

      $\underline{if}\ \neg(f\ \underline{is}\ \text{access-function} \wedge x\ \underline{is}\ domain(f)$

       $\wedge range(f) = domain(f))\ \underline{then}\ \underline{failure}\ \underline{end}$

      $\underline{prp}(domain(f),\ seen = \underline{afn}(0,\infty))$

      $seen :\ni x$

      $\underline{resume}(x)$

      $\underline{for}\ y \leftarrow closure1\ (f,x,seen)$

          $\underline{resume}(y)$

          $\underline{up}\ 1$

      $\underline{end}$

2.10. Contexts

2.10.1. Definition

We are now going to introduce the very important notion of context, enlarging upon its classical definition in ALGOL to the more sophisticated meaning it has in [6], [13] and [12]. Let us use an example :

    $g = \underline{prog}(x,y,z)$

```
┌─────────────────────────────┐
│ body of the program "g"     │
│ where one is using the      │
│ identifiers "x","y" and "z" │
└─────────────────────────────┘
```

    $f = \underline{prog}(x,y,z)$

```
┌─────────────────────────────┐
│ body of the program "f" where │
│ one is using the identifiers  │
│ "x","y" and "z" and where one │
│ is calling the program "g"    │
└─────────────────────────────┘
```

When "f" is called, the process "p" of executing it is able to give some meaning (internal names) to the identifiers "x", "y" and "z" defined in the body of "f". Now, when "p" calls "g", the new process "q" (executing "g") is using the same iden tifiers but they have not the same meaning as the one they had while executing "q". We will say that, at the same time, the meaning of these identifiers is different according to the various contexts in which they have to be evaluated (i.e. the con- text of process "p" or the context of process "q").

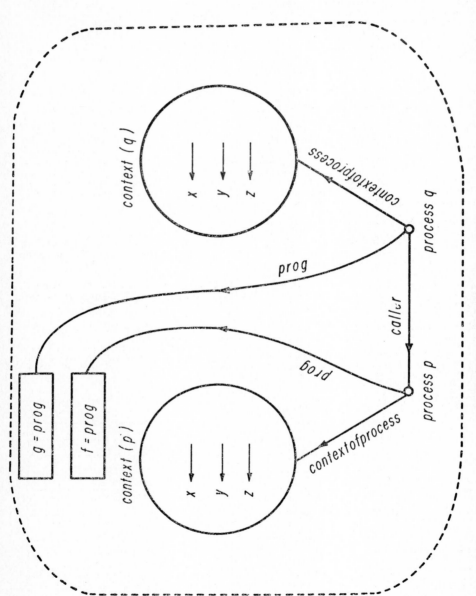

This notion seems to be very close to that of process : in fact every process when
created (by open) generates a new context but the contrary is not true : following
Fraser [13] we will say that a context is a concrete object that one can create
(using operator ctx) and kill independently of any process.

The relations between "program","context" and "process" can be formalized by the
following definitions :

$$\underline{rel}(process,\ program,\ prog\ =\ \underline{afn}(1,1),\ \underline{afn}(0,\infty))$$

$$\underline{rel}(process,\ process,\ caller\ =\ \underline{afn}(1,1),\ \underline{afn}(0,\infty))$$

$$\underline{rel}(process,\ context,\ cont\ =\ \underline{afn}(1,1),\ \underline{afn}(0,1))\quad (see\ section\ 4.2.)$$

Contexts are related to each other by a double hierarchy whose role is to define
the rules of evaluations for synonyms, nicknames and access functions. Let us introduce this hierarchy intuitively in the previous example : when the process "p"
has called the program "g" the dynamic situation is the one drawn on the schema on
the preceding page. We will say (i) that the "staticfather" of the context of "p"
(and of context of "q" as well) is the "global" context where the program "f" (and
"g") executed by "p" ("q") has been defined and (ii) that the "dynamicfather" of
the context of "q" is the context of "p" that invoqued "q".

Now the rules of evaluation are the followings :

identifiers are understood in a context while going up from (and including)
this context following the "staticfather" access function until the "global"
context is reached.

There exists a special context of name "global" which is the root of both hierar-
chies. While executing a process, the nickname "local" denotes the context of this
process.

What we have to define so far is not very different from what is usually done in
ALGOL, but the notion of context plays another very important role :

every action is supposed to have an effect in a certain context "c" and
this effect unless otherwise hidden by a reverse effect, is seen in the
dynamic descendants of this context "c".

For the actions defined so far, we have not defined explicitly in which context
they have their effects. These implicit effect contexts are the following :

Actions	Implicit effect context
ctx	global
cat, rel, afn open, close, prog	local
generate kill	The context where the corresponding categories are defined
:∋ , :∋ , ←	The context where the corresponding access functions are defined
for x ← ∀ x ← ∃ x ← x ←	local Notice also that these statements are introducing eventually "x" as a new nickname in "local"

If one wants to define <u>explicitly</u> the effect context of an action, one has to use the operator "<u>wrt</u>" followed by a context denotation ("<u>wrt</u>" stands for "with respect to" ; this terminology is taken from [6]).

<u>Example</u> :

$$\text{spouse}(x) \leftarrow y \ \underline{\text{wrt}} \ \underline{\text{local}}$$

"x" and "y" are now married but only in the "<u>local</u>" context and not in the one where "spouse" was defined.

It is important to notice here that by "effect of an action" we do not mean only the standard effect but also the <u>side effects</u> as defined by the semantic extension of the action : in the above example if there exists an "<u>updater</u>(spouse)", then the eventual side effects implied by this "<u>updater</u>" would only take place "<u>wrt</u> <u>local</u>".

Let us now give the rule for evaluating (in a "<u>local</u>" context) an access function "f(x)" defined in a certain context "c" (which is necessarily a static ascendant, as well as a dynamic ascendant of "<u>local</u>") : starting from "c" the model evaluates "f(x)" and then following down the unique dynamic descendant contexts path to "<u>local</u>", it <u>enlarges</u> or <u>restricts</u> the first evaluation of "f" by taking into account the various updating (f(x) :∋ y) or erasing (f(x) :∌ z) that took place "en route".

This is precisely the mechanism that allows us to speak of the model having imagination (section 1) : all effects done "<u>wrt</u> <u>global</u>" are the <u>direct consequence</u> of a change of the physical world whereas all effects that take place in innermost contexts are only the consequence of some <u>hypothetical changes</u> that have no counterpart in the physical world. This is particularly important when several users ("subject" see next section) are using the model at the same time : each user is able to access the "<u>global</u>" context and to perform hypothetical modifications in its own "<u>local</u>" context without interfacing on other users work. If a user wants to keep some hypothetical modifications (or partial results) from one session to another, he may create a new context (using the operator <u>ctx</u>) that will not be destroyed when he leaves the model. Therefore, when nobody is using the model there exists possibly several live contexts under the "<u>global</u>" one :

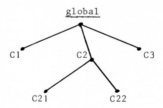

We will see in a next section that when a user enters the model he is informing it under which context he wishes to start.

All the elements introduced here will be defined precisely in section 4.

2.10.2. <u>Example</u>

This example is taken from the graph structure of university courses. Each course has a certain number of prerequisite courses among which some are mandatory and some are optional.

We can represent each course (and some dummy courses) by a node with the following relation :

$$\underline{rel}(node, node, prerequisite = \underline{afn}(0,\infty), previous = \underline{afn}(0,\infty))$$

With each node is associated a number which represents the number of prerequisite courses the student must have followed :

$$\underline{rel}(node, integer, param = \underline{afn}(1,1), \underline{afn}(0,\infty))$$

Of course, if the parameter of a certain node is equal to the cardinal of the pre-requisite courses of this node, this means that they are mandatory ; conversely if the parameter is equal to 1, this means that the student must have followed any course among the prerequisite courses.

The problem is to "validate" the wish of a certain student to follow a certain "course" provided he has "already" followed a certain set of other courses.

It can very well happen that a course belongs to the prerequisite set of several different courses : our goal is to look only once at each node that is to say to keep information about the student status regarding each node encountered while traversing the graph with the main "validate" program. But, in doing so, we do not want to modify the graph because of several "validate" processes running possibly simultaneously ; in other words, we would like that the graph has a reentrance property : we need therefore a specific context in which we are going to record the graph modifications.

The "validate" program is as follow :

```
          validate = prog(course, already, c)
      if ⌐(course is node ∧ already is property∧range(already) =
          node ∧ c is context)
          then failure end
      if course ∈ already then learnup(course, c)
                                    success
                                    return
                          end
      for x ← (prerequisite(course) wrt c)
          validate(x, already, c)
          if failure then for y ← previous(x)
                              previous(x) :∌ y wrt c
                              up 1
                          end
                          up 1
          else if param(course) wrt c = 0
                      then success
                            return
                      else up 1 end
                  end
      end
      failure
      return
```

```
learnup = prog(course, c)
   if ¬(course is node ∧ c is context)
       then failure end
   for x ← previous(course)
       if param(x) wrt c = 0
           then down 1
           else if param(x) wrt c = 1
                   then learnup(x, c) end
           end
       param(x) ← param(x) - 1 wrt c
       previous(course) :≯ x wrt c
       up 1
   end
   return
```

Let us now describe the run on the following example :

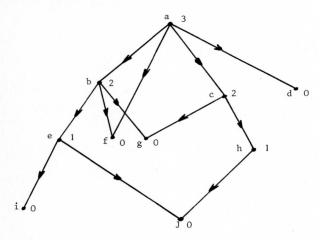

Suppose we have "already" = {g, j, d} , we then get the following trace for valida-
ting "a". Notice that (i) this program does not work if the graph has cycles (this
would be rather curious for a prerequisite relation and can be prevented by adding
an "updater" to the basic relation), and (ii) the behavior of this program is not
entirely consistent with the rules given in section 6.3.

I like to thank Mr. D. Portal for suggesting me this example.

```
validate(a)
   validate(b)
      validate(e)
         validate(i) failure
         previous(i) :∌ e wrt c
         validate(j) success (because j ∈ already)
            learnup(j)
               learnup(e)
                  param(b) ← 1 wrt c
                  previous(e) :∌ b wrt c
                  param(e) ← 0 wrt c  ◄─────────────┐
                  previous(j) :∌ e wrt c            │
                  learnup(h)                        │
                     param(c) ← 1 wrt c             │
                     previous(h) :∌ c wrt c         │
                  param(h) ← 0 wrt c                │
                  previous(j) :∌ h wrt c            │
      success (because of ──────────────────────────┘
      validate(f) failure
      previous(f) :∌ b wrt c
      previous(f) :∌ a wrt c ◄─────────────────────────────────────────┐
      validate(g) success  (because g ∈ already)                        │
         learnup(g)                                                     │
            learnup(b)                                                  │
               param(a) ← 2 wrt c                                       │
               previous(b) :∌ a wrt c                                   │
            param(b) ← 0 wrt c ◄──────────────────┐                     │
            previous(g) :∌ c wrt c                │                     │
            learnup(c)                            │                     │
               param(a) ← 1 wrt c                 │                     │
               previous(c) :∌ a wrt c ◄───────────┼──────────┐         │
            param(c) ← 0 wrt c                     │          │         │
            previous(g) :∌ c wrt c                 │          │         │
   success  (because of ───────────────────────────┘          │         │
   validate(d) success  (we know that "f" and "c" are disconnected)     │
      learnup(d)                              │          │              │
         learnup(a)                           └──────────┴──────────────┘
         param(a) ← 0 wrt c ◄──────┐
         previous(d) :∌ a wrt c    │
success  (because of ──────────────┘
```

2.11. Subjects and privacy

As already explained in the last section, the model representation of the model
users is done by objects belonging to a particular category called "subject".
A "subject" is not an object like others because its semantics is somehow more
deeply involved in the behavior of the model. In particular, when a user wishes to
start playing with the model (notice that we do not presume any special ways for
technically playing with the model, i.e. batch, conversational), he has :

    . to introduce himself as a particular "subject" "s"
    . to designate the context "c" under which he wants to start.

There exists a relation between "subject" and "context" which is the following :

    rel(subject, context, startingcontext = afn(0,1), afn(0,∞))

The login of a user "s" under a context "c" is therefore done by :

    startingcontext(s) :∋ c

Notice that if the subject "s" is already logged in, we get a failure.

There exists a relation between "process" and "subject" which is the following :

    rel(process, subject, p-user = afn(1,1), afn(0,∞))

Therefore when the user wants to make an "<action>" whose effect is only in the
context where he started, he can do the following :

    <action> wrt startingcontext(p-user (inv(cont)(local)))

With the following definition :

    usercontext ≡ startingcontext (p-user (inv(cont)(local)))

we get :

    <action> wrt usercontext

The following definition will also be useful :

    user ≡ p-user (inv(cont)(local))

As seen so far the notion of "subject" has a partially well defined semantics. It
is interesting however, for a particular model, to give some particular semantic
properties for "subjects", specially for defining privacy ; the semantical extension and the notion of failure can be used for this.

For example : suppose the following definition :

    rate = cat

    low = generate rate

    medium = generate rate

    high = generate rate

    rel(subject, qualitication = afn(1,1), afn(0,∞))

    and

    rel(person, number, salary = afn(1,1), afn(0,∞))

We wish to define the following restrictions in the usage of salary :
    . users of low qualification cannot access the salary nor update it
    . users of medium qualification can only access salaries smaller than 2000
      and cannot update any salary.

This is defined by :

> accessor(salary) ← prog(x)
>
>   if(qualification(user) = low) $\lor$ ((qualification(user) = medium
>
> $\land$std(x) $\geqslant$ 2000) then failure end
>
>   std(x)
>
> updater(salary) ← prog(x,y)
>
>   if $\neg$(qualification(user) = high) then failure end
>
>   std(x,y)

We can, using this method, define rigorously the rights of a particular "subject" defined by : "modeldesigner = generate subject" ; the "startingcontext" of "model-designer" is of course "global".

Another "subject" could be defined as :

> subjectcreator = generate subject

and we could have in particular :

> generator(subject) ← prog(x)
>
>   if $\neg$(user = subjectcreator) then failure end
>
>   std

3. A COMPLETE EXAMPLE

We will describe the semantics of a very simplified reservation system of places on a ship. Let us first define it informally : each ship is made up of a certain number of places of different classes ; each voyage is made by a ship, at a certain date, between two ports belonging to different countries. The state of the reservations for each voyage gives the number of places available in each class. A single reservation defines a port of departure, a port of arrival, a date and a class. The problem consists of making out a ticket corresponding to a given reservation.

If the system finds no place for the reservation requested, it must be capable of finding alternative solutions on its own, either in other classes, or on very close dates or for neighbouring departure or arrival ports (same countries). In other words, the system must be able to find the "nearest" voyage corresponding to the requested reservation.

We suppose that the system may evolve in that it is able to adopt different strategies to find the "nearest" voyage according to various preferences requested by the customer.

We can define these semantics with the following structure :
    (see figure on next page)

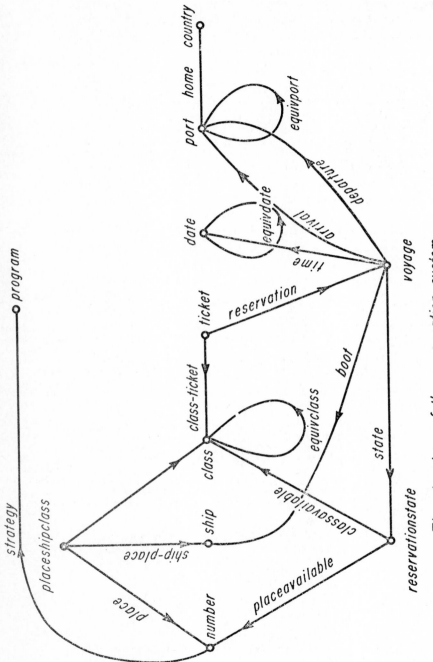

The structure of the reservation system

The above schema may be formalized into the following definitions :

$\underline{rel}$(placeshipclass, number, place = $\underline{afn}(1,1)$, $\underline{afn}(0,\infty)$))

$\underline{rel}$(placeshipclass, ship, shipplace = $\underline{afn}(1,1)$, $\underline{afn}(0,\infty)$))

$\underline{rel}$(placeshipclass, class, classplace = $\underline{afn}(1,1)$, $\underline{afn}(0,\infty)$))

$\underline{rel}$(reservationstate, number, placeavailable = $\underline{afn}(1,1)$, $\underline{afn}(0,\infty)$))

$\underline{rel}$(reservationstate, class, classavailable = $\underline{afn}(1,1)$, $\underline{afn}(0,\infty)$))

$\underline{rel}$(voyage, reservationstate, state = $\underline{afn}(1,\infty)$, $\underline{afn}(1,1)$))

$\underline{rel}$(voyage, ship, boot = $\underline{afn}(1,1)$, $\underline{afn}(0,\infty)$))

$\underline{rel}$(voyage, date, time = $\underline{afn}(1,1)$, $\underline{afn}(0,\infty)$))

$\underline{rel}$(voyage, port, departure = $\underline{afn}(1,1)$, $\underline{afn}(0,\infty)$))

$\underline{rel}$(voyage, port, arrival = $\underline{afn}(1,1)$, $\underline{afn}(0,\infty)$))

$\underline{rel}$(ticket, voyage, reservation = $\underline{afn}(1,1)$, $\underline{afn}(0,\infty)$))

$\underline{rel}$(ticket, class, class-ticket = $\underline{afn}(1,1)$, $\underline{afn}(0,\infty)$))

$\underline{rel}$(port, country, home = $\underline{afn}(1,1)$, $\underline{afn}(0,\infty)$))

$\underline{rel}$(class, class, equivclass = $\underline{afn}(1,\infty)$, equivclass)

$\underline{rel}$(date, date, equivdate = $\underline{afn}(1,\infty)$, equivdate)

$\underline{rel}$(port, port, equivport = $\underline{afn}(1,\infty)$, equivport)

$\underline{rel}$(number, program, strategy = $\underline{afn}(1,1)$, $\underline{afn}(0,\infty)$))

Let us now give some semantic extensions corresponding to our problem. We are going to define first the three "$\underline{generator}$" for "placeshipclass", "voyage" and "reservationstate".

$\underline{generator}$(placeshipclass) ← $\underline{prog}$(sh,cl,nb)

   $\underline{if}\ \lnot$(sh $\underline{is}$ ship$\land$cl $\underline{is}$ class$\land$nb $\underline{is}$ number) $\underline{then}$ $\underline{failure}$ $\underline{end}$

   $\underline{if}\ \lnot$(($\underline{inv}$(shipplace)(sh)$\cap$ $\underline{inv}$(classplace)(cl)   = $\underline{nothing}$)

      $\underline{then}$ $\underline{failure}$ $\underline{end}$

   x ← std

   shipplace(x) ← sh

   classplace(x) ← cl

   place(x) ← nb

This "$\underline{generator}$" expresses that for a given "ship" and a given "class" there is only one "placeshipclass". It defines "placeshipclass" as a ternary relation. In Codd's relational system [3] this would have been defined as :
   "$\underline{relation}$ placeshipclass(place, ship, class) $\underline{key}$(ship,class)"

$\underline{generator}$(voyage) ← $\underline{prog}$(sh,p1,p2,t)

   $\underline{if}\ \lnot$(sh $\underline{is}$ ship $\land$p1 $\underline{is}$ port $\land$p2 $\underline{is}$ port $\land$t $\underline{is}$ date)
      $\underline{then}$ $\underline{failure}$ $\underline{end}$
   $\underline{if}\ \lnot$(($\underline{inv}$(boot)(sh)$\cap$ $\underline{inv}$(time)(t)) = $\underline{nothing}$)
      $\underline{then}$ $\underline{failure}$ $\underline{end}$
   x ← $\underline{std}$
   boot(x) ← sh
   arrival(x) ← p1
   departure(x) ← p2
   time(x) ← t
   $\underline{for}$ y ← $\underline{inv}$(shipppace)(sh)
      $\underline{generate}$ reservationstate (x,place(y),classplace(y))
   $\underline{end}$ $\underline{up}^1$

This "generator" expresses that for a given "date" and "ship" there is only one "voyage" and it has the mean side effect of generating as much "reservationstate" as there are "placeshipclass" for the "ship" corresponding to the "voyage".

    generator(reservationstate) ← prog(v,nb,cl)
        if ¬(v is voyage∧nb is number∧cl is class) then failure end
        x ← std
        inv(state)(x) ← v
        placeavailable(x) ← nb
        classavailable(x) ← cl

This "generator" defines "reservationstate" as a 3-ary relation between a "voyage" a "number", and a "class".

It is interesting to notice here that the ternary relation "reservationstate" and the 5-ary relation "voyage" are related by the fact that they are a domain of each other.

Let us now define the three equivalence relations for "class", "date", and "port".

    accessor(equivclass) ← prog(cl)
        resume(cl)
        for x ← class
            if ¬(x=cl) then resume(x) end
            up 1
        end

This "accessor" defines the "classes" equivalent to a given "class" as this "class" and the other.

    accessor(equivport) ← prog(p)
        resume(p)
        for x ← inv(home)(home(p))
            if ¬(x=p) then resume(x) end
            up 1
        end

This "accessor" defines the "ports" equivalent to a given "port" p as all the "ports" of the "country" of p.

    accessor(equivdate) ← prog(t)
        resume(t)
        resume(nextday(t))
        resume(previousday(t))

This "accessor" defines the "dates" equivalent to a given "date" as this "date" and the two surrounding "dates".

Let us now define the "generator" of a "ticket".

<u>generator</u>(ticket) ← <u>prog</u>(cl,pl,p2,t,pref)

 <u>if</u> ⌐(cl <u>is</u> class ∧pl <u>is</u> port ∧p2 <u>is</u> port ∧t <u>is</u> date ∧pref <u>is</u> number)

  <u>then failure end</u>

 (v,cl1) ← strategy(pref)(cl,pl,p2,t)

 <u>if</u> ⌐ <u>failure then</u> x ← <u>std</u>

      reservation(x) ← **v**

      classticket(x) ← cl1

    <u>else failure end</u>

We are now going to define one (among other) "strategy" for finding a "voyage" and a "class" for a given reservation :

 strategy(1) ← <u>prog</u>(cl,pl,p2,t)

  <u>if</u> ∃ tl ← equivdate(t)

   (∃ cl1 ← equivclass(cl)

    (∃ pl1 ← equivport(pl)

     (∃ p21 ← equivport(p2)

      (∃ v ← (<u>inv</u>(time)(tl)∩ <u>inv</u>(departure)(pl1)

            ∩ <u>inv</u>(arrival)(p21))

       (∃ r ← (state(v)∩inv(classavailable)(cl1))

       (placeavailable(r) > 0))))))

  <u>then</u> placeavailable(r) ← placeavailable(r)−1

   <u>return</u>(v,cl1)

  <u>else failure end</u>

This "strategy" looks if there exists an available place on a voyage which is in the vicinity of the requested reservation.

Other strategies could be defined that look for a voyage using different orders of priority.

We will see in section 6.3. how this program has to be modified to allow simultaneous reservation requests.

4. FORMAL DESCRIPTION OF THE MODEL

Our purpose, in this section, is to define precisely the semantics of the model using the model itself. It is important to notice that this effort is <u>not an implementation but only a formal definition</u>.

We are going to give, in fact, the definition of the various operators introduced informally in section 3, namely :"=", "←", "cat", "<u>rel</u>", "<u>afn</u>","<u>generate</u>", "<u>kill</u>", ":∍", ":⫫", "<u>is</u>", "<u>∈</u>", "<u>open</u>", "<u>close</u>", "<u>ctx</u>", and also the relations of the various categories : "category", "relation", "access function", "program", "process", "context" and "subject".

4.1. Linking identifiers and objects

We will use the following structure :

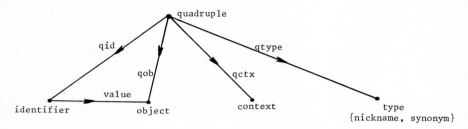

The category "object" represents the set of internal names of all the objects (whatever is their category). Formally we have :

    rel(quadruple, identifier, qid = afn(1,1), afn(0,∞))

    rel(quadruple, object, qob = afn(1,1), afn(0,∞))

    rel(quadruple, context, qctx = afn(1,1), afn(0,∞))

    rel(quadruple, type, qtype = afn(1,1), afn(0,∞))

    rel(identifier, object, value = afn(1,1), afn(0,∞))

Let us now define some semantical extensions :

    generator (quadruple) ← prog (i,o,c,t)

    if ¬(i is identifier ∧ o is object ∧ c is context ∧ t is type)

        then failure end

    q ← std

    qid(q) ← i

    qob(q) ← o

    qctx(q) ← c

    qtype(q) ← t

"quadruple" is defined as a 4-ary relation.

    accessor(value) ← prog(id)

        for c ← closure(staticfather, dynamicfather(local))

            if ∃q ← inv(qctx)(c) ∩ inv(qid)(id)

                (qob(q) ∈ aliveobject(dynamicfather(local)))

                then return(qob(q))

                else up 1 end

        end

        failure

The "closure" program is the one that has been defined in section 2.9.5. ; "dynamicfather(local)" denotes the context where the action takes place ; ("staticfather" and "dynamicfather" will be defined in the next section).

This "accessor" returns the value of an identifier as the internal name ("qob") of an object assigned to this identifier in the "local" context of in the static ascendance of it. Notice that the value to be returned must correspond to an object that is alive in "local" (see section 4.3. for the definition of "aliveobject").

We are going to define now the operator "=" as it is used in

      john = <u>generate</u> person

      spouse = <u>afn</u>(0,1)

      alpha = <u>prog</u> ... etc ...

      etc ...

    = = <u>prog</u>(id,ob)

        <u>if</u> ¬(id <u>is</u> identifier∧ob <u>is</u> object) <u>then</u> <u>failure</u> <u>end</u>

          <u>if</u> ∃q ← <u>inv</u>(qid)(id)

              (qctx(q) ∈ <u>closure</u>(staticfather, dynamicfather(<u>local</u>)))

              <u>then</u> <u>failure</u>

              <u>else</u> <u>generate</u> quadruple(id, ob, dynamicfather(<u>local</u>), synonym)

          <u>end</u>

"id" necessarily is an identifier that has no meaning in the "local" context. It becomes a "synonym" to the internal name "ob".

Let us now define the operator "←" as it appears in :

      x ← <u>generate</u> person

      for x ← ...

      ∀x ← ...

      etc ...

    ← = <u>prog</u>(id,ob)

        <u>if</u> ¬(id <u>is</u> identifier∧ob <u>is</u> object) <u>then</u> <u>failure</u> <u>end</u>

        <u>if</u> ∃q ← (<u>inv</u>(qid)(id) ∩ <u>inv</u>(qctx)(dynamicfather(<u>local</u>)))

            <u>then</u> <u>if</u> qtype(q) = synonym <u>then</u> <u>failure</u>

                            <u>else</u> qob(q) ← ob <u>end</u>

            <u>else</u> <u>generate</u> quadruple(id, ob, dynamicfather(<u>local</u>), nickname)

          <u>end</u>

4.2. Program, processes, contexts and subjects

These objects are defined with the structure shown on next page.

      <u>rel</u>(process, program, prog = <u>afn</u>(1,1), <u>afn</u>(0,∞))

      <u>rel</u>(process, process, caller = <u>afn</u>(0,1), <u>afn</u>(0,∞))

      <u>rel</u>(process, subject, puser = <u>afn</u>(1,1), <u>afn</u>(0,∞))

      <u>rel</u>(process, context, cont = <u>afn</u>(1,1), <u>afn</u>(0,1))

      <u>rel</u>(subject, context, startingcontext = <u>afn</u>(1,1), <u>afn</u>(0,∞))

      <u>rel</u>(context, context, staticfather = <u>afn</u>(0,1), <u>afn</u>(0,∞))

      <u>rel</u>(context, context, dynamicfather = <u>afn</u>(0,1), <u>afn</u>(0,∞))

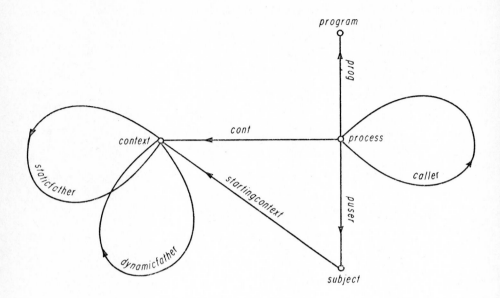

We have now the following semantic extensions :

    accessor(dynamicfather) ← prog(c)

      if ¬(std(c) = nothing)

        then return(std(c))

        else if ¬(inv(cont)(c) = nothing)

          then return(cont(caller(inv(cont)(c))))

          else return(staticfather(c)) end

      end

The "dynamicfather" of a context "c" is, unless explicitly defined, the context of
the "caller" of the process associated with "c" ; or if the context "c" is defined
independently of any process, the "staticfather" of "c".

We are now going to define the operators "open", "close", "get" and "ctx". "open"
is a synonym for the "generator" of a process.

    generator(process) ← open = prog(pr)

        if ¬(pr is program) then failure end

        p ← std

        q ← generate context

        prog(p) ← pr

        cont(p) ← q

        staticfather(q) ← generatingcontext(pr)

        puser(p) ← puser(inv(cont)(dynamicfather(local)))

The "staticfather" of the context of the new process is the context in which the program oxecuted by this process has been defined ("generatingcontext(pr)").

Notice that in case of "opening" "<u>wrt</u> c" we must add to this program the following statement :

        dynamicfather(q) ← c

Let us now define the operator "<u>close</u>(p)" whose main effect is to "<u>kill</u>" the processes called by the process "p" and also the context of "p".

    <u>killer</u>(process) ← <u>close</u> = <u>prog</u>(p)

        <u>kill</u> cont(p)

        <u>for</u> q ← <u>inv</u>(caller)(p)

            <u>kill</u> q

            <u>up</u> 1

        <u>end</u>

        <u>std</u>(p)

The statement "<u>get</u>(p)" is simply a short hand for :

    <u>caller</u>(p) ← <u>inv</u>(cont)(<u>local</u>)

    <u>local</u> ← cont(p)

Generating a new context indenpendently of any process is done by the operator :

    <u>ctx</u> = <u>prog</u>( )

    c ← <u>generate</u> context

    staticfather(c) ← dynamicfather(<u>local</u>)

    <u>return</u>(c)

In case of creating in a context c a new context c' independently of any process the "staticfather" of c' is c.

    <u>killer</u>(context) ← <u>prog</u>(c)

      <u>for</u> f ← access-function

      <u>if</u>(domain(f) = context)∧ ⌐ (<u>inv</u>(cont) = f)

          <u>then</u> <u>for</u> x ← f(c)

                <u>kill</u> x

             <u>end</u>

          <u>end</u>

        <u>up</u> 1

      <u>end</u>

      <u>std</u>(c)

Killing a context "c" has for side effect the killing of <u>all objects</u> connected to "c" (except its eventual process).

4.3. <u>Categories, relations, access functions and the corresponding operators</u>

Let us define the following structure :

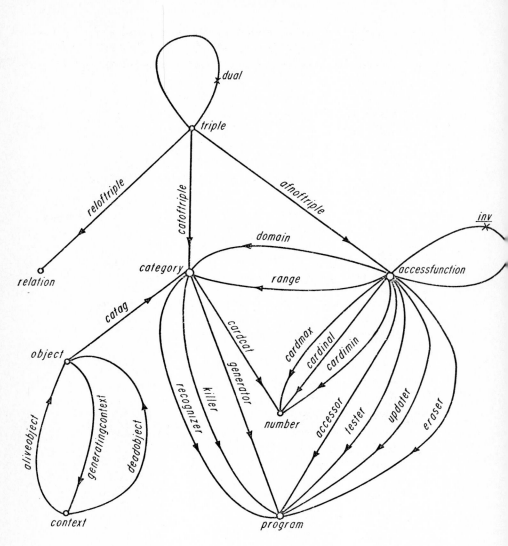

This can be defined formally as :

        rel(triple, relation, reloftriple = afn(1,1), afn(2,2))
        rel(triple, category, catoftriple = afn(1,1), afn(0,∞))
        rel(triple, access-function, afnoftriple = afn(1,1), afn(1,2))
        rel(triple, triple, dual = afn(1,1), dual)
        rel(access-function, category, domain = afn(1,1), afn(0,∞))
        rel(access-function, category, range = afn(1,1), afn(0,∞))

$\underline{rel}$(access-function, number, cardmin = $\underline{afn}$(1,1), $\underline{afn}$(0,∞))

$\underline{rel}$(access-function, number, cardmax = $\underline{afn}$(1,1), $\underline{afn}$(0,∞))

$\underline{rel}$(access-function, number, cardinal = $\underline{afn}$(1,1), $\underline{afn}$(0,∞))

$\underline{rel}$(access-function, access-function, inv = $\underline{afn}$(1,1), $\underline{inv}$)

$\underline{rel}$(category, number, catcard = $\underline{afn}$(1,1), $\underline{afn}$(0,∞))

$\underline{rel}$(object, category, catag = $\underline{afn}$(1,1), $\underline{afn}$(0,∞))

$\underline{rel}$(object, context, generatingcontext = $\underline{afn}$(0,1), $\underline{afn}$(0,∞))

$\underline{rel}$(context, object, aliveobject = $\underline{afn}$(0,∞), $\underline{afn}$(0,∞))

$\underline{rel}$(context, object, deadobject = $\underline{afn}$(0,∞), $\underline{afn}$(0,∞))

The seven other relations between "category" or "access-function" and "program" have been defined in section 2.7.

Let us now define some trivial semantic extensions :

        $\underline{accessor}$(dual) ← $\underline{prog}$(t)

            $\underline{for}$ t1 ← $\underline{inv}$(reloftriple)(reloftriple(t))

                $\underline{if}$ t1 = t $\underline{then}$ $\underline{up}$ 1

                                $\underline{else}$ $\underline{return}$(t1) $\underline{end}$

            $\underline{end}$

        $\underline{accessor}$(inv) ← $\underline{prog}$(f)

            $\underline{return}$(afnoftriple(dual($\underline{inv}$(afnoftriple)(f))))

        $\underline{accessor}$(domain) ← $\underline{prog}$(f)

            $\underline{return}$(catoftriple($\underline{inv}$(afnoftriple)(f)))

        $\underline{accessor}$(range) ← $\underline{prog}$(f)

            $\underline{return}$(catoftriple(dual($\underline{inv}$(afnoftriple)(f))))

        $\underline{tester}$(aliveobject) ← $\underline{prog}$(x,c)

            $\underline{if}$(generatingcontext(x) = $\underline{nothing}$) $\underline{then}$ $\underline{return}$ ($\underline{false}$) $\underline{end}$

            $\underline{for}$ C1 ← $\underline{closure}$(dynamicfather,c)

                $\underline{if}$ C1 = generatingcontext(x)

                        $\underline{then}$ $\underline{return}$ ($\underline{true}$) $\underline{end}$

                $\underline{if}$ (C1 = generatingcontext(catag(x))) $\lor$ (x deadobject(C1))

                        $\underline{then}$ $\underline{down}$ 1

                        $\underline{else}$ $\underline{up}$ 1 $\underline{end}$

            $\underline{end}$

            $\underline{return}$ ($\underline{false}$)

"x ∈ aliveobject(c)" means that the object "x" is "alive" (that is has not been killed) in context "c" or in its dynamic ascendant contexts. For the definition of "deadobject" see the definition of "$\underline{standardkiller}$" in section 4.4.

        $\underline{generator}$(triple) ← $\underline{prog}$(r,c,f)

            $\underline{if}$ ¬(r $\underline{is}$ relation ∧ c $\underline{is}$ category ∧ f $\underline{is}$ access function)

                $\underline{then}$ $\underline{failure}$ $\underline{end}$

            t ← $\underline{std}$

            reloftriple(t) ← r

> catoftriple(t) ← c
>
> afnoftriple(t) ← f
>
> return(t)

This "generator" simply defines "triple" as a ternary relation.

We are now in a good position for defining the three operators "cat", "rel", and "afn".

To follow the implicit effect context rules stated in section 2.10., we must admit that the "cat", "rel", "afn" actions have to be done "wrt local" when no context is explicitly written.

> generator(category) ← cat = prog( )
>
>   c ← std
>
>   return(c)
>
> generator(relation) ← rel = prog(C1, C2, f12, f21)
>
>   if ¬(C1 is category∧ C2 is category ∧ f12 is access function
>
>   ∧f21 is access function) then failure end
>
>   r ← std
>
>   generate triple(r,C1,f12)
>
>   generate triple(r,C2,f21)
>
>   return(r)
>
> generator(access-function) ← afn = prog(n1,n2)
>
>   if ¬(n1 is number ∧n2 is number) then failure end
>
>   f ← std
>
>   cardmin(f) ← n1
>
>   cardmax(f) ← n2
>
>   return(f)

Let us now define both operators "generate" and "kill". In order to follow the implicit effect context rules stated in section 2.10. we must admit that a statement like :

> generate person

is a short hand for

> generate person wrt generatingcontext(person)

and similarly that

> kill x

is a short hand for

> kill x wrt generatingcontext(catag(x))

With these facts in mind we have :

> generate = prog(c)
>
>   if ¬(c is category) then failure end
>
>   if¬(generator(c) = nothing)
>
>   then return (generator(c)( ) wrt dynamicfather(local))
>
>   else return (standardgenerator(c)( ) wrt dynamicfather(local))end

```
kill = prog(x)
        if ¬(x ∈ aliveobject(dynamicfather(local))
            then return
            else if ¬(killer(catag(x)) = nothing)
                then killer(catag(x))(x) wrt dynamicfather(local)
                else standardkiller(catag(x))(x) wrt dynamicfather(local)
                end
        end
```

"standardgenerator" and "standardkiller" will be defined in section 4.4. and also in section 5. These programs are the one invoqued when one finds "std" in "generator" or "killer" programs.

Let us now define the operators ":∋" and ":∌". To follow the implicit effect context rules, we must admit that

$$f(x) :∋ y$$

is a short hand for :

$$f(x) :∋ y \; \underline{wrt} \; generatingcontext(f)$$

It is obviously the same thing for the operator ":∌".

```
:∋ = prog(f,x,y)
if ¬(f is access-function ∧ x is domain(f) ∧ y is range(f)) then failure end
if y ∈ f(x) then return end
if (cardinal(f) = cardmax(f) ∨ cardinal(inv(f)) = cardmax(inv(f)))
        then failure end
if ¬(updater(f) = nothing)
        then updater(f)(x,y) wrt dynamicfather(local)
        else if (updater(inv(f)) = nothing)
            then updater(inv(f))(y,x) wrt dynamicfather(local)
            else standardupdater(f)(x,y) wrt dynamicfather(local)
                standardupdater(inv(f))(x,y) wrt dynamicfather(local)
            end
        end
```

```
:∌ = prog(f,x,y)
if ¬(f is access-function ∧ x is domain(f) ∧ y is range(f)) then failure end
if ¬(y ∈ f(x)) then return end
if ¬(eraser(f) = nothing)
        then eraser(f)(x,y) wrt dynamicfather(local)
        else if ¬(eraser(inv(f)) = nothing)
            then eraser(inv(f))(y,x) wrt dynamicfather(local)
            else standarderaser(f)(x,y) wrt dynamicfather(local)
                standarderaser(inv(f))(y,x) wrt dynamicfather(local)
            end
        end
```

"standardupdater" and "standarderaser" will be defined in section 4.4. and also in section 5. They are invoqued when one encounters "std" in "updater" or "eraser" programs.

Both operators "∈" and "is" could be defined using the same schema. Let us finally define the way of evaluating an access function using the (transparent) "eval" operator :

$$\text{eval} = \underline{\text{prog}}(f,x)$$

        $\underline{\text{if}}\ \neg(f\ \underline{\text{is}}\ \text{access-function} \wedge x\ \underline{\text{is}}\ \text{domain}(f))\underline{\text{then}}\ \underline{\text{failure}}\ \underline{\text{end}}$

        $\underline{\text{if}}\ \neg(\text{accessor}(f) = \underline{\text{nothing}})$

            $\underline{\text{then}}\ p \leftarrow \underline{\text{open}}(\text{accessor}(f)(x))$

            $\underline{\text{else}}\ p \leftarrow \underline{\text{open}}(\text{standardaccessor}(f)(x))$

        $\underline{\text{do}}\ \underline{\text{resume}}(\underline{\text{get}}(p))$

            $\underline{\text{if}}\ \underline{\text{failure}}\ \underline{\text{then}}\ \underline{\text{down}}\ 1$

                   $\underline{\text{else}}\ \underline{\text{up}}\ 1$

                   $\underline{\text{end}}$

      $\underline{\text{end}}$

      $\underline{\text{failure}}$

The "standardaccessor" will be defined in sections 4.4. and 5. It is invoqued when one encounters "std" in an "accessor" program.

4.4. Formal implementation

Let us now define the following programs : "standardgenerator(c)", "standard-killer(f)", "standarderaser(f)" and "standardaccessor(f)". We need the following structure :

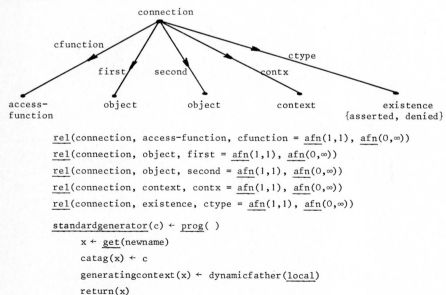

    $\underline{\text{rel}}(\text{connection}, \text{access-function}, \text{cfunction} = \underline{\text{afn}}(1,1), \underline{\text{afn}}(0,\infty))$

    $\underline{\text{rel}}(\text{connection}, \text{object}, \text{first} = \underline{\text{afn}}(1,1), \underline{\text{afn}}(0,\infty))$

    $\underline{\text{rel}}(\text{connection}, \text{object}, \text{second} = \underline{\text{afn}}(1,1), \underline{\text{afn}}(0,\infty))$

    $\underline{\text{rel}}(\text{connection}, \text{context}, \text{contx} = \underline{\text{afn}}(1,1), \underline{\text{afn}}(0,\infty))$

    $\underline{\text{rel}}(\text{connection}, \text{existence}, \text{ctype} = \underline{\text{afn}}(1,1), \underline{\text{afn}}(0,\infty))$

    $\text{standardgenerator}(c) \leftarrow \underline{\text{prog}}(\ )$

        $x \leftarrow \underline{\text{get}}(\text{newname})$

        $\text{catag}(x) \leftarrow c$

        $\text{generatingcontext}(x) \leftarrow \text{dynamicfather}(\underline{\text{local}})$

        $\underline{\text{return}}(x)$

"newname" is a process whose program generates a new internal name each time it is invoqued.

<u>standardkiller</u>(c) ← <u>prog</u>(x)

<u>if</u> generatingcontext(x) = dynamicfather(<u>local</u>)

    <u>then</u> <u>for</u> f ← <u>inv</u>(domain)(c)

           <u>for</u> cn ← (<u>inv</u>(cfunction)(f) ∩ <u>inv</u>(first)(x)) ∩

                (<u>inv</u>(cfunction)(<u>inv</u>(f)) ∩ <u>inv</u>(second)(x))

              <u>kill</u> cn

              <u>up</u> 1

           <u>end</u>

           <u>up</u> 1

        <u>end</u>

    <u>else</u> deadobject(dynamicfather(<u>local</u>)) :∋ x <u>end</u>

When the killing takes place in the context where the object was generated one can do some cleaning (killing the corresponding "connections"), otherwise it is a hypothetical killing and one just asserts that the object is not alive any more in the corresponding context (using "deadobject") (see section 6.4.).

<u>standardupdater</u>(f) ← <u>prog</u>(x,y)

    c ← <u>generate</u> connection

    cfunction(c) ← f

    first(c) ← x

    second(c) ← y

    contx(c) ← dynamicfather(<u>local</u>)

    existence(c) ← asserted

<u>standarderaser</u>(f) ← <u>prog</u>(x,y)

    <u>if</u> ∃c ← <u>inv</u>(cfunction)(f) ∩ <u>inv</u>(first)(x) ∩

           <u>inv</u>(second)(y) ∩ <u>inv</u>(cntx)(dynamicfather(<u>local</u>))

      <u>then</u> <u>kill</u> c

      <u>else</u> c ← <u>generate</u> connection

           cfunction(c) ← f

           first(c) ← x

           second(c) ← y

           contx(c) ← dynamicfather(<u>local</u>)

           existence(c) ← denied

    <u>end</u>

If the connection "c" between "x" and "y" through "f" was asserted in "dynamicfather(local)" one can do some cleaning (killing "c") otherwise one is denying the existence of the connection (in this case we have a hypothetical erasing).

standardaccessor(f) ← prog(x)

$\quad$ prp(range(f), good = afn(0,∞))

$\quad$ prp(range(f), bad = afn(0,∞))

$\quad$ for c ← closure(dynamicfather, dynamicfather(local))

$\quad\quad$ for cn ← inv(cfunction)(f) ∩ inv(first)(x) ∩ inv(contx)(c)

$\quad\quad\quad$ if ¬ (second (cn) ∈ aliveobject(dynamicfather(local))) then up 1

$\quad\quad\quad$ if ctype(cn) = asserted   end

$\quad\quad\quad\quad$ then if ¬(second(cn) ∈ bad)

$\quad\quad\quad\quad\quad\quad$ then good :∋ second(cn) end

$\quad\quad\quad\quad\quad$ else bad :∋ second(cn) end

$\quad\quad\quad$ up 1

$\quad\quad$ end

$\quad\quad$ if c = generatingcontext(f) then down 1

$\quad\quad\quad\quad\quad\quad\quad\quad\quad$ else up 1 end

$\quad$ end

$\quad$ for z ← good

$\quad\quad$ resume(z)

$\quad\quad$ up 1

$\quad$ end

$\quad$ failure

The "standardaccessor" goes up the "dynamicfather" chain selecting the "asserted" connections objects (in "good") unless they have been killed or previously hidden (in "bad") by some corresponding "denied" connections. It also selects the "denied" connections and asserts the corresponding objects as well as the dead objects as "bad". The final result is the elements of "good".

4.5. Comments on the formal definition of the model

I do not pretend that this formal definition is "bug" free !...

Most of the complications come from the dynamic context handling and the rules of evaluation through the "dynamicfather" context chain. This formal definition is not complete : in particular we have not defined the rule for evaluating a program. For doing so, it would have been necessary to define programs as concrete objects and to formalize the relation between a statement and the next statement (a statement would have been also a concrete object). The statements like "if ... then ... else ...", "do", "up i","down i", "end", "return", and "resume" would also require some attention, but no special difficulties.

5. SOME ELEMENTS FOR AN IMPLEMENTATION

We have seen in the last section in the definitions of "generate", "kill", ":∍",
":∌", "is", "∊" and "eval", the usage of the seven following programs :

standardgenerator(c)

standardkiller(c)(x)

standardupdater(f)(x,y)

standarderaser(f)(x,y)

standardrecognizer(c)(x)

standardtester(f)(x,y)

standardaccessor(f)(x)

These standard programs are in fact the linkage between the formal system and an
eventual implementation :

> implementing a model is to give a physical interpretation on
> a computer system for these programs.

Notice that the parameters "c" and "f" may be considered as applications category
or access functions (like "person" or "spouse") as well as model elements (like
"category", "access function", "context","process", etc .. or "cardinal", "relof-
triple", "cont", etc ..).

It would have been possible, of course, to give a formal implementation by defining these programs within the model itself (see section 4.4.).

The important thing to notice here is that these programs may be physically interpreted by any method such as pure programs, core memory management programs, file
handling programs, classical input-output programs, or a mixture of these. Notice
also that these physical interpretations may themselves lead to some physical
failure.

Another important remark is the following : at the model level we have defined binary relations by two access functions "f" and "inv(f)" inverse of each other. One,
then, could believe that the physical interpretation of these access functions will
lead to a totally inverted system (like T.D.M.S.). This is not true at all : the
model only is a totally inverted system in that the inverse function of an access
function may always be denoted by a name or using the "inv" operator. In fact, at
the physical interpretation level, it is always possible to define the interpretation of "standardaccessor(inv(f))" using the interpretation of "standardaccessor(f)"
in this case the interpretation of "standardupdater(inv(f))" is done by no program.
Notice also that "standardaccessor(inv(f))" could very well have some optimization
mechanism for storing in a working area some of the results of its interpretation
for future usage thereby achieving the third mechanism we were pointing out in
section 1.4. for answering questions (learning).

Our opinion, as far as implementation is concerned, is that actual computer system
have enough mechanisms to interpret these programs. The goal of such a model in
building a Data Base computer application would be the better one of a formal specifications tool ; it is quite obvious that a direct implementation of the formal
"metamodel" described in section 4 would lead to very poor efficiency with today's
technology !...

6. FURTHER INVESTIGATIONS

In this section we are going to develop some mechanisms that for some reasons (probably because they are not well defined in our mind !) we did not cover in the main
stream of sections 2 and 4.

6.1. Ordering and repetition

The first ones are the very important notions of ordering (vs disordering) and repetition (vs uniqueness). In sections 2 and 4 we did not speak of any ordering of
the elements enumerated by an access function but in fact when an access function
is defined by an "accessor" the elements are enumerated according to the occurences of the various "resumes" the process encounters in executing the program. In
the same case we did not speak of the possibility of an "accessor" to "resume"
twice (or several times) the same object.

Sometimes the ordering is not important, as in the following example :

    for y ← grandparent(x)

        up 1

    end

But sometimes it is in fact part of the semantics of the access function as in the
following example taken from section 3 :

    for x ← equivdate(date)

        up 1

    end

Remember that the "accessor" for "equivdate" was the following :

    accessor(equivdate) ← prog(t)

        resume(t)

        resume(previousday(t))

        resume(nextday(t))

In this case it is important that at least the first "resume" comes out the first.

Sometimes the repetition of an object as the output of an access function is
meaningful. Example :

    Suppose we want to calculate the sum of the age of all persons using the
    general procedure described in section 2.8.3. ("sigma"). We can define for
    this the following program :

    ageset = prog( )

        for x ← person

            resume(age(x))

            up 1

        end

    Then we can compute the sum of the ages by calling :

        sigma(ageset)

We see that in this case the repetition of the same number is important whereas the
order is not important (because in fact the "+" operation is commutative).

For all these reasons it seems important to give to an access function a "settype" which could be one of the following :

>   set, multiset, orderedset, tuple

(these notions are very well defined in QA-4 [6]).

The semantics of these elements are given in the following table :

Settype	the elements of the access function are :
set	all different and unordered
multiset	possibly identical and unordered
orderedset	all different and ordered
tuple	possibly identical and ordered

When an access function is a set or a multiset this does not mean that the elements it enumerates are not ordered (by some internal mechanism) ; the only thing it means is that this internal order is meaningless. The internal ordering of a set or a multiset can be considered as normalization mechanism (like the one for floating point numbers in computers).

The mechanism introduced so far can be formalized by requiring the "settype" of an access function when defining it : example :

>   f = afn(orderedset,0,∞)

Of course, the usage of the operator ":∋" is changed a little when dealing with orderedset or tuple.

Example : if "f" is the previously defined access function :

>   f(x)(3) :∋ y

means that "y" now becomes the third element of "f(x)" (eventually changing all higher orders).

>   y ← f(x)(3)

means that "y" is a nickname for the third element of "f(x)".

>   f(x) :∋ y

means that "y" is a now new element of the orderedset "f(x)" and that it is inserted in the proper rank according to the ordering defined necessarily in the "updater(f)". The identifier "last" is the rank of the last element : in "f(x)(last)", "last" is a short hand for "cardinal(f)".

Example : stacks and queues are particular "tuples"

>   f = afn(tuple,0,∞)

is a stack if :

>   updater(f) ← prog(x,y,rank)
>   if ⌐ (rank = cardinal(f)+1) then failure end
>   std(x,y,rank)
>   eraser(f) ← prog(x,y,rank)
>   if ⌐(rank = cardinal(f)) then failure end
>   std(x,y,rank)

$$f = \underline{afn}(tuple,0,\infty)$$

is a queue if :

    $\underline{updater}(f) \leftarrow \underline{prog}(x,y,rank)$

        $\underline{if} \neg (rank = cardinal(f)+1) \underline{\ then\ } \underline{failure}\ \underline{end}$

        $\underline{std}(x,y,rank)$

    $\underline{eraser}(f) \leftarrow \underline{prog}(x,y,rank)$

        $\underline{if} \neg (rank=1) \underline{\ then\ } \underline{failure}\ \underline{end}$

        $\underline{std}(x,y,rank)$

According to tradition, when "f" is a stack :

    $f(x)(\underline{last}+1) :\ni y$

is rewritten "$\underline{push}(f(x),y)$"

    $f(x)(\underline{last}) :\not\ni f(x)(\underline{last})$

is rewritten "$\underline{pull}(f(x))$"

After a "$\underline{pull}$" the empty stack case is therefore tested by :

    $\underline{pull}(f(x))$

    $\underline{if}\ \underline{failure}\ \underline{then}$ <empty stack case>

              $\underline{else}$ <non empty stack case > $\underline{end}$

6.2. Parallelism

When defining programs in section 2.8.3. we have said that the body of a program was a sequence of actions. We did not separate the various <actions> by ";" as is usual. We dit it, in fact, on purpose.

There exists a strong analogy between the notions of ordering (vs disordering) studied in last section and the one of sequentiality (vs parallelism). When the <actions> of a program are separated by ";" this means that they must be executed following their order in the program, whereas when they are separated by "," this means that they may be executed in any order. In the first case the order is meaningful while meaningless in the second case.

In order to enlarge this notion to the repetition of a block of statements ("for" or "do" loops) we must split these operators into "$\underline{seqfor}$" and "$\underline{parfor}$" (for "$\underline{for}$") and into "$\underline{seqdo}$" and "$\underline{pardo}$" (for "$\underline{do}$")

With these extensions we have the link between ordering (vs disordering) and sequentiality (vs parallelism) : the "$\underline{accessor}$" of a $\underline{set}$ or $\underline{multiset}$ (vs $\underline{orderedset}$ or $\underline{tuple}$) is a sequential (vs non sequential) program.

Example : the "ageset" program given in last section can be better rewritten by :

    $ageset = \underline{prog}(\ )$

    $\underline{parfor}\ x \leftarrow person\ ;$

        $\underline{resume}(age(x))\ ;$

        $\underline{up}\ 1\ ;$

    $\underline{end}$

The "accessor" for "equivdate" is now :

     accessor(equivdate) ← prog(t)

        resume(t) ;

        do resume(previousday(t)),

          resume(nextday(t)),

      end

We have here a case where an access function is only partially ordered.

An interesting consequence of the operators ",", "parfor" and "pardo" is that they introduce "miniprocesses" that may be physically interpreted by several processors at the same time.

(Notice that both notations ";" and ",", and their meaning, come from the language ALGOL 68 [7]).

6.3. Sharing of the model by various users

As we have already seen in section 2.10., when several users are playing simultaneously with the model, they can protect each other by performing their actions with respect to their "local" contexts. Unfortunately this is not sufficient at all when they want to do some action "wrt" some shared contexts.

The general problem is the following : when a user is executing the process of accessing a set (by going through the elements of a category as well as iterating on the elements defined by the evaluation of an access function) this set, as understood in the dynamic context hierarchy, must be well defined ; in other words its composition must not be modified (by adding or removing elements).

The problem could be stated in a more general way as a reentrance rule : when a process is executing a program, this program must be well defined, therefore not changed by any process. A process is executing a program from its birth (open) until its death (close).

An immediate consequence of this rule is that such statements like :

     for x ← person

        kill x

        up 1

    end

or

     for y ← car(x)

        car(x) :≢ y

        up 1

    end

are forbidden.

Therefore the above rule seems to be too restrictive and would have to be restated as :

Rule 1 : if, while accessing a set, there is an attempt to modify it, this change will be taken into account only when the accession is terminated. Or, in other words : when a process is created the corresponding program (or set) is frozen for the process until its death.

This rule must be completed by the following :

<u>Rule 2</u> : a process is given the right to access a set only when all pending modifications, requested before the access demand, are completed. Or in other words : a process is only opened when the corresponding program is in a well defined state.
An elegant solution to this problem of concurrent control has been given in [14] .

<u>Example</u> :

Suppose the following actions on the same set S :

time	accessing	accessing	modifying	modifying	accessing
action	accessing	accessing	modifying	modifying	accessing
process	P1	P2	P3	P4	P5

Processes P1 and P2 may access simultaneously the set S ; the process P5 may only access S when the modifications requested by P3 and P4 have been performed, that is to say not before the end of P1 and P2.

Are these rules able to lead to some deadlock situation ? The rules 1 and 2 may be abstracted into :

<u>Rule 1</u> : "all accessions, asked <u>before</u> the next modification, completed "⤳" all modifications, asked until the next accession, may be performed".

<u>Rule 2</u> : "all modifications, asked <u>before</u> the next accession, completed "⤳" all accessions, asked until the next modification, may be performed".

A set modification can be considered an instantaneous operation, whereas it is, of course, not the case for a set accession. Therefore when a process is asking for a set modification that is not yet possible, this process is not stopped (the set modification will be taken into account later on), whereas when a process is asking for a set access function that is not yet possible this process is stopped until the right is given to it.

Therefore there exists a risk of deadlock only when a process is asking for an access that is refused because some modifications on the same set are pending. Now, these modifications are pending until all accesses asked before are completed. It could be possible that the completion of one of these accessions is implied by the execution of the pending access if and only if they are all requested by the same process.

<u>Example</u> :

        <u>for</u> y ← car(x)
            car(x) :∌ y
            <u>for</u> z ← car(x)
                <u>up</u> 1
            <u>end</u>
            <u>up</u> 1
        <u>end</u>

The inner loop is never given right because the "car(x) :∌ y" action is pending until the completion of the outer loop which is only possible after the completion of the innerloop !...

<u>This case must be considered as a programming error.</u>

The question is now the following : is it possible to detect such a programming error only by looking at the program ? The answer is <u>no</u> because the statement :

    car(x) : $\exists$ y

can very well be a <u>side effect</u> implied by some semantic extension and is therefore not apparent explicitly in the program. The situation is even worse because this side effect could have been added after the writing of the program ..

The moral of the story is that (i) this programming error can be only detected at execution time, (ii) this situation is not in fact a deadlock but only an interlock which is a less serious case because it does not disturb other users.

The rules we have given so far are the <u>implicit</u> protection rules. They consider the <u>resources</u> are the sets and <u>not the objects themselves</u>. Is this realistic ? The answer is certainly <u>no in some cases</u> where <u>semantically</u> it is necessary that the modifications of <u>several</u> access functions of the <u>same object</u> are completed before any attempt to access one of these access functions is made.

<u>Example</u> : suppose the following structure :

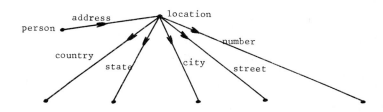

The accession to any access function of a "location" must be done only when <u>all</u> eventual modifications have been performed otherwise we could very well get an inconsistent "address".

Another case where the implicit protection rules are not sufficient is when the modification of the access function of an object is conditioned by the accession of another (or the same) access function of this object.

<u>Example</u> : Let's take the program "strategy" defined at the end of section 3.

    strategy(1) $\leftarrow$ <u>prog</u> ...

      <u>if</u> ...

       ...

       ...

      (placeavailable(r) > 0)

      <u>then</u> placeavailable(r) $\leftarrow$ placeavailable(r)-1

      <u>else</u> ...

It could very well happen that <u>two</u> users reserve the <u>unique</u> last place ! ..

Our opinion concerning such cases is that the right rule of protection is part of the semantics of the concerned objects and that it cannot be done by any general implicit mechanism. We need an <u>explicit mechanism</u>.

Let us, for this, introduce the following operators : "$\underline{lock}$(x)" and "$\underline{unlock}$(x)" whose meaning is the following :

a) "x" is supposed to be an object denotation

b) when a process encounters "$\underline{lock}$(x)" it stops until $\underline{all}$ accessions or modifications concerning all access functions of the object "x" are completed

c) "$\underline{lock}$" and "$\underline{unlock}$" operators are parenthesis like operators

d) when a process is wanting to access or to modify any access function of a locked object "x" (that is to say such that there is a process inside the "$\underline{lock}$(x)" .. "$\underline{unlock}$(x)" parenthesis) it is stopped at least until the "$\underline{unlock}$(x)" operation is executed (this last rule is a partial rewriting of rule b)).

Example : the above "strategy" program can be rewritten :

$$\text{strategy(1)} \leftarrow \underline{prog} \cdots$$

          ⋮

     $\underline{if} \cdots$
       $\cdots$

     $\cdots$

          (placeavailable(r) > 0)

     $\underline{then}$ $\underline{lock}$(r)
          $\underline{if}$ (placeavailable(r) > 0)
               $\underline{then}$ placeavailable(r) ← placeavailable(r)-1
                    unlock(r)
                    return(v,c11)
               end
          unlock(r)

     end

     $\underline{failure}$

This program is in fact not correct because in case of falsity of the second "placeavailabel(r) > 0" the backtracking must restart. Correcting it would be done by using "$\underline{for}$" loops.

Is the "$\underline{lock}$" ... "$\underline{unlock}$" operator able to generate deadlock situations ? The answer is $\underline{Yes}$. We have in fact the classic deadlock situation when several such parenthesis are nested.

Example :

User 1	User 2
$\underline{lock}$(a)	$\underline{lock}$(b)
$\underline{lock}$(b)	$\underline{lock}$(a)
$\underline{unlock}$(b)	$\underline{unlock}$(a)
$\underline{unlock}$(a)	$\underline{unlock}$(b)

In order to avoid such a case we could introduce a generalized "$\underline{lock}$" operator allowing to lock simultaneously several objects :

$$\underline{lock}(a_1, a_2, \cdots, a_n)$$

with the restriction that nested locks are now forbidden.

The semantics of the multiple locks is the following : lock them all together or wait (without any partial locks) until it is possible. With this operator and this restriction, we may avoid the deadlock situation depicted above at the risk of having a process "p" indefinitely suspended in the case of a continuous conflictual situation between several processes and "p".

Notice that the problem of detecting nested locks is not obvious (as above for detecting the interlock situation).

Unfortunately we may still very easily enter a deadlock situation when there are conflicts between the explicit and the implicit mechanisms.

Example :

User 1	User 2
lock(a,b)	lock(c)
for x ← f(c)	for x ← g(a)
end	end
unlock	unlock

"User 2" cannot access "g(a)" because "a" is locked until "User 1" has completed accession to "f(c)" which is suspended because "User 2" is locking "c" !...

A very restrictive solution is to have a total "lock" ... "unlock" operator working at the level of the entire model. At first glance this total lock seems to be too drastic but if it is used only in the right cases and for short programming sequences it could be very well the good, though not intellectually satisfactory, solution. It seems, in fact, that a combination of this solution with the usage of the context protection mechanism is a good balance.

Another solution that is inbetween the multiple objects lock and the model lock is the context lock. Further studies have to be made in this direction.

6.4. Killing objects and cleaning the model

We have seen in section 4.4. that the "standardkiller" program has for an eventual side effect the modification of all access functions concerned by the killed object. This general cleaning could be very time-consuming specially when some access functions are interpreted physically by the interpretation of the inverse access functions (see section 5). In fact, this cleaning is not necessary if we suppose that the "newname" process is really giving a new internal name each time it is invoqued (this new internal name is in fact a kind of a date of birth).

The "standardkiller" program may be rewritten as :

     standardkiller(c) ← prog(x)

        if generatingcontext(x) = dynamicfather(local)

            then generatingcontext(x) : ∌ dynamicfather(local)

            else deadobject(dynamicfather(local)) : ∋ x end

The cleaning can now take place when accessing an access function : each time the "standardaccessor" discovers that an object involved in a "connection" is really dead then it kills the "connection". We could call this method a distributed garbage collection or cleaning by exception.

The price we have to pay for this simplification is the continual testing of the livestatus of all objects (as it is done in fact in the formal description in section 4. see the "accessor(value)", and the "standardaccessor(f)").

CONCLUSION

The model we have described in this paper is <u>not a language nor a new generalized Data Base Management System proposal</u>.

We could merely consider it (as already said in section 5) as a specification tool that could (?) help people in writing programs. In this sense, this paper belongs to the "structured programming" area more than to the "Data Base"literature ...

ACKNOWLEDGMENTS

I would like to thank C. DELOBEL, J.C. FAVRE and R. COUTO-BARBOSA for numerous very helpful and pleasant discussions, M. HOLLETT for correcting my English, Mrs. C. CHALAND for her patience in typing this paper and S. RASOLONJATOVO for the beautiful drawings.

REFERENCES

[1]   C. HEWWIT : Description and Theoretical Analysis (using schemata) of
                   PLANNER : A language for proving theorems and manipulating
                   models in robot.
                   Ph.D. Thesis. MIT, February 1971

[2]   CODASYL Systems Committee Technical Report
                   Feature Analysis of generalized Data Base Management Systems
                   A.C.M., May 1971

[3]   E.F. CODD : A relational model of data for large shared data banks
                   C.ACM, vol. 13, n° 6, June 1970

[4]   M. MINSKY (editor) : Semantic information processing
                   MIT Press, 1968

[5]   R.M. BURSTALL : Programming in POP-2
                   University Press Edinburgh, 1971

[6]   J.F. RULIFSON : QA4 : a procedural calculus for intuitive reasoning
                   SRI Artificial Intelligence Center, Technical note 73,
                   Menlo Park, November 1972

[7]   A. VAN WIJNGAARDEN : Report on the algorithmic language ALGOL 68
                   MR101 Mathematish Centrum Amsterdam, February 1969

[8]   Ch. J. PRENNER : Multi-path control structures for programming languages
                   Ph.D. Thesis, Center for research in computing technology,
                   Harvard University, October 1972

[9]   P. SUPPES : Axiomatic set theory
                   Van Nostrand Company, 1960

[10]   J. VUILLEMIN : Proof techniques for recursive programs
                   Ph.D. Thesis, Stanford University, 1973

[11]   J. McCARTHY : LISP-1.5. Programmer's manual
                MIT Press, 1962

[12]   A.G. FRASER : On the meaning of name in programming systems
                C. ACM, vol. 14, n° 6, June 1971

[13]   V. McDERMOTT : The CONNIVER reference manual
                MIT Artificial Intelligence Laboratory, Memo 259, May 1972

[14]   P.J. COURTOIS : Concurrent control with "readers" and "writers"
                C. ACM, vol. 14, n° 10, October 1971

DISCUSSION

Bayer : Please clarify the concept of category. Is it a type or mode ?

Abrial : Initially it is typeless. The only applicable operators at this stage are generate and kill. Properties may be added to a category as time progresses by the rel operator. Then the operators : $\ni$ and : $\not\ni$ become applicable.

Bayer : There is a vast implementation distinction between the addition of a new relation and the addition of a new value. This difference appears to be overlooked in your semantic model.

Abrial : This is intentionally so. Implementation distinctions are not our concern in describing the semantics.

Codd : My question has two parts. First, you stated there were situations in which one needed to use one relation as a domain for another relation, because an identifier (or key) was not available. Surely, one can always arrange for the system to generate externally-usable unique identifier values for any relation one chooses. Second, in the reservation example in your paper, you have a cycle in the declarations -- specifically, reservation-state is a domain of voyage, and voyage is a domain of reservation-state. If you request a listing of either one of these relations, how do you avoid a non-terminating output ?

Abrial : With regard to the first question, the user should not be burdened with identifiers that are system generated. In the second case, to avoid non-terminating output, the system would have to print out an internal identifier.

Data Base Management, J. W. Klimbie and K. L. Koffeman, (eds.)
© *North-Holland Publishing Company (1974)*

CONCEPTUAL FOUNDATION OF THE INFOLOGICAL
APPROACH TO DATA BASES

BO SUNDGREN
National Central Bureau of Statistics,
Stockholm, Sweden

Abstract: The paper summarizes some basic ideas in my PhD thesis, "An infological approach to data bases". The infological framework and theory comprises concepts facilitating

A. at <u>design time</u>   1) for the future users of the data base to define precisely <u>what</u> information a planned data base should contain, without anticipating the datalogical design decisions, i e the decisions about <u>how</u> the information structure should be efficiently represented by data structures

2) for the computer experts to transform systematically, step by step, any specified information structure into an efficient data/storage structure

B. at <u>operation time</u> 1) for the users of the data base to define in a non-procedural way what information they want to retrieve, without having to refer to the datalogical structure of the data base

2) for the data base management system to interpret the information request and select dynamically an efficient processing strategy

1   Introduction

The purpose of a data base is to receive, retain, and produce information, knowledge, about a slice of reality, S. S will be called the object system of the data base. The infological approach to data bases starts out from the assumption that S will often satisfy the following general description:

(1)   "S contains different kinds of objects. At any point of time every object in S possesses a set of properties. Some of the properties of an object are local, i e they are independent of the existence and properties of other objects in S. Other properties of an object are relational, i e they are dependent upon the object's relations to other objects in S."

It is seen that this general description of an object system rests upon four fundamental concepts: "object", "property", "object relation", and "time". A fifth
fundamental concept within the infological framework is "reference". In much the
same way as objects, properties, object relations, and times are supposed to be
the building-blocks of the object system, references to object system entities
may be combined into structured information, messages, about the object system.
References and messages are conceptual, non-physical entities, which may however
be represented by data and datalogical structures like file entries, files, and
file complexes. Datalogical structures are allocated to memories and thus have to
reflect both the infological structure of the represented information and the
physical storage and access structure of the representing medium.

Thus the infological theory of data bases makes a clear distinction between (a)
the object system, (b) information about the object system, (c) data representations of information, and (d) the storing and accessing medium to which the data
are allocated. During the design of a data base we have to define an efficient
mapping of (a) into (d). According to the infological view, this task may be
performed in a more systematical way and with more constructive assistance from
the ultimate users of the data base, if we sub-divide the (a) → (d) mapping into
the partial mappings (a) → (b), (b) → (c), and (c) → (d). While defining (a) → (b)
we are only concerned with the infological aspect of the data base. Datalogical
considerations are deliberately postponed to later design steps.

What we actually do when we define the (a) → (b) sub-mapping is that we individual-
ize the general description (1) with respect to a particular object system S' and
a particular data base DB(S'). In principle this is done by telling what objects
in S' are of interest, what properties these objects may have, what relationships
may prevail between different kinds of objects, and by what names we want to refer
to different object system entities. A statement of this kind will be called a
specification of the particular infological model IM(S') underlying the data base
DB(S'). Whereas the statement (1) is assumed to be valid for all object systems
of all data bases, an IM specification will usually only be valid for one
particular data base.

Infological theory does not uniquely determine one particular infological model
IM(S') for a particular object system S'. If two different project teams were
given the same specification task, they are likely to get slightly different results. Thus the same slice of reality may be looked at through different "infological glasses". However, adherence to the infological vocabulary and syntax will
make it easy for any project team member, or even for an outsider to put the
finger on the differences and to argue for one view or the other.

2   The infological framework

In the previous section we identified the five fundamental concepts of the
infological framework. Figure 1 shows how these concepts are logically related to
some important derived concepts, i e concepts which are formally defined in terms
of the fundamental concepts. In the subsequent sections the concepts referred to
in the figure will be briefly commented upon. For a detailed analsyis, see Sundgren
(1973), chapters 2 and 3.

2.1   Objects, properties, object relations and time

An object is an entity or a phenomenon that we are interested in, something that
we want to gather information about. Objects may or may not be physical entities.
Enterprises, departments, educations, leisure activities, and car accidents are as
good "object candidates" as are persons, buildings, areas, pets, and motor
vehicles. A particular object may either be formally undefined, atomic, or defined
in terms of other specified entities. The latter kind of objects are called
compound objects. A household, consisting of a set of persons, is a good example
of a compound object. A trade transaction is a more sophisticated example which
will be treated in section 2.2.

Objects are characterized by their properties and by the relations which hold
between n-tuples of objects (n $\geq$ 2). Formally we may regard properties as object
relations of degree n = 1. Properties and object relations may generate other
properties and object relations according to certain generation rules. For example,
the properties "to be tall" and "to be lean" may generate properties like "to be
both tall and lean" and "to be either lean or not tall". The property "to have a
father who is a millionaire" is an example of a relational property, i e a property
which is generated by another property ("to be a millionaire") and an object
relation ("to be father of").

Objects have properties and are related to each other at points of time or during
time intervals. The infological time concept covers both points of time and time
intervals. This means among other things that regardless of whether a data base
user prefers so-called "stock models" or "flow models", he should be able to
express his model within the infological framework.

Properties and object relations may be time-dependent. For example, the property
"to be in London 1970-01-01" is a time-dependent property which is generated by the
time-independent property "to be in London" and the time "1970-01-01". Time-
dependent properties are always stable in the sense that if an object has such a

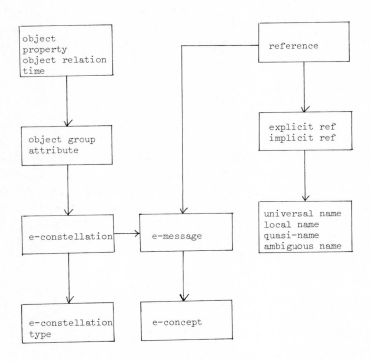

<u>Figure 1</u>

property p(t) at t' then it will have the same property at any other time t"
during its life-time.

Example. Suppose A marries B at time t. For some time after t, A will then have
the property of being married to B. However, this property may be highly instable.
On the other hand, the time-dependent property of A of having married B at t is
perfectly stable. A may very well escape B, but he may never escape the fact that
he once married B.

Properties which are used as general identifiers of objects should be stable. This
is a rule which is often violated in practice with a lot of trouble as a result.
The rule implies that unless one chooses "informationless" registration numbers
for object identification purposes, one should generate identifiers from stable
(e g time-dependent) properties which may be easily and undoubtedly established.

2.2   Constellations, constellation types, object groups, and attributes

According to the infological theory, objects, properties, object relations, and
times form certain basic structures, called elementary constellations, or
e-constellations, which together define the whole structure and contents of the
object system.

Definition 1. If x is an object or an n-tuple of objects, y is a property or an
n-ary object relation, and z is a time, then the triple $\langle x, y, z \rangle$ is called an
e-constellation. If x is a single object and y is a property, then the e-constellation is said to be of property type. Otherwise it is said to be a relational
e-constellation.

Remark. As has been suggested in section 2.1 compound structures, like e-constellations, may themselves be strong object candidates.

A sales transaction, for instance, may be primarily thought of as a relational
e-constellation

  $\langle\langle$seller, buyer, product$\rangle$, sell, time$\rangle$

However, the transaction as such may very well be "something that we are interested
in, something that we want to gather information about". For example, we may be
interested in the quantity sold or the transportation mode for the consignment.
Thus the sales transaction may be the natural object part of property type

e-constellations like

<sales transaction, quantity, time>
<sales transaction, transportation mode, time>

Note that the quantity and the transportation mode cannot in general be regarded
as a property of any one of the object constituents of the sales transaction. The
quantity could not be regarded as a property of the product, provided that
different quantities of the product can be bought. Neither could it be regarded as
a property of the buyer, provided that the buyer may buy different quantities on
different occasions. Etc. Thus in connection with phenomena like transactions
there are properties for which there is no feasible object smaller than the
transaction itself.

End of remark.

For a particular infological model IM(S') we should distinguish between

C = the set of all e-constellations
V = the set of valid e-constellations
F = the set of facts

F is a subset of V which is a subset of C. C contains all triples which are
e-constellations according to definition 1. However, when we specify an infological model, we also specify restrictions which make certain e-constellations
invalid. For example, we may specify that a particular property is only relevant
for a particular kind of objects, or that a certain object relation requires the
time component to be a time interval and not a point of time. Thus V could be
interpreted as the set of all "imaginable" situations in the object system, when
the latter is looked upon through our particular part of "infological glasses".
All "imaginable" situations do not actually occur. Those which do are called facts
and belong to F. Thus F is the set of e-constellations which have occured, are
occurring, or will occur.

One way of specifying the object system part of an infological model would be to
state explicitly, e-constellation by e-constellation, the contents of V. This
specification method is not practically feasible, however. Instead an infological
model should be specified by enumeration of a number of so-called e-constellation
types which implicitly determine the contents of V. The "e-constellation type"
concept is central within the infological theory and will be discussed below, but
first we have to define "object group" and "attribute".

Definition 2. The object group $O(p)$ generated by a property p, the so-called group property, is the set of all objects which have, have had, or will have the property p, i e

$$O(p) = \{o_i \mid \exists t: <o_i, p, t> \in F\}$$

A set of objects O is an object group if and only if there is a property p which generates $O = O(p)$.

Definition 3. The time slice $O_t(p)$ of the object group $O(p)$ is the subset of $O(p)$ characterized by

$$O_t(p) = \{o_i \mid <o_i, p, t> \in F\}$$

It is easy to prove that any object group $O(p)$ is the union set of all time slices $O_t(p)$, i e that

$$O(p) = \bigcup_t O_t(p)$$

$O_t(p)$ is the set of objects having property p at time t. If t is incompatible with p because of the restrictions defined for the infological model, then $O_t(p) = \emptyset$.

For time-dependent properties $p = p(t_1, \ldots, t_n)$ all non-empty time-slices are identical with the whole object group.

Example. The object group $O(p)$

"persons born in 1900, working in 1920 as miners, and being still alive"

is generated by a time-dependent property $p = p(t_1, t_2, t_3)$, where t_1 = 1900, t_2 = 1920, and t_3 = "now". It follows from definition 3 and the definition of "time-dependent property" that $O_t(p) = O(p)$ or $O_t(p) = \emptyset$ for any t.

Intuitively, some object groups are more "natural" classes of objects than others. For example, "persons", "enterprises", and "motor vehicles" may seem to be more "natural" object groups than the object group $O(p)$ in the example above. Without stating a formal definition here, we shall use the term "object type" for "natural" object groups. When we specify infological models it is often practical to talk in terms of (permanent) object types as distinct from the more ephemeral object groups, which are (temporarily) defined by an information consumer at data base operation time.

Now that we have discussed groups of objects we shall turn our interest to <u>attri-butes</u>, which will be defined as particular groups of properties.

<u>Definition 4</u>. If

(a) $O(p)$ is an object group generated by the property p, and

(b) $A = \{v_i\}$ is a set of properties, and

(c)   for every time slice $O_t(p)$, every object which is contained in $O_t(p)$ is
             also contained in at least one of the corresponding time slices $O_t(v_i)$
             generated by the properties v_i in A,

then

(d) A is said to be an <u>attribute</u> which is <u>relevant</u> to the object group $O(p)$,
             and

(e)   the elements v_i of A are called the <u>values</u> of the attribute A.

A set of properties A is an <u>attribute</u> if and only if there is an object group for
which A is relevant. The object group is called a <u>relevance group</u> of the attribute.

If we substitute "exactly one" for "at least one" in condition (c) above, we get
the definition of a <u>single-valued attribute</u>. Single-valued attributes will also be
called <u>variables</u>. Attributes which are not variables will be called <u>multiple-valued attributes</u>.

Suppose A is a single-valued attribute, i e a variable, with the relevance group
$O(p)$. Also suppose that the object o_i is a member of $O(p)$ at time t. Then,
according to the definition, there is exactly one property, one value v_j, of A,
which o_i has at t. We shall say then that the attribute takes the value v_j for the
object o_i at time t.

We may now give the earlier announced definition of "e-constellation type".

<u>Definition 5</u>. If x is an object group or an n-tuple of object groups, and y is an
attribute or an n-ary object relation, then the pair $\langle x, y \rangle$ is called an
e-constellation type.

A property type e-constellation $\langle o, p, t \rangle$ and an attributive <u>e-constellation
type</u> $\langle 0, A \rangle$ are said to <u>correspond</u> to each other if and only if $o \in 0$ and $p \in A$.

Similarly a relational e-constellation $\langle\langle o_1, \ldots, o_n\rangle, r, t\rangle$ and a <u>relational e-constellation type</u> $\langle\langle O_1, \ldots, O_n\rangle, R\rangle$ are said to correspond to each other if and only if $o_1 \in O_1, \ldots, o_n \in O_n$, and $r = R$.

Sometimes it may be useful to talk about different <u>time versions</u> of e-constellation types. A time version of an attributive e-constellation type has the structure $\langle O, A, t\rangle$, whereas $\langle\langle O_1, \ldots, O_n\rangle, R, t\rangle$ shows the structure of a time-version of a relational e-constellation type. The number of time-versions per e-constellation type, which the ultimate data base users consider to be of interest, may be an important input parameter to the design process.

Enumeration of e-constellation types is a convenient and precise method for specification of the object system part of an infological model $IM(S')$. Such an enumeration does not anticipate any datalogical design decisions. Yet it constitutes a sound basis for the file formation part of the design process. Files corresponding to e-constellation types will be called elementary files, e-files. During the design process several e-files may be consolidated into larger files, c-files, for the sake of storage and retrieval efficiency. Cf section 5.

2.3   References, messages, and message types

<u>References</u> are conceptual, mental entities which human beings use when they perceive and think about an object system. Each reference refers to an object system entity, the <u>target</u> of the reference. Thus there are e g object references, property references, attribute references, object relation references, and time references with objects, properties, attributes, object relations, and times respectively as targets.

References may be combined into <u>reference expressions</u>. An elementary message, or <u>e-message</u>, is a reference expression which has an e-constellation as the object system target. An e-message of <u>property type</u> has the structure

$$\langle \rho(\text{object}), \rho(\text{property}), \rho(\text{time})\rangle$$

whereas

$$\langle\langle \rho(\text{object 1}), \ldots, \rho(\text{object n})\rangle, \rho(\text{obj rel}), \rho(\text{time})\rangle$$

shows the structure of a <u>relational</u> e-message. The "$\rho(\text{property})$" sub-reference of a property type e-message will often be a reference expression itself, with the structure

$$\langle \rho(\text{attribute}), \rho(\text{value}) \rangle$$

Such a property reference will be called a <u>complex property reference</u>.

Different references and reference expressions may have the same object system target. For example figure 2 shows how the reference expression, or <u>implicit reference</u>,

"THE FAIR-HAIRED SISTER OF BILL"

may indirectly, via other object system entities, refer to the same object as the <u>atomic</u>, or <u>explicit</u>, reference

"ANNE"

In general, reference expressions and object system structures are isomorphic according to the following pattern

$$\text{expr } (\rho_1, \ldots, \rho_n)$$
$$\updownarrow \quad \updownarrow \qquad \updownarrow$$
$$g \ (e_1, \ldots, e_n)$$

where $\rho_1, \ldots, \rho_n$ are atomic references, $e_1, \ldots, e_n$ are object system entities, and g is generation rule, for example a property generation rule of the kind discussed in section 2.1.

The structure of a reference expression determines for any sub-reference of the expression what kind of object system entity it refers to. For example, the structure of the reference expression

"THE YOUNGEST COUSIN OF GEORGE MARRIED THE FAIR-HAIRED SISTER OF BILL THE SAME DAY AS MARY´S GRANDMOTHER DIED"

determines that "THE YOUNGEST COUSIN OF GEORGE" refers to an object, that "MARRIED" refers to an object relation, and that "THE SAME DAY AS MARY´S GRANDMOTHER DIED" refers to a time.

The structure of a reference expression may be stated explicitly, separately from the reference itself, but at least partially it may alternatively be implied by the sub-references of the expression. Suppose, for instance, that the sub-reference "MARRIED" of the reference expression above is <u>universally unique</u> within a

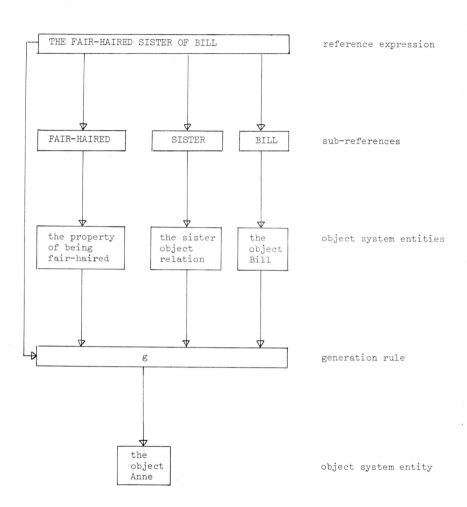

THE FAIR-HAIRED SISTER OF BILL	reference expression
FAIR-HAIRED SISTER BILL	sub-references
the property of being fair-haired / the sister object relation / the object Bill	object system entities
g	generation rule
the object Anne	object system entity

Figure 2

particular infological model, i e in whatever infological context "MARRIED" occurs,
it refers to one and the same uniquely identified object system entity, in this
case a binary object relation. Then wherever "MARRIED" occurs, it imposes a
certain structure upon its infological context, i e upon the reference expression
of which it is a sub-reference. More precisely the occurrence of the sub-reference
"MARRIED" in a reference expression implies, under the conditions just stated, the
co-occurrence in the same reference expression of two sub-references referring to
objects.

An explicit reference which is universally unique will be called a universal name.

An explicit reference, which is not universally unique, but which in its infological context refers to one particular object system entity, will be called a
context-dependent name, or a local name.

In communication - between people or between people and data bases - it may be
convenient to use references as though they were names, albeit one does not know
it they actually are unique. One then expects constructive feed-back from the
person (the data base), should the reference not be unique within his (its)
infological model. After one or more interactions it will hopefully be possible
to replace the tentative name, or quasi-name, with a universal name or local name
in the original reference expression.

Example. Suppose a person asks a data base for the income of somebody. Then he
might use "INCOME" as a preliminary, quasi-name substitute for a lot of slightly
differently defined income attributes. Thus he might get the return question from
the data base, whether he means for instance "GROSS INCOME", with the definition
..., or whether he rather means "INCOME NET OF TAX", with the definition ..., or
... . Note that procedures like this one make it possible for a user to communicate
with a data base, even if he is not perfectly familiar with the details of the
particular infological model underlying the data base.

The sub-references, or conceptual terms, of an e-message are the building-blocks
of information, but they are not themselves information. The complete e-message
is the smallest information structure. If we remove any of its terms, it will not
convey well-defined knowledge any longer.

E-messages refer to e-constellations. In particular, e-messages which refer to
valid e-constellations will be called meaningful e-messages, whereas e-messages
which refer to e-facts will be called true e-messages. E-messages referring to
members of the difference set $V \setminus F$ will be called false e-messages. It follows

from the definitions in section 2.2 that all true e-messages and all false e-messages are meaningful, and that all meaningful e-messages are either true of false.

For the same reasons and in much the same way as we classified e-constellations into e-constellation types, we shall classify e-messages into e-message types, or e-concepts to speak with Langefors [1].

Definition 6. If $\rho(x)$ refers to an object group or an n-tuple of object groups, and $\rho(y)$ to an attribute or an n-ary object relation, then the reference expression $\langle \rho(x), \rho(y) \rangle$ is called an e-message type, or e-concept.

It should be obvious how we may now define attributive e-concepts $\langle \rho(0), \rho(A) \rangle$ with time-versions $\langle \rho(0), \rho(A), \rho(t) \rangle$, and relational e-concepts $\langle\!\langle \rho(0_1), \ldots, \rho(0_n) \rangle, \rho(R) \rangle$ with time-versions $\langle\!\langle \rho(0_1), \ldots, \rho(0_n) \rangle, \rho(R), \rho(t) \rangle$; cf section 2.2.

3   The data base and its environment

3.1   The infological data base concept

At the present state of the art it does not seem to be possible to give a short definition covering all aspects of the complex data base concept. It seems justified and necessary for users, systemeers, computer specialists, and information system researchers to have slightly different opinions as to what a data base really is. On the other hand, if different categories of people are to be able to communicate constructively with each other in a data base design project, their respective conceptualizations of the data base have to be compatible with each other, even if they are not identical. We think that the infological view of the data base as being basically a black box reservoir of information is a view which promotes the development of a relevant common kernel of ideas and attitudes among those who take part in a data base project.

The infological data base concept is based upon the ultimate user's view of the data base. The ultimate user of a data base is an information consumer, e g a planner or a decision-maker, and to him the data base is an information source among other information sources. If we adopt the infological view of the data base concept, we realize that the ultimate user of a data base is up to essentially the same interpretation and confidence problems as he is up to when we uses any artificial or human source of information which is external to his own mind. The retrieved information may be more or less uncertain, and this in

turn may or may not affect the solution to the user´s problem. The information
could be deliberately or inadvertently biased for some reason. The definitions,
assumptions, and models underlying the information contents of the data base may
not be what the information consumer believes them to be. Thus the user of a data
base should not only request the information which he needs to solve his problem.
He should also request information about quality and other properties of the
directly needed information. We shall refer to such information as "information on
information". Information on information is made up by messages, the object parts
of which are themselves messages.

Information on information is one important category of meta-information. The
latter concept also covers

-          information about the basic constituents of the particular infological
           model underlying the data base; example: formal and informal definitions
           of attributes and object types

-          information about the data representations of the information contents
           of the data base; example: file descriptions

Remark. Data representations of meta-information will be called meta-data. Subsystems of data bases containing meta-information and data representations thereof
may be called meta-data-bases.

A well designed data base should stimulate the user to request meta-information.
At least it should assist the user in his search for such information. We shall
call these tasks "the semantic mission of the data base".

By adopting the infological view of the data base as being a black box reservoir
of information with which the information consumer communicates we gain several
advantages. One advantage is that the interest of the designers is focused upon
non-datalogical problems like the quality and interpretation problems mentioned
above. Thus the infological data base concept could help the designers to avoid
the common mistake of jumping too soon into vivid discussions about what file and
data structures to choose, what programming language or software package to use,
and other similar problems which concern internal properties of the system to be
designed and constructed. Before such datalogical problems are tackled, the
external, infological properties of the planned system should have been settled
upon as far as possible. In other words: the designer of a data base, like the
designer of any other system should consider very carefully what the system should
do, before he devotes too much energy to "how?"-questions.

Figure 3 visualizes the data base black box, its environment, and the communication which is assumed to take place between the data base and its environment. Applying the black box approach to the data base means that we do not care about the internal details of the data base. Instead we discuss input and output to and from the system, and the relations between input and output.

The environment of a system may be defined as the set of conditions that are relevant to but not under the control of the managers of the system. However, we have to be careful when we use such a definition in general discussions of data base design, because what is under the control of the goalsetters and designers will vary from one data base design situation to another. A data base is often a component in a broader information system, which may or may not be designed or redesigned in connection with the design of the data base. Thus in a practical situation the boundaries between the controllable main system and the uncontroll-able environment should perhaps be drawn in a different way than is done in the subsequent discussion.

The input and output transactions of a data base system usually appear in pairs: an input transaction causes the appearance of an output transaction. What kind of input transactions a data base should be ready to accept, what kind of output transaction a particular input transaction should result in, and how long time the intervening processing may take in different situations are good examples of external properties of the planned data base. Thus they are good examples of problems which could and should be discussed in infological terms at an early design stage.

3.2   The data base environment

Figure 4 is a revised version of figure 3, where the data base environment has been broken down into eight subsystems. The arrows indicate the principal informa-tion and control flows between the environment and the data base and between the different environment subsystems.

The nine "system boxes" in figure 4 may be grouped in the following way. The two upper left boxes represent the object system to be observed by the information suppliers of the data base and/or controlled by information consumers like planners and other decision-influencers. The data base designer is faced with different kinds of design problems depending upon the degree and character of overlapping between the observed and the controlled object system.

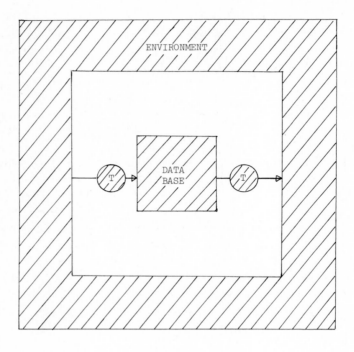

Figure 3

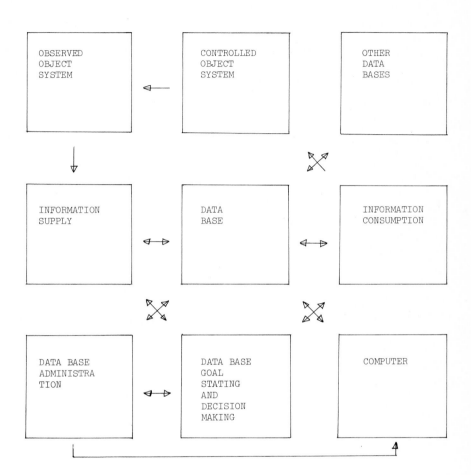

Figure 4

The six boxes at the bottom of the figure represent the <u>information system</u> of
which the data base is a part. Depending upon the level of ambition, which is set
for a particular data base, one and the same task, say coding of input information,
error elimination or "intelligent analysis" of retrieved information, may be
allocated to the data base itself or to one of the environment subsystems within
the surrounding information system. Sometimes the task may be most efficiently
performed in "conversational mode" as a joint effort between the data base and its
environment.

The tasks of the <u>data base administration</u> function are good examples of tasks which
should often be performed "semiautomatically", in close cooperation between the
data base and its environment. Among other things the data base administrator is
responsible for infological as well as datalogical restructuring of the data base.
<u>Datalogical restructuring</u> may be for example changes of the file structure of the
data base in order to speed up response times or save secondary storage. <u>Infologi-
cal restructuring</u> will mean such things as the introduction or elimination of an
object type or an e-concept, or the changing of the secrecy status of a particular
attribute, i e changes which concern the infological model IM(S') underlying the
data base..

Finally, the upper right box in figure 4 represents <u>other data bases</u>, belonging
to other information systems, which are connected to "our" data base and "our"
information system. The different parties involved in a data base network may often
have a lot to gain by coordination activities like integration of their respective
infological models

$$IM_1(S_1), \ldots, IM_n(S_n)$$

into one joint model

$$IM(S) \text{ where } S = \bigcup_{i=1}^{n} S_i$$

Infological integration is often much more important than physical integration.

3.3   Basic subsystems of the infological data base: the schema, the nucleus,
             and the filter

Still regarding the data base from an infological point of view we may identify
three principal functions, or subsystems, within the data base: the schema, the
nucleus, and the filter; cf figure 5.

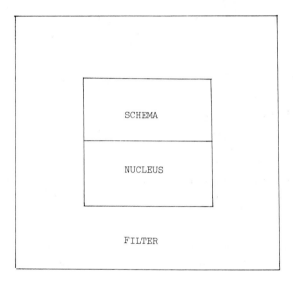

Figure 5

The <u>nucleus</u> is the set of e-messages which are explicitly represented by data in physically existing file entries.

The <u>schema</u> may be thought of as a statement of the particular infological model which is underlying the data base. The schema has a <u>deductive</u> mission and a <u>semantic</u> mission. In its deductive capacity the schema "amplifies" the information contents, N, of the nucleus so as to become the total information contents, M, of the data base. The deductive function of the schema is tied to a set of derivation rules, which determine how some messages in the data base generate other messages. Formal definitions stating how the value of one attribute may be calculated from the values of other attributes are typical examples of such derivation rules. More sophisticated data bases may contain message generation rules of probabilistic nature. An advanced data base might even be able to induce such rules automatically from its own contents.

The semantic mission of the schema consists in conveying to the information consumer the true meaning of the messages contained in the data base. This is a non-trivial task, in which the names chosen for attributes etc as well as informal definitions and descriptions play important roles. The task is complicated by the circumstance that there are usually many different persons involved in the creation, maintenance, and use of the information potential of a data base. Almost certainly all these persons have non-identical frames of reference. Not even the frame of reference of one single person is invariant over time.

The <u>filter</u> function of the infological data base should protect the data base and its users against false messages and messages which are not meaningful according to the specifications and definitions embedded in the schema.

The actions of the filter may take several guises. For instance it could make the data base refuse input messages which are not meaningful within the particular infological model underlying the data base. Similarly, the filter could monitor the output messages, assembled by the data base, for oddities. Not only could the filter act upon the in- and out-going transactions. Whenever the data base system is idle, i e when it does not interact with its environment, it could, through its filter function, try to "purify" itself by carrying out different kinds of consistency checks, thus utilizing the redundancy that may exist in the base.

Beside performing quality control kind of actions, the data base filter could also do things like preventing disclosure of confidential information to un-authorized interactors. In this capacity the filter may in effect make the same physical data base appear infologically different to different users.

Remark. A data base with a selective filter, as described above, may be regarded as a special case of a multi-schema data base, i e a data base with several schemas, equivalent to several infological models, which make the same physical data appear as different infological data bases. Note, however, that among the multiple schemas of such data bases there has to be one schema which is more fundamental than the others, namely the schema which is assumed when the data base assimilates information from its environment. Compare the general impossibility of observing without categories in which to observe, i e without a model of the observed!

3.4   Data base dynamics

By changing the schema, the nucleus, or the filter, we also change the information contents of the data base. Naturally the typical, most frequent way of changing the data base will be to add or delete a particular message, i e to change the nucleus of the data base. In so doing, we change immediately the information contents of the base except in certain redundancy situations. By changing the schema we may or may not change the information contents of the data base at once. For example, the substitution of one definition for another will probably directly affect the set of messages contained in the base, whereas the introduction of a new attribute will not have any effects upon the information contents of the data base, until messages involving references to the new attribute arrive. A filter change, finally, will typically have indirect, mediate effects only. However, e g an alteration of the filter's selectivity towards confidential messages may immediately and drastically change the effective data base from a particular user's point of view.

Figure 6 provides an alternative starting point for the discussion of data base dynamics. It shows two different ways of classifying the set of all messages, $M\Omega$. According to classification A, $M\Omega$ consists of the three subsets

$A_1 =$ the set of false messages

$A_2 =$ the set of meaningless messages

$A_3 =$ the set of true messages

According to the other classification, B, $M\Omega$ consists of the subsets

$B_1 =$ the set of unknown messages, i e messages which neither are at present in the information contents of the data base under consideration, nor have been so at any earlier point of time

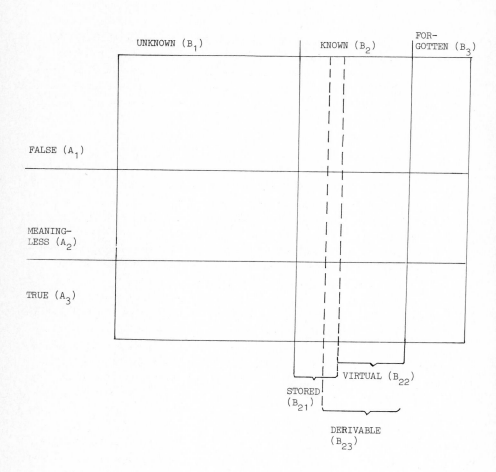

<u>Figure 6</u>   A cross-classification of the set of all
              messages (MΩ)

B_2 =   the set of <u>known messages</u>, i e messages which are at present contained
               in the data base

B_3 =   the set of <u>forgotten messages</u>, i e messages which are not at present
               in the data base, but which have been so at some earlier point of time

The set B_2 of known messages may be further subdivided into

B_{21} =   the set of <u>stored messages</u>, i e messages which are contained in the
               data base nucleus

B_{22} =   the set of <u>virtual messages</u>, i e messages which are contained in the
               data base without being stored in the nucleus

The subsets B_{21} and B_{22} are exclusive. We may also define

B_{23} =   the set of <u>derivable messages</u>, i e messages which derivable from other
               messages in the data base by means of the derivation rules in the data
               base schema

Note that B_{22} is a subset of B_{23}. The data base (nucleus) is <u>non-redundant</u> if and
only if $B_{22} = B_{23}$. If $B_{22} = B_{23} = \phi$, the data base has no deductive power.

It is obvious that classification B is tied to the particular data base under
consideration. Classification A is not data base independent either, however. We
can see this if we analyze what happens if we change the data base schema, i e if
we modify the particular infological model underlying the data base.

For data bases which are based upon identical infological models, and thus have
identical schemas, the $M\Omega$-sets are identical, and so are the subsets according to
classification A, because (i) the common schema uniquely determines a common
subset A_2 of meaningless messages, and (ii) if we assume the existence of one
unique reality, the same meaningful messages has to belong either to the subset
A_1 of false messages in both data bases or to the subset A_3 of true messages in
both bases. However, the classification B need not coincide for two data bases,
even if they are based upon the same infological model and have a common schema,
because one of the bases may have got to know (or forgotten) a lot of messages
which the other data base has not learnt (forgotten) yet.

The information contents $M(t)$ of a data base $DB(t)$ at a particular point of time
t can easily be identified as the subset B_2 of known messages. The assimilation

by the data base of an unknown message implies a $B_1 \to B_2$ transition. If the
message was already known by the data base, the addition transaction might lead
to nothing or to a transition from B_{22} to $B_{21} \cap B_{23}$; in the latter case the
message is redundantly stored although it is derivable. Similarly a deletion
transaction might lead to one of the transitions $B_2 \to B_3$, or $B_{21} \cap B_{23} \to B_{22}$.

From figure 6 we find immediately that

$$M(t) = B_2 = (A_1 \cap B_2) \cup (A_2 \cap B_2) \cup (A_3 \cap B_2)$$

Remark. The mission of the data base filter may be expressed as

(a)   keeping down the number of messages in $(A_1 \cap B_2)$; "consistency checking"

(b)   keeping down the number of messages in $(A_2 \cap B_2)$; "syntax checking"

(c)   preventing confidential messages in $(A_3 \cap B_2)$ from being disclosed to
           unauthorized users; "secrecy checking"

(d)   preventing $(A_3 \cap B_2) \to (A_3 \cap B_3)$ transitions, unless they are desired
           by the data base owner; "security checking"

4   Data base interaction

4.1   Different kinds of interactors and interactions

If we look back at figure 4, we realize that the data base environment contains
several quite different categories of data base interactors, e g

- information suppliers,
- information consumers, or ultimate users, and
- data base administrators

Each category may be further subdivided. For example, some of the data base
administrators are information structures, others are data structurers; cf
section 3.2.

Different interactor categories may require access to the data base for quite
different reasons, and this in combination with educational and other differences
could well motivate the design of different interaction languages for different
kinds of interactions and interactors. So far most development efforts within the

realm of data base interaction languages have been concentrated upon the needs of
"application programmers" and "parametric users". Information consumers with
complex information needs but without programming knowledge have been more or less
neglected, and so have several other interactor categories, e g information
suppliers, and infological and datalogical restructurers.

Data base interaction languages may be classified along several dimensions, e g

- degree of conversation
- degree of procedurality
- degree of reality-orientation

It is felt that the infological approach to data bases will in particular facilitate the development of non-procedural, reality-oriented data base languages for
the expression of complex information requests.

As an alternative classification basis for interactions and transactions between
the data base and its environment we shall borrow the so-called S-O-R model from
psychology. In a particular interaction

(S)   a _stimulus_ from the environment may or may not occur
(O)   the _organism_, i e the data base, may or may not be transformed
(R)   a _response_ from the data base may or may not appear

As a situation characterized by a "null stimulus", $S = \emptyset$, a "null transformation",
$O \rightarrow O$, and a "null response, $R = \emptyset$, cannot very well be regarded as interactive,
this leaves us with $2^7 - 1 = 7$ basic interaction types. A structuring of these
interaction types is shown in figure 7.

4.2   Data base transactions

It is by means of data base transactions that the exchange of data, information,
and control between the data base and its environment takes place. Formally a data
base transaction has the structure

- dbt = ⟨operator, parameter⟩

where

- the _operator_ is a stimulus which initiates a certain _kind of behavior_, or
action, on part of the data base or the environment interactor, depending upon

S - O - R	INTERACTION TYPE
$\emptyset$ - * - *	Spontaneous behavior
$\emptyset$ - 1 - *	- modified data base
$\emptyset$ - $\emptyset$ - *	- invariant data base
1 - * - *	Triggered behavior
1 - 1 - *	- modified data base
	. nucleus modification
	- addition of message
	- deletion of message
	- substitution
	. schema modification
	. filter modification
1 - $\emptyset$ - *	- invariant data base
	. query
	- about the object system proper[1]
	- about the information[1]
	. modification failure

Figure 7   A classification of interactions based upon the
            S - O - R model

Legend:

"$\emptyset$" = null stimulus (transformation, response)
"1" = other than null stimulus (transformation, response)
"*" = any kind of stimulus (transformation, response)

---

[1] Queries about the information request meta-information (cf section
3.1), whereas queries about the object system proper request information about the observed object system (cf figure 4)

the direction of the transaction

- the <u>parameter</u> modifies the behavior of the data base or interactor by providing
the process, initiated by the operator, with certain input.

Naturally, the operator need not be represented by a specific string of characters
or the like. Just as often the stimulus may be inseparable from the string of
characters representing the parameter. For instance, a query operator may be
explicitly represented by a question mark ("?"), or implicitly represented by the
grammatical structure of the message supplying the parametrical input to the
query process.

The number and scope of the operators we define for a specific data base task will
depend upon whether we choose to achieve a certain total amount of "<u>communication
variety</u>" by means of a few operators allowing a wide range of parametrical input
or by means of a larger number of operators, each of them with more rigid
requirements upon the parametrical input.

There are three major transaction types, which all concern nucleus modification:

(a) $<$ ADD, message $>$, information addition
(b) $<$ DELETE, message $>$, information deletion
(c) $<$ SUBSTITUTE, message 1, message 2 $>$, information substitution

Suppose that the message part of an addition (or a deletion) transaction contains
n e-messages. Then it is not at all certain that the effective information contents
of the data base will be increased (decreased) by n e-messages. For example, the
amplification power of the schema may cause more than n e-messages to be added
(deleted).

A substitution transaction is equivalent to a deletion of one set of e-messages,
immediately followed by an addition of another set of e-messages. In tradtional
update situations in connection with situational (as distinct from historical)
data bases, the former set of messages will seldom be explicitly stated.

4.3   Query transactions

According to figure 7 the query type of interaction is a kind of triggered
behavior which leaves the data base invariant. The triggering stimulus is
contained in a <u>query transaction</u> which normally results in a non-trivial <u>reply
transaction</u> from the data base to the interactor.

There are several kinds of query transactions. First of all, we may distinguish
between queries about the object system proper, and queries about the data base
contained information about the object system proper. However, if the meta-data
bases containing the meta-information are designed according to the same infological principles as the data base proper – and there is no reason why they should not
be – then there is no structural differences between the two kinds of queries.

If we are looking for structural differences between different kinds of queries,
we may instead distinguish between

(a)   yes/no-queries,
(b)   retrieval queries, and
(c)   process queries

What is typical of yes/no-queries is that the parameter part of such a transaction
will always be a complete message, m. If m is contained in the data base, the
obvious reply to the query is "yes", and if a message, which logically contradicts
m, is contained in the data base, the latter will certainly reply "no" to the
query. If neither m, nor its contradiction is contained in the data base some kind
of qualified "I don´t know" response should be expected. What exactly will happen
in such a situation is dependent upon our infological design of the data base
schema. A sophisticated data base might give an answer in terms of probabilities.

In retrieval queries the parameter will be an incomplete message, m. The reply is
expected to contain messages, referring to all e-constellations, which satisfy m.
Naturally, the "I don´t know" problem mentioned above is present in connection with
retrieval queries, too.

In process queries the operator part will contain a processing request, meaning
that not only should a specified set of messages be retrieved, they should also
be processed in a certain way before presentation. For instance, the processing
request could imply aggregation and statistical analysis.

Let us return to the retrieval queries for some further considerations. They are
particularly important, because in fact most transactions from an interactor to a
data base will, among other things, imply processing that is equivalent to the
processing of a retrieval query.

Many retrieval queries conform to the pattern

(2)   "For all objects having the property P , retrieve the values of the
             attributes A_1^β, ..., A_m^β at the times t_1^β, ..., t_m^β, respectively."

This query may be formally described as a set of m incomplete e-messages

(3) $< P^\alpha, \; < A_i^\beta, \; ? >, \; t_i^\beta >$ i = 1, ..., m

where P^α is an ambiguous object reference, and $< A_i^\beta, \; ? >$ is an ambiguous property
reference. We see that the query consists of an α-part and a β-part. The α-part,
P^α, may be a very complex reference expression involving a lot of attribute
references, A_j^α, time references, t_j^α, and object relation references. Note that the
difference between α-attributes and β-attributes is not inherent in the attributes.
It is rather a functional difference, depending upon the infological contexts of
the respective attributes within the query reference expression.

(4)   "What are the addresses of the textile-manufacturing enterprises with
             more than 15 employees and producing articles containing the poison
             with the industrial name POI?"

is an example of an αβ-query, i e a retrieval query conforming to the pattern (2),
(3).

Figure 8 shows how (4) and other αβ-queries may be analyzed and graphically
represented. By adopting a few conventions, we may instead get the much simpler
representation shown in figure 9.

An αβ-query requests the retrieval of a single e-message or an unstructured
conjunction of e-messages. More general retrieval requests will possess one or
more of the following characteristics:

(a)   The query requests the retrieval of a stuctured conjunction of e-
             messages, sorted by one or more arguments.

(b)   The query requests the fabrication of aggregate messages from sets of
             e-messages. An aggregate message is a message, the object part of which
             refers to a compound object, and the predicate part of which is a
             function of predicate parts of messages, the object parts of which refer
             to individual member objects of the compound object referred to in the
             aggregate message.

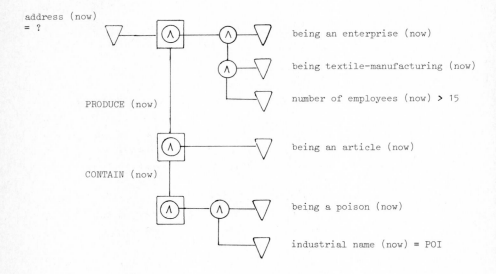

being an enterprise (now)

being textile-manufacturing (now)

number of employees (now) > 15

being an article (now)

being a poison (now)

industrial name (now) = POI

Figure 8

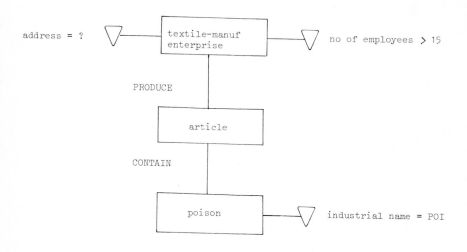

Figure 9

(c)   The query requests the retrieval of a structured conjunction of
           aggregate messages, e g a table of averages sorted by one or more
           arguments.

Queries possessing one or more of these characteristics may be formally described
as structured sets of $\alpha\beta$-queries. Examples:

(5)   "List the names and telephone numbers of all employees by department."

(6)   "Compute average income 1971 for different social classes in Stockholm."

The α-parts of the $\alpha\beta$-queries making up these and similar requests may be
formalized in the following way:

(7) $$P^\alpha_1 = P^\alpha_o \wedge (v^\gamma = a_1)$$
           $$\vdots$$
           $$P^\alpha_n = P^\alpha_o \wedge (v^\gamma = a_n)$$

In (5) the common α-property P^α_o is "to be an employee", and in (6) it is to be an
inhabitant in Stockholm". The common attribute, which we shall call a γ-attribute,
v^γ, is "department" in (5) and "social class" in (6). "n" is equal to the number
of departments and the number of social classes, respectively, i e the number of
values of v^γ.

More generally the α-parts of the set of $\alpha\beta$-queries making up a complex transaction
may contain several, say k, common γ-attributes. Then the set of α-parts may be
formalized in the following way:

(8) $$P^\alpha_{1\ldots1} = P^\alpha_o \wedge (v^\gamma_1 = a_{11}) \wedge \ldots \wedge (v^\gamma_k = a_{k1})$$
           $$P^\alpha_{1\ldots2} = P^\alpha_o \wedge (v^\gamma_1 = a_{11}) \wedge \ldots \wedge (v^\gamma_k = a_{k2})$$
           $$\vdots$$
           $$P^\alpha_{1\ldots n_k} = P^\alpha_o \wedge (v^\gamma_1 = a_{11}) \wedge \ldots \wedge (v^\gamma_k = a_{kn_k})$$
           $$\vdots$$
           $$P^\alpha_{n_1\ldots1} = P^\alpha_o \wedge (v^\gamma_1 = a_{1n_1}) \wedge \ldots \wedge (v^\gamma_k = a_{k1})$$
           $$\vdots$$
           $$P^\alpha_{n_1\ldots n_k} = P^\alpha_o \wedge (v^\gamma_1 = a_{1n_1}) \wedge \ldots \wedge (v^\gamma_k = a_{kn_k})$$

There are $\displaystyle\prod_{i=1}^{k} n_i$ rows in (5); n_i = the number of values that V_i^γ can take.

Example. In the request

(9)   "Compute the average length of life for human beings by nationality
           and sex."

P_0^α = "to be a human being", V_1^γ = "nationality", V_2^γ = "sex", k = 2, n_1 = the number
of nationalities, n_2 = 2.

Remark. In the formulas above we have not made explicit reference to "time",
because we thoght it would only obscure the main line of analysis here. However,
we may easily think of all involved properties and variables as time-dependent.
Similarly, the properties and variables may very well be relation-dependent.

Definition. A data base transaction, which may be dissolved into a set of αβ-
queries, the α-parts of which conform to pattern (8), will be called an αβγ-query.

αβ-queries and αβγ-queries are thoroughly analyzed in Sundgren (1973), chapters
5 and 6. An outline of a non-procedural language for such queries is also
presented there.

5   Datalogical extensions to the infological framework and theory

For those who are to perform the computer-dependent, datalogical design of a
data base, the infological "black box view" will not be sufficient. However, it
is highly desirable that the datalogical concepts and models, which computer-
oriented designers use, are compatible with the infological framework. Only then
will it be possible to "translate", in a systematical way, the external, user-
oriented requirements, as they manifest themselves in a particular infological
model IM(S'), into internal, datalogical data base properties. Thus we should
prove that the infological framework may be extended in a natural way so as to
cover the computer-oriented, representational aspect of a data base as well. There
is not room for such a proof in this paper. However, the interested reader may find
a thorough discussion of the topic in Sundgren (1973), chapter 8-9. Here we shall
only give a few indications of the contents of that discussion.

In order to bridge the gap between the infological and the datalogical sphere of
the general data base design theory, an elementary file, or e-file, is defined
in Sundgren (1973) as a certain "normal" representation of an e-concept. There
are three basic types of e-files: object e-files, property e-files, and relational

e-files. Which type we choose for a particular e-concept, ec, is dependent upon such infological parameters as the respective frequencies and response time requirements for (a) αβγ-queries where ec occurs in the α-part, (b) αβγ-queries where ec occurs in the β-part, and (c) αβγ-queries where ec occurs in the γ-part of the query.

Thus the initial datalogical design step according to the extended infological theory consists in a transformation of the set of e-concepts of the infological model into a set of object, property, and relational e-files. Then, according to Sundgren (1973) there is a set of formally well-defined file structuring operators by means of which we may transform the initial file structure into a file structure which better fits (a) the expected infological pattern of the transactions which will hit the operative data base, and (b) the storage and access structure of available memories.

After a number of applications of the file structuring operators we will arrive at the file structure which is to be implemented. The final file structure, or file system, will contain a number of subsystems called αβ-complexes, or directory/file-complexes. The internal structure of such a complex may or may not conform to some well-known file organization technique. Anyhow we will have designed our file system in a much less arbitrary and much more user-influenced way than is common today.

In summary we hope to have convinced the reader of this paper that the infological approach to data bases is an approach which a little better than alternative approaches looks after the justified interests of the ultimate data base users, at design time as well as at operation time. In this last section we have also indicated that the scope of the infological framework could in a natural way be extended so as to include all the "traditional" datalogical design problems as well. Thus even strictly computer-oriented data base designers would at least not have to sacrifice anything by re-indoctrinating themselves in the direction of an infological view. Finally, we believe that the infological framework and theory lays a long missing solid ground for further research on data bases and data base design.

Literature

[1]   Langefors, B.: Theoretical Analysis of Information Systems, Lund 1966, 1973

[2]   Sundgren, B.: An Infological Approach to Data Bases, Stockholm 1973 (PhD thesis)

DISCUSSION

<u>Durchholz</u> : You told us that the basic concepts must be first of all
meaningful to the end-user. A theory could very well use primitive
concepts, which are not intended for direct application by the user.
The goal should be to find primitives which are appropriate as a conceptual base on which concepts can be developed that lend themselves for
direct application. A good example is that of physics, where you have
primitives which are not directly observable.

<u>Sundgren</u> : It is a question of strategy for the theory development.
I think that we need intuitively meaningful concepts when we develop
a theory for the first time. In a second pass it might be worthwhile
to reduce the set of primitive concepts to a smaller number of theoretical
constructs; we have seen this in the past in other sciences.

<u>Steel</u> : Would it not be profitable to embed at once a data base
theory within a known formal framework, like set theory in order to
draw upon the guaranteed consistency and the set of theorems which
already exist in that theory ?

<u>Sundgren</u> : As I said to the previous question, it is a question of
strategy in theory development. Embedding data base theory formally
and completely within that theory is not an undertaking which I considered to be of highest priority.

<u>Falkenberg</u> : a) I doubt that it is possible to state exact formal
criteria to differentiate between objects and properties.

b) Have you considered that the same entity might very
well be regarded as an object within one "infological " model and as
a property within another one ?

Sundgren : a) You are right in saying there are no formal criteria.

However, I am convinced that useful informal rules of thumb can be
given. Moreover, my experience is that it is not a big problem for
the user to make a satisfactory intuitive distinction between objects
and properties.

        b) Yes, I have considered that and it is permitted by the
theory.

Olle :   We studied query languages in the CODASYL Systems Committee
work. We arrived at a similar structuring to your α β α queries but
we used the terms selection, extraction, processing for α_9 β_9 γ
respectively and a fourth are formatting. However, I do not believe in
your statement such a structure is adequate for 90% of the user queries
in a typical business environment. I would estimate the figure at something
more like 15 to 20%.

Sundgren : My environment is the National Central Bureau of Statistics
in Sweden. I think my estimate is correct for that environment. I am not
in a position to argue on your estimate for business applications actually
have the structure of statistical tables, even if this is not immediately
evident. Even if you are right and only 50% of business application queries
were to adhere to the α β γ pattern I think it would be worthwhile to
develop languages and software covering these.

Data Base Management, J. W. Klimbie and K. L. Koffeman, (eds.)
© *North-Holland Publishing Company (1974)*

CONCEPTS FOR DATA BASE MANAGEMENT SYSTEMS

R. DURCHHOLZ and G. RICHTER

Gesellschaft fuer Mathematik und Datenverarbeitung

St. Augustin, Germany

> We have spent the last 50 years with
> almost Ptolemaic information systems.
> These systems, and most of the thinking
> about systems, were based on a 'computer
> centered' concept.
> (Charles W. Bachman, 1973)

1. The objective

When one has to talk about Data Base Management Systems (DBMS) in general rather than about a particular DBMS, one is bound to find a conceptual basis common to all DBMS. This situation arises most convincingly in the following three areas:

- Teaching about DBMS
- Evaluation of DBMS
- Technology of producing DBMS.

In an attempt to obtain such a conceptual basis one is faced with the remarkable fact that there is a general dearth of commonly accepted and sufficiently clear concepts with which to talk about DBMS. Although every existing DBMS of course has its own concepts and terminology to communicate about its achievements and behaviour, those concepts are not only ill-defined but also vary considerably among the various DBMS.

So we undertook to look for appropriate concepts, for which task we received valuable support from work already known in the literature. However, for reasons given in section 3, we did not think previous conceptual systems, as they were, to be suitable for our aim. Therefore it became our goal to develop a coherent, consistent and adequate conceptual system for the world of Data Base Management Systems.

2. The approach

Once the goal to find such a conceptual basis is accepted, the first question is, what objects to take into consideration, that is: What is considered to be a DBMS? The criterion for this is based very much on 'feelings' such as considerations on intended use. Rigid formulation of such a criterion cannot be expected to be possible, because the concepts for doing so are exactly the thing to be developed. Feelings about DBMS tell us for instance that IMS is one, whereas the Data Management System of OS/360 is not. There are several software systems where different people may feel differently. It is legitimate to discard such systems to simplify the task in the first attempt.

Having agreed upon which software systems can be called DBMS, the next step is to detect regularities. Similarly as in the above case of selecting DBMS, simplification - that is abstraction from confusing detail - is legitimate and a well established method of natural science. Simplification led us to the hardly surprising conclusion, that the only unquestionably common feature of DBMS is that they are software systems dedicated to storing and retrieving information for some class of users. Thus the attention was focussed on the interface between DBMS and user. Considerations of architectural properties were postponed.

A close look at this interface however revealed, that by no means it was clear which features emerged from the desire to support users in their problem of storing and retrieving information and which were consequences of restrictions from technical feasibility or from lack of imagination of the DBMS-designers. We tried to reflect upon what really happens at the interface between user and DBMS. We wanted to see the rationale behind the things as they are now and thus be able to distinguish which features are intrinsic to the problem and which can be attributed to more accidential circumstances of history and technical availability. By what we saw we were caused to risk a bold leap into the hypothesis, that the DBMS we know of are a biased sample of a population of software systems mostly hidden behind the curtains of the future.

To guess by which concepts these future DBMS could be described, the only way was to explore the commonalities found in the interface with the user. Consequently, the concepts invariant in that assumed population should be expected to be rooted in the user's requirements of storing and retrieving information. So we tried to find concepts to describe the user's requirements. It should be clear from the above discussion that it was considered most important to refer to a user who is n o t biased by the knowledge of current (or, for that matter, also ancient) data processing techniques. Of course such a person is not really available, so that we had to build up an ideal user as someone with bulk information to manage and with a clear intuitive idea of what he needs, but in want of concepts to express his ideas concisely and properly. We want to provide him with concepts adequate to his way of thinking and suitable to organize the information. We expect, that a logically consistent description of processes designed to help the user handle his information will be relatively easy to make when it is based on those concepts.

3. Relation to other work

There have been quite some efforts towards general concepts for DBMS (see references). These however did not fit exactly our purpose in at least one of the following respects: 1. Restriction to a particular class of DBMS. 2. Insufficient regard of the user's view. 3. Close relation to machine features.

The second point does need some explanation. For a conceptual system, it should not be expected that the very basic concepts are readily digested by people interested in more complex units of thought, much the same as fundamental concepts in mathematics (e.g. natural numbers) need not to be considered by mathematicians solving differential equations. However, the basic concepts should form a convenient point of departure for the development of a consistent conceptual system at the top of which the notions emerge the user is in need of.

Just this was the aspect we felt to be insufficient in existing conceptual systems. We can not see for instance how records or repeating groups can be defined using the relational model without stretching the principle. A similar remark holds with respect to the DBTG data model when one tries to define general relations. Of course, in both examples it is p o s s i b l e to obtain the desired definitions, but the result seems to be artificial in the sense that the power of the basic concepts is not fully exploited, but instead secondary, quasi-basic concepts are defined. This entails unnecessary, hence unnatural, complications. The Feature

Analysis of Generalized Data Base Systems of CODASYL [6] - although
it caused some trouble to give it a consistent appearance (see [10])
- is of particular historical importance in the strive for DBMS-
concepts. In this work the attempt was made to extract concepts from
a set of given DBMS. Although there is no direct relation to our
concepts, we have to acknowledge, that a great deal of our ideas
were developed during the discussion about the Feature Analysis.

4. Concepts developed so far

The way a user wants to organize his information is not only given
by its 'natural structure' but will certainly depend on the way he
intends to handle it. Therefore to set up an information structure
the user must have in mind the anticipated interaction with this
structure. Nevertheless information organization and information
handling can and should be distinguished conceptually to achieve a
clean picture. This distinction is reflected in the next two
subsections.

4.1. Information organization

Let us look first at the kind of information transmitted at the
interface between user and DBMS.

Imagine a person - the user - who has some knowledge of other
persons, say employees. The user has some intention, some purpose in
mind, of how to make use of this knowledge. But for the intended
purpose the user does not need all the information, which by the way
is incomplete in any case. Therefore the user reduces the
information to that portion that is relevant with respect to the
considered purpose. This way the knowledge about an employee may be
reduced to - say - his names, his date of birth, his home address
etc.

The user now has a sort of model information about the employee in
his mind. That is the way the user sees the employee on a mental or
'logical' level.

It is this model information on which we focus our interest and for
the description of which we developed our terminology.

The process of abstraction from the initial information to the model
information has two effects:
- It is a selection, that is a reduction of initial information and
- it introduces a certain structure to the information.
As model information is constructed from inital information with an
intended purpose in mind, we use the term   c o n s t r u c t   for
model information, which by choice of the user and as result of the
abstraction process is considered to possess an inner structure.

Constructs, that is information, can be represented in any of the
usual ways. Several representations of the same construct are
possible: There is a representation in our brain (which we do not
consider here), on the paper, in the air (when speech is used), and
last but not least in the computer. But even on the same kind of
medium there can be different representations of the same construct.
Representations are necessary for the communication of model
information.

It is obvious that representation only makes sense, if we can regain
the represented constructs from the representation. Therefore we
have to consider a process of interpretation as well.

Summarizing what has been said so far yields the following picture:

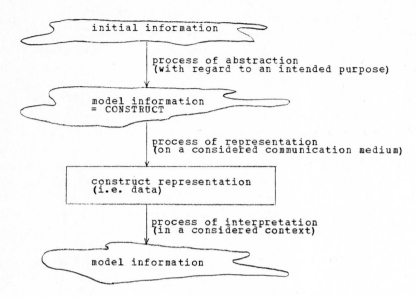

Figure 1

In the following sections concepts are introduced which are located at the level of model information. But nevertheless representations on paper have to be used as well. For graphic representation we developed conventions which are explained when they are used.

4.1.1. Constructs

It is the experience of the authors, that in particular data processing professionals tend to think of 'types' or 'classes' quite automatically when they deal with data. Therefore it seems appropriate to emphasize that in the current section no such connotation is implied. Only single constructs are considered. The very important concept of 'type' is based on the concept of single constructs and is discussed in the next section (4.1.2).

It was mentioned already that in model information the user expresses the structure of information which is relevant for his purposes. In some contexts he wants to consider a construct as elementary, that is, not composed of other constructs. Such an elementary construct we call a v a l u e . To be precise the user does not necessarily consider the construct as elementary but he wants the system to consider it as an elementary construct.

On the other hand it is possible to form (in the user's mind) a construct by combining several constructs into a larger one. Such a compound construct we call an a g g r e g a t e , and the constructs combined together are the i m m e d i a t e c o m p o n e n t s - or c o n s t i t u e n t s as we choose to say - of the aggregate.

A simple example of an aggregate could be composed from the values '1964', '7', 'NOV'. According to our graphic conventions this would be represented by combining three boxes into one box - each of them representing a single construct:

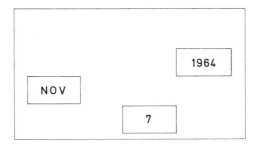

Figure 2

To provide for a convenient selection of constructs among other constructs, it is often desirable to assign n a m e s to them, which are unique within a given context. It is important to notice that names are not present in the initial information. They are created during the abstraction process and first appear in the model information. They are a means of introducing structure to the model information and to support mnemonic convenience.

Returning to the above example we can assign the following names to the values (using a circle for indicating the presence of a name):

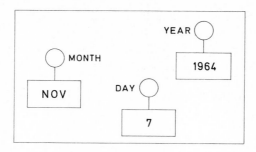

Figure 3

In other cases names are not necessary. A trivial example is the case where in some environment only one single construct is considered. Another example is a set of constructs, each being the model information on one employee. If the user chooses to select constructs concerning employees via the specification of properties (e.g. by specifying some values which are components of the wanted constructs), then there is no need for names for these constructs. Yet another example is the set of descriptors for one document in a document retrieval system. There is no reason why descriptors should have names.

At this point it should be made clear, that a name is not the only means for selecting constructs, or the other way round, that not every unique criterion for accessing constructs as constituents of a given construct is a name. If e.g. the value named NAME OF STATE is a unique criterion for selecting a record in a population file, this value is not a name in the above sense, whereas NAME OF STATE is one.

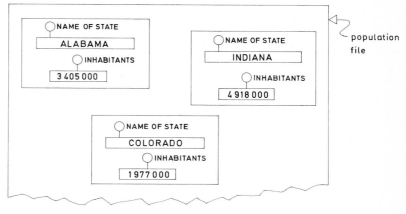

Figure 4

Now we have two classes of aggregates with respect to their composition from immediate components:
- Aggregates having named constructs as constituents. These we call
    n o m i n a t i o n s.
- Aggregates having unnamed constructs as constituents. These we call c o l l e c t i o n s.
As long as there is no need for it, we do not admit aggregates consisting of a mixture of named and unnamed constituents.

Nominations can be described by the concept of a mathematical function: as the mapping of names onto constructs. Collections can be described by the concept of an unordered finite set.

We can now represent a more complex example of a construct which shows nominations as well as a collection.

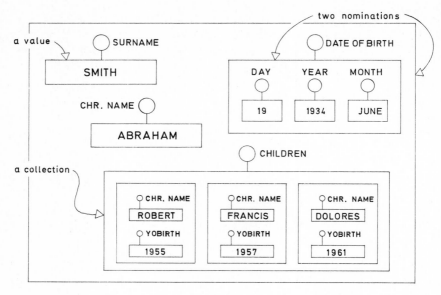

Figure 5

The reader should note that by definition (see 4.1.1, second paragraph) the constituents of a nomination are constructs rather than pairs of names and constructs. Thus a name can be considered as being similar to a label or sticker which in some context is useful to attach to the construct.

Within a construct with several levels of aggregation a name may not be unique. If a construct has to be selected within a context where the name is not unique, we compose an i d e n t i f i e r from names of the higher levels (i.e. qualification). Thus a name can be regarded as a simple identifier.

In many applications we find collections of nominations the immediate components of which have the same set of names. A construct of this kind we call a c o l l e c t i v e with regard to the uniformity of the immediate components of such a collection. The concept of a collective seems to us a very important one with respect to the mass of similar things or facts from which constructs are derived to enter a data base. Homogenuous files, as used in many computer applications are examples of a collective. Moreover, a collective is the adequate concept for the description of relations between constructs. (Cf. e.g. [4],[9])

Describing e.g. the relation 'ownership' between persons and cars we have a collective like this in mind:

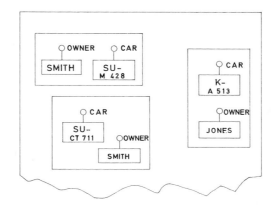

Figure 6

In the above collective the set of names of its constituents (= nominations) is {OWNER, CAR}.

If we add some information about the collective itself and combine this with the collective to form a nomination we get a 'data structure', which in the terminology of the Feature Analysis [6] e.g. is called a relation (not mathematical).

Expanding the above example, such a relation could be represented as follows:

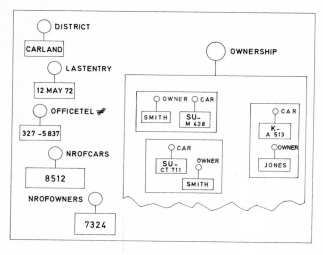

Figure 7

Here we have an example to draw the attention to the multiple occurrence of one construct as a component in different constructs. A person may have more than one car. That means that the same construct (for the considered person) occurs in as many nominations as this person owns cars. These are several contexts in the user's mind, therefore several mental models are represented. Of course, another view would be conceivable. So the user could think of sets of cars associated with the respective user. This would be represented in the following way:

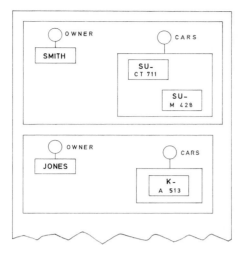

Figure 8

Generally, we have to be aware
- that one construct can be component of many constructs,
- that one construct can be component of nominations and collections at the same time (that is, in different contexts a name is attached or is not),
- that one construct can have different names (in the same or in different contexts).

We feel that all these features are to be found in the user's mind, when he is forming constructs from his knowledge of the 'real world'. The problems in connection with storing representations of constructs on data media are up to the computer system and constitute a problem in its own right.

4.1.2. Types

One can look upon a set as an a s s e m b l y of things. This view was held in the previous section (4.1.1), where sets were called 'collections'. A different way of set interpretation is to regard it as an a b s t r a c t i o n. When talking about a set one deals with properties which all elements have in common and one disregards properties which distinguish set elements from one another. However, when attention is restricted to the interior of the set, the view is reversed: Properties distinguishing set elements are considered and properties common to all elements are no longer interesting. Thus a third aspect for sets arises: a set s e p a r a t e s between set-specific properties and element-distinguishing properties. It is the abstraction and separation aspect for sets we are concerned with in this section.

Property separation and abstraction are important processes in any systematic approach. It is reasonable to assume that in particular the user of DBMS is interested in a systematic treatment of his bulk information. Thus - apart from and in addition to the aggregation of constructs - he will want to talk of sets of constructs expressing property separation and abstraction. When the intention is to refer to this aspect, a set of constructs is called a t y p e. [1]

For illustration consider the user mentioned above (see 4.1) who has to keep record of employees. The collection embodying the model information will change daily as employees are entering and leaving the company. However certain properties - mainly of a structural nature - are common to all those collections. When he extracts those properties from the entire possible set of employees, the user must have in mind not only the information he has about the current employees, but also he must guess what will be invariant through all changes in the future. This is an abstraction process of paramount practical interest, as many painful reorganizations of data bases suggest.

When the user agrees upon invariant properties with the DBMS he can gain two advantages:
- He does not need to repeat information about these properties upon every change.
- The DBMS is able to check for the particular kind of errors violating the invariance agreement.
The gain from the second advantage can be quite considerable if the DBMS is smart enough to understand rather subtle properties (such as arise in so-called consistency conditions for data validation).

The last remark leads us to a methodically important observation: Of course the user can obtain agreement with the DBMS only about things that are in the comprehension of the DBMS. The conceptual capacity

----

[1] For layout reasons, the footnote appears 4 pages ahead

of the DBMS is made manifest in the language the user employs to communicate with it. The entirety of linguistic elements with which to talk about types we call the type description language (TDL). The TDL therefore defines what sets of constructs can be considered types by the DBMS. It appears that the notion of type is relative to a TDL, and, as each DBMS has its own TDL, also relative to the DBMS.

An element of a type is called an i n s t a n c e of that type. A description of a type in a considered TDL is called a s c h e m a. One can imagine a variety of ways to describe a type. If the type is very small the instances could be enumerated. Thus we could think of a type 'month of the year', the instances of which are given in tabular form. Otherwise the type could be given by a decision machine based on the schema, which accepts constructs that belong to the type and rejects others. If types are mainly defined by structural properties of their instances - such as aggregation and name assignment - it is natural to have a type definition in analogy to the composition of the instances. That is, the type is described by the way its instances are built up from their constituents, where the constituents may range over different types described in the same way. The recursion is repeated until types of values are encountered. This technique is a very usual one in existing DBMS. One has to take into account however, that by this method it is not possible to exclude individual combinations of constructs taken from the constituent types. It may well be, that in cases of more complex consistency conditions radically different type description methods are more appropriate.

For the 'normal' case where recursive definition of types from constituent types is adequate, we extend our graphic notation for constructs to graphic schema representation.

To indicate that a type is represented, we add a small box in the upper right corner of the construct symbol. This small box provides a place for inserting the name of the type or the t y p e d e s i g n a t i o n as we prefer to say.

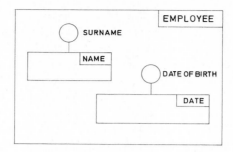

Figure 9

The concept of type enables us to say what a 'repeating construct'
(e.g. 'repeating group') is. If several constituents of a construct
are of the same type, this type is said to be r e p e a t i n g
within the construct. Thus 'repeating' is a concept for describing a
structure property of the type of constructs of which the 'repeating
constructs' are constituents. Consequently 'repeating' is not a
property of the repeated construct - which, by the way, does not
make sense anyway, because no construct is repeated in the strict
sense. Consider the part of a personnel record containing the names
and years of birth of an employee's children (cf. Figure 10). The
entries for the children are all constructs of the same type (e.g.
CHILD). Constructs of this type may occur zero, one or more times as
constituents of a next higher construct, say of type CHILDREN. So
the term 'repeating' expresses a property of the type CHILD with
respect to a construct of type CHILDREN.

In the graphic representation we use three dots, attaching them
close to the right upper corner of the box representing a construct
type, to indicate the multiple occurrence of constructs of the
'dotted' type.

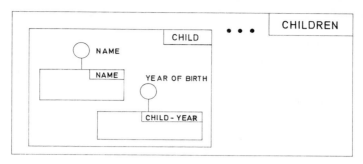

Figure 10

Defining a type of nominations the set of names is equal or similar
to a certain degree in each instance of the nomination type. In the
case of a repeating type we provide for generation rules to produce
names for the instances of this type within a considered nomination
(cf. names for constructs of type PJ and DPT in Figures 11 and 12
below).

For reference and representation purposes we assign, as was
previously done, to each type a t y p e d e s i g n a t i o n,
which names the set of constructs as a whole. Conceptually, this
type designation is completely different from a name, even when for
mnemonic reasons some names correspond with some type designations.
Remember that a name is a means for selecting a constituent of a
considered construct among other constituents, whereas a type
designation identifies the set of constructs defined as a construct
type (cf. YEAR OF BIRTH vs. CHILD-YEAR in Figure 10).

In developing our theory we recognized a strong relationship between
the concept of construct type and the problem of consistency. A type
definition implies a set of requirements which the members of the
type have to meet. This is well known for the value level, but it
holds also for higher levels.

Example:

Construct type definition in graphic notation (graphic schema):
                        (incomplete)

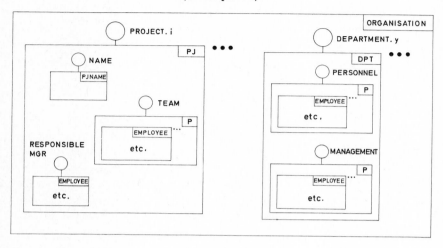

Figure 11

Footnote for second paragraph of this section

[1] The intensional distinction between type and construct is, that a
    type is used to express a restriction of the universe of
    discourse - that is, an agreement with respect to the
    communication between user and DBMS -, whereas a construct is
    model information. A consequence of this is, that the concept of
    a type makes reference to a TDL, as discussed in the fifth
    paragraph of this section. This also implies a formal distinction
    between these concepts (binary and unary predicate). In addition
    there is the less important formal distinction that a construct
    is always finite, whereas no such condition exists for types.

Example (continued):

Graphic representation of a single construct (instance):

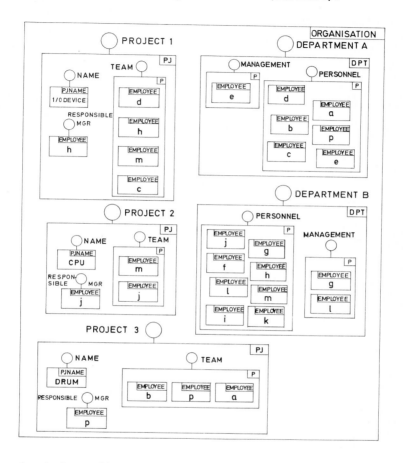

Remark: For graphic reasons lower case letters (a,b,...) stand for
        individual representations of EMPLOYEE type constructs

Figure 12

4.2. Information handling

After having achieved an understanding about what the things are a
DBMS can handle, one will ask which manipulations it can perform on
them.

A DBMS is considered a device that inter alia has information stored
within itself. We agreed to talk about information exclusively as
given in (abstracted into) the form of constructs. Simultaneous
presence of constructs within a data base is of significance for the
user (e.g. for availability, combinability and consistency reasons).
So it seems useful to suppose an all-embracing aggregate containing
all these constructs as components. We call it the
f r a m e w o r k   c o n s t r u c t. Communication between the
user and the DBMS refers to the framework construct and to
constructs exchanged between the user and the DBMS. Exchange of
constructs takes place at the interface between user and DBMS and
requires representation generated and interpreted by both the user
and the DBMS. Therefore the representation itself is an issue of
interface behaviour and thus - as we choose to focus our interest
onto this interface - will take influence on our concepts.

What are now the terms on which the communication about construct
manipulation is based? Besides construct exchange there are
basically the aspects of pointing to components in the framework
construct and of requests to change it.

Strictly speaking, 'change' means replacement of the entire
framework construct. However small the difference of the new
framework construct to the former one may be, the fact is that it
i s different. Of course we want to keep the term 'change',
meaning that significant portions of the framework construct are
retained. But to be precise one has to say now what significant
portions are. It is our opinion that this can only be decided in a
specific way for every individual DBMS.

To tell the DBMS which of the components of the framework construct
the user wants to talk about (and vice versa) he needs concepts to
point to components. We have mentioned identifiers, but one cannot
pass through the skin of a collection with an identifier.

Constituents of collections are identified by their properties. Thus we can use a sequence of names and properties leading to exactly one component of the construct to identify this component within a particular environment. Such a sequence defines or leads to a s p o t , as we say.

Look at the example of Figure 12. We want to point at the spot, where the j occurs as constituent of the collection named TEAM (in the middle of the figure). This spot is defined by the sequence (framework construct / PROJECT2 / TEAM / construct of type EMPLOYEE with property j). On other hand, the spot on the left, where the construct j is located too, is defined by (framework construct / PROJECT / MGR), whereas the sequence (framework construct / DEPARTMENT B / PERSONNEL / construct of type EMPLOYEE with property j) leads to the third occurrence of the construct j in the considered example. So the concept of spot makes it possible to distinguish occurrences of the same construct in different environments.

As we require that any spot is defined by exactly one sequence, we need a general and with certainty identifying property. Such a property is the one, to be the constituent in question itself. Thus for the spot defining sequence we replace properties by the constructs themselves. (Mind that this is a concept, not a linguistic element, for which it would certainly be to bulky.)

The user now wants to talk of spots, to remember them and to refer to them. That is, we need identifiers for spots. We call such identifiers l a b e l s and we assume, that there is at any time a partial mapping of labels onto the spots of the framework construct. An example for a label could be the 'last accessed spot of run unit', which would allow quick reference to the just accessed construct together with its just considered environment.

Besides the concept of spot and label there is another complex of questions concerning the processes in a DBMS by which the handling of information is done. The results achieved so far concerning these problems can not be discussed here. But to give an idea of the course we pursue, an overview of the DBMS functions is shown. These functions we chose for b a s i c functions

... on constructs:
1. Input construct (to DBMS)
2. Output construct (from DBMS)

... on constructs at spots:
3. Insert component (generate a spot)
4. Delete component (discard a spot)
5. Replace component (at a given spot)

... on labels:
6. Attach label (to a spot)
7. Remove label (from a spot)
8. Shift label (from one spot to another)

... on spots:
9. Lock spots (against access)
10. Unlock spots

...on DBMS processes:
11. Cancel (current execution)
12. Stop (current execution)
13. Continue (current execution)

5. Conclusion and further development

The emphasis of this presentation of our work was put on general aspects rather than on technical detail of the concepts already developed.   For an overview it seems appropriate to give an indication of the prominent features of the conceptual system we are developing and of the expectations we have.

Features that bear on generality and applicability are:
- no apriori distinction of particular levels of structuring
- recursive concepts
- only one kind of construct composition
- no anticipation of storage techniques and optimization considerations
- adequate to the associative way of thinking of users
- suitable for the description and comparison of various data

structure and data manipulation concepts

Whereas the first four features can be recognized directly from the definitions, adequacy and suitability are properties not intrinsic to the conceptual system, but they refer to its relation to the user of the concepts. They can only be validated by experience, when the concepts are applied to existing and future DBMS. Our first experiments in this direction were encouraging. Not only were we able to describe various data structures (e.g. those of [6] and of STAIRS), but we also gained insights into the nature of well-known concepts such as record, repeating group, file, relation, set, currency status information and update.

On the other hand, it has to be taken into account, that the development is still under way and that there are several problems to be tackled. E.g. the mutual dependence of type and schema is not entirely clear yet. Also the role of the schema in construct representation (on media) needs some more clarification. Furthermore much more thought must be given to the concept of a DBMS itself, in particular when problems of causality and concurrency are touched upon.

Besides progress in the fundamental ideas all the concepts have to be developed further to bring them nearer to the world of immediate use, which means that concepts have to be derived that are as closely related as possible to the familiar unprecise ideas in data processing.

6. Index_of_terms

This is a list of terms for the concepts introduced in this paper. As the subject is discussed also in German language, the German terms are included too.

aggregate	4.1.1	Aggregat
collection	4.1.1	Kollektion
collective	4.1.1	Kollektiv
component	4.1.1	Komponente
constituent	4.1.1	Bestandteil
construct	4.1	Gebilde
framework construct	4.2	Rahmengebilde
identifier	4.1.1	Identifikator
instance	4.1.2	Exemplar
label	4.2	Marke
name	4.1.1	Name
nomination	4.1.1	Nomination
repeating type	4.1.2	Wiederholungstyp
schema	4.1.2	Schema
spot	4.2	Stelle
type	4.1.2	Typ
type designation	4.1.2	Typenbezeichnung
value	4.1.1	Wert

7. References

[1] CODASYL: An information algebra. CACM April 62

[2] Childs: Description of a set-theoretic data structure. AFIPS Conference Proceedings FJCC 68

[3] McGee: Generalized file processing. Annual Review in Automatic Programming 5, 1969

[4] Codd: A relational model of data for large shared data banks. CACM 13(6), June 70

[5] CODASYL: Data Base Task Group Report April 71

[6] CODASYL: Feature analysis of generalized data base management systems. CODASYL Systems Committee Technical Report May 71

[7] Senko: Details for a scientific approach to information systems. Courant Computer Science Symposium 6, Data Base Systems, May 71

[8] Turski: A model for data structures and its applications. Acta Informatica 1, 1971/72

[9] Codd: Further normalization of the data base relational model. IBM Research Aug. 71

[10] Durchholz, Richter: Das Datenmodell der 'Feature Analysis of Generalized Data Base Management Systems' (German). Angewandte Informatik 12, Dec. 72

[11] Senko, Altman, Astrahan, Fehder: Data structures and accessing in data base systems. IBM Systems Journal 12(1) 1973

DISCUSSION

Mc Gee :   Can names and types be considered to be attributes of constructs
           Do you have any additional attributes you did not mention ?

Durchholz : The concept developed here are meant to be appropriate for
explanation of any of the concepts usually employed with DBMS. This also
applies to attributes which can be explained by the concept of a name.
In fact we made a description of the data structure chapter of the Feature
Analysis of Generalized DBMS, where we used a fixed set of names for the
attributes of a given data structure class.

Taylor :   Do you also provide the concept of a null-construct ?

Durchholz : Yes. Collections can be empty. But as in set theory, there is
only one empty collection. However, it may be desirable to distinguish
between "no persons" and " no cars ". Such a distinction can actually be
made when you discuss it on the type level.

Data Base Management, J. W. Klimbie and K. L. Koffeman, (eds.)
© *North-Holland Publishing Company (1974)*

A CONTRIBUTION TO THE STUDY OF DATA EQUIVALENCE

W. C. McGEE
IBM Corporation
Palo Alto, California USA

1. Introduction

Data processing is replete with examples of transformations in which one collection of data is transformed or mapped into a second collection which, while not identical to the first, is equivalent to the first in the sense that every fact which can be deduced from the first collection can also be deduced from the second collection, and vice versa. When such a transformation takes place, we say that information has been preserved, or equivalently that no information has been lost. A common example of this kind of equivalence can be found in the familiar card-to-tape conversion process. When we transcribe a deck of cards onto a blank tape, we recognize that the resultant objects are not identical (for one thing, they must be accessed through different hardware devices), but we assert with some confidence that they are equivalent: everything that can be deduced from the data punched in the cards can also be deduced from the data recorded on the tape; and (assuming the tape contains no other data) everything deducible from the tape is deducible from the cards.

Data processing also contains numerous examples of transformations in which one collection of data is transformed or mapped into a subset of that collection. The source and target collections in this case are clearly not equivalent in the sense of the preceding paragraph, since there will in general be facts deducible from the main collection which cannot be deduced from the subcollection, simply because data is omitted from the subcollection. On the other hand, we can state that the collections are equivalent in the sense that every fact which can be deduced from the subcollection can also be deduced from the main collection. This is a "one-sided" version of the equivalence of the preceding paragraph. A prominent example of this type of equivalence can be found in data base systems which provide different views or "subdatabases" of a single data base. The data base and its subdatabases are equivalent (in the sense of this paragraph), since everything derivable from a subdatabase can also be derived from the database. Other examples of one-sided equivalence include the relation between an unabridged dictionary and an abridged version thereof; and the relation between a book and its table of contents.

The subject of data equivalence assumes particular importance when dealing with data objects from different <u>data structure classes</u>. A data structure class (or DSC) may be defined as the class of all structures which can be constructed from a given set of primitives using a given set of operators. Because the primitives and operators of different DSC's tend to be different, the structures in the classes also look different--sometimes quite different. Yet we believe that the notion of data equivalence applies to structures in different classes just as well as to structures in the same class. For example, we believe it is possible to show that a file with hierarchic entries is equivalent to a set of files whose entries have no hierarchic structure.

Whether or not we are dealing with one or with many DSC's, the subject of data equivalence has a number of unresolved questions whose answers are of considerable practical importance. For example:

(1) How can the equivalence of two structures be demonstrated? E.G., what algorithm can I use to determine whether it is "safe" to replace an old file with a more current version?

(2) Given one structure, how can an equivalent structure be derived? E.g., how can I represent a graph in a linear address space?

(3) Assuming that two DSC's are equivalent when every structure in one is equivalent to at least one structure in the other, how can the equivalence of two DSC's be demonstrated? E.g., how can I prove that everything I can do with graphs, I can do with sets of trees?

This paper is concerned with the second of the questions posed in the preceding paragraph, namely, the question of deriving equivalent structures. The paper presents a set of techniques for transforming structures of one particular DSC into equivalent structures of a second DSC. As the first DSC, we will take the Flat Data Structure Class (FDSC), to be defined in this paper. The FDSC is so named because it is comprised of "flat" files, i.e., files with single-level entries. This class is one of the oldest extant in computer work, and is currently receiving renewed interest due to the work of Codd on the relational data model (Codd 1970) and the work of Engles (Engles 1972), Senko (Senko 1973), and others on the entity set model. The FDSC presented here is similar in concept to both the relational model and the entity set model.

As the second DSC, we will take the class implicit in the data description language of the CODASYL Data Description Language Committee (CODASYL DDLC 1973), which we will refer to as the Data Description Language Class (DDLC). The DDLC is also receiving considerable attention currently by virtue of its use in several data base system implementations, and by virtue of a proposal to integrate it into the DSC of the COBOL language (CODASYL DBLTG 1973).

The sense in which equivalence is used in this paper is the first of the senses previously discussed, namely, an FDSC structure and a DDLC structure are equivalent if every fact derivable from one is also derivable from the other, and vice versa. The transformations we show will be unidirectional only, namely, from FDSC structures to DDLC structures. Transformations in the opposite direction should be easily obtained by methods similar to those employed herein.

This paper does not show how one may demonstrate the equivalence of structures in FDSC and DDLC, nor does it prove that the target structures of the transformation methods given are equivalent to the source structures. However, as the reader will see, there are strong intuitive arguments for believing that the source and target structures are in fact equivalent. Hopefully, these arguments will be useful in motivating further study of the equivalence of these two classes in particular, and of data structure classes in general.

This paper should also be of practical value to designers of systems which provide DSC's similar to FDSC and DDLC, and which provide for the mapping or transformation between structures in the two classes.

The plan of the paper is as follows. First, we define the FDSC and show an example of a "data base" from the class. Next, we identify several major alternative techniques for representing FDSC structures as DDLC structures, and discuss the factors to be considered in choosing between the alternatives.

Finally, we show how these techniques might be applied to the sample FDSC data base to produce an equivalent DDLC data base, and we comment briefly on the nature of this equivalence.

2.   The Flat Data Structure Class

In FDSC, a data base is composed of one or more named <u>files</u>, each file having a schema of the form

$$F = \left\{ D_1, D_2, \ldots, D_n \right\}$$

in which the D_i represent <u>field</u> schemas.

An instance of a file schema (i.e., a file) is defined by

$$I(F) = \left\{ \begin{array}{l} \left\{ I_1(D_1), I_1(D_2), \ldots, I_1(D_n) \right\}, \\ \left\{ I_2(D_1), I_2(D_2), \ldots, I_2(D_n) \right\}, \\ \vdots \\ \left\{ I_m(D_1), I_m(D_2), \ldots, I_m(D_n) \right\} \end{array} \right\}$$

where $I_i(D_j)$ represents an instance of field schema D_j, and where for no i,j is it true that

$$I_i(D_1) = I_j(D_1)$$

$$\underline{and} \quad I_i(D_2) = I_j(D_2)$$

$$\underline{and} \quad \ldots$$

$$\underline{and} \quad I_i(D_n) = I_j(D_n)$$

(i.e., if I(F) is viewed as a matrix, the rows must be distinct). The set of field schemas $D_{k1}, D_{k2}, \ldots, D_{kr}$ is called a <u>key</u> of the file if for no i,j is it true that

$$I_i(D_{k1}) = I_j(D_{k1})$$

$$\underline{and} \quad I_i(D_{k2}) = I_j(D_{k2})$$

$$\underline{and} \quad \ldots$$

$$\underline{and} \quad I_i(D_{kr}) = I_j(D_{kr})$$

(i.e., in the matrix formed by extracting from I(F) the columns corresponding to the key fields, all rows are distinct). From the definition of I(F) it follows that the set of all fields $\left\{ D_1, D_2, \ldots, D_n \right\}$ is a key of F.

An important subdivision of the file I(F) is the set of fields having a common subscript, e.g.,

$$\left\{ I_i(D_1), I_i(D_2), \ldots, I_i(D_n) \right\}$$

This set is called an <u>entry</u>. A file can thus be viewed as a set of entries, all distinct and each containing exactly one instance of each field schema. For generality, we allow a file to be empty, i.e., to contain no entries.

A field schema D is atomic (i.e., has no component structures), and has the attributes <u>name</u> and <u>value set</u>. An instance of a field schema (i.e., a field) I(D) has the attributes <u>name</u> and <u>value</u>, whose values satisfy

$$\underline{name} \ (I(D)) = \underline{name} \ (D)$$

$$\underline{value} \ (I(D)) \in \underline{value \ set} \ (D)$$

The following is an example of a field schema and a field instance:

$$D = (\underline{name}=PARTY, \ \underline{value \ set}= \left\{ \begin{array}{l} INDEPENDENT, \ NATIONAL \\ REPUBLICAN, \ WHIG, \\ FEDERALIST \end{array} \right\})$$

$$I(D) = (\underline{name}=PARTY, \ \underline{value}=WHIG)$$

The names of the field schemas comprising a file schema must be distinct.

(In exhibiting examples of constructs we use the following notation:

$$construct\text{-}composition \ (construct\text{-}attribute\text{-}list)$$

In the case of fields, the construct-composition part is absent since fields are atomic.)

While not normally done in the relational model or entity set model, it is convenient to introduce into FDSC another structure type, namely, the <u>group</u>. A group schema has the composition

$$G = \left\{ D_1, \ D_2, \ . \ . \ ., \ D_r \right\}$$

where each of the constituent field schemas D_i must be taken from the same file schema F. The group schema has the attribute <u>name</u>, whose value must be different from the names of every other group schema associated with F. An instance of a group schema has the same name as G, and has the composition

$$I \ (G) = \left\{ I(D_1), \ I(D_2), \ . \ . \ ., \ I(D_r) \right\}$$

The following is an example of a group schema and instance:

$$G = \left\{ YEAR, \ MONTH, \ DAY \right\} \ (DATE)$$

$$I(G) = \left\{ 1892, \ July, \ 4 \right\} \ (DATE)$$

The following is an illustration of a file from FDSC:

$$D_1 = (\underline{name}=\text{ADMINISTRATION-NUMBER}, \underline{value\ set}= \{ 1,2,\ldots \} \ )$$

$$D_2 = (\underline{name}=\text{INAUGURATION-YEAR}, \underline{value\ set}= \{ 1789,1790,\ldots \} \ )$$

$$D_3 = (\underline{name}=\text{INAUGURATION-MONTH}, \underline{value\ set}= \{ \text{Jan.,Feb.,}\ldots\text{Dec.} \} \ )$$

$$D_4 = (\underline{name}=\text{INAUGURATION-DAY}, \underline{value\ set}= \{ 1,2,\ldots,31 \} \ )$$

$$D_5 = (\underline{name}=\text{PRESIDENT-NAME}, \underline{value\ set}= \{ \text{Washington,J.Adams,}\ldots \} \ )$$

$$G= \{ D_2, D_3, D_4 \} \ (\text{INAUGURATION-DATE})$$

$$F= \{ D_1, D_2, D_3, D_4, D_5 \} \quad (\text{ADMINISTRATION})$$

$$I(F) = \left\{ \begin{array}{l} \{ 1,\ 1789,\ \text{April},\ 30,\ \text{Washington} \}, \\ \{ 2,\ 1793,\ \text{March},\ \ 4,\ \text{Washington} \}, \\ \qquad\qquad \cdot \\ \qquad\qquad \cdot \\ \qquad\qquad \cdot \\ \{ 53,\ 1965,\ \text{January},\ 20,\ \text{L.Johnson} \} \end{array} \right\}$$

3. A Sample Data Base in FDSC

Figure 1 gives an informal definition of a data base consisting of a set of FDSC files. This data base was derived from the "presidential data base" example developed by A. Vorhaus and A. Weinert as part of their work in the CODASYL Systems Committee. The data base is concerned with entities of a dozen or so different kinds (presidents, elections, states, etc.). A separate file is established for each kind of entity, with fields appropriate to the attributes of that entity.

In devising the data base of Figure 1, two guidelines were followed:

(1) Each file is the equivalent of a third normal form relation (simply stated, each file contains only data which pertains to the entity represented by the file key); and

(2) The amount of redundant data has been kept to a reasonable minimum (data is redundant if it can be derived from other data).

These guidelines were adopted in order to keep the example as simple and compact as possible and still provide a suitably rich vehicle for illustrating transformation techniques. Despite guideline (2), certain redundancies are present in the data base. An example can be found in the CABINET-OFFICER file; the field ADMINISTRATION-NUMBER is redundant, since it can be obtained from the ADMINISTRATION file through a suitable comparison of TENURE-START-DATE in the CABINET-OFFICER file and the inauguration date (INAUGURATION-YEAR, etc.) in the ADMINISTRATION file.

PRESIDENT   PRESIDENT-OCCUPATION
  PRESIDENT-NAME   PRESIDENT-NAME
  DATE-OF-BIRTH   OCCUPATION
  HEIGHT
  PARTY
  COLLEGE   PRESIDENT-MARRIAGE
  ANCESTRY   PRESIDENT-NAME
  RELIGION   WIFE-NAME
  DATE-OF-DEATH   DATE-OF-MARRIAGE
  CAUSE-OF-DEATH   NO-OF-CHILDREN
  FATHER-OF-PRES
  MOTHER-OF-PRES
  STATE-BORN-IN

ELECTION   CANDIDATE
  ELECTION-YEAR   ELECTION-YEAR
  WINNER-NAME   CANDIDATE-NAME
                                         CANDIDATE-PARTY
                                         VOTES-FOR-CANDIDATE

ADMINISTRATION   CABINET-OFFICER
  ADMINISTRATION-NUMBER   OFFICE-NAME
  INAUGURATION-YEAR   TENURE-START-DATE
  INAUGURATION-MONTH   ADMINISTRATION-NUMBER
  INAUGURATION-DAY   TENURE-END-DATE
  PRESIDENT-NAME   OFFICE-HOLDER-NAME

CONGRESS   SENATE-PARTY
  CONGRESS-NUMBER   CONGRESS-NUMBER
  ELECTION-YEAR   PARTY-NAME
                                         NO-OF-SENATORS

                                       HOUSE-PARTY
                                         CONGRESS-NUMBER
                                         PARTY-NAME
                                         NO-OF-REPS

STATE   STATE-CITY
  STATE-NAME   STATE-NAME
  DATE-ADMITTED   CITY-NAME
  CAPITAL   CITY-POPULATION
  AREA
  POPULATION
  ELECTORAL-VOTE

Figure 1

FDSC Data Base Schema
(Underlined fields are collective identifiers)

4. The Representation of FDSC Structures as DDLC Structures

The problem of representing FDSC structures as DDLC structures can be divided into two sub-problems:

(1) the representation of individual files, and

(2) the representation of sets of files.

A file in FDSC can be represented in DDLC structures in basically three ways. For ease of reference, we will call these representation schemes direct, network, and hierarchic.

4.1 Direct Representation of Files

In a direct representation, the file schema $F = \{D_1, D_2, \ldots, D_n\}$ carries over directly to a DDLC record schema $R = \{I_1, I_2, \ldots, I_n\}$, in which each item schema I_i is derived from the corresponding field schema D_i. Each entry in the file then gives rise to an instance of R. For example:

$$F = \{ \text{ELECTION-YEAR, CANDIDATE-NAME, CANDIDATE-PARTY, VOTES-FOR-CANDIDATE} \}$$
$$\Longrightarrow R = \{ \text{ELECTION-YEAR, CANDIDATE-NAME, CANDIDATE-PARTY, VOTES-FOR-CANDIDATE} \}$$

$$I(F) = \left\{ \begin{array}{l} \{1892, \text{Cleveland, Democratic, 277}\}, \\ \{1892, \text{Harrison, Republican, 145}\}, \\ \{1892, \text{Weaver, Peoples, 22}\}, \\ \{1896, \text{McKinley, Republican, 271}\}, \\ \{1896, \text{Bryan, Democratic, 176}\}, \\ \{1916, \text{Wilson, Democratic, 277}\} \end{array} \right.$$

$$I_1(R) = (1892, \text{Cleveland, Democratic, 277})$$
$$I_2(R) = (1892, \text{Harrison, Republican, 145})$$
$$I_3(R) = (1892, \text{Weaver, Peoples, 22})$$
$$I_4(R) = (1896, \text{McKinley, Republican, 271})$$
$$I_5(R) (1896, \text{Bryan, Democratic, 176})$$
$$I_6(R) = (1916, \text{Wilson, Democratic, 277})$$

4.2 Network Representation of Files

In a network representation, the field schemas of the file schema $F = \{D_1, D_2, \ldots, D_n\}$ are first partitioned into $m>1$ group schemas $G_1, G_2, \ldots, G_m$ in such a way that at least one of the group schemas, say G_m, is a key for the file. Subsidiary file schemas are then defined as follows:

$$F_1 = \{G_1, G_m\}$$
$$F_2 = \{G_2, G_m\}$$
$$\vdots$$
$$F_{m-1} = \{G_{m-1}, G_m\}$$

Note that since G_m is a key for the original file, it will also be a key in each of these subsidiary files.

Next, a DDLC record schema R_i is associated with each group schema G_i, in the manner of the direct representation technique:

$$G_1 \Longrightarrow R_1$$
$$G_2 \Longrightarrow R_2$$
$$\vdots$$
$$G_m \Longrightarrow R_m$$

Finally, a DDLC set schema S_i is associated with each of the subsidiary file schemas $F_i = \{G_i, G_m\}$ in such a way that the record associated with G_i is the set owner, and the record associated with G_m is the set member:

$$F_1 = \{G_1, G_m\} \Longrightarrow S_1 = \langle R_1, R_m \rangle$$
$$F_2 = \{G_2, G_m\} \Longrightarrow S_2 = \langle R_2, R_m \rangle$$
$$\vdots$$
$$F_{m-1} = \{G_{m-1}, G_m\} \Longrightarrow S_{m-1} = \langle R_{m-1}, R_m \rangle$$

In diagram form, the DDLC schema has the following appearance:

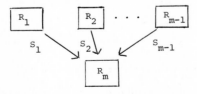

Each unique value of G_i in the file $I(F_i)$ gives rise to an instance of record schema R_i. Similarly, each unique value of G_m in the same file gives rise to an instance of R_m, which is paired with the appropriate instance of R_i. Since G_m is a key, there can be no duplicate instances of G_m in a file, and each such instance can therefore be paired with at most one instance of R_i (in this set), as required by the DDLC data structure class.

The following is an example of network representation:

$$F = \left\{ \text{ELECTION-YEAR, CANDIDATE-NAME, CANDIDATE-PARTY, VOTES-FOR-CANDIDATE} \right\}$$

$$I(F) = \left\{ \begin{array}{l} \{ 1892, \text{Cleveland, Democratic, } 277 \}, \\ \{ 1892, \text{Harrison, Republican, } 145 \}, \\ \{ 1892, \text{Weaver, Peoples, } 22 \} \quad , \quad \cdot \\ \{ 1896, \text{McKinley, Republican, } 271 \}, \\ \{ 1896, \text{Bryan, Democratic, } 176 \}, \\ \{ 1916, \text{Wilson, Democratic, } 277 \} \end{array} \right\}$$

Let $G_1 = \left\{ \text{CANDIDATE-PARTY} \right\}$

$\quad G_2 = \left\{ \text{VOTES-FOR-CANDIDATE} \right\}$

$\quad G_3 = \left\{ \text{ELECTION-YEAR, CANDIDATE-NAME} \right\}$

Then:

$$F_1 = \left\{ G_1, G_3 \right\} = \left\{ \text{CANDIDATE-PARTY}, \left\{ \text{ELECTION-YEAR, CANDIDATE-NAME} \right\} \right\}$$

$$I(F_1) = \left\{ \begin{array}{l} \left\{ \text{Democratic, } \left\{ 1892, \text{Cleveland} \right\} \right\}, \\ \left\{ \text{Republican, } \left\{ 1892, \text{Harrison} \right\} \right\}, \\ \left\{ \text{Peoples, } \left\{ 1892, \text{Weaver} \right\} \right\}, \\ \left\{ \text{Republican, } \left\{ 1896, \text{McKinley} \right\} \right\}, \\ \left\{ \text{Democratic, } \left\{ 1896, \text{Bryan} \right\} \right\}, \\ \left\{ \text{Democratic, } \left\{ 1916, \text{Wilson} \right\} \right\} \end{array} \right\}$$

$$F_2 = \left\{ G_2, G_3 \right\} = \left\{ \text{VOTES-FOR-CANDIDATE}, \left\{ \text{ELECTION-YEAR, CANDIDATE-NAME} \right\} \right\}$$

$$I(F_2) = \left\{ \begin{array}{l} \left\{ 277, \left\{ 1892, \text{Cleveland} \right\} \right\}, \\ \left\{ 145, \left\{ 1892, \text{Harrison} \right\} \right\}, \\ \left\{ 22, \left\{ 1892, \text{Weaver} \right\} \right\}, \\ \left\{ 271, \left\{ 1896, \text{McKinley} \right\} \right\}, \\ \left\{ 176, \left\{ 1896 \text{ Bryan} \right\} \right\}, \\ \left\{ 277, \left\{ 1916, \text{Wilson} \right\} \right\} \end{array} \right\}$$

The representations are:

$$G_1 \Longrightarrow R_1 = \left\{ \text{PARTY-NAME} \right\} \text{ (PARTY)}$$
$$G_2 \Longrightarrow R_2 = \left\{ \text{VOTE-VALUE} \right\} \text{ (VOTES)}$$
$$G_3 \Longrightarrow R_3 = \left\{ \text{ELECTION-YEAR, CANDIDATE-NAME} \right\} \text{ (ELECTION-CANDIDATE)}$$
$$F_1 \Longrightarrow S_1 = \left\langle \text{PARTY, ELECTION-CANDIDATE} \right\rangle \quad \text{(S1)}$$
$$F_2 \Longrightarrow S_2 = \left\langle \text{VOTES, ELECTION-CANDIDATE} \right\rangle \quad \text{(S2)}$$

(continued next page)

In diagram form, the representation is:

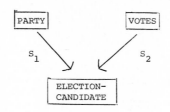

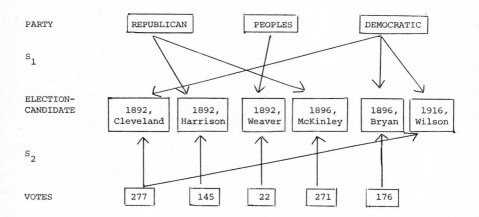

The requirement that at least one of the group schemas in a file schema be a key would seem to be a limitation on the use of network representation. This limitation can always be circumvented, however, by introducing a "dummy" field schema whose instances guarantee that it is a key; for example, the set of positive integers. The dummy field schema may then be grouped with any of the remaining field schemas to form the required key group schema G_m. For example, suppose we add the field schema

$$(\underline{name} = INTEGER, \underline{value\ set} = \left\{1,\ 2,\ \dots\right\})$$

to the previous file schema F, so that it now becomes

$$F = \left(ELECTION\text{-}YEAR, CANDIDATE\text{-}NAME, CANDIDATE\text{-}PARTY, VOTES\text{-}FOR\text{-}CANDIDATE, INTEGER\right)$$

$$I(F) = \left\{ \begin{array}{l} \left\{1892,\ \text{Cleveland, Democratic, 277, 1}\right\}, \\ \left\{1892,\ \text{Harrison, Republican, 145, 2}\right\}, \\ \left\{1892,\ \text{Weaver, Peoples, 22, 3}\right\}, \\ \left\{1896,\ \text{McKinley, Republican, 271, 4}\right\}, \\ \left\{1896,\ \text{Bryan, Democratic, 176, 5}\right\}, \\ \left\{1916,\ \text{Wilson, Democratic, 277, 6}\right\} \end{array} \right\}$$

We can now let

$$
\begin{aligned}
G_1 &= \Big\langle \text{ELECTION YEAR} \Big\rangle \\
G_2 &= \Big\langle \text{CANDIDATE-NAME} \Big\rangle \\
G_3 &= \Big\langle \text{CANDIDATE-PARTY, VOTES-FOR-CANDIDATE, INTEGER} \Big\rangle
\end{aligned}
$$

and be assured that G_3 is a key because of the presence of the field INTEGER. (The group $\{$CANDIDATE-PARTY, VOTES-FOR-CANDIDATE$\}$ by itself is not a key; see, for example, entries 1 and 6 in I(F).)

The subsidiary file schemas become

$$
F_1 = \Big\langle G_1, G_3 \Big\rangle = \Big\langle \text{ELECTION-YEAR,} \Big\langle \text{CANDIDATE-PARTY,VOTES-FOR-CANDIDATE,INTEGER} \Big\rangle \Big\rangle
$$

$$
I(F_1) = \left\{
\begin{array}{l}
\Big\langle 1892, \{ \text{Democratic, 277, 1} \}\Big\rangle , \\
\Big\langle 1892, \{ \text{Republican, 145, 2} \}\Big\rangle , \\
\Big\langle 1892, \{ \text{Peoples, 22, 3} \}\Big\rangle , \\
\Big\langle 1896, \{ \text{Republican, 271, 4} \}\Big\rangle , \\
\Big\langle 1896, \{ \text{Democratic, 176, 5} \}\Big\rangle , \\
\Big\langle 1916, \{ \text{Democratic, 277, 6} \}\Big\rangle
\end{array}
\right\}
$$

$$
F_2 = \Big\langle G_2, G_3 \Big\rangle = \Big\langle \text{CANDIDATE-NAME,} \Big\langle \text{CANDIDATE-PARTY, VOTES-FOR-CANDIDATE, INTEGER} \Big\rangle \Big\rangle
$$

$$
I(F_2) = \left\{
\begin{array}{l}
\Big\langle \text{Cleveland,} \Big\langle \text{Democratic, 277, 1} \Big\rangle\Big\rangle , \\
\Big\langle \text{Harrison,} \Big\langle \text{Republican, 145, 2} \Big\rangle\Big\rangle , \\
\Big\langle \text{Weaver,} \Big\langle \text{Peoples, 22, 3} \Big\rangle\Big\rangle , \\
\Big\langle \text{McKinley,} \Big\langle \text{Republican, 271, 4} \Big\rangle\Big\rangle , \\
\Big\langle \text{Bryan,} \Big\langle \text{Democratic, 176, 5} \Big\rangle\Big\rangle , \\
\Big\langle \text{Wilson,} \Big\langle \text{Democratic, 277, 6} \Big\rangle\Big\rangle
\end{array}
\right\}
$$

The record schemas become

$$
\begin{aligned}
G_1 &\Longrightarrow R_1 = \Big\langle \text{ELECTION-YEAR} \Big\rangle \; \text{(ELECTION)} \\
G_2 &\Longrightarrow R_2 = \Big\langle \text{CANDIDATE-NAME} \Big\rangle \; \text{(CANDIDATE)} \\
G_3 &\Longrightarrow R_3 = \Big\langle \text{PARTY-NAME, VOTE-VALUE} \Big\rangle \; \text{(PARTY-VOTES)}
\end{aligned}
$$

Note that an item schema corresponding to INTEGER is not needed in R_3, since it carries no real information; its presence in G_3 is needed only to force the creation of a separate instance of R_3 for each entry in the files $I(R_1)$ and $I(R_2)$. The set schemas become

$$
\begin{aligned}
F_1 &\Longrightarrow S_1 = \Big\langle \text{ELECTION, PARTY-VOTES} \Big\rangle \; \text{(S1)} \\
F_2 &\Longrightarrow S_2 = \Big\langle \text{CANDIDATE, PARTY-VOTES} \Big\rangle \; \text{(S2)}
\end{aligned}
$$

In diagram form, the representation is:

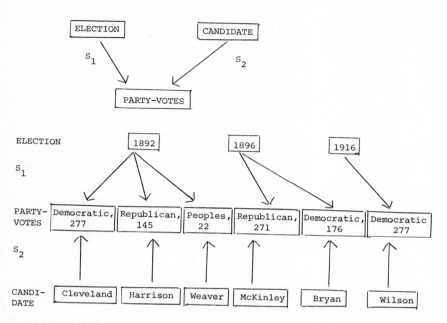

Note that two instances of PARTY-VOTES are identical, viz., $\{$Democratic,277$\}$; this was forced by the presence of INTEGER in the subsidiary file schemas.

An important special case of the foregoing technique results when the dummy field is taken by itself to be the key G_m. The corresponding record schema R_m then becomes an "empty" record whose only function is to relate other records.

4.3 Hierarchic Representation of Files

In a hierarchic representation, the field schemas of a file schema are partitioned into m group schemas G_1, G_2,..., G_m as in a network representation, except that now we drop the requirement that at least one of these groups be a key. We then form the following subsidiary file schemas:

$$F_1 = \left\{ G_1, \ G_2 \right\}$$
$$F_2 = \left\{ G_2, \ G_3 \right\}$$
$$\vdots$$
$$F_{m-1} = \left\{ G_{m-1}, \ G_m \right\}$$

In effect, we are hierarchically ordering the groups G_1, G_2,...,G_m.

Next, we associate a record schema R_i with each group schema:

$$G_1 \Longrightarrow R_1$$
$$G_2 \Longrightarrow R_2$$

$$\vdots$$

$$G_m \Longrightarrow R_m$$

and then associate a set schema with each subsidiary file schema:

$$F_1 = \left(G_1,\ G_2 \right) \Longrightarrow \quad S_1 = \left\langle R_1,\ R_2 \right\rangle$$
$$F_2 = \left(G_2,\ G_3 \right) \Longrightarrow \quad S_2 = \left\langle R_2,\ R_3 \right\rangle$$

$$\vdots$$

$$F_{m-1} = \left(G_{m-1},\ G_m \right) \Longrightarrow \quad S_{m-1} = \left\langle R_{m-1},\ R_m \right\rangle$$

In diagram form, this is a hierarchy of record schemas:

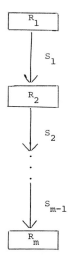

The hierarchy schema is populated according to the following rules: each unique value of G_1 in F_1 gives rise to an instance of R_1. Then, each value of G_2 in F_1 (including duplicates) gives rise to an instance of R_2, which is paired with the appropriate instance of R_1. Then, each value of G_3 in F_2 gives rise to an instance of R_3 which is paired with the appropriate instance of R_2. And so on until the entire tree has been built. Note that except at the first level, there will in general be duplicate records in the structure.

The following is an example of hierarchic representation:

In $F = \Big\{$ ELECTION-YEAR, CANDIDATE-NAME, CANDIDATE-PARTY, VOTES-FOR-CANDIDATE $\Big\}$

let

$$
\begin{aligned}
G_1 &= \Big\{ \text{ELECTION-YEAR} \Big\} \\
G_2 &= \Big\{ \text{CANDIDATE-NAME} \Big\} \\
G_3 &= \Big\{ \text{CANDIDATE-PARTY, VOTES-FOR-CANDIDATE} \Big\}
\end{aligned}
$$

Then

$$F_1 = \Big\{ G_1, G_2 \Big\} = \Big\{ \text{ELECTION-YEAR, CANDIDATE-NAME} \Big\}$$

$$
I(F_1) = \left\{ \begin{array}{l}
\big\{ 1892, \text{Cleveland} \big\} , \\
\big\{ 1892, \text{Harrison} \big\} , \\
\big\{ 1892, \text{Weaver} \big\} , \\
\big\{ 1896, \text{McKinley} \big\} , \\
\big\{ 1896, \text{Bryan} \big\} , \\
\big\{ 1916, \text{Wilson} \big\}
\end{array} \right\}
$$

$$F_2 = \Big\{ G_2, G_3 \Big\} = \Big\{ \text{CANDIDATE-NAME}, \big\{ \text{CANDIDATE-PARTY, VOTES-FOR-CANDIDATE} \big\} \Big\}$$

$$
I(F_2) = \left\{ \begin{array}{ll}
\big\{ \text{Cleveland}, & \big\{ \text{Democratic, 277} \big\} \big\} , \\
\big\{ \text{Harrison}, & \big\{ \text{Republican, 145} \big\} \big\} , \\
\big\{ \text{Weaver}, & \big\{ \text{Peoples, 22} \big\} \big\} , \\
\big\{ \text{McKinley}, & \big\{ \text{Republican, 271} \big\} \big\} , \\
\big\{ \text{Bryan}, & \big\{ \text{Democratic, 176} \big\} \big\} , \\
\big\{ \text{Wilson}, & \big\{ \text{Democratic, 277} \big\} \big\}
\end{array} \right\}
$$

The representations are:

$$
\begin{aligned}
G_1 &\Rightarrow R_1 = \Big\{ \text{YEAR} \Big\} \ (\text{ELECTION}) \\
G_2 &\Rightarrow R_2 = \Big\{ \text{NAME} \Big\} \ (\text{CANDIDATE}) \\
G_3 &\Rightarrow R_3 = \Big\{ \text{PARTY-NAME, VOTE-VALUE} \Big\} \ (\text{PARTY-VOTES})
\end{aligned}
$$

$$
\begin{aligned}
F_1 &\Rightarrow S_1 = \big\langle \text{ELECTION, CANDIDATE} \big\rangle \ (\text{S1}) \\
F_2 &\Rightarrow S_2 = \big\langle \text{CANDIDATE, PARTY-VOTES} \big\rangle \ (\text{S2})
\end{aligned}
$$

In diagram form, these become:

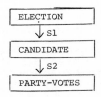

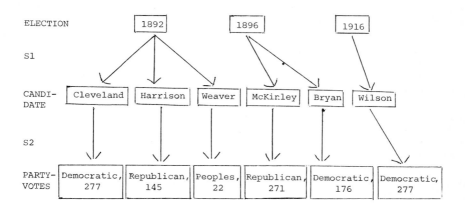

A variation on the hierarchic representation scheme is made possible through the DDLC facility for repeating groups within records. Instead of building a hierarchy of record schemas, we can build a hierarchy of repeating group schemas, as follows:

$$G_3 \Longrightarrow RG_1 = \left\{ \text{PARTY-NAME, VOTE-VALUE} \right\} \text{ (PARTY-VOTES)}$$
$$G_2 \Longrightarrow RG_2 = \left\{ \text{NAME,} RG_1 \right\} \text{ (CANDIDATE)}$$
$$G_1 \Longrightarrow R = \left\{ \text{YEAR,} RG_2 \right\} \text{ (ELECTION)}$$

A sample record might be

$$\left\{ 1892, \left\{ \begin{array}{l} \text{Cleveland,} \left\{ \text{Democratic, 277} \right\} \\ \text{Harrison,} \left\{ \text{Republican, 145} \right\} \\ \text{Weaver,} \left\{ \text{Peoples, 22} \right\} \end{array} \right\} \right\}$$

4.4   Remarks on the File Representation Techniques

The foregoing techniques for representing individual files are meant to be schematic only; in practice, the techniques could be modified and combined in a number of different ways. For example, in using the hierarchic technique, hierarchic record schemas can be used down to a certain point in the hierarchy, and nested repeating groups from that point on. As another example, the network and hierarchic techniques can be combined to yield structures such as the following:

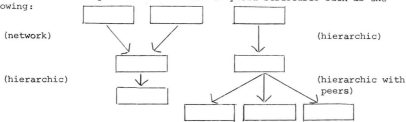

The three techniques differ in two important respects: (1) degree of item value repetition and (2) accessibility. The direct technique introduces the most repetition since item values can potentially be repeated in every record instance. The network technique introduces the least, and it is in principle possible, through the dummy record tactic, to have no repetition at all (each record would consist of a single item). The hierarchic technique is intermediate in repetition, since the items at the top of the hierarchy occur just once, whereas those at lower levels occur a number of times. It is clear that item value repetition can be controlled in this approach by putting the items with greatest variability in the upper part of the hierarchy.

The techniques probably also differ with respect to accessibility, i.e., given one field value, how difficult is it to find another field value in the same entry? Assuming that records are implemented in contiguous storage, and that sets are implemented with some sort of pointer technique, it would seem that the direct technique would provide the greatest degree of accessibility. The network and hierarchic techniques would have less, with the edge going to hierarchic to the extent that physical hierarchic storage techniques were used.

4.5 Representing Sets of Files

The general procedure for representing a set of FDSC files as DDLC structures consists of two steps: (1) representing the individual files in the set by one or more of the techniques presented in the preceding sections; and (2) consolidating the record schemas which result from step (1). Step (2) is not essential, but is desirable from the standpoint of reducing the repetitious representation of data. An example should make this clear.

Suppose we use the network technique to represent the file CANDIDATE (as we did in the preceding examples), with the result that we produce the following DDLC schemas:

$$R_1 = \{ \text{ELECTION-YEAR} \}$$
$$R_2 = \{ \text{CANDIDATE-NAME} \}$$
$$R_3 = \{ \text{CANDIDATE-PARTY, VOTES-FOR-CANDIDATE} \}$$

$$S_1 = \langle R_1, R_3 \rangle$$
$$S_2 = \langle R_2, R_3 \rangle$$

Suppose further that we use the direct technique to represent the file ELECTION, with the result that we have the additional record schema

$$R_4 = \{ \text{ELECTION-YEAR, WINNER-NAME} \}$$

Note that R_1 and R_4 have a common item schema. If it happens (as it does in this case) that every instance of R_1 has a corresponding instance of R_4, we can consolidate these record schemas by taking their union:

$$R_1' = R_1 \cup R_4 = \{ \text{ELECTION-YEAR, WINNER-NAME} \}$$

The consolidated set of schemas then becomes

$$R_1' = \{ \text{ELECTION-YEAR, WINNER-NAME} \}$$
$$R_2 = \{ \text{CANDIDATE-NAME} \}$$
$$R_3 = \{ \text{CANDIDATE-PARTY, VOTES-FOR-CANDIDATE} \}$$

$$S_1 = \langle R_1', R_3 \rangle$$
$$S_2 = \langle R_2, R_3 \rangle$$

Set schemas are not consolidated; the only change required in the set schemas is to replace record schemas which are consolidated with their con- solidated equivalent (e.g., replacing every appearance of R_1 and R_4 in the preceding example by R_1').

The effect of consolidating record schemas of course is to minimize repetitive data representation (e.g., not carrying the same item schema in two or more record schemas). We can minimize repetition if we anticipate the consolidation step during the initial file representation step. For example, if we have a choice of representing a file in two ways, one of which produces record schema R_1 and the other of which produces record schema R_2; and R_1 can be consolidated with some other record schema already (or to be) produced, but R_2 cannot be so consolidated; and the choice between the two methods is otherwise arbitrary; then we should choose the method which produces R_1, since it minimizes item repetition.

5. Representation of the Presidential Data Base

Figures 2 through 4 illustrate the application of the representation techniques discussed in Section 4 to the FDSC schema of Figure 1. Figure 2 shows the first step in the representation process, i.e., the representation of the individual files of Figure 1. Figure 3 shows the result of the second step, i.e., the consolidation and naming of schemas produced in the first step. Figure 4 is the data structure diagram equivalent of Figure 3.

For any given instance S of the FDSC schema of Figure 1, it is possible, using the rules previously given, to generate a corresponding instance S' of the DDLC schema of Figure 3. It is our contention that the structures S and S' in every pair produced in this manner are equivalent, in the sense that every fact which can be derived from S can also be derived from S', and vice versa.

It should be emphasized that the DDLC schema shown here is only one of many representations possible using the given representation techniques. The one shown is not believed to have any special merit, other than it appears relatively straightforward and seems to have a low degree of item repetition.

6. Summary and Discussion

In this paper we have introduced the notion of data equivalence, and have developed techniques for transforming structures of one particular class into what purport to be equivalent structures of another class. We have not proved this equivalence, but we have hopefully introduced sufficient material to suggest its plausibility.

One possible concern over the equivalence of DDLC and FDSC structures is the lack in FDSC of any facility for explicitly defining relations between entries, i.e., any facility equivalent to the set facility of DDLC. Because of this, it might be supposed that information carried in sets is lost in representing data as FDSC structures. A moment's study of Figure 1, however, should make it clear that set information is preserved by replicating certain field schemas in various file schemas and by adopting the reasonable convention that two entries are related whenever the values of their common field schema are the same. For example, the relationship between a president and his administrations, achieved in the DDLC schema through the set PRESIDENTIAL- ADMINISTRATIONS, is achieved in the FDSC schema by carrying the field PRESIDENT- NAME in both the PRESIDENT and ADMINISTRATION entries. Given a certain

PRESIDENT entry, associated ADMINISTRATION entries can be located by (conceptually) searching the ADMINISTRATION file for entries with a matching value for PRESIDENT-NAME. Similarly, given a certain ADMINISTRATION entry, we can locate the associated PRESIDENT entry by searching the PRESIDENT file for a matching value of PRESIDENT-NAME.

To achieve relationships in FDSC structures, of course, it is necessary to introduce repetition in the form of replicated keys. In developing the techniques of Section 4, we noted that some if not all of this type of repetition can be avoided in DDLC structures by using sets to represent relationships. Whether this is a significant advantage is not at all clear, since in the absence of an implementation we have no way of assessing the impact of repetition on storage or performance. At the logical level, repetition of this type seems to have some merit inasmuch as it affords a straightforward and easily understood way of defining the relationships among file entries. On the other hand, in formulating complex queries against FDSC structures, key names have a tendency to proliferate more rapidly than is the case with queries directed against hierarchic and network structures. The latter suggests that there is a tradeoff between the complexity of a data structure, and the complexity of queries directed against it.

(1) $F = \{$ PRESIDENT-NAME, DATE-OF-BIRTH,...,STATE-BORN-IN $\}$ (PRESIDENT)
$$\implies R_1 = \{ \text{PRESIDENT-NAME, DATE-OF-BIRTH,...,}\ \text{STATE-BORN-IN} \}$$

(2) $F = \{$ PRESIDENT-NAME, OCCUPATION $\}$ (PRESIDENT-OCCUPATION)
$G_1 = \{$ OCCUPATION $\}$ $\implies$ $RG_1{}^* = \{$ OCCUPATION $\}$
$G_2 = \{$ PRESIDENT-NAME $\implies$ $R_2 = \{$ PRESIDENT-NAME, RG_1 $\}$

(3) $F = \{$ PRESIDENT-NAME, WIFE-NAME, DATE-OF-MARRIAGE, NO-OF-CHILDREN $\}$
(PRESIDENT-MARRIAGE)

$G_1 = \{$ WIFE-NAME, DATE-OF- MARRIAGE, NO-OF- CHILDREN $\}$ $\implies$ $RG_2 = \{$ WIFE-NAME, DATE-OF- MARRIAGE, NO-OF- CHILDREN $\}$

$G_2 = \{$ PRESIDENT-NAME $\}$ $\implies$ $R_3 = \{$ PRESIDENT-NAME, RG_2 $\}$

(4) $F = \{$ ADMINISTRATION-NUMBER, INAUGURATION-DATE, PRESIDENT-NAME $\}$
(ADMINISTRATION)

$G_1 = \{$ PRESIDENT-NAME $\}$ $\implies$ $R_4 = \{$ PRESIDENT-NAME $\}$
$G_2 = \{$ ADMIN-NUMBER, INAUGURATION-DATE $\}$ $\implies$ $R_5 = \{$ ADMIN-NUMBER, INAUGURATION-DATE $\}$

$F = \{ G_1, G_2 \}$ $\implies$ $S_1 = \langle R_4, R_5 \rangle$

(5) $F = \{$ OFFICE-NAME, TENURE-START-DATE, ADMINISTRATION-NUMBER, TENURE-END-DATE, OFFICE-HOLDER-NAME $\}$ (CABINET OFFICER)

$G_1 = \{$ ADMIN-NUMBER $\}$ $\implies$ $R_6 = \{$ ADMIN-NUMBER $\}$
$G_2 = \{$ OFFICE-NAME $\}$ $\implies$ $R_7 = \{$ OFFICE-NAME $\}$
$G_3 = \{$ TENURE-START-DATE, TENURE-END-DATE, OFFICE-HOLDER-NAME $\}$ $\implies$ $R_8 = \{$ TENURE-START-DATE, TENURE-END-DATE, OFFICE-HOLDER-NAME $\}$

$F_1 = \{ G_1, G_2 \}$ $\implies$ $S_2 = \langle R_6, R_7 \rangle$
$F_2 = \{ G_2, G_3 \}$ $\implies$ $S_3 = \langle R_7, R_8 \rangle$

(6) $F = \{$ ELECTION-YEAR, WINNER-NAME $\}$ (ELECTION)
$$\implies R_9 = \{ \text{ELECTION-YEAR, WINNER-NAME} \}$$

Figure 2
(Page 1 of 2)

Individual File Representation,
Presidential Data Base

---

*DDLC schemas are numbered sequentially for later reference

(7) $F = \Big\{$ ELECTION-YEAR, CANDIDATE-NAME, CANDIDATE-PARTY, VOTES-FOR-CANDIDATE $\Big\}$ (CANDIDATE)

$G_1 = \Big\{$ ELECTION-YEAR $\Big\}$ $\Longrightarrow$ $R_{10} = \Big\{$ ELECTION-YEAR $\Big\}$

$G_2 = \Big\{$ CANDIDATE-NAME $\Big\}$ $\Longrightarrow$ $R_{11} = \Big\{$ CANDIDATE-NAME $\Big\}$

$G_3 = \Big\{$ CANDIDATE-PARTY, VOTES-FOR-CANDIDATE, INTEGER $\Big\}$ $\Longrightarrow$ $R_{12} = \Big\{$ CANDIDATE-PARTY, VOTES-FOR-CANDIDATE $\Big\}$

$F_1 = \Big\{ G_1, G_3 \Big\}$ $\Longrightarrow$ $S_4 = \Big\langle R_{10}, R_{12} \Big\rangle$

$F_2 = \Big\{ G_2, G_3 \Big\}$ $\Longrightarrow$ $S_5 = \Big\langle R_{11}, R_{12} \Big\rangle$

(8) $F = \Big\{$ CONGRESS-NUMBER, ELECTION-YEAR $\Big\}$ (CONGRESS)

$\Longrightarrow$ $R_{13} = \Big\{$ CONGRESS-NUMBER, ELECTION-YEAR $\Big\}$

(9) $F = \Big\{$ CONGRESS-NUMBER, PARTY-NAME, NO-OF-SENATORS $\Big\}$ (SENATE-PARTY)

$G_1 = \Big\{$ CONGRESS-NUMBER $\Big\}$ $\Longrightarrow$ $R_{14} = \Big\{$ CONGRESS-NUMBER $\Big\}$

$G_2 = \Big\{$ PARTY-NAME $\Big\}$ $\Longrightarrow$ $R_{15} = \Big\{$ PARTY-NAME $\Big\}$

$G_3 = \Big\{$ NO-OF-SENATORS, INTEGER $\Big\}$ $\Longrightarrow$ $R_{16} = \Big\{$ NO-OF-SENATORS $\Big\}$

$F_1 = \Big\{ G_1, G_3 \Big\}$ $\Longrightarrow$ $S_6 = \Big\langle R_{14}, R_{16} \Big\rangle$

$F_2 = \Big\{ G_2, G_3 \Big\}$ $\Longrightarrow$ $S_7 = \Big\langle R_{15}, R_{16} \Big\rangle$

(10) $F = \Big\{$ CONGRESS-NUMBER, PARTY-NAME, NO-OF-REPS $\Big\}$ (HOUSE-PARTY)

$G_1 = \Big\{$ CONGRESS-NUMBER $\Big\}$ $\Longrightarrow$ $R_{17} = \Big\{$ CONGRESS-NUMBER $\Big\}$

$G_2 = \Big\{$ PARTY-NAME $\Big\}$ $\Longrightarrow$ $R_{18} = \Big\{$ PARTY NAME $\Big\}$

$G_3 = \Big\{$ NO-OF-REPS, INTEGER $\Big\}$ $\Longrightarrow$ $R_{19} = \Big\{$ NO-OF-REPS $\Big\}$

$F_1 = \Big\{ G_1, G_3 \Big\}$ $\Longrightarrow$ $S_8 = \Big\langle R_{17}, R_{19} \Big\rangle$

$F_2 = \Big\{ G_2, G_3 \Big\}$ $\Longrightarrow$ $S_9 = \Big\langle R_{18}, R_{19} \Big\rangle$

(11) $F = \Big\{$ STATE-NAME, ..., ELECTORAL-VOTE $\Big\}$ (STATE)

$\Longrightarrow$ $R_{20} = \Big\{$ STATE-NAME, ..., ELECTORAL-VOTE $\Big\}$

(12) $F = \Big\{$ STATE-NAME, CITY-NAME, CITY-POPULATION $\Big\}$ (STATE-CITY)

$G_1 = \Big\{$ CITY-NAME, CITY-POPULATION $\Big\}$ $\Longrightarrow$ $RG_3 = \Big\{$ CITY-NAME, CITY-POPULATION $\Big\}$

$G_2 = \Big\{$ STATE-NAME $\Big\}$ $\Longrightarrow$ $R_{21} = \Big\{$ STATE-NAME, RG_3 $\Big\}$

Figure 2
(Page 2 of 2)

$RG_1 = \left\{ \text{OCCUPATION} \right\}$ (OCCUPATION)

$RG_2 = \left\{ \text{WIFE-NAME, DATE-OF-MARRIAGE, NO-OF-CHILDREN} \right\}$ (MARRIAGE)

$RG_3 = \left\{ \text{CITY-NAME, CITY-POPULATION} \right\}$ (CITY)

$R'_1 = R_1 \cup R_2 \cup R_3 \cup R_4$
     $= \left\{ \text{PRESIDENT-NAME,...,STATE-BORN-IN}, RG_1, RG_2 \right\}$ (PRESIDENT)

$R'_2 = R_5 \cup R_6$
     $= \left\{ \text{ADMINISTRATION-NUMBER, INAUGURATION-DATE} \right\}$ (ADMINISTRATION)

$R'_3 = R_7$
     $= \left\{ \text{OFFICE-NAME} \right\}$ (CABINET-OFFICE)

$R'_4 = R_8$
     $= \left\{ \text{TENURE-START-DATE, TENURE-END-DATE, OFFICE-HOLDER-NAME} \right\}$ (OFFICE-TENURE)

$R'_5 = R_9 \cup R_{10}$
     $= \left\{ \text{ELECTION-YEAR, WINNER-NAME} \right\}$ (ELECTION)

$R'_6 = R_{11}$
     $= \left\{ \text{CANDIDATE-NAME} \right\}$ (CANDIDATE)

$R'_7 = R_{12}$
     $= \left\{ \text{CANDIDATE-PARTY, VOTES-FOR-CANDIDATE} \right\}$ (VOTES-BY-PARTY)

$R'_8 = R_{13} \cup R_{14} \cup R_{17}$
     $= \left\{ \text{CONGRESS-NUMBER, ELECTION-YEAR} \right\}$ (CONGRESS)

$R'_9 = R_{15} \cup R_{18}$
     $= \left\{ \text{PARTY-NAME} \right\}$ (PARTY)

$R'_{10} = R_{16}$
     $= \left\{ \text{NO-OF-SENATORS} \right\}$ (SENATORS)

$R'_{11} = R_{19}$
     $= \left\{ \text{NO-OF-REPS} \right\}$ (REPS)

$R'_{12} = R_{20} \cup R_{21}$
     $= \left\{ \text{STATE-NAME,...,ELECTORAL-VOTE}, RG_3 \right\}$ (STATE)

Figure 3   (page 1 of 2)

Consolidation and Naming of Schemas

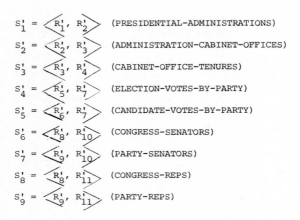

$S_1' = \langle R_1', R_2' \rangle$ (PRESIDENTIAL-ADMINISTRATIONS)

$S_2' = \langle R_2', R_3' \rangle$ (ADMINISTRATION-CABINET-OFFICES)

$S_3' = \langle R_3', R_4' \rangle$ (CABINET-OFFICE-TENURES)

$S_4' = \langle R_5', R_7' \rangle$ (ELECTION-VOTES-BY-PARTY)

$S_5' = \langle R_6', R_7' \rangle$ (CANDIDATE-VOTES-BY-PARTY)

$S_6' = \langle R_8', R_{10}' \rangle$ (CONGRESS-SENATORS)

$S_7' = \langle R_9', R_{10}' \rangle$ (PARTY-SENATORS)

$S_8' = \langle R_8', R_{11}' \rangle$ (CONGRESS-REPS)

$S_9' = \langle R_9', R_{11}' \rangle$ (PARTY-REPS)

Figure 3   (page 2 of 2)

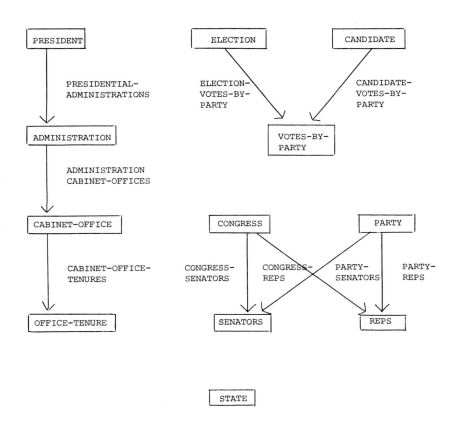

Figure 4

Data Structure Diagram of Consolidated Schemas

REFERENCES

CODASYL Data Base Language Task Group (1973), The COBOL Data Base
Facility Proposal

CODASYL Data Description Language Committee (1973), Journal of
Development

E. F. Codd (1970), "A Relational Model of Data for Large Shared Data
Banks", Comm. ACM 13, 377.

R. W. Engles (1972), "A Tutorial in Data-Base Organization", Annual
Review in Automatic Programming 7, 1.

M. E. Senko, E. B. Altman, M. M. Astrahan, and P. L. Fehder (1973),
"Data Structures and Accessing in Data Base Systems", IBM Systems
Journal 12, 30.

DISCUSSION

<u>Langefors</u> : I would like to make two remarks on this topic :

a) I agree that this subject has not been given as much explicit attention as it deserves. However, I would point out that the "infological " approach discussed by Bo Sundgren yesterday does in fact consider this problem in some depth.

b) You suggest that one of the things which was wrong with your first definition of data equivalence was that the concept of <u>fact</u> was undefined. The "infological " approach, again, gives a precise definition of "elementary fact ", and I believe that it is very important to be able to .talk about "facts" when designing an information system. You should not try to eliminate the concept of "fact" from your scheme of things.

<u>Mc Gee</u> : Points accepted; agreed.

<u>Neuhold</u> :The paper you mentioned which discusses the transformation of hierarchical structures into relational structure is :

" Data Mapping : a Hierarchical and Relational View "

by E.J. Neuhold (Report n°. 10, 1973, Institut für Angewandte

Informatik, Univ. of Karlsruhe, W. Germany)

Another relevant paper is :

"Formal View on Schema/Sub-schema Correspondance"

by H. Billier & E.J. Neuhold (to be presented at IFIP Congress

1974, Stockholm)

This paper shows that if the schema and sub-schema possess certain (very general) properties then any operation in terms of the sub-schema can be reflected in suitable operations in terms of the schema. The DBTG schema/sub-schema constructs are a rather simple special case of the general situation.

<u>Bayer</u> : Your general concept of data equivalence is perhaps too ambitious. It is very important to realize that two data structures can only be said to be equivalent with respect to certain well-defined (and considerably

constrained) sets of <u>operators</u>. The problem is the same as the mathematical problem of demonstrating isomorphism.

<u>Mc Gee</u> : I agree. However, different data structure classes tend to have disparate sets of operators, and to prove the equivalence of classes we need the notion of operators which somehow transcend classes.

<u>Bayer</u> : No : this is done just as in demonstrating isomorphism, namely by establishing equivalence between the operators in the different classes.

<u>Olle</u> : We have learnt that the world is not black and white but grey : in other words, there is not a simple division between data structure on the one hand and storage structure on the other, but a spectrum of possible data structures; and the problem is, not to show the equivalence of two structures on the spectrum, but rather to decide the point in the spectrum at which the optimal structure lies. The " flat data structure class " is probably at one end of the spectrum. In the last analysis the problem is one of optimization.

<u>Abrial</u> : I agree that the problem is one of optimization -- and eventually of <u>dynamic</u> optimization. We need to be able to define an evaluation function so that we can prove that one structure is better than another, and thus pare the way for systems which can dynamically organize themselves for optimal performance.

<u>Mc Gee</u> : I did not wish to imply that optimization is not important : but I believe that we can and should study the equivalence problem independently of the optimization problem.

FORMALIZATION OF THE NOTIONS OF DATA,

INFORMATION AND INFORMATION STRUCTURE

Claude PAIR, UNIVERSITY OF NANCY II

1. INTRODUCTION

What is an information processing problem ? One can say that it is
the transition from one information entity to another. Let us take the
simple example of the computation of pay starting from an hourly salarly
(sh), a number of hours of work (nh), and considering the deduction for
Social Security, that is :

$$(1) \quad \begin{cases} pay = sh - ss \\ sh = nh \times sh \\ ss = sb \times 0.06 \end{cases}$$

The system (1) represents the problem. It passes from one information
entity X (nh = 39 ; sh = 10) to a result R (pay = 366.60). Moreover,
with every other information entity of the same type as X, the problem
associates a result of the type of R.

The mechanism of 'transition' from X to R consists of completing the
system (1) with the information X, then to be concerned with a consequence
R of the system thus obtained.

It is appropriate to define precisely the term 'information'. One speaks
also of data. Are the two words synonymous ? A problem is applicable
to information of a certain type ; can one formalize the notion of type
by speaking of information structure (or data structure) as one speaks
of group structure ? An important part of information processing consists
of representing information, modifying it, having access to it ; in particular, starting from given elementary accesses, one can construct
derived accesses. Can all these operations be defined with precision ?
Later in this paper we present the major lines of a formalization
attempting to answer these questions. We hope that such work will permit
a better understanding of the concepts relative to such domains as : data
banks, semantics of programming languages, compilation, operating systems,
etc. ...

2. EXAMPLES OF DATA

The information X of the introduction is composed of elementary information
entities nh and sh. More generally, let us try first of all to understand
composite information, using examples less simple than the preceding.

a) An array of real numbers is sometimes considered as a grouping of real
numbers. In reality, the important thing is the manner by which one has
access to these real numbers : each one of them is determined by indexes.
An array of real numbers, with two dimensions for example, can therefore
be considered as a function which associates a real number with a pair of
integers, in a certain domain of definition.

b) In a file of addresses, each article can be diagrammed in the following
manner :

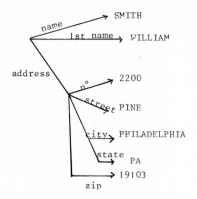

name, first name, address ... are functions which permit access to a chain
of characters, to an integer or to another element which serves only a
relay, or reference.

c) The table of identifiers (symbols) of an assembler is again a function
which passes from an identifier to the address which it represents.

d) The task queue in a system can be diagrammed as :

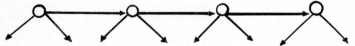

each task, except the last, has one following in the queue ; moreover,
it is characterized here by two elementary information entities.

e) Let us consider the following declarations in the language Algol 68,
(A. Van Wijngaarden, 1969) :

$$\underline{real}\ x := 3.14\ ;\ \underline{compl}\ z := (1.2,\ 3.14)\ ;\ \underline{compl}\ u = z$$

The identifier x gives access to
(one says possesses) a name which,
in turn, refers to the value 3.14
(after a new assignment, it can refer
to another value). Similarly, z possesses a name which refers to a
complex number formed of two components:
its real part 1.2 and its imaginary
part 3.14. Finally, u possesses a
complex number (which cannot vary),
that which is referred to by z.
The state of the 'Algol 68 machine'
after these declarations is diagrammed in the adjoining figure.
Possesses, refers to, re, im are
here again functions permitting
accesses.

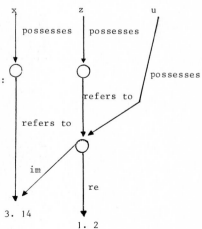

f) A polyhedron, for example a tetrahedron ABCD, can be diagrammed in the following manner :

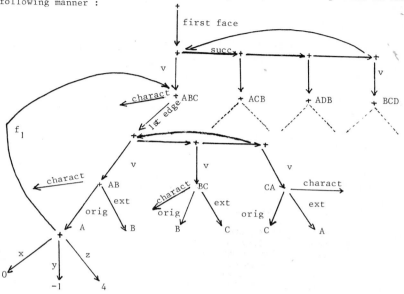

first face (resp. first edge) gives access, via an intermediate v, to the first face (resp. first edge) of the tetrahedron considered (resp. of the face considered), faces and edges being ordered arbitrarily. Charact is a function associating with a face (resp. edge) the characteristics of that face (resp. edge), for example color, form ... Each edge has an origin and an extremity which are vertices. With each vertex are associated its coordinates by means of three functions x, y, z and the three faces to which it belongs by three functions f_1, f_2, f_3.

Data thus appears, in these examples, as being composed of elementary objects (elementary values and 'relays', belonging to given sets) connected by access functions (functions of one or several variables). The essential operation on these functions is the composition which, starting from elementary accesses, constructs more elaborate accesses. This is what the following formalization conveys.

3. FUNCTIONAL FORMALIZATION, NOTION OF DATA

3.1 Definition

A <u>datum</u> is an m+1 -uple $(E_1, \ldots, E_m, \Lambda)$, where E_i (i=1,...,m) is a set of elementary objects ; Λ is a set of (partial) functions defined in sets of the form $E_{j_1} \times \ldots \times E_{j_q}$ (q ≥ 0 and $1 \leq j_i \leq m$), with values in one of the $E_i (1 \leq j_1 \leq m)$; such a function will be called an elementary access with q variables, a function with 0 variable being identified with its value.

3.2 Example

a) list :

A list on a set E is a finite sequence of elements of E. To state precisely this notion of sequence, and in particular to express the accesses to the elements of such a sequence, we introduce a totally ordered set F (the set of 'places' in the sequence considered), of which the first element $\mathcal{C}$ is called the head of the list and the last $\mathcal{S}$ is the tail of the list. The total ordering is conveyed by giving a function of succession in F, denoted by σ, which is a bijection from $F - \{\mathcal{S}\}$ into $F - \{\mathcal{C}\}$. Then every element of F is the image of $\mathcal{C}$ under σ^i $(=\sigma \circ \sigma \circ \sigma ... \circ \sigma)$ for a certain i. Furthermore a mapping γ assigns to each element of F a value in E. Thus a list is the triplet $(F, E, \wedge)$ where $\wedge = \{\sigma, \gamma, \mathcal{C}\}$ and

- σ is a bijection from $F - \{\delta\}$ onto $F - \{\mathcal{C}\}$ satisfying :
$$(\forall x \in F) \ (\exists i \geq 0) \ (x = \sigma^i \ (\mathcal{C}) \ )$$

- γ is a (total) function from F into E

- $\mathcal{C}$ is an element of F   (function of 0 variable)

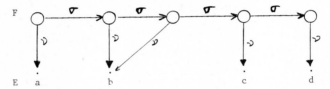

Diagram of the list abbcd

We will often use this notion of list in the examples.

b) table :

examples : - table of identifiers of an assembler which associates an address with an identifier

- two-dimensional array of real numbers which associates a real number with a pair of integers.

Formally, a table is a triplet $(Id, E, \wedge)$ where
Id is the set of indicators present (entries) in the table
E is the set of values of the table

$\wedge = \{\mathcal{C}\} \cup$ Id : $\mathcal{C}$ is a function defined in Id, with values in E ; the elements of Id are functions of 0 variable.

c) memory :

The notion of addressable memory can be formalized in the following manner :
an addressable memory is a quadruplet $(M, U, A, \wedge)$ where :

- M is a set of words,
- U is the set of values that can be contained in these words (for example, the set of sequences of 32 bits)
- A is a subset of U : the set of addresses (for example, elements of U of which the first 15 bits are 0)
- $\wedge = \{\gamma, \mu\} \cup U \cup \wedge'$, the set of elementary functions where :
γ is the function content defined on M with values in U
μ is the function addressing defined on A with values in M (injective).

One does not have access directly to the words but to the values of U ; in other words, among the elementary access functions are the elements of U as functions of 0 variable.

- Λ' is a set of operations in U, that is, of functions of one or more variables of U with values in U ; for example, an addition or a successor function :

$$u \longrightarrow u + 1$$

3.3 Remarks

1) It is always possible to reduce a datum to one for which m=1 by considering that the elements of Λ are partial functions from E into itself with E = $\cup E_i$. ($1 \leqslant i \leqslant m$).
It is then necessary to express which sets are the domain and the codomain of the elements of Λ; a convenient manner consists of adjoining to Λ some 'predicate' functions pr_i (i=1, ..., m) of which E_i is the domain of definition, with : $pr_i^i(x)=x$ for all $x \in E_i$.
Then to say that ℓ is defined in E_j with values in E_k is equivalent to :

$$\ell \circ pr_j = \ell \qquad (*)$$
$$pr_k \circ \ell = \ell$$

2) It is also possible to consider total functions instead of partial functions by introducing an element $\perp \in E$ which is interpreted as 'undefined'.

Example: a function pr_j defined in E_j with values in E_j is extended into a total function $\overline{pr}_j$ defined by :

$$\overline{pr}_j (x) = \underline{if}\ x \in E_j\ \underline{then}\quad x\ \underline{else}\ \perp$$

Thus, for a list, $\sigma (\delta) = \perp$; for a list with 4 elements $\sigma^4(\mathscr{C}) = \perp$. More generally, the extension of a partial function g into a total function $\overline{g}$ is made in the following manner :
for $x \in E$: $\overline{g} (x) = \underline{if}\ g(x)$ is defined $\underline{then}\ g(x)\ \underline{else}\ \perp$
and $\overline{g} (\perp) = \perp$

3.4   Notion of data structure :

We have thus formalized the notion of data ; but we have not answered the other questions posed in the introduction.

For lists, for example, we want to be able to express certain transformations such as :

- change in value of an element
- adjunction of an element at the head of the list
- suppression of an element, etc.

(*) The equality of two partial functions means that they have the same domain of definition and that on this domain they take the same values.

Any such modification transforms the initial list into a new list ;
furthermore, the description of this transformation is independent of
the source list. Thus, with the preceding definition of a list, to
change the value of an element is tantamount to changing the function ϑ;
to add or suppress an element is tantamount to changing the set F and
the functions ϑ and σ .
In the preceding transformations what matters is the type of the datum
much more than the datum itself. A type is, intuitively, a class of
data having the same integer m and 'similar' sets $\wedge$.
The two fundamental notions of type of a datum and modification defined
on data of a certain type are incorporated in the notion of data structure ; here 'structure' has the same sense as in group structure : it is
the framework in which one can express certain properties characterizing
certain objects. It is for the data structures that the problem of representation, especially in memory, is posed. To express more precisely
these notions of type, modification and structure, by stating in particular what is meant by 'similar sets $\wedge$', one is led to a more formal
definition, replacing the functions by function symbols, the notion of
function schema formalizing the composition of functions.

4. FORMALIZATION OF LOGICAL TYPE, INFORMATION AND INFORMATION TYPE

4.1 Introduction

In the preceding approach a datum $(E_1, E_2, \ldots, E_m, \wedge)$ is a 'concrete'
object. By contrast we will consider an information entity as being
an 'ideal' object which permits assertions ; in brief, an information
entity will be a set of theorems of a certain form. Furthermore an
information entity will be able to be realized concretely (interpreted,
in the logical sense) by a datum.
Examples :

a) In an information entity of list type, if s (resp. v,t) represents
the unary (resp. unary, 0-ary) function symbol interpretable as the
function σ (resp. ϑ, $\mathcal{E}$) and if ω is the 0-ary function symbol interpreted as 'undefined', the list diagrammed in 3.2 a) is characterized
by the following theorems :

$$\begin{cases} vt \equiv a & (\equiv \text{ represents formal equality}) \\ vst \equiv b \\ vs^2t \equiv b \\ vs^3t \equiv c \\ vs^4t \equiv d \end{cases}$$

Furthermore, one expresses that σ is an injection by the following set
of theorems :

for $i \neq j$, i, j $\in$ N we have $s^i t \equiv s^j t \supset s^i t \equiv \omega$

Finally, we make precise that $s^4 t$ is the last element by :

$$s^5 t \equiv \omega$$

b) In an information entity of memory type ($\S 8$), we express that the
function symbol mem must be interpreted as an injective function (μ)
by :

mem x $\equiv$ mem y $\supset$ x $\equiv$ y for all function symbols x and y.

c)Let us consider the following Algol 68 declarations :

<u>real</u> x : = 3.2 ; <u>rep real</u> y = <u>loc real</u> : = 4.1 ;
<u>compl</u> z = (x,y) ;

The information representing the state of the memory after their ela-
boration contains the theorems :

$$\left\{ \begin{array}{l} \text{poss } x \equiv 3.2 \\ \text{rep poss } y \equiv 4.1 \\ \text{re poss } z \equiv 3.2 \\ \text{im poss } z \equiv 4.1 \end{array} \right.$$

where poss (resp. rep, re, im) is a function symbol interpreted as
the function possesses (resp. refers to, real part, imaginary part),
A.VAN WIJNGAARDEN (1969). An information type is therefore, at first
sight, a framework for these theorems. This will be a formal system
$\mathcal{F}$ = (Alph, F,X,R) ,   JR SHOENFIELD (1967),expressing the general
properties common to all of the information entities of the type.(Alph
is the alphabet of $\mathcal{F}$, F the set of formulas, X the set of axioms, and
R the set of rules of inference).
To obtain an information structure, we will later on ($\mathcal{F}$7) adjoin to $\mathcal{F}$
a set Mod of elementary modifications.

4. 2 <u>Formal systems associated with information structures</u> :

The formulas of the formal system are constructed in several steps.
One defines successively :
- a set L of function symbols (or accesses)
- a set S of function schemata on L and a subset A of $S \equiv S$ (set of
  atomic formulas)
- the set F of the formulas of the system, the minimal solution of the
  equation
$$F = A \cup \neg F \cup (F \supset F)$$

4.2. 1 <u>Alphabet</u>

The alphabet contains :
- a set L of function symbols
- the symbol $\equiv$
- the symbols $\neg$, $\supset$, (,)

To interpret the function symbols, we must introduce m sets E_1, ...,
E_m and interpret each symbol as a function from E_{i_1} x... x E_{j_q} into E_k.
This leads us to specifying an integer m and associating with each
element f of L a q+1 - uple, pl (f)= (j_1,..., j_q, k) with q $\geqslant$ 0 and
$1 \leq j_i \leq$ m for $1 \leq$ i $\leq$ q. pl (f) will be called the <u>profile</u> of f.

<u>Example</u> : For lists, m= 2 and L contains :

  - s (which will be interpreted as the successor function σ:
    pl (s) = (1,1)
  - v (which will be interpreted as the 'value' function ν :
    pl (v) = (1,2)
  - t (interpreted as the head $\mathcal{C}$, a 0-ary function):pl(t) = (1)
  - ω (interpreted as the element 'undefined' $\perp$) : pl(ω)= (1)
  - a set V of symbols, interpreted as the values of the list
    (elements of E) : the profile of each of these is (2).

The alphabet is therefore characterized by the triplet (L,m,pl) formed of the set L, the integer m and the mapping _profile_ pl.

Definition 1 : An _interpretation_ of (L,m,pl) is an m+1 -uple
$(E_1, \ldots, E_m, r)$ where the E_i are sets and r is a mapping associating with each $f \in L$ such that $pl(f)=(j_1,\ldots,j_q,k)$ a mapping from $E_{j1} \times \ldots \times E_{jq}$ into E_k.

4. 2.2 Function schemata of the system

Let us recall that for every set L of function symbols with each one of which is associated an integer q (its number of arguments), we know how to define _function schemata_ : their set is generated by the grammar with rules :

$$S ::= \quad f\ S^q \quad \text{for every f with} \quad q \quad \text{arguments.}$$

Here we will consider only certain function schemata, those which are obtained by taking the profiles into account in the composition.

Definition 2 : We call _function schemata compatible with (L,m,pl)_ the elements of the language S on L defined by :

$$S = \bigcup_{k=1}^{m} S_k$$

where $(S_1, \ldots, S_m)$ is the unique solution of the system

$$S_k = \bigcup_{q \geqslant 0} \{ f\ S_{j1}\ S_{j2} \ldots S_{jq} \mid pl\ (f)=(j_1,j_2,\ldots,j_q,k) \}$$

$$(1 \leqslant k \leqslant m)$$

Theorem : Let $(E_1,\ldots, E_m, r)$ be an interpretation of (L,m,pl). r determines a unique mapping $\hat{r}$ from S into $E = \bigcup_{1 \leq i \leq m} E_i$ such that
for all $f \in L$ satisfying $pl(f)= (j_1, \ldots, j_q, k)$ and for all
$(x_1,\ldots, x_q) \in S_{j1} \times \ldots \times S_{jq}$ we have :

$$\hat{r}\ (fx_1 \ldots x_q) = r(f)\ (\hat{r}\ (x_1), \ldots, \hat{r}(x_q)\ ).$$

The proof is immediate and analogous to the proof for the function schemata in general (G.KREISEL - 1966).

Example: The set S of the function schemata of the list on V structure is $S = S_1 \cup S_2$ where S_1 and S_2 form the minimal solution of the system with fixpoint :

$$\begin{cases} S_1 = s\ S_1 \cup \{t,\omega\} \\ S_2 = v\ S_1 \cup V \end{cases}$$

Here $S_1 = \{ s^i t \mid i \geqslant 0\} \cup \{ s^i \omega \mid i \geqslant 0\}$
$S_2 = \{ vs^i t \mid i \geqslant 0\} \cup \{ v\ s^i \omega \mid i \geqslant 0\} \cup V$

4.2.3 Atomic formulas

Using the preceding notation, the set A of atomic formulas is defined by the system :

$$A = \bigcup_{1 \leqslant k \leqslant m} S_k \equiv S_k$$

(One compares the function schemata f and f' with $pl(f)=(j_1,\ldots,j_q,k)$ and $pl(f')=(j_1,\ldots,j_q,k')$ only if $k=k'$).

Example : For lists, we do not want to compare a place $(s^i t)$ and a value $(v s^j t)$. We also have !

$$A = S_1 \equiv S_1 \cup S_2 \equiv S_2$$

4.2.4 Formulas

The set F is the minimal solution of the system with fixpoint

$$F = A \cup \neg F \cup \quad (F \supset F)$$

This is equivalent to saying :

1) every atomic formula is a formula
2) if φ is a formula, $\neg \varphi$ is also a formula
3) if φ and ψ are formulas, $(\varphi \supset \psi)$ is a formula
4) every formula is obtained by application of the preceding 3 rules.

Furthermore, parentheses are omitted with the convention of evaluating the expressions from right to left.

example : $\varphi \supset \psi \supset \rho$ replaces $\varphi \supset (\psi \supset \rho)$.

4.2.5 Axioms

We distinguish in the set X of axioms :

. logical axioms, valid for every information structure
. axioms particular to the structure considered.

The logical axioms are :

- the axioms of the propositional calculus, regrouped into three schemata

$$SH_1 = \{\varphi \supset (\psi \supset \varphi) \mid \varphi, \psi \in F\}$$
$$SH_2 = \{(\varphi \supset (\psi \supset \rho)) \supset ((\varphi \supset \psi) \supset (\varphi \supset \rho)) \mid \varphi, \psi, \rho \in F\}$$
$$SH_3 = \{(\neg \varphi \supset \neg \psi) \supset (\psi \supset \varphi) \mid \varphi, \psi \in F\}$$

- and the axioms of equality

$$SH_4 = \{x \equiv x \mid x \in S\}$$
$$SH_5 = \{x_1 \equiv y_1 \supset \ldots \supset x_n \equiv y_n \supset fx_1 \ldots x_n \equiv fy_1 \ldots y_n \mid$$
for every $i \leqslant n$, $x_i \equiv y_i \in A$ and $fx_1 \ldots x_n \equiv fy_1 \ldots y_n \in A\}$
$$SH_6 = \{x_1 \equiv x_2 \supset x_1 \equiv x_3 \supset x_2 \equiv x_3 \mid x_i \equiv x_j \in A \text{ if } 1 \leqslant i \leqslant j \leqslant 3\}$$

Example : The axioms peculiar to the list on V structure are regrouped into three schemata.
          To express them, we distinguish in V an element ω', to be interpreted as the undefined value.

$$SH_7 = \{ s^i t \equiv s^j t \supset s^i t \equiv \omega | i \neq j \}$$

$$SH_8 = \{ s \omega \equiv \omega , v \omega \equiv \omega ' \}$$

$$SH_9 = \{ \neg a \equiv b | a,b \in V \; ; \; a \neq b \}$$

SH_7 and SH_8 express that either all the $s^i t$ are 'distinct' (infinite list), or else there exists an integer n such that t, st, ..., $s^{n-1} t$ are 'distinct' and $s^n t$, $s^{n+1} t$, ... are 'undefined' (list of length n).

4.2.6 Rules of inference of the formal system

The only rule of inference is the rule of detachment or 'Modus Ponens'. For every formula φ , ψ of F, one can deduce ψ from φ and $\varphi \supset \psi$:

$$\varphi , \; \varphi \supset \psi \longmapsto \psi$$

Finally, the formal system of a structure is completely defined by the set L of accesses, the integer m, the profile function pl and the set of the axioms peculiar to the structure.

4.2.7 Information entities of the structure

Definition 3

An information entity of the structure is a subset of F containing the theorems of the formal system and closed under the application of the rule of detachment. I is therefore an information entity of the structure if and only if :

   i) $X \subset I$

   ii) For all φ, ψ of F, $\varphi \in I$ and $\varphi \supset \psi \in I$ imply $\psi \in I$

Example : information entity of the list structure.
A finite list I, of length n, is specified by a given sequence (a_i), $1 \leqslant i \leqslant n$, of elements of V. It can be defined formally by the following set of axioms X_1 :

$$X_1 = \{ v \; s^i t \equiv a_i \; | \; 0 \leqslant i \leqslant n \} \cup \{ s^n t \equiv \omega \}$$

An infinite list is specified by giving an infinite sequence $(a_i), i \geqslant 0$, of elements of V. It can be defined by :

$$X_1 = \{ v s^i t \equiv a_i \; | \; i \geqslant 0 \}$$

Remark :
Let T be the set of theorems of the formal system and $\mathcal{J}$ the set of information entities of the structure. T belongs to $\mathcal{J}$ as does F. Every intersection of elements of $\mathcal{J}$ is an element of $\mathcal{J}$. Therefore, given a family $\{ I_\lambda \}$ of information entities, there exists a smallest information entity I containing all the I_λ. $\mathcal{J}$ is therefore a complete lattice,   (D. SCOTT 1972) for the relation of inclusion, with minimal element T and maximal element F.

The rest of the paper briefly studies information structures, in order to answer the questions posed in the introduction concerning the manner of defining derived accesses starting from elementary accesses, the modifications of information entities of one structure, and the representation of information structures.
A certain number of results are stated without proof. The proofs use the properties of the propositional calculus (see for example JR SHOENFIELD, 1967). They appear in J.L.REMY - J.P. FINANCE (1973).

5. CONSISTENT, COMPLETE INFORMATION ENTITIES - REALIZATIONS

This paragraph is a study of the lattice of the information entities of a structure. The following notation is used : if I designates an information entity and φ a formula, $I(\varphi)$ is the information entity obtained starting from I by adding φ to the axioms, in other words the smallest information entity containing I and φ .

5.1 Consistent information entities

<u>Definition 1</u> : an information entity I is <u>consistent</u> if $I \neq F$

<u>Proposition 1</u> : An information entity I is consistent if and only if it satisfies one of the following equivalent properties

  i) For every formula φ of F, $\varphi \in I \Rightarrow \neg \varphi \notin I$

  ii) For every atomic formula α of A, $\alpha \in I \Rightarrow \neg \alpha \notin I$

<u>Proposition 2</u> : Let I be an information entity. A formula φ belongs to I if and only if $I (\neg \varphi)$ is not consistent.

5.2 Complete information entities

<u>Definition 2</u> : An information entity I is <u>complete</u> if it is maximal in the set of consistent information entities.

<u>Proposition 3</u> : A consistent information entity I is complete if and only if it satisfies one of the following equivalent conditions :

  i) For every formula φ of F, $\varphi \notin I \Rightarrow \neg \varphi \in I$

  ii) For every atomic formula α of A, $\alpha \notin I \Rightarrow \neg \alpha \in I$

<u>Definition 3</u> : Let $\mathscr{S}$ be a structure and I an information entity of $\mathscr{S}$. A simple extension of I is an information entity I' of $\mathscr{S}$ containing I.

<u>Proposition 4</u> : Every consistent information entity I admits a complete simple extension.

One can summarize the preceding study by a lattice diagram of the information entities of a structure :

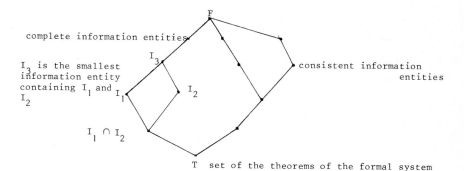

complete information entities

I_3 is the smallest
information entity
containing I_1 and
I_2

consistent information
entities

$I_1 \cap I_2$

T set of the theorems of the formal system

Lattice of information entities

5. 3 Realization of an information entity

Definition 4 : Let I be an information entity of a structure and let
$R = (E_1, E_2, \ldots, E_m, r)$ be an interpretation of the triplet
(L, pl, m) of the structure (4.2.1). Let us define a
truth function $\tilde{r}$ on the set of atomic formulas :

$$\tilde{r}\ (\alpha \equiv \beta)\ = \quad \underline{\text{true}}\ \text{if}\ \hat{r}\ (\alpha)\ =\ \hat{r}\ (\beta)$$

$$\underline{\text{false}}\ \text{otherwise} \quad (\text{see } 4.2.2 \text{ for the definition of } \hat{r})$$

$\tilde{r}$ is extended in a natural way to all the formulas.
We say that R is a realization of I if, for every $\varphi \in I$, $\tilde{r}\ (\varphi) =$ true.
The m+1-uple $(E_1, \ldots, E_m, r(L)\ )$ is a datum in the sense of 3.1 ; One
can say that this datum realizes the information entity I.

Example : Let us again take the list of order n considered in 4.2.7.
We can associate with it the following realization :

$E_1 = \{0, 1,\ \ldots,\ n-1,\ \perp \}$; $E_2 = V$;

$r(t) = 0$; $r(s) = \sigma$;

$r(\omega) = \perp$; $r(v) = \nu$;

$r(a) = a$ for $a \in V$; where the functions σ and ν are defined by
(3.2 b) :

$$\begin{cases} \sigma(i) = i+1 & \text{for } 0 \leqslant i \leqslant n-1 \\ \sigma(n-1) = \perp \\ \sigma(\perp) = \perp \end{cases}$$

and $\begin{cases} \nu(i) = a_i & \text{for } 0 \leqslant i \leqslant n-1 \\ \nu(\perp) = \omega' \ (\text{'undefined' element in V}) \end{cases}$

Definition 5 : Two realizations $(E_1, \ldots, E_m, r)$ and $(E'_1, \ldots, E'_m, r')$
are equivalent if $\tilde{r}(\varphi) = \overset{\sim}{r'}(\varphi)$ for every formula φ
of F.

One can then prove the following theorem :

Theorem : An information entity is consistent if and only if it admits
a realization. It is complete if and only if it admits a
realization and all its realizations are equivalent.

6. DERIVED ACCESSES

6.1 Extension of an information structure

Let $\mathcal{S}$ and $\mathcal{S}'$ be two information structures, F and F' their sets of
formulas, T and T' their sets of theorems, $\mathcal{T}$ and $\mathcal{T}'$ their sets of
information entities.

Definition 1: One says that $\mathcal{S}'$ is an extension of $\mathcal{S}$ if $F \subset F'$ and
$T \subset T'$.

Consequence : Every information entity of $\mathcal{S}'$ contained in F is an
information entity of $\mathcal{S}$; otherwise expressed :
$$\mathcal{T}' \cap \mathcal{P}(F) \subset \mathcal{T}$$

Definition 2 : Let I be an information entity of $\mathcal{S}$; the extension of I
to $\mathcal{S}'$ is the smallest information entity $\overline{I'}$ of $\mathcal{S}'$
containing I. We write $I' = \& (I)$.

<u>Definition 3</u> : Let I' be an information entity of $\mathcal{J}$' ; the <u>restriction</u> of I' to $\mathcal{S}$ is the information entity I = I'$\cap$ F of $\mathcal{S}$. We write I = $\mathbf{R}$ (I').

<u>Proposition</u> : If $\&$ preserves completeness

$\mathbf{R}$ o $\&$ (I)= I   for every complete information entity I of $\mathcal{S}$

$\&$ o $\mathbf{R}$ (I')= I'   for every complete information entity I' of $\mathcal{S}'$.

<u>Remark</u> : If $\&$ preserves completeness, it preserves consistency :indeed every consistent information entity I has a single complete extension I_1. $\&$ (I_1) being complete,$\&$ (I) is consistent for it is contained in $\&(I_1)$.

<u>Proof</u> :

a) Let I be a complete information entity. $\&$ (I) is consistent as is $\&$ (I) $\cap$ F. $\&$ (I) $\cap$ F contains I. Because I is maximal, we have the equality.

b) Let I' be a complete information entity of $\mathcal{S}'$. I'$\cap$ F is also complete in $\mathcal{S}$ (from 5.2, prop.3), as is $\&$ (I' $\cap$ F) in $\mathcal{S}'$. Because I' contains $\&$ (I' $\cap$ F) we have the equality.

<u>Definition 4</u> : If $\&$ preserves completeness, we say that $\mathcal{S}'$ <u>is deduced</u> from $\mathcal{S}$.

6. 2 <u>Structure deduced from another by definition of new symbols (or accesses)</u>

Let $\mathcal{S}$ be an information structure and f_1, $\ldots$,f_n function symbols not belonging to L. We consider an extension $\mathcal{S}'$ of $\mathcal{S}$ such that L' = L $\cup$ $\{f_1 \ldots, f_n\}$. The set of particular axioms of $\mathcal{S}'$ is formed from the particular axioms of $\mathcal{S}$ and a set X $[f_1,\ldots,f_n]$ of axioms "defining" f_1, $\ldots$, f_n.

<u>Example</u> : Given a structure $\mathcal{S}$, one can define a 4-ary symbol cond1 with profile (1,1,1,1,1,) by the set of axioms :

X [cond 1] = $\{$ x$\equiv$y $\supset$ cond1 (x,y,z,t)$\equiv$ z, $\daleth$ x $\equiv$ y $\supset$ cond1 (x,y,z,t)$\equiv$ t | x,y,z,t $\in$ $S_1\}$ (S_1 is defined in 4.2.2 : it is the set of function schemata 'with result in the first set').

Let I be an information entity, and I' the information entity obtained by adjoining the symbol cond 1.

If R = ($E_1,\ldots,E_m$,r) is a realization of I, one can obtain a realization R'=($E_1,\ldots,E_m$, r') of I' by putting :

r' (f) = f for f $\in$ L

r' (cond1) = Cond 1

where Cond 1 (a,b,c,d) = <u>if</u> a=b <u>then</u> c <u>else</u> d for a,b,c,d in E_1. One can show that for every structure $\mathcal{S}$, $\mathcal{S}'$ is deduced from $\mathcal{S}$. $_1$

6.3 <u>New accesses defined by a system of axioms with fixpoint</u>

Let us first study this type of definition by means of an example.

<u>Example:</u> Let $\mathcal{S}$ be the structure deduced from the list on V structure by adjoining the symbol cond1 and a symbol cond2 with profile (2,2,1,1,1) and an analogous set of axioms. Let $\mathcal{S}'=\mathcal{S}$ (assoc) be the structure obtained by adjoining the axiom schema:

$$X_1 = \{assoc\ (s^i\ t,a) \equiv cond\ 2\ (vs^i t,a,s^i t,$$
$$cond\,1\ (s^{i+1}\ t,\ \omega\ ,\ \omega\ ,\ assoc\ (s^{i+1}\ t,a)))\,|\,i \rangle\ 0, a \in V\ \}$$

(Parentheses and commas have been inserted in order to render this schema readable). The symbol assoc formalizes the associative access in a list starting from any element.

Let I be a consistent information entity of $\mathscr{A}$, for example a finite list of length n. Is $\&$ (I) consistent ? Yes, indeed, let R be the realization of I described in paragraph 5.3. To obtain a realization of $\&$(I) extending R, we must choose r(assoc) such that for every axiom φ of X_1, $\tilde{r}$ (φ) = <u>true</u>. For this, it is necessary and sufficient that r (assoc) satisfy the equation with unknown λ :

$$\begin{cases} \lambda\ (i,a) = \underline{if}\ \nu\ (i) = a\ \underline{then}\ i\ \underline{else}\ \underline{if}\ \sigma\ (i) =\ \perp\ \underline{then}\ \perp \\ \qquad\qquad \underline{else}\ \lambda\ (\ \sigma(i),a) \\ if\ i=0,\ 1,\dots,\ n-1\ and\ a \in V \\ \lambda\ (\perp,\ a) = \perp \end{cases}$$

We can order the sets E_1 and E_2 by the relation

a $\langle$ b if and only if a=b or a= $\perp$

Likewise, we can order the set of mappings from $E_1 x E_2$ into E_2 by the relation

$\lambda\ \langle\ \lambda'$ if and only if, for every a $\in E_1 x E_2$, λ (a) $\langle\ \lambda'$ (a).
$\perp$ being the "undefined" symbol, $\lambda\ \langle\ \lambda'$ if and only if, for every a such that λ(a) is defined, we have λ (a) = λ' (a). The function r(assoc) must be a solution of the equation described above,

$$\lambda = \mathscr{C}\ (\lambda).$$

For the ordering defined as in the preceding, the mapping $\mathscr{C}$ is continuous. Therefore this equation admits a minimal solution. In fact every solution can be chosen as an image of assoc under r.

For example, let us now consider the infinite list of axioms :
$v\ s^i\ t \equiv b$ for i $\rangle$ 0

It is easy to see that λ is a solution of the equation if and only if
λ (i,b) = i for i $\rangle$ 0 , and
λ (i,a) = λ (i',a) for a$\neq$b, i $\rangle$ 0, i' $\rangle$ 0

Indeed, for a $\neq$ b the equation reduces to :

λ (i,a) = λ (i+1,a).

The multiplicity of solutions of the system conveys the fact that $\&$(I) is not complete, or more concretely the fact that the associative access is not defined for the infinite lists. For this example, a program seeking the smallest integer i such that ν (i) = a does not terminate if a is different from b.

In order to give a general definition of this type of extension, we must first generalize the notion of function schema by permitting arguments in it. For that, it suffices to add to the set L of accesses, for j=1,2, ...,m, a denumerable set Z_j of formal parameters of profile (j). We thus define new sets of function schemata (cf.4.2.2),S'_1, ...,S'_m. Let us consider one of them, h $\in$ S'_k, and a sequence of formal parameters $z_1 \in Z_{j1}$, $z_q \in Z_{jq}$, among which are all those which are used in h : we say that $(j_1,\dots j_q,k)$ is a profile associated with h ; furthermore, if $x_1 \in Sj_1, \ldots, x_q \in S_{j_{q}}$, we will denote by h $[x_1, \ldots, x_q]$ the result of the substitution in h of x_1 for $z_1, \ldots, x_q$ for z_q.

For each new access f_i, we then give a profile $(j_{i1}, \ldots, j_{iq_i}, k_i)$ and a function schema with arguments h, on $L \cup \{f_1, \ldots, f\}$ with which this profile is associated. We take as the set of new axioms

$$\mathbf{X} [f_1, \ldots, f_n] = \bigcup_{i=1}^{n} \mathbf{X} [f_i]$$

with $X [f_i] = \{ f_i x_1 \cdots x_{qi} \equiv h_i [x_1, \ldots, x_{qi}] | x_1 \in S_{j_{i1}}, \ldots x_{q_i} \in S_{j_{iq_i}} \}$

In the preceding example, n=1 and
$h_1 = \text{cond2} (vz_1, z_2, z_1, \text{cond1} (sz_1, \omega, \omega, \text{assoc} (sz_1, z_2)))$

Let I be an information entity of the given structure $\mathscr{S}$. A realization of I permits us to write a system of equations(S), associated with the axiom schemata defining the new accesses $f_1, \ldots, f_n$: we have defined this system in the preceding example (it was there reduced to a single expression) ; it permits us to extend the given realization to $\mathscr{E}$ (I). One then can prove the following theorem :

Theorem :
If the system (S) admits at least one solution, $\mathscr{E}(I)$ is a consistent information entity. If the system (S) admits several solutions, $\mathscr{E}$ (I) is not complete.

7. ELEMENTARY MODIFICATIONS OF A STRUCTURE

We have said that an information structure is defined by giving a formal system $\mathscr{S}$ and a set of elementary modifications.

7.1 Elementary modifications

Let $\mathscr{S}$ be a structure and $\mathscr{T}$ its set of information entities.

Definition 1 : A modification is a mapping from $\mathscr{T}$ into $\mathscr{T}$. To be given a set of modifications amounts to deciding which elementary modifications are acceptable in the framework of the information structure.

Example 1 : We want to adjoin, in a list on $\mathbf{V}$, an element after a given element x. Intuitively, this means that sx is going to become the successor of the successor of x, ssx.

To convey that, we introduce the structure $\mathscr{S}'$ obtained from $\mathscr{S}$ by replacing s by s', then the structure $\mathscr{S}''$ 'containing' $\mathscr{S}$ and $\mathscr{S}'$. More precisely,

$$L'' = \{t, v\} \cup \{s, s'\} \cup \{\omega\} \cup V.$$

$\mathscr{S}''$ conveys the coexistence of $\mathscr{S}$ and $\mathscr{S}'$. The adjunction of an element is then conveyed by the axioms :

$$\begin{cases} s's'x \equiv sx \\ (\neg x \equiv y) \supset s'y = sy \end{cases}$$

Let us examine how these axioms define a modification as a mapping from $\mathcal{S}$ into $\mathcal{S}$. Let I be an information entity of $\mathcal{S}$; we consider in turn :

- the information entity I", the extension of I in the structure $\mathcal{S}$", denoted by $\mathcal{E}$ " (I)

- the information entity I', the restriction of I" in the structure $\mathcal{S}$', denoted by R' (I")

- the information entity I_1, obtained from I' by replacing s' by s. I_1 is an information entity of $\mathcal{S}$, the result of the modification defined by the axioms written just above. We will denote this modification by adj(x). Let us now return to the general framework.

Definition 2:

Let $\mathcal{S}$ be a structure defined by the set of accesses L, the integer m, the function profile pl, and the set of particular axioms X. Let η be a bijection from L onto a set L', of which the restriction to $L \cap L'$ is the identity mapping. We define a profile function pl' in L' by :

$$pl'(\eta(f)) = pl(f) \text{ for } f \in L.$$

η is naturally extended into a mapping from the set of formulas F onto a set F': F' is the set of formulas of the structure $\mathcal{S}$' defined by L',m,pl' and X'= η(X). Let $\mathcal{S}$" be the structure defined by $L \cup L'$, the integer m, the profile function equal to pl on L and to pl' on L', as well as a set of axioms containing X and X' :

$$X" = X \cup X' \cup Y$$

The modification π, defined by η and the set of axioms Y, is :
$$\pi = \eta^{-1} \circ R' \circ \mathcal{E}"$$

where R' and $\mathcal{E}$ " have the same meaning as in the preceding example.
$$I \xrightarrow{\mathcal{E}"} I" \xrightarrow{R'} I' \xrightarrow{\eta-!} \pi(I)$$

Example 2 :

The modification π = asg (x,a) which assigns the value a to the element x of a list is associated with the bijection changing v into v' (and leaving unchanged the other symbols of L)and with the set Y of axioms :

$$Y = \{ v'x \equiv a, \quad (\neg x \equiv y) \supset v'y \equiv vy \}$$

7.2.Schemata of modifications

In the preceding example 2, π depends on x and a : we have in fact defined a schema of modifications with two parameters, asg.
A structure of information entities is defined by a formal system $\mathcal{F}$ and a finite number of schemata of elementary modifications. The elementary modifications are mappings and their composition permits us to define that of schemata of modifications.
Let M_1 and M_2 be two schemata of modifications with k arguments. We denote by $M_1 \circ M_2$ the schema composed of M_1 and M_2 defined by :
$$M_1 \circ M_2 (x_1, \ldots, x_k) = M_1(x_1, \ldots, x_k) \circ M_2(x_1, \ldots, x_k).$$

One can always be brought back to the case where M_1 and M_2 have the same number of arguments by composing them, if necessary, with projection functions. One can also use permutations of the arguments.

Thus starting from the set Sch of the schemata of elementary modifications of an information structure, one can, by compositions as well as projections and permutations of arguments, obtain the set, denoted by Sch, of the schemata of modifications of the structure.

8. REPRESENTATION OF ONE STRUCTURE IN ANOTHER

8. 1 Introduction

The last problem posed in the introduction and not yet treated is that of the representation of one information structure in another, and in particular that of the representation of an information entity of a structure $\mathscr{E}$ by an information entity of a structure $\mathscr{E}'$.

For example : how to define the representation of a list with n elements in a memory structure ? Let us quickly state precisely that, for a memory structure : the set of function symbols is

$$L = \{ \ c, \ mem, \ succ \ \} \cup U$$

. U is interpreted as the set of values that can be contained in a memory word :

. c, mem are interpreted respectively as γ, μ (paragraph 3.2.example c)

. finally, succ is interpreted as the mapping (3.2. example c) which associates with a value a of U its successor a+1.

8.2 Prerepresentation of an information structure

To represent a structure $\mathscr{E}$ in a structure $\mathscr{E}'$, one must first completely define the accesses of $\mathscr{E}$ starting from those of $\mathscr{E}'$. One can therefore give the following definition.

Definition :

A prerepresentation of a structure $\mathscr{E}$ in a structure $\mathscr{E}'$ is a structure $\mathscr{E}$ " containing $\mathscr{E}$ and which is deduced from $\mathscr{E}'$ (6.1. definition 4).

There exists then an extension $\&$ from $\mathscr{E}$ to $\mathscr{E}$" and a restriction R ' from $\mathscr{E}$" to $\mathscr{E}'$. Given an information entity I of $\mathscr{E}$, its representation in $\mathscr{E}'$ is the information entity R ' o $\&$ (I)

We will put $\rho = R$ ' o $\&$.

Example :

If $\mathscr{E}$ is the list on V structure and $\mathscr{E}'$ the memory structure described in 8.1, a prerepresentation of $\mathscr{E}$ in $\mathscr{E}'$ is obtained by adding to the axioms of $\mathscr{E}$ and $\mathscr{E}'$:

$$\{ \ t \equiv c \ mem \ a_0 \ \} \cup \{ \ vx \equiv \theta \quad c \ mem \ x, \ sx \equiv c \ mem \ succ \ x \mid x \in S_1 \ \}$$

where a_0 is a particular element of U, θ is a mapping from a subset of U into V ; S_1 is defined in 4.2.2.

The added axioms express in particular that s is represented by linking.

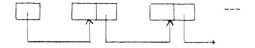

8.3. Representation of an information structure

It remains to consider modifications.

Let $\mathscr{S}$ and $\mathscr{S}'$ be two information structures. We denote by Sch (resp. Sch') the set of schemata of elementary modifications of $\mathscr{S}$ (resp. the set of schemata of modifications of $\mathscr{S}'$).

A prerepresentation $\boldsymbol{\rho}$ of $\mathscr{S}$ in $\mathscr{S}'$ is a <u>representation</u> of $\mathscr{S}$ in $\mathscr{S}'$ if there exists a mapping $\bar{\rho}$: Sch $\rightarrow$ Sch' such that, for every $M \in$ Sch with n arguments and for every information entity I of $\mathscr{S}$: $\rho \circ M\ (x_1, \ldots, x_n) \qquad = \bar{\rho}\ (M)\ (\rho\ (x_1), \ldots, \rho\ (x_n)\ ) \circ \boldsymbol{\rho}$

(ρ being defined in 8.2.)

In other words, the following diagram must be commutative :

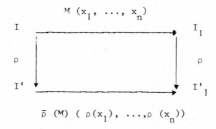

$$\bar{\rho}\ (M)\ (\rho(x_1), \ldots, \rho\ (x_n))$$

ACKNOWLEDGEMENT

I am indebted to J.P. FINANCE, J.L. REMY and J.BERGER for their aid in the preparation of the manuscript.

REFERENCES
==========

D.L. CHILDS
Feasibility of a set- theoretical data structure
Proc. I.F.I.P. Congress 1968, North-Holland, p. 162-172

E.F. CODD
A relational model of data for large shared banks
Comm. ACM 13 (1970), p.377-387

G. KREISEL - J.L. KRIVINE
Eléments de logique mathématique - Théorie des modèles-Dunod (1966)

C. PAIR
Structures d'informations - Cours de l'Ecole d'été d'Informatique de
l' A.F.C.E.T. - Alès (1971)

J.L. REMY - J.P. FINANCE
Structures d'information et sémantique d'un langage de programmation -
Ecole d'été d'Informatique de l' A.F.C.E.T. - Grenade (1973)

D. SCOTT
Data types as lattices - Cours de l'Ecole d'été d'Amsterdam (juin 1972)

JR SHOENFIELD
Mathematical logic - Addison - Wesley (1967)

A. VAN WIJNGAARDEN (ed)
Report on the Algorithmic language Algol 68, MR 101 - Mathematical
Centrum - Amsterdam (1969)

DISCUSSION

Codd : I would like to make the comment that different models have

advantages in different areas of applicability; and yours

seems to have the right kind of properties for tackling McGee's

data equivalence problem.

Data Base Management, J. W. Klimbie and K. L. Koffeman, (eds.)
© *North-Holland Publishing Company (1974)*

SPECIFYING QUERIES AS RELATIONAL EXPRESSIONS[*]

by

R. F. Boyce, D. D. Chamberlin, W. F. King III, M. M. Hammer[**]
IBM Research Laboratory
San Jose, California

ABSTRACT: (Specifying Queries As Relational Expressions) is a set oriented data sublanguage for expressing queries (access, modification, insertion, and deletion) to a data base consisting of a collection of time-varying relations. The language mimics how people use relations or tables to obtain information. It does not require the sophisticated mathematical machinery of the predicate calculus (bound variables, quantifiers, etc.) in order to express simple references to tables. However, the language has been shown to be complete, i.e., any query expressible in the predicate calculus is expressible in SQUARE.

1. Introduction

In a series of papers E. F. Codd [1-5] has introduced the relational model of data which appears to be the simplest possible data structure consistent with the semantics of information and which provides a maximum degree of data independence.

Given sets $S_1, S_2, ..., S_n$ (not necessarily distinct), $R(S_1, S_2, ..., S_n)$ is a relation of degree n on these n sets if it is a set of n-tuples each of whose elements has its first component from S_1, its second component from S_2, etc. In other words $R(S_1, S_2, ..., S_n)$ is a subset of the Cartesian product $S_1 \times S_2 \times ... \times S_n$. In this paper we will deal only with underlined relations [1]. A relation is normalized if each of its domains is simple, i.e., no domain is itself a relation.

A normalized relation can be viewed as a table of n columns and a varying number of rows as is apparent in Figure I.

A normalized relation has the following properties:

1) Column homogeneity - in any particular column all items are of the same type;

2) All rows of the table are distinct;

3) The ordering of the rows is immaterial; and

4) If distinct names are given to the columns the ordering of the columns is immaterial.

The concept of a relation has its present day analog in the notion of a file. The rows or tuples can be thought of as records. The entire data base may be viewed as a collection of time-varying relations of assorted degree upon which inserts, deletes, and updates can be made.

---

[*] This paper appeared in the proceedings of the SIGPLAN/SIGIR Interface Meeting, Gaithersburg, Maryland, November 1973, copyright held by the Association of Computing Machinery.
[**] Project MAC, MIT.

EMP	NAME	SALARY	MANAGER	DEPARTMENT
	SMITH	10K	JONES	TOY
	JONES	12K	DAHL	FURNITURE
	LEE	10K	THOMAS	APPLIANCE

Figure I: Employee Relation

In addition to introducing the relational data structure, Codd has defined a
language [5] which allows for the accessing or referencing of data represented
relationally. This language and similar ones (COLARD [6], RIL [7]) are based
on the first order predicate calculus. Queries in these languages typically
require:

1)   The user to define extra variables which have as values rows or portions
      of rows of a relation, and

2)   The user to state the query using Boolean expressions, and quantifiers
      (universal and existential).

Knuth [8] has shown that the majority of statements in FORTRAN are rather simple.
We believe this is also true of queries to a data base. SQUARE is a language
which attempts to mimic how people use tables to obtain information. It does
not require the sophisticated mathematical machinery of the predicate calculus
(extra variables, quantifiers) in order to do relatively simple references to
tables. However, it is not hard to show [9] that the SQUARE language is
complete, i.e., any query expressible in the predicate calculus is expressible
in SQUARE.

The user's perception of a query expressed in the predicate calculus is very
different from the SQUARE perception. This is a rather illusive concept to
define (section 3 treats it in detail including examples) but for introductory
purposes it is sufficient to note that the calculus machinery requires the user
to express the query in the form –

1)   Select rows of tables

2)   Apply a predicate, if true return the rows (or portions of rows)

3)   Iterate.

In SQUARE the user expresses the query in the form –

1)   Scan a column (or columns) of a table looking for a value (or set of
      values)

2)   For any such values found return the corresponding element(s) of a certain
      column(s) in the same row.

Put another way, SQUARE enables the user to describe data selection in terms of
set oriented table look-ups rather than in a row-at-a-time fashion. This
capability makes possible the elimination of quantifiers and the elimination of
explicit "linking terms" when the query requires the correlation of information
from several tables.

Before proceeding to illustrate the key components of the subject language
(section 2) we must comment on the relation of SQUARE to current data base
languages, e.g., DML of DBTG [10], DL/1 of IMS [11]. In general terms both the
predicate calculus languages and SQUARE are much higher level in the sense of

being less procedural. These higher level languages allow the user to specify
what are the properties of the data to be accessed, modified, inserted, or
deleted rather than how the relevant data is to be found. Hence by moving to
such higher level languages, user productivity is greatly increased.

2. Data Manipulation Description

As we introduce the facilities of SQUARE, we will illustrate them by examples.
The examples of this section are drawn from a data base describing the operation
of a department store, as follows:

$$\begin{array}{ll} \text{EMP} & \text{(NAME, SAL, MGR, DEPT)} \\ \text{SALES} & \text{(DEPT, ITEM, VOL)} \\ \text{SUPPLY} & \text{(COMP, ITEM, VOL)} \end{array}$$

The EMP relation has a row for every store employee, giving his name, salary,
manager, and department. The SALES relation gives the volume (yearly count) in
which each department sells each item. The SUPPLY relation gives the volume
(yearly count) in which the store obtains various items from its various supplier
companies. We assume that the SALES and SUPPLY relations have no zero-volume
entries (e.g., if the Toy Department does not sell dresses, there is no 'TOY,
DRESS, 0' entry in the SALES relation.)

In this paper we do not deal with the data description language. The questions
of unique names, comparability of domains, units, authorization, etc., are not
described. For a discussion of these issues, see [6].

We now proceed to describe the syntax of a relational expression, i.e., an
expression which evaluates to a relation. The simplest form of relational
expression is called a "mapping," and is illustrated by Q1.

   Q1. Find the names of employees in the Toy Department.

$$\underset{\text{NAME}}{\overset{\text{EMP}}{}}\quad \underset{\text{DEPT}}{}\quad \text{('TOY')}$$

A mapping consists of a relation name (EMP), a domain name (DEPT), a range name
(NAME), and an argument ('TOY'). The value of the mapping is the set of values
in the range column of the named relation whose associated values in the domain
column match the argument. This mapping evaluates to a unary relation (in this
case, a list of names.) Mapping emulates the way in which people use tables.
In this example, to find the names of employees in the Toy Department, a person
might look down the DEPT column of the EMP relation, finding 'TOY' entries and
making a list of the corresponding NAME entries.

The argument of a mapping may be either a single value (e.g., 'TOY') or a set
of values. If the argument is a set, the mapping returns all those range-values
whose corresponding domain-values match any element of the argument. Formally,
if the argument S is a set of individual values s_i,

$$\underset{B\ \ A}{R}\ (S) \equiv \bigcup_i \underset{B\ \ A}{R}\ (s_i)$$

For this reason the mapping is generally called a disjunctive mapping. For
simplicity the term mapping in this paper always refers to a disjunctive mapping.

Mappings may be "composed" by applying one mapping to the result of another, as
illustrated by Q2.

   Q2. Find those departments which sell items supplied by Revlon.

$$\underset{\text{DEPT}\quad\text{ITEM}}{\text{SALES}}\quad \text{o} \quad \underset{\text{ITEM}\quad\text{COMP}}{\text{SUPPLY}}\quad \text{('REVLON')}$$

The company 'REVLON' is first mapped to the items it supplies, and then to the departments which sell those items. The range of the inner mapping must be compatible with the domain of the outer mapping, but they need not be identical, as illustrated by Q3.

Q3. Find the salary of Anderson's manager.

$$EMP_{SAL\ NAME} \circ EMP_{MGR\ NAME} \text{ ('ANDERSON')}$$

Q2 is repeated in section 3 in order to demonstrate the different perception of the query that is required in order to answer the query in a predicate calculus-like language.

The next important building block of relational expressions is called a free variable. A relational expression containing a free variable takes the following form:

free-variable-list : test

On the left side of the colon are listed the free variables to be used in the query and the relations to which they belong. Each free variable represents a row of a relation. Free variables may be given arbitrary names provided they do not conflict with the names of relations. On the right side of the colon is a logical test which may be true or false for each set of values of the free variables. The value of the expression is the set of free-variable values for which the test is true. A subscripted free variable represents a particular field-value from the row represented by the free variable. For example:

Q4. Find the names of employees who make more than their managers.

$$x_{NAME} \ \varepsilon\ EMP : x_{SAL} > EMP_{SAL\ NAME} (x_{MGR})$$

The following types of operators are permissible in tests:

numeric comparisons:	$= \neq > \geq < \leq$
set comparisons:	$= \neq \supset \supseteq \subset \subseteq$
arithmetic operators:	$+ - \times /$
set operators:	$\cup \cap -$
logical connectives:	$\wedge \vee$
parentheses for grouping:	$( )$
built-in functions:	SUM, COUNT, AVG, MAX, MIN, etc.

The following example constructs a binary relation:

Q5. List the name and salary of all managers who manage more than ten employees.

$$x_{NAME, SAL} \ \varepsilon\ EMP : COUNT (EMP_{NAME\ MGR} (x_{NAME})) > 10$$

The free variable is introduced into queries where it becomes necessary to correlate information pertaining to a specific row in a table with another row or set of rows from some table. Consequently, this variable is introduced only for queries that are more complex than simple selection. As can be seen in section 3, all queries regardless of complexity require free variables in predicate calculus based languages.

Another important concept is that of projection. If a relation-name appears subscripted by one or more column-names, it represents the set of unique tuples of values occurring in those columns of the relation. For example, $SUPPLY_{ITEM}$ is the set of all item-values in the SUPPLY relation. This feature is useful in constructing expressions like the following:

Q6. Find those companies, each of which supplies every item.

$$x_{COMP} \; \varepsilon \; SUPPLY_{ITEM} : \; SUPPLY_{COMP}(x_{COMP}) = SUPPLY_{ITEM}$$

Note that equality here is set equality.

We will now discuss some extensions to the concept of mapping. A mapping may specify more than one domain field in which case each domain field must be compatible with its respective argument. If an argument is a set then the value of the domain field must match some element of the set. This facility is useful in dealing with n-ary associations. For axample:

Q7. Find the volume of guns sold by the Toy Department.

$$SALES_{VOL}{}^{DEPT, ITEM} \; ('TOY', 'GUN')$$

Similarly, a mapping may specify more than one range field, in which case it returns tuples of values from the fields specified.

When one of the numeric comparison operators $=, <, \leq, >, \geq$, is used as a prefix to the argument of a mapping, the argument effectively becomes the set of all values which compare by the given operator with the given argument. This type of mapping often avoids the use of a free variable, as illustrated in Q8.

Q8. List the names and managers of employees in the Shoe Department with salary greater than 10000.

$$EMP_{NAME, MGR}{}^{DEPT, SAL} \; ('SHOE', > '10000')$$

The six numeric comparison operators may also be extended so that a number may be compared to a set, or a set to a set. This is done by placing the work SOME or ALL on the side(s) of the comparison operator which is a set. For example, X > ALL Y is true if the number X is greater than all elements of the set Y, and Y ALL < SOME Z is true if all elements of Y are less than some element of Z. This facility is useful in queries like the following:

Q9. Find those departments which sell some item in greater volume than any single company supplies it.

$$x_{DEPT} \; \varepsilon \; SALES_{VOL} : x_{VOL} > ALL \; SUPPLY_{VOL}{}^{ITEM}(x_{ITEM})$$

In understanding Q9, it is important to remember that the free variable x represents a row of the SALES relation. If the test (which uses the VOL and ITEM values of the row) is true, the DEPT value of the row is returned. All rows of the relation are tested in this way, and duplicate values are eliminated from the returned set.

It should be noted that many of the functions of ALL and SOME could be
accomplished equally well by the built-in functions MAX and MIN. For example:

$$X > ALL\ Y \Longleftrightarrow X > MAX\ (Y)$$

$$Y\ SOME < ALL\ Z \Longleftrightarrow MIN\ (Y) < MIN\ (Z)$$

Another language feature which is occasionally useful is a special type of
mapping called a conjunctive mapping. As in a normal mapping, a relation name,
domain, range, and argument are specified, but the relation name is underlined
to denote the conjunctive mapping. The conjunctive mapping differs from a
disjunctive mapping only when the argument is a set. In this case, the
conjunctive mapping returns the set of range values whose corresponding domain
values match all elements of the argument set. Formally, we write the following
definitions for a disjunctive mapping and a conjunctive mapping on a set S of
values s_i:

$$\underset{B\ \ A}{R}\ (S) \equiv \underset{i}{\bigcup}\ \underset{B\ \ A}{R}\ (S_i)$$

$$\underset{B\ \ A}{\underline{R}}\ (S) \equiv \underset{i}{\bigcap}\ \underset{B\ \ A}{R}\ (S_i)$$

As an example of the use of a conjunctive mapping, we might express Q6 as follows,
eliminating the free variable:

$$\underset{COMP}{\underline{SUPPLY}}\ \underset{ITEM}{}\ (\underset{ITEM}{SUPPLY})$$

This concludes our discussion of the basic accessing facilities of SQUARE.
Additional notions of assignment, returning values from functions computed on
data, insert, delete, and updates are described in detail elsewhere [9].

3. Comparison With Predicate Calculus Based Languages

In this section we illustrate the difference in perception between queries
expressed in the calculus and those expressed in SQUARE. As we have already
mentioned the ALPHA language [5], COLARD [6], and RIL [7] are examples of
relational languages based on the first order predicate calculus. They permit
the description of sets of data but require the description to be in terms of
tests on individual rows of the relations in question. This assumes a certain
degree of mathematical sophistication on the part of the programmer.

In the predicate calculus Q1 is expressed as follows:

$$\{v[NAME]\ \epsilon\ EMP : v\ [DEPT] = \text{'TOY'}\}$$

Where v is a variable which ranges over rows of EMP and v[X] is the projection
of v on the (set of) domain(s) X. Even for this simple query the user must
invent a variable to be used as a cursor for selection of rows.

Q2 shows how this notation is extended for functional composition.

$$Q2:\ \ \{v_0\ [DEPT]\ \epsilon\ SALES : \exists(v_1\ \epsilon\ SUPPLY)\ [(v_1\ [COMP] = \text{'REVLON'})\wedge$$
$$(v_1\ [ITEM] = v_0\ [ITEM])]\}$$

Here the distinctions between the programmer's perception of the languages
becomes clearer. In section 2 we saw that the SQUARE programmer could view this
query as a simple combination of table look-ups. The calculus programmer must
be concerned with:

1) Setting up two variables, v_0 and v_1, to sequence through each table;

2) The notion of existential quantifier and bound variable;

3) The explicit linking term, "v_1 [ITEM] = v_0 [ITEM]," which describes the interrelationship between the variables;

4) The actual matching criteria to be satisfied for membership in the set.

As the queries become more complex the differences between the languages become greater. More variables and linking terms are required in the calculus and the management of quantifiers become more complex.

Of course, we do not suggest that really complex queries are simple to express in SQUARE; rather we stress the relative difference between the two approaches and perceptions. As an example of a complex query the following data base and query is presented:

        SUPPLIER (SNAME, NAME, JNAME)
        JOB (JNAME, LOC)
        PART (PNAME, TYPE)

Q10:   Find the supplier names, who supply a job located in 'NY' with every
        part of type 'A'.

SQUARE

$$x \quad \epsilon \text{ SUPPLIER} : \quad \underset{\text{SNAME, JNAME}}{\overset{\text{SUPPLIER}}{}} \quad (x \underset{\text{SNAME, JNAME}}{}) \supseteq \underset{\text{PNAME}}{\overset{\text{PART}}{}} \quad ('A')$$
(SNAME / PNAME)

$$\Lambda \quad \underset{\text{LOC} \quad \text{JNAME}}{\overset{\text{JOB}}{}} \quad (x \underset{\text{JNAME}}{}) = \text{'NY'}$$

CALCULUS

$$\{v[\text{SNAME}] \ \epsilon \ \text{SUPPLIER} : \ \forall(p\epsilon\text{PART}) \ [(p[\text{TYPE}] = \text{'A'}) \ \Rightarrow \ \exists(s \ \epsilon \ \text{SUPPLIER})$$

$$((s[\text{SNAME}] = v(\text{SNAME}]) \ \Lambda(s[\text{JNAME}] = v[\text{JNAME}])$$

$$\Lambda(s[\text{PNAME}] = p[\text{NAME}]))]$$

$$\Lambda \ \exists(j \ \epsilon \ \text{JOB}) \ [(v[\text{JNAME}] = j[\text{JNAME}]) \ \Lambda \ (j[\text{LOC}] = \text{'SJ'})]\}$$

4. Conclusions

This paper has presented the data accessing portion of a data sublanguage based on the relational model of data. This query facility corresponds to the way people use tables. The language does not require the user to have the mathemtical sophistication demanded by the previous languages based on the first order predicate calculus. The user describes the relevant data to be accessed by set expressions rather than row-at-a-time iteration. Consequently, the queries are more concise, use fewer temporary variables, and do not require the quantifiers of the predicate calculus.

ACKNOWLEDGMENT

The authors wish to thank L. Y. Liu and B. M. Leavenworth for their useful discussions.

REFERENCES

1. E. F. Codd, "A Relational Model of Data for Large Shared Data Banks,"
    Comm. ACM, vol. 13, no. 6 (June 1970), pp. 377-387.

2. E. F. Codd, "Further Normalization of the Data Base Relational Model,"
    Courant Computer Science Symposia, vol. 6, Data Base Systems, Prentice-Hall,
    New York, May 1971.

3. E. F. Codd, "Relational Completeness of Data Base Sublanguages," Courant
    Computer Science Symposia, vol. 6, Data Base Systems, Prentice-Hall, New York,
    May 1971.

4. E. F. Codd, "Normalized Data Base Structure: A Brief Tutorial," Proc. 1971
    ACM SIGFIDET Workshop on Data Description, Access and Control, San Diego,
    November 1971.

5. E. F. Codd, "A Data Base Sublanguage Founded on the Relational Calculus,"
    Proc. 1971 ACM SIGFIDET Workshop on Data Description, Access and Control,
    San Diego, November 1971.

6. G. Bracchi, et al., "A Language for a Relational Data Base Management System,"
    Proc. of the Sixth Ann. Princeton Conf. on Infor. Sci. and Systems, March 1972,
    pp. 84-92.

7. P. L. Fehder, "The Representation - Independent Language," IBM Technical
    Report, RJ 1121, November 1972.

8. D. E. Knuth, "An Empirical Study of FORTRAN Programs," Software - Practice
    and Experience, vol. 1, no. 2 (April 1971), pp. 105-133.

9. R. F. Boyce, et al., "Specifying Queries As Relational Expressions: SQUARE,"
    IBM Technical Report, July 1972.

10. CODASYL Data Base Task Group Report, April 1971.

11. Information Management System 1360, Application Description Manual H20-0524-1,
    IBM Corp., White Plains, N. Y., July 1968.

DISCUSSION

Olle : I am glad to hear that you see both the programmer and non-programmer interacting with the same data base -- interruption -- I agree with different _views_ of the data, which is important of course.

This touches on what I may refer to as the problem of peaceful cohabitation between these different classes of user. What is your philosophy on this ?

King : There are some knotty problems to be solved : for example, the case of what DBTG calls MANUAL membership. If the programmer INSERTS a record at a procedurally-specified point (i.e. the positioning is not value-controlled), how does the system know whether to include it in the non-programmer user's view or not ? There are several problems of this nature. However, I am hopeful that they can be solved.

Data Base Management, J. W. Klimbie and K. L. Koffeman, (eds.)
© *North-Holland Publishing Company (1974)*

SEVEN STEPS TO RENDEZVOUS WITH THE CASUAL USER

by

E. F. Codd
IBM Research Laboratory
San Jose, California

ABSTRACT: If we are to satisfy the needs of casual users of data bases, we must
break through the barriers that presently prevent these users from freely
employing their native languages (e.g., English) to specify what they want.   In
this paper we introduce an approach (already partially implemented) that permits
a user to engage a relational data base system in a dialog with the objective of
attaining agreement between the user and the system as to the user's needs. The
system allows this dialog to be in unrestricted English so long as it is able to
extract a viable quantum of information from the user's response. Immediately
the system finds that the user's response is inadequately decipherable or clearly
inadequate, it confronts the user with a multiple choice question. As soon as
possible, the conversation reverts to unrestricted English.

1. Introduction

The aim of the work reported in this paper is to bring casual users into effective
communication with formatted data bases. A casual user is one whose interactions
with the system are irregular in time and not motivated by his job or social
role. Such a user cannot be expected to be knowledgeable about computers,
programming, logic, or relations. Neither can he be expected to be willing to
learn an artificial language (even if it is oriented towards non-programmers) or
artificial constraints placed upon a natural language such as English (and English
is used as an example throughout this paper).   The class of casual users is
quite broad -- it includes almost all of institutional management (private or
public) and housewives.

The only way to entice such a user to interact with a computerized data base is
to permit him free use of his native tongue -- or at least the illusion of free
use. The irregularity of his interactions implies that it would be unsafe to
assume that he remembers anything he may have learned from his previous
interactions with the system. Computer-assisted instruction techniques are
therefore inapplicable.

It is very unlikely that any two English-speaking persons understand precisely
the same English.   In a sense, each of us understands a private (and usually
extensible) subset of the language.   We enjoy the illusion of using English
freely as a consequence of our ability and willingness to participate in
clarification dialog: that is, dialog that includes queries about previous
utterances in the dialog.

Certain experimental systems (such as the Rapidly Extensible Language System [1]
and Converse [2]) have been designed to support one-way communication (from the
user to the system) in restricted English. The freedom in their English is orders
of magnitude superior to that of the software products that support "English-like"
query languages. Nevertheless, this freedom is generally considered to be
adequate only for the kind of user whose involvement with the data base is of
such a professional or job-oriented nature that he is willing to invest the effort
of learning to live with the restrictions.

The few systems that do support dialog in English appear to be oriented towards
other kinds of dialog (not the clarification type). To understand the distinction
between these types, consider the following utterance by person A:

A: "I went to a downtown dealer yesterday and bought a very expensive car.
     Afterwards, I felt I should not have done it."

Now consider three alternative responses:

B1: "I am sorry you have feelings of regret. What will you do now?"

B2: "I also bought a car recently and discovered that it has a very high gas
     consumption"

B3: "A downtown dealer? Which one, and what do you mean by 'very expensive'?"

Response B1 is a stroking response -- it assures A that B1 has been listening to
A and invites him to continue his story.   The conversational pattern
illustrated by A's utterance and B1's response is typical of stroking dialog.
This is the kind of dialog supported by Weizenbaum's ELIZA [3].   Response B2 is
a contributive response -- entirely new information is introduced. Winograd's
SHURDLU [4] supports dialog involving contributive utterances and questions about
changes of state in the given environment, but not questions about the meaning
of previous utterances. Response B3 is a clarification response, an essential
component of clarification dialog. In section 3 we discuss the introduction of
a specific kind of clarification dialog as one of seven steps needed to support
the casual user. First, however, we must introduce a sample data base and dialog
about it for expository reasons.

2.   Sample Data Base and Dialog

Consider a somewhat limited data base for expository purposes. Let it contain
information about suppliers, parts, projects, and shipments of parts by suppliers
to projects.   The relation names appearing in the relational schema are SUPPLIER,
PART, PROJECT, and SHIP.   The attributes associated with each of these
relations are shown in Table 1.

RELATION	D	ATTRIBUTE	COMMENT	
supplier	s	snumber	supplier serial no.	key
	x	sname	name	
	l	sloc	city (location)	
	r	rating	integer-coded rating	
part	p	pnumber	part serial no.	key
	y	pname	name of part	
	q	qoh	quantity on hand	
	q	qoo	quantity on order	
	t	ptype	classification of part	
project	j	jnumber	project serial no.	key
	z	jname	project name	
	l	jloc	city (location)	
ship	s	snumber	supplier serial no.	key
	p	pnumber	part serial no.	key
	j	jnumber	project serial no.	key
	d	date	shipdate	key
	q	qship	quantity shipped	

       Table 1:   Relational Schema

The comment gives a brief interpretation of the corresponding attribute and
indicates whether or not it participates in the primary key of the designated
relation.   The column labelled D indicates the underlying domain from which the
designated attribute draws its values. Note, for example, that qoh, qoo, qship
are all defined on the same underlying domain, whereas supplier rating is defined

on a distinct domain, even though it too is a non-negative integer. This indicates to the system that any query that entails comparing supplier rating (for equality or inequality) with any of the attributes qoh, qoo, qship is semantically invalid.

Now consider the following sample dialog between a casual user and the data base as described above. We shall assume for this example that the user has an adequate idea of what each relation name and attribute denotes. However, we do not assume he knows what a relation is in the abstract sense. Neither do we assume he knows anything about the concepts of attribute, domain, relational algebra, etc.

SYSTEM: Please proceed

USER: Give me a list of the part numbers, quantities, and suppliers of Houston parts

SYSTEM: You are requesting (among other things) a listing of quantities of parts.   Do you want:
          1. quantities on hand
          2. quantities on order
          3. quantities shipped ?

USER: I want quantities on order

SYSTEM: Fine! Now, with regard to "Houston parts", do you mean:
          1. parts supplied by Houston suppliers
          2. parts supplied to Houston projects
          3. parts associated with Houston in some other way ?

USER: I mean item 2

(Note: nothing prevents the user from responding in a manner which is incomprehensible to the system   -- for example, "le deuxieme" -- but if he does, the system tightens up the dialog by: "Please reply by means of one of the numerals 1 or 2 or 3". How response 3 would be treated is discussed later.)

SYSTEM: Good! I need one more piece of information. In the listing of part numbers, quantity on order, and suppliers, how do you want suppliers to be identified:
          1. by number
          2. by name
          3. some other way ?

USER: By name and by city

SYSTEM: O.K. This is what I understand your query to be: "Find all combinations of part number, quantity on order, supplier name, and supplier city <u>such</u> <u>that</u> the supplier supplied the part to a project located in Houston". Is this what you intended ?

(We now follow two possibilities. Case 1: the user is satisfied)

USER: Yes

SYSTEM: Do you want the listing to be ordered in any special way?

USER: Yes, by part number and then by supplier number

This ends the dialog in Case 1. The system now proceeds to interpret the relational calculus formula for the user's query -- a formula that it has been

synthesizing in its store, partly from the original statement by the user, and
partly from the succeeding dialog.

(Case 2: the user is not satisfied)

USER: I have changed my mind

(Note: the system does not understand this idiom, but is fully aware of its
inability to understand, so it tightens up the dialog as follows)

SYSTEM: Please select item 1 or 2 below:
         1. the re-statement is satisfactory
         2. the re-statement is not satisfactory

USER: 2

SYSTEM: If your intent can be expressed by making minor changes in my
         re-statement, please type it in with your changes incorporated. If your
         change is major, you may re-state your query in your own terms.

This is where we leave the dialog in Case 2.

We may now ask: is it feasible to support this kind of dialog at this stage of
the software art? Can the program that attempts to analyze the user's statements
and generate questions for the user be independent of the particular data base
description (and hence work just as well for medical applications as for
self-service airline reservations)? Can the program be sufficiently
language-independent that it could be readily applied to dialog in any
Indo-European language? The only way to provide convincing answers to these
questions is to implement a system and attempt to apply it in several environments
of quite different character and with different languages. We outline below
seven steps that we believe will yield a subsystem that does support dialog of
the type illustrated above, and that will be readily applicable in a wide variety
of environments. It is too early to predict how language-independent the code
will be. The author is implementing such a subsystem and it is already in partial
operation.

3. The Seven Steps

Step 1: Select a simple data model

The user's view of the data in a formatted data base has a fundamental impact on
the way he conceives and formulates queries and other types of transactions.
For his sake, this view or data model should have enough structure to enable him
to rapidly and concisely identify the part of the data base he is interested in
-- hence, more structure is needed than that of the Rand Relational Data File
[5]. At the same time, the data model clearly should not have a multiplicity of
structural alternatives for representing data. Such a multiplicity is
incompatible with the casual user's unwillingness to consciously engage in a
learning process and with his tendency to forget what he may have learned
unconsciously, because of the irregularity of his interactions. The relational
model [6], in which the data is structured as a collection of non-hierarchic
relations of assorted degrees,   appears to provide the right balance between
too little structure and too much.   It also requires very little in the way
of description, as can be seen in the example of a relational schema exhibited
in Table 1.

Step 2: Select a high level logic as internal target

When users (especially casual ones) are given freedom of expression in
interrogating data bases in their native tongue, we can expect a large proportion

of their queries to be poorly formulated. These queries may be ambiguous, semantically incomplete, semantically incompatible with the data base description, or (perhaps most sinister of all) well-formed, complete, unambiguous, and meaningful, but not what the user really intended.   The last of these possibilities is treated in step 4.

To enable the system to detect semantic incompleteness, incompatibility, or ambiguity, the user's source statements should be translated into an internal, precise language that is of the highest possible level.   Data sublanguage ALPHA [7] is an example of such a language. It is based on the relational calculus for relations of arbitrary degree [8] and permits simpler tests for the semantic anomalies cited above -- much simpler than a procedural-level target language would permit. An additional advantage of selecting a high level, precise language as internal target is that the translation scheme can be oriented very heavily towards the semantics of the user's query rather than its syntax. For example, the translation scheme in the RENDEZVOUS system in its present implemented form is capable of interpreting English queries expressed in a large number of distinct ways, yet it is unable to distinguish a noun from a verb! By de-emphasizing syntax to a maximal extent, the RENDEZVOUS analyzer is able to interpret discontiguous fragments of a query that are separated by an undecipherable fragment. This capability is extremely important in that it permits the generation of more meaningful dialog for finding out what the undecipherable fragment is all about. This brings us to the third step.

Step 3:   Introduce clarification dialog of bounded scope

Having a very limited understanding of English, the system must play the dialog game with finesse. It must keep the dialog closely tied to the data base description and the user's intended query. We call this clarification dialog of bounded scope, and discuss the tactics for it below for cases of incomprehensible words and constructions, semantic ambiguities, incompatibilities with the data base description, and semantic incompleteness. Underlying all these tactics is the following general rule: all questions to the user must be framed in the context of his utterances. Note that, although there is an attempt to limit the semantic range of user responses, there is no need to limit (and it is psychologically advantageous not to limit) the syntactic range, unless and until the user employs obscure modes of expression.

To illustrate tactics for incomprehensible words, suppose the system encounters the word "concerning" in a user's query and discovers that neither "concerning" nor "concern" is in its lexicon.   It would be a tactical blunder of the first magnitude to ask the user: "What does 'concerning' mean?". This kind of system response encourages the user to display his talents for poetry or philosophy or linguistic analysis or profanity. Whether the user's response is banal, inarticulate, or erudite, it is extremely likely to be beyond the system's power of comprehension.

A less risky system response is a request to the user to re-phrase his query (or part of it) so as to avoid use of the word "concerning" (and any other words the system failed to understand). The disadvantage of this tactic is that it fails to provide the user with any clues as to what alternative modes of expression the system might be able to understand. Furthermore, it gives the user no reassurance that the system has understood any other part of what he said. The user cannot be expected to tolerate such sensory deprivation!

The most promising tactic for dealing with incomprehensible words appears to be that of temporarily ignoring them, translating the remaining comprehensible fragments into formal fragments, and piecing these together to determine what kinds of things are missing. In the case of incomprehensible constructions, any comprehensible components would naturally be exploited, but the overall construction would be temporarily ignored. If the piecing together of formal fragments yields a complete query, the system can enter a verification phase to see if it satisfies the user without further embellishment (step 4 reveals how this is accomplished without exposing the user to the formal query itself).

If parts are missing from the collection of formal fragments generated so far, the system attaches priorities to the different kinds of missing parts and proceeds to discover these parts through dialog in order of priority. This problem will be discussed further in step 7.

An example of a simple ambiguity and the way it can be handled was illustrated in the sample dialog of section 2. To be able to detect the ambiguity of "quantities" and list its possible denotations in the context of the given data base, the system must have a table of such synonyms. Such a table can be thought of as an extension to the data base description -- specifically for casual user support, however. While the synonyms for "quantities" were all attributes, in general synonyms may be of various types (consider "number" for example, which may denote the function COUNT or various attributes such as PNUMBER).

To illustrate an incompatibility with the data base description, suppose that serial numbers of parts are required to have at least one digit and one letter. The phrase "part number 417" (or even "part 417") is, in all probability, a loose way of specifying the part with serial number 417.   Since "417" contains no letter, it is invalid as a part serial number with this data base description. The system can point out this incompatibility and request the user to supply a proper substitute.

A more interesting case of suspected incompatibility is that of "Houston parts" in the sample dialog of section 2. While the incompatibility above was between an attribute (PNUMBER) and its value (417), the incompatibility here is between a relation name and a domain name, since PART does not have a domain LOCATION (the system can detect that "Houston" belongs in the domain LOCATION through inclusion in the data base description of a table of attribute-implying -- and hence domain-implying -- values for every attribute that has relatively few distinct values). Exploiting these tables, the system can offer to the user possible ways of associating "Houston" with "parts", suggesting first the simplest ways and then, if the user is not satisfied, more complicated ways. A simple metric can be placed on the attributes in the data base description for this purpose. In cases of suspected incompatibility, the system has to be prepared for outright rejection of its suggestions, and for responses of the following kind:

    "I meant 'projects' instead of 'parts'"
    "I should have said 'heavy' instead of 'Houston'"
    "The query is correct as it stands"

In the last case, the system must assume that, for one reason or another, it has made an inadequate analysis of the associations between relation names, attributes, and values occurring both in the phrase under consideration and elsewhere in the user's query. Accordingly, it must now gain this information through further dialog with the user.

A simple example of incompleteness occurs in the dialog of section 2. In his original query the user asked for suppliers to be listed, but failed to indicate how they were to be identified. This omission was easily rectified by means of a simple question to the user.   A more complicated case (and one of suspected rather than known incompleteness) is that in which combinations of things are requested without supplying an adequate specification of the combining criterion.   For example, if the sample data base were extended to include information about employees and their assignments to projects, and the user asked for names of people and names of parts in combination without giving a criterion for associating people with parts, it would be reasonable for the system to point this out and offer the user first the simplest possibilities of doing this, and then, if the user is not satisfied, the more complicated possibilities as discussed earlier in connection with incompatibility.

Step 4: Introduce system re-statement of user's query

Suppose the system has extracted whatever meaning it can from the user's query, and through clarification dialog has rectified suspected or known incompatibilities, ambiguities, and logical gaps. How can we be sure that the system has correctly interpreted the user's intent? It may have correctly interpreted the user's query, although even this is not certain. It is useless to expose the internally generated formal query to the casual user. The most appropriate check appears to be that of synthesizing from the formal query a precise re-statement in system English of the user's query as modified by subsequent dialog. Except for the simplest kinds of queries, the system's re-statement is likely to differ quite a bit in mode and precision of expression from the user's original formulation. This forces the user to consider his intent, and to examine carefully whether the system's version has captured that intent. If the user does not agree that his intent is properly reflected in the system's re-statement, the dialog must be pursued with fresh vigor. It can now be based on the re-statement if the user feels that would be the most expeditious way of getting the system to understand his intent.

Step 5: Separate query formulation from data base search

Notice that the combination of clarification dialog and re-statement of the query in precise English does not entail access to the main body of data in the data base. The actual search for the desired data is commenced only after the user and system are in complete agreement on the user's intent. In this manner the user can be protected from what may be expensive searches for information he does not want, and from the possibly embarrassing consequences of not realizing that either he has mis-formulated his intent or the system has failed to understand his query correctly.

Step 6: Employ multiple choice interrogation as fall-back

A casual user is likely to be impatient and unwilling to tolerate a long string of multiple choice questions concerning his query. Consequently, the use of such stylized dialog should be kept to a minimum. Nevertheless, when a user employs idioms or obscure words, this is the price he can expect to pay.

Because the domain of discourse is restricted to the data base description and because the possible types of components of a formal query are pre-determined, a finite (and more importantly a manageable) number of multiple choice questions can serve to extract a user's query if his only intelligible input is selection numbers, providing that the query does not require for its correct interpretation a function, relation, attribute, or definition not listed in the data base description.

Step 7: Provide a definition capability

In a non-dialog environment, it is the user who must observe the need for a definition and he or some other user acting for him must take the initiative in framing it and supplying it to the system's library of definitions. The Rapidly Extensible Language System [1] has an excellent definition capability for such an environment.

In the dialog environment we are discussing, the system must take on an extra burden: namely, that of detecting the need for a definition and engaging in clarification dialog to extract it from the user. Since definitions can be arbitrarily complex, we cannot expect to provide a complete multiple choice fall-back for this aspect of understanding a user's query. However, casual user interaction will rarely involve complicated definitions, so the comprehension failure rate on this account will be quite low.

Consider the sample query: "Are any east coast suppliers supplying part 3G25?". Suppose the catalog of definitions does not include any definition for "east coast", "coast", or "east", and the lexicon does not include these words. According to the tactics discussed in Step 3, the system temporarily ignores these words in the query and attempts to decipher the remainder. In this case, the residual query is: "Are any suppliers supplying part 3G25?" and, let us assume, this is comprehensible.   Accordingly, the system makes a re-statement and the user immediately expresses his dissatisfaction, noting that "east coast" has been left out (to guard against user oversight of this omission, the system can easily list words and phrases that it finds incomprehensible). At this point, the system may assume (with very little risk) that the phrase "east coast" is not only information bearing, but that it somehow qualifies "suppliers" in the original query. Drawing upon the data base definition, the system can now ask the user whether "east coast" has anything to do with a supplier's rating, location, etc. (all the non-identifying attributes of SUPPLIER), serial number, name (all the identifying attributes), or what he is supplying or capable of supplying (all the relations other than SUPPLIER that have the SUPPLIER key SNUMBER as an attribute). The user would select "location", and the system would then ask the user to tell it which supplier locations are "east coast".

Note that the system avoids asking the user point blank: "What is the meaning of east coast?", because a definition of "east coast" outside of the specific context of supplier locations would be too abstract for the system to comprehend and, in all probability, would cause the casual user a good deal of unnecessary mental anguish in trying to frame such a definition.

Now consider detection of the need for a definition when the residual query (after removal of incomprehensible words) is incomplete. We take the query: "Find the suppliers whose rating exceeds 5" and suppose that "exceeds" is not in the system's lexicon.   In this case, the residual query clearly lacks a relational connective (e.g., =) to associate "rating" and "5" adequately.   It can therefore offer the user the following initial options: "rating is (greater than) (equal to) (less than) 5". The user will always have to be given an escape option: "something else, if so what?".   For example, a user who is a bit eccentric in his use of "exceeds" might respond: "I mean rating is much greater than 5". We now encounter two serious problems:

1. "Much greater than" is a fuzzy concept in the sense of Zadeh [9];
2. User eccentricity implies that a definition supplied by one user cannot be assumed to reflect the intent of another user -- it can, however, be used as an option for another user to select if he so desires.

Introduction of support for fuzzy denotations presents interesting and challenging problems that will not be discussed here.

4.   The RENDEZVOUS Implementation

We shall only provide an outline of the implementation of the RENDEZVOUS query formulation subsystem. It should nevertheless be adequate for the reader to observe the marked differences between this and other systems that handle English input.

In Fig.1 we show the three principal components -- the analyzer, synthesizer, and dialog control -- and the four types of communication with the user -- statement of query by user, interrogation of user by system, response by the user to this interrogation, and re-statement by the system of its understanding of the query.   Let us examine the operation of these components one by one.

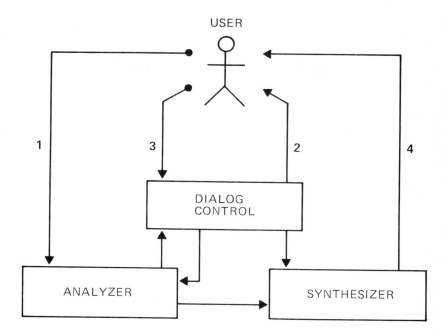

1. User makes initial statement of his query (unrestricted English)
2. System interrogates user *about* his query (to obtain information which is missing or hidden in language the system does not understand, and to resolve ambiguities)
3. User responds to system interrogation
4. System provides a re-statement of user's query in system English (in a very precise way, based on the n-ary relational calculus)

Figure 1. RENDEZVOUS Subsystem

4.1 The Analyzer

The principal function of the analyzer is that of translating as much as possible of the user's original statement of his query into data sublanguage ALPHA. Other functions include the discovery and analysis of translation difficulties together with the generation of sufficient dialog parameters to enable the dialog control to piece together clarification dialog appropriate to the state of translation and the state of user interaction. The analyzer also provides interpretation service on the user's responses.

The analyzer has as its components the word transformer, the phrase transformer, and the diagnostic component.   We now consider each of these.

4.1.1 Word Transformer

The word transformer is the first component of the analyzer to be invoked. Its
first act is to store a copy of the user's query on one side, so that, as the
need arises for dialog with the user, questions can be generated using as far as
possible the very same terms he used. The word transformer then proceeds to
reduce each word (independently of other words) to a normalized form, partly by
means of standard suffix transformations and partly by replacing words that have
a single canonical synonym by that synonym. Noise words, such as "please", are
dropped altogether.

4.1.2 Phrase Transformer

The second component of the analyzer to be activated is the phrase
transformer. It attempts, by means of phrase transformation rules, to recognize
certain types of phrases in the text, and replace these by other phrases that
are syntactically closer to the form required by data sublanguage ALPHA. The
syntax of ALPHA is tabulated in the appendix. For an introductory description
of ALPHA, see [8]; and for its foundation, see [9]. To facilitate the
step-by-step transition from ENGLISH text to ALPHA and the handling of
discontiguous decipherable fragments separated by an undecipherable fragment, we
introduce the concept of a transition language INTER-ALPHA, whose syntactic types
include all those of ALPHA plus certain additional ones that are extremely
convenient as temporary "working" types. For example, INTER-ALPHA permits
relation names to be used in many cases where ALPHA would require dummy variables
having these relations as their ranges. We shall say that an English phrase has
been inter-alpha-typed if its INTER-ALPHA type has been recognized, and
alpha-typed if its ALPHA type has been recognized. Note that a very large number
of English phrases are not alpha-typable, and need not be for this system to
operate effectively.

The phrase transformation rules of RENDEZVOUS are multi-purpose. They always
specify replacement of one kind of phrase (if it occurs in the text being
examined) by another. However, in RENDEZVOUS many of the rules have either
one or both of the following additional capabilities: first, the discovery in
the text being examined of ambiguities, apparent incompatibilities, etc. that
need to be resolved by dialog together with the generation of appropriate
linguistic fragments for the dialog control to piece together into questions for
the user; second, the storing of inter-alpha-typed phrases in a phrase dump,
accompanied by their replacement in the text itself by surrogate symbols that
identify their types and positions in the dump. Phrase dumping is reversible.

To understand the RENDEZVOUS phrase transformation rules it is necessary to
observe that, after word normalization, the system assigns two lexical classes
to every text word that it encounters. If the word is already in the lexicon,
the appropriate pair of classes is found there. Otherwise the lexical class pair
is computed and reflects only elementary properties of the word (such as whether
it is composed of nothing but letters, nothing but digits, or a mixture of both).
Most of the lexical classification reflects semantic, rather than English
syntactic, properties of words. For example, lexical class 21 consists of names
of linking relations -- a linking relation is one that has two or more attributes,
each of which is a key of some other relation. A list of the presently existing
lexical classes is included in the appendix.

Various kinds of values may appear in a query: for example, 'JONES' as the name
of a supplier, 'X3' as a part number, and '15' as a quantity on order. Values
that contain digits are easily distinguished from English words and are therefore
easily recognized as values. On the other hand, values such as 'JONES' and
'BOSTON' will normally appear without quotes or other distinctive marks. This
makes it difficult for the system to distinguish them from English words that do
not happen to be included in the lexicon. Why not search the data base? With

the large data bases that we are assuming, query formulation would become
unnecessarily expensive if a data base search had to be conducted to recognize
every purely alphabetic value cited in the query.   Now, certain domains (such
as sex, cities in which suppliers and projects are located, etc.) have relatively
few distinct values. For these domains we can afford a search at query
formulation time, and accordingly we shall treat these values as belonging to
the data base description -- they are called <u>cataloged</u> <u>values</u> and appear in the
lexicon as lexical class 2, while non-cataloged values have a computed lexical
class of 1. For each domain the catalog indicates the known syntactic properties
of its values, regardless of whether these values are cataloged or not.
Nevertheless, there still remains a problem when the system encounters a
non-cataloged, purely alphabetic value -- as in the phrase 'SUPPLIER JONES'.
When such values occur in contexts that indicate a reasonable probability that
they are values of this kind, the phrase transformation rules call (via dialog
control) for dialog with the user to clarify the situation -- as in "IS JONES
THE NAME OF A SUPPLIER?".

In the present implementation, there are eight classes of phrase transformation
rules: the series 100 rules are the first to be candidates for application; when
a state is reached in which no more series 100 rules are applicable, the series
200 rules become candidates; and so on, until no more of the series 800 are
applicable. Roughly speaking, progression from one class of rules to its
successor class corresponds to an advance of one level in the ALPHA syntax tree
(see appendix).   By this we mean that the goal of the successor class of rules
is recognition of a higher level phrase type in INTER-ALPHA and, finally, in
ALPHA. We have to say "roughly speaking", because the great variety of
permissible word orderings in English is the source of some of the separation of
rule classes, and also because the series 100 rules are solely concerned with
ascertaining the query type (find set, test existence, or test truth other than
existence) and the quota (if any).

Some of the phrase transformation rules entail checks of the semantic
compatibility of phrase components with one another (using the data base
description as the guide). As will be observed from the example below, apparent
incompatibility can give rise to dialog with the user. Because of their strong
semantic orientation, we call the left-hand sides of transformation rules <u>semantic</u>
<u>templates</u>.

The example is intended to illustrate several features (but not all) of the phrase
transformer. It is actual input to and print-out from an execution of RENDEZVOUS
on November 1, 1973. The sample of dialog is not representative of the full
dialog capability implemented at that time; also, it is only for expository
purposes that we set the print control to provide intermediate print-out of rule
number, text position (or origin) at which the rule is applied, the rule itself,
and the new text after successful application.

Lines 1-2
The user types in his query. The word transformer converts the plural forms
NAMES, SUPPLIERS to singular, and replaces SUPPLY by its canonical synonym SHIP
(a relation name peculiar to this data base). A terminating symbol ω is appended,
and the origin for template matching is set to word # 1 in the text. The phrase
transformer is invoked with the series 100 rules activated.
Line 3
The word at the origin (GIVE) is used to find an applicable rule, the search time
being kept small by appropriate indexing of the rules. Rule 128 is found to be
applicable because GIVE is in lexical class 8, ME is in lexical class 19, THE is
in lexical class 25.   Note that, if THE had been omitted, a match would still
have been obtained due to the presence of the null symbol '*' as an option in
the template term '(25,*)'.

```
     HSCAN Q08

     GIVE ME THE NAMES OF SUPPLIERS WHO SUPPLY PART J5 TO A PROJECT
     IN DETROIT
     128 01    8 19 (25,°) → F
     F NAME OF SUPPLIER WHO SHIP PART J5 TO A PROJECT IN DETROIT ω
5    132 01    8 → F ↓
     F NAME OF SUPPLIER WHO SHIP PART J5 TO A PROJECT IN DETROIT ω
     216 07    4 *(15,°) *1 → 1 ( B13↑E631H31 = 3 )
     F NAME OF SUPPLIER WHO SHIP PART ( PNUMBER = J5 ) TO PROJECT IN
     DETROIT ω
10   ↑220 PROJECT IN DETROIT?
     IGNORE? NO
     NEW PHRASE: PROJECT IN FRESNO
     220 14    4∧20 *(15,°) *2 → 1 ( B13↑E2311V31F31A3R3 = 3 )
     F NAME OF SUPPLIER WHO SHIP PART ( PNUMBER = J5 ) TO PROJECT (
15   JLOC = FRESNO ) ω
     405 02    6 OF (25,°) 20T1 → 4 B41↑E341R1
     F SUPPLIER SNAME WHO SHIP PART ( PNUMBER = J5 ) TO PROJECT (
     JLOC = FRESNO ) ω
     508 05    21 20 ( U ) (15,°) 20L1 ( U ) → 1 ( 2 ( 4 ) ∧ ( 7 ( 9 )
20   F SUPPLIER SNAME WHO SHIP ( PART ( PNUMBER = J5 ) ∧ ( PROJECT (
     JLOC = FRESNO ) ) ω
     604 02    4 3 → 1 [ 2 ] ρ
     F SUPPLIER [ SNAME ] WHO SHIP ( PART ( PNUMBER = J5 ) ∧ (
     PROJECT ( JLOC = FRESNO ) ) ω
25   603 05    ] (17,°) (10,°) 21 → 1 [] 4 ρ
     F SUPPLIER [ SNAME ] [] SHIP ( PART ( PNUMBER = J5 ) ∧ ( PROJECT
     ( JLOC = FRESNO ) ) ω
     702 02    20 [ U ] → α62
     F SUPPLIER [ SNAME ] [] SHIP ( PART ( PNUMBER = J5 ) ∧ (
30   PROJECT ( JLOC = FRESNO ) ) ω
     704 04    21 ( U ) → α61
     F SUPPLIER [ SNAME ] [] SHIP ( PART ( PNUMBER = J5 ) ∧ (
     PROJECT ( JLOC = FRESNO ) ) ω
     701 07    20 ( U ) → α60
35   F SUPPLIER [ SNAME ] [] SHIP ( PART ( PNUMBER = J5 ) ∧ (
     PROJECT ( JLOC = FRESNO ) ) ω
     F SUPPLIER [ SNAME ] [] SHIP ( PART ( PNUMBER = J5 ) ∧ (
     PROJECT ( JLOC = FRESNO ) ) ω
```

Sample Input to and Print-out from RENDEZVOUS

November 1, 1973

Line 4
Application of rule 128 has resulted in the replacement of GIVE ME THE by F (a
system-generated, non-English word denoting a find type query). The origin is
kept at position 1 and the series 100 indexes are searched again.
Lines 5-6
Application of rule 132 has no effect on the text, but does terminate the series
100 rules with the origin still at position 1.
Line 7
The phrase transformer is invoked again, but now with the series 200 rules
activated. Finding no matching rule for position 1, the system advances the

origin to 2, and so on, until at position 7 the template of rule 216 matches the phrase PART J5. We can account for this match as follows: PART is a relation name (lexical class 4); J5 is a non-cataloged value (lexical class 1). Note that no preposition (lexical class 15) is discovered in the text, but the null symbol '*' in the template permits a match in spite of this.

The right hand side of rule 216 specifies how the replacing phrase (P say) is to be constructed.   The first RHS term '1' specifies as the first word in P the text word which matched the first term in the template (in this case, it was PART in the text which matched lexical class 4 specified by the first template term).   The second RHS term '(' calls for a left parend to be appended to P. The third RHS term has two parts: B13 and   E631H31. The first part B13 invokes a broadly applicable compatibility checking function B on arguments that, in this case, are the text words matching the first and third template terms -- the relation name PART and the value J5 respectively..   Referring to the data base description, the function B finds that PART has at least one attribute for which J5 is a legal value (as evidenced by the syntax of this value), and that PNUMBER is the most likely attribute of the several with this property. Accordingly, PNUMBER is appended to the replacing phrase P.

If the value J5 had been invalid as a part number or as a part name, generation of the replacing phrase P would have been suspended, the code E631H31 would have been interpreted, and information compiled for communication to the dialog control (we shall consider an E code in more detail in section 4.3).

Since J5 was found to be valid, generation of P continues. The fourth RHS term calls for the symbol '=' to be appended to P, while the fifth and final RHS term calls for the text word (in this case J5) which matched template term 3 to be appended to P.
Lines 8-9
Application of rule 216 has resulted in the replacement of PART J5 by PART(PNUMBER=J5).
Lines 10-11
The template of rule 220 matches the text phrase beginning with PROJECT (word number 14, since each parend in the text counts as a word). In attempting to construct the replacing phrase, the function B discovered an incompatibility between PROJECT and DETROIT. Now, DETROIT is a cataloged value and the catalog indicates that it is a valid supplier location, but not a valid project location.   Accordingly, information is passed to dialog control, which in turn emits the message to the user: PROJECT IN DETROIT? IGNORE? The user responds NO, because he discovers that he did make a mistake. In the fully supportive mode, dialog control provides significantly more information to the user (this will be discussed in section 4.3).
Line 12
Dialog control now requests the user to supply a new phrase, and the user responds with PROJECT IN FRESNO (once again, the fully supportive dialog mode would offer options).
Line 13
Rule 220 can now be successfully applied, because the catalog indicates that FRESNO is a valid project location.
Lines 14-15
PROJECT IN FRESNO has been replaced by PROJECT(JLOC='FRESNO').
Line 16
The phrase transformer discovers that no further rules in the 200 series or in the 300 series are applicable. The template of rule 405 matches the text phrase NAME OF SUPPLIER, since NAME is a synonym for at least one catalog item, OF in the text matches OF in the template, lexical class 25 is not matched, but the null alternative * permits matching to proceed, and 20T1 calls for the name of a non-linking relation (which SUPPLIER is) compatible with the text word matching the first template term (namely NAME).

The RHS of rule 405 generates first the word SUPPLIER (the text word matching the fourth template term) and then, by invoking B, the word SNAME (the most likely attribute of SUPPLIER synonymous with NAME, the text word matching the first template term).

Lines 17-18
NAME OF SUPPLIER has been replaced by SUPPLIER SNAME.

Line 19
The next rule found to be applicable is rule 508. The template term U matches the shortest phrase between the text word matching the template term immediately preceding the U and the text word matching the template term immediately succeeding the U. The template of rule 508 accordingly calls for a linking relation name (lexical class 21) followed by a non-linking relation name (lexical class 20) followed by a phrase enclosed in parends followed by a preposition or null followed by a non-linking relation name having a key attribute that is an attribute of the first-mentioned relation followed by a phrase enclosed in parends. The text phrase beginning with SHIP and terminating with the right parend immediately preceding the symbol ω fulfills these requirements.

The RHS of rule 508 generates a replacing phrase which places PART and PROJECT in the scope of the linking relation SHIP (by introducing extra parends) and which introduces logical AND to replace the preposition TO.

Lines 20-21
The substitution specified by rule 508 has now been effected.

Lines 22-24
The next applicable rule 604 now introduces some structure into the target list.

Lines 25-27
At this stage, rule 603 causes WHO to be replaced by a symbol that separates the target list from the qualification expression in a find type query. The resulting text is now completely converted to INTER-ALPHA. The extra steps needed to make the final conversion to data sublanguage ALPHA are quite straightforward, but were not yet implemented as of November 1973.

4.1.3 The Diagnostic Component

In the example described above, dialog was generated solely as a result of the invocation of compatibility-checking functions cited in the phrase transformation rules. Fortuitously, dialog generated in this way proved to be adequate to obtain a complete translation from the English source to INTER-ALPHA, and therefore to the ALPHA target language. A fundamental assumption in the RENDEZVOUS system is that, no matter how hard the designer of the lexicon and transformation rules may try to make these components complete with respect to all possible queries, he is going to fail. There will always be the possibility of strange words or constructions that contain information significant to the precise formulation of the user's query. Accordingly, we associate with certain classes of rules a recognition goal (for example, the separation of the target list from the qualification expression in a find type query). At the end of application of such a class of rules, the diagnostic component of the analyzer is invoked. It checks whether the corresponding goal has been attained and, if not, supplies appropriate parameters to the dialog control for the generation of dialog with the user.

Consider the following example: "Which parts have quantity on hand greater than 100, if we ignore parts of type X3?". Suppose the word and phrase transformers are incapable of deciphering the phrase "if we ignore", but can interpret the remaining fragments. Although translation of the first fragment by itself would yield a complete and sensible query, and although the phrase "if we ignore" contains no catalog items ("if" and "we" are, however, in the lexicon), this undecipherable phrase cannot be ignored by the analyzer, because of the isolated, dependent, and clearly information-bearing phrase at the end of the query. Detection of this situation comes about when the phrase transformer has completed the application of the series 600 rules. At this point, the diagnostic component discovers that the present (partially translated query) consists of the following phrases and types:

Phrase	INTER-ALPHA Type
F	query type designator
PART	inter target list
:	separator
QOH > 100	qualification expression
IF WE IGNORE	undetermined
PART(PTYPE='X3')	qualified relation expression

Through table look-up the diagnostic component determines the various permissible ways of uniting the first contiguous sequence of recognized INTER-ALPHA expressions with the second (in this example there are only two such sequences). The options for _unification sites_ are reduced to one, namely that the qualified relation expression be absorbed into the qualification expression, because the relation name PART is common to the two sequences (had this not been the case, absorption of the relation name in the second sequence into the inter target list of the first sequence would have been a second option).   The options for _unification linkages_, in this example, are the 16 possible boolean connectives (keep in mind that the phrase "if we ignore" is completely unintelligible to the system).   These options are obviously not exposed to the user all at once -- the most likely options are exposed first, and a reasonably painless English phrasing is adopted rather than the more concise logical symbols.

More generally, when two INTER-ALPHA expressions are being united, they may be linked up as peers or one expression may be made a subexpression of the other. The linking may entail concatenation of (sub)expressions with or without the accompanying insertion of a boolean connective, relational connective, comma, period, or colon.

4.2   The Synthesizer

When the analyzer and dialog control have generated a complete query in data sublanguage ALPHA, the synthesizer takes over to translate back from the ALPHA statement to a version in English that is (hopefully) equally precise.   To accomplish this, it employs additional sets of transformation rules, but essentially the same machinery as the analyzer.

No dialog is needed to complete this translation.   The major problem encountered is that of generating reasonably fluent English, while not sacrificing precision. A minor problem is that of avoiding the generation of ambiguous English.   In the case of intermixed ANDs and ORs (and possibly NOTs also) the very weak indications of scope that English affords can be augmented to advantage by judicious indentation of phrases on the output display.

When the RENDEZVOUS implementation is completed, it will be possible to type in a query in user-chosen English and observe on the display terminal the gradual step-by-step modification (a word or a phrase at a time) as the query is first translated into ALPHA and then back into English.   The combination of these two translations represents a normalization in English that is not merely many-to-one -- it is very-many-to-one.

4.3   Dialog Control

Dialog control provides a base for experimentation with dialog styles and tactics. Style includes such items as:
1.   how fully the user is kept informed of the system's progress in understanding his inputs;
2.   the extent to which a user is constrained in the way he can express his responses;

3.   the amount of stroking or encouragement given to the user.
Users who have gained confidence in the system will often prefer the system to
adopt a very brief style and omit stroking altogether.

Tactics include when to switch from one style to another, and whether to postpone
posing a question to the user until more content has been examined.   Development
of alternative styles and tactics is still in a rudimentary state.

Now we propose to illustrate how the analyzer and dialog control work together
to question the user about his query. We shall take the same query as cited in
section 3.1.1. However, we select a more supportive dialog mode.

The phrase PROJECT IN DETROIT matches the template of rule 220.   In evaluating
the RHS of rule 220, function B is invoked with the relation name PROJECT and
cataloged value DETROIT as arguments. A low-level subroutine B24 (where the
digits 2, 4 are the primary lexical class numbers of the two arguments) constructs
the internal message:
     B24A DETROIT PROJECT
where B24 identifies the routine originating the message, A is a code indicating
that the relation under consideration (PROJECT) does have an attribute (JLOC)
defined on the domain (LOCATION) to which the cataloged value (DETROIT) belongs.

Upon receiving this message, a higher level routine in the analyzer uses the code
A in B24A to select the first (E2311V31) of the two E-codes in the current RHS
term of the current rule (220). The first part (E2) of this E-code is left
undecoded at this stage. The second part (311V31) is decoded as follows:
     '3' refers to the text word DETROIT matching the third term in the template;
     '1' similarly refers to the text word PROJECT;
     'V31' invokes a function that generates the set of all cataloged values in
     the domain LOCATION (the domain to which DETROIT belongs) that are admissible
     as values for the LOCATION attribute (JLOC) of PROJECT.
The resulting parameter list is accordingly:
     3   DETROIT
     1   PROJECT
     1   PROJECT
     V31 BOSTON, SEATTLE, FRESNO, HOUSTON
These parameters together with the rule number (220) and the E-code prefix (E2)
are passed to dialog control.

In the supportive mode, dialog control uses the prefix E2 to select the message
template:
     WE HAVE NO INFORMATION ON U1 U2S, BUT WE DO HAVE U3S IN U4.
The symbols U1,U2,U3,U4 in this template are "slots" to be replaced by the four
parameters from the analyzer. Replacement yields:
     WE HAVE NO INFORMATION ON DETROIT PROJECTS, BUT WE DO HAVE PROJECTS IN BOSTON,
     SEATTLE, FRESNO, HOUSTON.
Dialog control now completes the message by concatenating the one above with:
     SELECT ONE OR SUPPLY AN ALTERNATIVE PHRASE OR ASK FOR HELP.
This message is then displayed at the user's terminal.

5. Conclusion

Natural languages have evolved so far in an environment that places very little
survival value on precision of expression. Consequently, we have to agree with
Montgomery's position (which she stated with impressive erudition in [10]) that
"natural language is not a natural query language". Nevertheless, for many (and
probably the vast majority) of future users of computers, there is no alternative
at this stage of evolution.

Previous work in interpreting queries stated in English -- at least, the work of
which this author is aware -- has been based on two unstated assumptions:

1. whenever a user conceives a query, he is able to formulate it accurately in English right away -- that is, he will be able to convey his intent to the system faithfully and precisely at his first attempt;
2. if the user's English is beyond the restricted English understood by the system, it is the responsibility of the user alone to re-state his query in system-comprehensible English, whatever that is!

The first assumption might be tolerable in an application field such as document retrieval where the data retrieved in response to a query normally provides adequate feedback to the user for him to determine whether he has asked the right question. Unfortunately, the formatted, operating data bases of large institutions and enterprises do not have this reassuring property. When casual users are brought into contact with these data bases, we must decisively reject this first assumption.

The second assumption must also be discarded, because of the large psychological impact on the casual user when his query is rejected for what appears to him to be arbitrary reasons. If these two assumptions were applied together to the casual user, it would be tantamount to asking him to engage in blind flying without instruments!

In this paper we have outlined seven steps -- and described an implementation -- intended to bring casual users into effective interaction with large, formatted databases. The seven steps are:

1. Select a simple data model
2. Select a high level logic as internal target
3. Introduce clarification dialog of bounded scope
4. Introduce system re-statement of user's query
5. Separate query formulation from data base search
6. Employ multiple choice interrogation as fall-back
7. Provide a definitional capability.

These steps, particularly the clarification dialog and re-statement steps executed prior to accessing the main body of data, should protect users from the many pitfalls of applying a non-precision-oriented language to the precision-demanding task of query formulation.

6. Acknowledgment

The author is indebted to Professors Frederick Thompson and Bozena Thompson of the California Institute of Technology and to Mr. Charles Kellogg of the System Development Corporation, Santa Monica for explaining their respective systems (REL and CONVERSE) and for providing demonstrations of them in operation.

REFERENCES

1. F. P. Thompson, P. Lockeman, B. H. Dostert, R. Deverill, "REL: A Rapidly Extensible Language System", Proc. 24th ACM National Conference, New York, ACM 1969 pp 399-417.
2. C. H. Kellogg, J. Burger, T. Diller, K. Fogt, "The CONVERSE Natural Language Data Management System: Current Status and Plans", Proc. ACM Symposium on Information Storage and Retrieval, Univ. of Maryland, College Park 1971 pp 33-46.
3. J. Weizenbaum, "ELIZA -- A Computer Program for the Study of Natural Language Communication between Man and Machine", Comm. ACM 9, No. 1, January 1966 pp 36-45.
4. T. Winograd, "Procedures as a Representation for Data in a Computer Program for Understanding Natural Language", MIT Project MAC, Cambridge, Mass., MAC TR-84 1971.

5. R. E. Levien, M. E. Maron, "A Computer System for Inference Execution and
    Data Retrieval", Comm. ACM 10, No. 11, November 1967.
6. E. F. Codd, "A Relational Model of Data for Large Shared Data Banks", Comm.
    ACM 13, No. 6, June 1970 pp 377-387.
7. E. F. Codd, "A Data Base Sublanguage founded on the Relational Calculus",
    Proc. 1971 ACM-SIGFIDET Workshop on Data Description, Access, and Control,
    San Diego, available from ACM New York.
8. E. F. Codd, "Relational Completeness of Data Base Sublanguages", Courant
    Computer Science Symposia 6, "Data Base Systems", New York City, May 24-25,
    1971, Prentice Hall.
9. L. A. Zadeh, "A Fuzzy-Set-Theoretic Interpretation of Linguistic Hedges",
    Journal of Cybernetics 2, 1972 pp 4-34
10. C. A. Montgomery, "Is Natural Language an Unnatural Query Language?", Proc.
    ACM National Conference, New York, ACM 1972 pp 1075-1078

ADDITIONAL BIBLIOGRAPHY

11. Randall Rustin (ed.), "Natural Language Processing", Courant Computer Science
    Symposia 8, New York City, December 20-21, 1971, Prentice Hall
12 R. F. Simmons, "Natural Language Question-Answering Systems: 1969", Comm.
    ACM 13, No. 1, January 1970 pp 15-30
13. S. R. Petrick, "Semantic Interpretation in the REQUEST System", IBM Research
    Report RC4457, IBM Research Center, Yorktown Heights, New York
14. F. P. Palermo, "A Data Base Search Problem", Fourth International Symposium
    on Computer and Information Science, Miami Beach, December 1972; also
    available as IBM San Jose Research Report RJ1072
15. J. B. Rothnie, "The Design of Generalized Data Management Systems", Ph.D.
    Dissertation, Dept. of Civil Engineering, MIT, September 1972
16. R. F. Boyce, D. D. Chamberlin, W. F. King III, M. M. Hammer, "Specifying
    Queries as Relational Expressions: SQUARE", Proc. ACM SIGPLAN-SIGIR Interface
    Meeting, Gaithersburg, Maryland, November 4-6, 1973; also available as IBM
    San Jose Research Report RJ1291

APPENDIX 1

ALPHA Syntax

Terminal Symbol Class	Class Abbreviation	Class Members
function names	F	
relation names	R	
tuple variables	T	
values	x	
attributes	A	
relational connectives	r	$= \neq < \leq > \geq$
logical connectives	l	$\land \lor \longrightarrow$
quantifiers	Q	$\forall \; \exists$
query type symbols		f e t
punctuation		: . , ( )
negation		$\neg$

```
attribute term          term = T . A
argument list           arglist = term or arglist,term
function term           fterm = term or F(arglist)
join term               jterm = (fterm r x)
                        or (fterm r fterm)
boolfunction expression bfexp = F(arglist)
        where F denotes a truth-valued function
boolean expression      boolexp = jterm or bfexp
                        or    boolexp
                        or (boolexp) l (boolexp)
qualification expression qexp = boolexp or Q T (qexp)
target list             tlist = fterm or tlist,fterm
alpha expression        alphexp = tlist : qexp
        where tuple variables appearing in target list
        are those which are free in qualification exp
range expression        rgexp = RANGE R T
range specification      rgspec = rgexp or rgspec,rgexp
quota                   quota = integer
ordering expression     ordexp = arglist
find type query         fquery = f quota rgspec:alphexp:ordexp
        where tuple variables in ordering expression must
        appear in target list of alpha expression
exist type query        equery = e r quota T:rgspec:qexp
truth test query        tquery = t rgspec:qexp
alpha query             alphaquery = fquery or equery or tquery
```

Note 1: all tuple variables appearing in the alpha expression of a find type
    query must also appear in the corresponding range specification
Note 2: similarly, all tuple variables appearing in the qualification expression
    of an exist type or truth test query must also appear in the corresponding
    range specification
Note 3: workspace names have been intentionally omitted from this syntax, because
    of their irrelevance to the topic of this paper

APPENDIX 2

RENDEZVOUS Lexical Classes

```
01    non-cataloged value
02    cataloged value
03    attribute
04    relation name
05    function name
06    cataloged synonym
07    do type word
08    find type word
09    units word (e.g., dollars, meters)
10    is type word
11    boolean word
12    comparator
13    location word
14    noise
15    preposition
16    quantifier
17    target-qualification separator
18    time word
19    pronoun
20    non-linking relation name
21    linking relation name
22    general synonym
23    fuzzy word
24    case type word
25    article

31    all-digits word
32    all-letters word
33    alphanumeric word

41    less type word
42    equal type word
43    greater type word
44    parends
45    system word (non-English)
```

Lexical classes 50 and up are the syntactic classes of INTER-ALPHA (these include the syntactic classes of ALPHA).

APPENDIX 3

<u>Sample Queries</u>

     QPRINT 'Q'

01 *FIND THE NUMBER OF TYPES OF PARTS SUPPLIED BY TORONTO
SUPPLIERS WHO ARE CURRENTLY SUPPLYING OAKLAND PROJECTS*
02 *FIND OUT WHETHER PART X4 IS ON ORDER FROM DETROIT*
03 *FIND THE PART NUMBERS AND QUANTITIES ON HAND OF HOUSTON
PARTS*
04 *OF ALL THE PARTS SUPPLIED FROM DETROIT, WHICH ONES ARE
SHIPPED TO PROJECT HOPE?*
05 *IN WHAT QUANTITIES IS PART NUMBER 3 SUPPLIED?*
06 *DISPLAY SUPPLIER NAMES AND PROJECT NAMES INVOLVING THE
SUPPLY OF PART NUMBER 400*
07 *WHEN DID SUPPLIER JONES SUPPLY PART NUMBER 5 AND TO WHICH
PROJECTS?*
08 *DID SUPPLIER JONES SUPPLY PART 5 TO A PROJECT IN DETROIT?*
09 *IS IT TRUE THAT ALL SUPPLIERS WHO SUPPLY PART 2 ARE LOCATED
IN HOUSTON?*
10 *GIVE ME A LIST OF THE PARTS SUPPLIED IN 1971 ALONG WITH
THEIR SUPPLIERS*
11 *WHAT WAS THE TOTAL QUANTITY OF PART 4 SHIPPED BETWEEN APRIL
1972 AND JANUARY 1973?*
12 *PART NUMBERS, PTYPE, QUANTITIES SUPPLIED TO HOUSTON PROJECTS*
13 *HOW MANY SUPPLIERS SUPPLY PART 6?*
14 *WHERE IS PROJECT 8 LOCATED?*
15 *DOES THERE EXIST A SUPPLIER WHO IS SUPPLYING MORE THAN 50
KINDS OF PARTS?*
16 *FIND ALL THOSE CASES IN WHICH HOUSTON SUPPLIERS SUPPLY
TORONTO PROJECTS*
17 *GIVE ME A LIST OF PARTS SHIPPED TO PROJECT 8*
18 *ARE THERE NOT SUPPLIERS WHO SHIP PART 5 TO PROJECT 8?*
19 *IS IT THE CASE THAT SUPPLIER JONES SUPPLIES PROJECT 5?*
20 *WHO SUPPLIES PARTS OF TYPE 9?*
21 *HOW MANY PARTS NUMBERED 3 ARE SUPPLIED FROM HOUSTON?*
22 *FIND OUT HOW MANY OF PART X4 ARE ON ORDER*
23 *HOW MANY SUPPLIERS SUPPLYING PART M6 ARE LOCATED IN HOUSTON?*
24 *FIND THE PARTS HAVING QOH IN EXCESS OF 10 AND NONE ON ORDER*
25 *I WANT AT MOST 5 INSTANCES OF A TORONTO SUPPLIER SUPPLYING
A HOUSTON PROJECT*

DISCUSSION

Delobel : In your example how can your system know that HOUSTON is a city name?

Codd : For those domains which have few distinct values, these values are stored with the Data Base Description along with the relevant attribute so that the system is able to recognize them as values.

Delobel : Is it possible to include dynamically new words in the Data Base Description?

Codd : No, not at present.

Tsichritzis : Can you make a comparison between your system and several other systems developed by Artificial Intelligence People?

Codd : This system is much less ambitious than the A.I. projects in that its domain of discourse is quite narrow and well-defined. One does not need much knowledge to interact with a formatted Data Base. On the other hand I am taking pains to avoid user frustration. the system takes very careful steps to keep the user there.

Langefors : How is your system helping the user understand what he wants?

Codd : There are two kinds of assistance : first the restatement mechanism and second simple display of informal explanation.

Data Base Management, J. W. Klimbie and K. L. Koffeman, (eds.)
© *North-Holland Publishing Company (1974)*

PROBLEMS OF HIGH LEVEL DATA BASE
ACCESS LANGUAGE IMPLEMENTATION
IN INVERTED STORAGE STRUCTURE
ENVIRONMENT

.L.A.Kalinichenko, V.M.Ryvkin

Complex Computer Control Institute

Vavilova 24, Moscow, GSP 312, USSR

Abstract:

Some preliminary results obtained in course of experimental research concerning dialogue data base access language (DALD) of high level are considered. DALD selective features are based on first order predicate calculus and data base structure is represented by set of relations /3/.It is planned to implement DALD chosen on the basis of formatted data management system with inverted storage structure. The intention of this research consists in

- proper choice of DALD selective features effectively implementable in inverted storage structure environment;
- choice of relational operator set for DALD selective features interpretation.

Introduction:

Characteristic feature of contemporary data base management system /1,2/ consists in several levels of data base (DB) logical structure description languages. Here we take into account two language levels- system level and functional level.

System level of data structure description language (DDLS) is oriented on independent of functional programs and corresponding programming languages definition of integrated DB logical structure. By means of DDLS DB logical structure is defined in terms of entities (being images of real world objects) and their relations.

Functional level of data structure description language (DDLF) is
used for definition of logical structure of integrated DB subsets.
Such subsets may be processed by functionally-oriented programs or
may be used by non-programmer in course of dialogue. Thus
functional level is dependent on programming and dialogue
language and for this reason includes several data description
languages-schema DDL in well-known proposals /1/corresponds to the
systems level language and subschema DDLs correspond to
functional level languages.
DB access languages have also several levels. By analogy with
data structure description languages the distinction between
functional and system DB access language levels exists.
DB access languages of functional level (DALF) are programmer
oriented and syntactically conform to corresponding programming
languages. DALF statements should be elementary to the extent that
fficient DB processing (DB is defined by corresponding DDLF)
y functional program be possible.
In fact all DB processing operations are accomplished on integrated
DB level defined by DDLS. That is why DB access language of system
level (DALS) should be included into the DB management system.
DALS is the language that is used to express DB processing
operations. DALF and DALS levels are very close, and DALF→DALS
conversion should be executed by DB management system in order to
interpret DALF operations.

Particular place among DALF is occupied by non-programmer-oriented dialogue DB access languages (DALF). It is convenient to subdivide DALF features on <u>selective</u> features used for expressing criterion satisfiable by data being extracted or stored into DB and <u>directive</u> features which include set of statements to express actions (e.g., STORE,GET,INCLUDE,REPLACE etc.). DB <u>queries</u> are expressed by selective features of DALD.

DALD level and its selective capabilities in particular should be much higher than those of DALS. It's also obvious that DALD selective features should reflect data structures defined by dialogue-oriented DDLF. Such structures may be interpreted in terms of trees, networks or set of relations. DALD selective features may be based on first order predicate calculus characterised by high selective capability /4/. The intention of this research consists in
- proper choice of DALD selective features effectively implementable in inverted storage structure environment,
- choice of DALS operator set for DALD selective features interpretation (set of algebraic operators on relations is used),
- development of methods of DALD interpretation.

2. DB LOGICAL STRUCTURE AND DALS OPERATORS

DB logical structure will be defined in the following way.

<u>Set of DB relations</u> $\rho_1 = \{R_i\}$ is collection of normalized relations /3/ Ri   where Ri is n_i -ary relation which is contained in DB.

<u>Set of DB variables</u> $X = \{x_1, x_2, \ldots, x_m\}$ is union of different domain names of all relations from ρ_1.

<u>Set of DB universums</u> is collection of unary relations $\mu = \{Mx_1, Mx_2, \ldots Mx_m\}$ where universum Mx_i is union of sets of all different x_i variable values through all relations from ρ_1 in which variable x_i is used as domain name. The triple $<\rho_1, X, \mu>$ defines DB logical structure.

<u>Generalized variable</u> X $\subset$ X defines a subset of set of DB variables if there exist such relation Ri that all variables from X are domain names in this relation. <u>Generalized variable value</u> $\overline{X}$ is any tuple of corresponding variable values in this relation.

For example, if X $= \{x_{i_1}, x_{i_2}, \ldots, x_{i_k}\}$ then
$$\overline{X} = <\overline{x}_{i_1}, \overline{x}_{i_2}, \ldots, \overline{x}_{i_k}> \in Mx_{i_1} \times Mx_{i_2} \times \ldots \times Mx_{i_k}$$

DALS operators on relations oriented on interpretation of selective features of dialogue DB access languages are considered further. The part of DALS considered here does not include operators which increase relation degree.

First of all unary operator of projection and binary operator of restriction are included into DALS operator set. These operators defined in /3/ are denoted here by $\pi_X(R_i)$ and $R_i \mathbin{\mathpalette\@underrel{\ominus}{x}} R_i$ correspondingly.

By $\mathcal{O}_2 = \{r_j\}$ we denote set of all possible derivative relations being a result of successive application of projection and restriction operators on relations $R_i \in \mathcal{O}_1$ set-theoretical operators of union (U) intersection $(\cap)$ and difference $(\backslash)$ are also included into DALS and represent binary operators on relations from $\mathcal{O}_2$ having equal degrees and equal domain names.

By $\mathcal{O}_3 = \{q_k\}$ we denote set of relations which may be derived from relations $r_j \in \mathcal{O}_2$ by means of set - theoretical operators and by $\mathcal{O} = \mathcal{O}_1 U \mathcal{O}_2 U \mathcal{O}_3$ set of all relations which are included into DB and may be created by operators observed. It's obvious that $\mu \subset \mathcal{O}$ and any DB universum may be derived from $\mathcal{O}_1$ by means of projection and union operators. Taking into account interpretation efficiency of relational operators in inverted storage structure environment it is natural to include μ in DB as an independent set of relations.

Additionally three relational operators having common name <u>conditional</u> projection are included into DALS. Generalized variables are denoted by X, Y and DB variables - by x,y.

<u>Conditional projection</u> $\mathcal{E}$ is binary operator on relations $R_1, R_2 \in \mathcal{O}$ where $R_2 \subseteq \pi_Y(R_1)$ The result of $\mathcal{E}$ -operator $R_3 = \mathcal{E}_{X,Y}(R_1, R_2)$ is such maximal subset of relation $\pi_X(R_1 \mathfrak{S}_Y R_2)$ that $(\forall \bar{x} \in \pi_X(R_1 \mathfrak{S}_Y R_2))(\pi_Y(R_1 \mathfrak{S}_x \bar{X}) \subseteq R_2)$.

<u>Conditional projection</u> λ is unary operator on relation $R_1 \in \mathcal{O}$ The result of λ -operator $R_2 = \lambda_{X,Y}(R_1)$ is such maximal subset of relation $\pi_X(R_1)$ that $(\forall \bar{x} \in \pi_X(R_1))(\pi_Y(R_1 \mathfrak{S}_x \bar{X}) = M_y)$.

$\mathcal{E}$ - and λ -operators are used for interpretation of queries in which universal quantifiers are used.

<u>Conditional projection</u> $\mathcal{Y}$ is unary operator on relation $R_1 \in \mathcal{O}$. The result of $\mathcal{Y}$ operator $R_2 = \mathcal{Y}_{X,Y}(R_1)$ is such maximal subset of relation $\pi_X(R_1)$ that $(\forall \tilde{x} \in \pi_X(R_1))(f_y(\pi_y(R_1 \mathfrak{S}_x \bar{x})) \gtreqless N)$, where $f_y(L) :: = COUNT_y(L) / MAX_y(L) / TOTAL_y(L) / AVERAGE(L) / MIN_y(L)$, defined in /4/.

COUNTY$_y$(L) -function counting the number of the elements y in relation L,

MAX$_y$(L)   -   function selecting maximal value of y in relation L,

MIN$_y$(L)   -   function selecting minimal value of y in relation L,

TOTALy(L)   -   function counting the sum of y values in
                        relation L,
AVERAGEy(L)   -   function counting the arithmetic mean of
                        y in relation L,
N   -   real value

Thus part of system level DB access language oriented on interpretation of selective features of dialogue languages in inverted
storage structure environment includes operators collection
$\pi, \subseteq, \mathcal{E}, \lambda, \mathcal{Y}, \cup, \cap, \setminus$.
Application of the operators considered .above and their interpretation will be described further.

3. RELATIONAL OPERATORS INTERPRETATION IN INVERTED STORAGE
   STRUCTURE ENVIRONMENT

   All relations from $\mathcal{O}_1$ are stored by formatted data management
system (FDMS) having inverted storage structure. All domains
of every relation are inverted. FDMS makes possible to retrieve
tuples from relations $R_i \in \mathcal{O}_1$ by query which may contain values
of variables corresponding to domains of relation Ri and logical
combinations of such values. FDMS allows also to retrieve DB
universum corresponding to any DB relation domain. Besides that
FDMS makes possible to count the number of relation Ri tuples which
satisfy the query without retrieving Ri tuples from DB.

Intermediate relations from $\mathcal{O}_2 \cup \mathcal{O}_3$ sets are stored in working
areas (WA) containing temporary files which are created during
dialogue query interpretation. These files are created dynamically
and every file corresponds to some relation. In such environment
relational operators introduced above may be implemented in the
following way.

Projection operator $\pi(R_1, R_2, X)$

Here R_1 is initial relation, X is generalized variable, R_2 is
result of operator.
If $R_1 \in \mathcal{O}_1$ and X contains only one variable then corresponding
universum is retrieved by FDMS. In case when X contains more than
one variable and $R_1 \in \mathcal{O}_1$ usage of this operator in dialogue
language interpretator is restricted because of low efficiency
of π - operator.

If initial relation $R_1 \in (\rho_2 \cup \rho_3)$ projection is found by sorting
relation file R_1 by X variable and by transferring $\overline{X}$ -tuples
of R_1 into file R_2 without duplications. Number n_j showing how
many tuples of initial relation include $\overline{X}$-tuple of projection is
put into correspondence to every tuple of projection.

Restriction operator $\sigma(R_1, R_2, R_3, X)$

Here relation $R_1 \in \rho_1$ is restricted by relation $R_2 \in (\rho_2 \cup \rho_3)$
and by generalized variable X. R_3 is the result of operator.
During the interpretation the query to FDMS is formed. This query
is constructed from the relation R_2-tuples in the following manner

$$(\overline{x}_1^1 \& \overline{x}_1^2 \& \ldots \& \overline{x}_1^k) \vee (\overline{x}_2^1 \& \overline{x}_2^2 \& \ldots \& \overline{x}_2^k) \vee \ldots$$

where $\overline{x}_i^j$ is the value of variable corresponding to domain j
in tuple i and K is degree of the relation R_2.
R_3 is formed on the basis of data retrieved by this query.

Set - theoretical operators $(\cup, \cap, \setminus)$.

These operators are applied to relations belonging $(\rho_2 \cup \rho_3)$
which are represented by equally ordered sequential files.
Interpretation of such operators is obvious.
Conditional projection operator $\varepsilon(R_1, R_2, R_3, X, Y)$
Here $R_1 \in \rho_1$ and $R_2 \in (\rho_2 \cup \rho_3)$ are initial relation, R_3 is the result
of operator, X, Y are generalized variables, Y being quantified in
query by quantifier $\forall$. During the first interpretation step
relation $R_4 = \pi_X(R_1 \sigma_Y R_2)$ being set of tuples $\langle \overline{x}, n_j \rangle$ is created.
For every tuple of R_4 relation the query to FDMS is constructed
in order that the number of tuples which include value $\overline{x}$ be found.
If this number is equal to n_j this R_4 tuple is transferred to R_3.

Conditional projection operator $\lambda(R_1, R_2, X, y)$

Here $R_1 \in \rho$ is initial relation, R_2 is the result of operator, y
is the variable quantified by $\forall$ in query. Interpretation of this
operator begins with retrieving of universum My by FDMS and
putting it into WA. If $R_1 \in \rho_1$ then for every value $\overline{y} \in My$ the query
to FDMS is constructed in order that subset of R_1 every tuple
of which contains $\overline{y}$ be found. Next operation consists in
building of π_X for this subsets. Relation R_2 is produced by intersection of all such projections.
If $R_1 \in (\rho_2 \cup \rho_3)$ preliminary operation of file R_1 sorting on y
values should be done. After that it's possible to retrieve
necessary subsets of R_1 for every $\overline{y}$.

Conditional projection operator $\mathcal{P}(R_1, R_2, x, y, z, N)$.

Here $R_1 \in \mathcal{O}$ is initial relation, R_2 is the result of operator, x, y
are DB variables. During the first step of operator $\mathcal{P}$ interpretation universum Mx is retrieved by FDMS. After that if $R_1 \in \mathcal{O}_1$
then for every value $\bar{x} \in Mx$ the query to FDMS is constructed
in order that the subset of R_1 every tuple of which contains $\bar{x}$
be found. Then projection Π_y of this subset is constructed.
If $f_y(\Pi_y(R_1 \ominus_x \bar{x})) \lessgtr N$ where f is one of the functions COUNT, MAX
MIN, TOTAL, AVERAGE then $\bar{x}$ is transferred to R_2.
In case when $R_1 \in (\mathcal{O}_2 \cup \mathcal{O}_3)$ relation R_1 is sorted on x and after that
for every $\bar{x} \in M_x$ the subset of R_1 every tuple of which contains
$\bar{x}$ is found. Further operations are analogous to the case $R_1 \in \mathcal{O}_1$.

4. DIALOGUE LANGUAGE FEATURES

Any query includes a list of DB target variables. The target
variable is DB variable values of which should be retrieved by the
query. All the target variables from this query list should be
included in one generalized variable denoted here by Y.
Besides that any query includes selective criterion which must
be satisfied by target generalized variable Y values.
Such criterion is expressed by some formula of first order
predicate calculus. In queries only such subset of all wff of first
order predicate calculus may be chosen that set of satisfying
tuples of values of every wff be retrieved from DB relation by
finite sequence of relational operators defined above.
The selective criterion is formula from this subset in which all
DB variables included into generalized variable Y are free and all
remaining variables of this formula are bound. The selective
criterion may also be constructed as a logical combination of
permissible formulae.
To every relation $R \in \mathcal{O}$ some predicate arguments of which are
variables the names of which match with corresponding domain
names in relation R may be put into correspondence.

The definition of formulae given below is recursive. FORMULA(Z)
is logical combination of permissible formulae in which Z is
free generalized variable. Z may be also considered as a union
of two nonintersecting generalized variables X and Y, that are
included into the same relation $R \in \mathcal{O}$ The predicates are denoted
by names of the corresponding relations.

Basic formula types which may be used in queries are given below.

$R(Y)$ & FORMULA $(X \subset Y)$

Here Y and X are generalized variables, Y is target variable, $R(Y)$ is the predicate which corresponds to the relation $R \in \mathcal{O}_1$. The meaning of this formula type consists in selecting such subsets of relation R that X - component of any its tuples satisfies the condition expressed by FORMULA(X).

FORMULA 1 (Y) & FORMULA 2 $(X \subseteq Y)$.

This formula type is such extension of previous one that instead of $R(Y)$ formula is used.

$\exists X (\text{FORMULA }(X,Y))$

Interpretation of this formula type consists in constructing of the relation being set of satisfying tuples of FORMULA (X,Y) and then in building of the projection of this relation by X.

$\forall X (\text{FORMULA 1 }(X,Y) \longrightarrow \text{FORMULA 2 }(X))$

The meaning of this formula type consists in selecting those values from the set of generalized variable Y values that satisfy FORMULA1 only together with those X values which satisfy FORMULA 2 (X). Implementation of this formula type consists in restricting set of satisfying tuples of FORMULA 1 by set of satisfying tuples of FORMULA 2 with application of $\mathcal{E}$ -operator afterwards.

$\forall X (\text{FORMULA}(X,Y))$

The meaning of this formula type is obvious. Formula is implemented by λ -operator.

$f(\text{FORMULA}(X,Y),x) \gtrless N)$,

where f is one of the functions described above, N-value and symbol of relational operation $(> | < | = | \geqslant | \leqslant)$ is given by the user. In this formula type y is free variable and x is bound by f. By this formula type such subset of y values from set of satisfying tuples of FORMULA (x,y) is retrieved that x values which are included in tuples together with y value satisfy condition that $fx \gtrless N$ over the set of satisfying tuples of FORMULA (x,y).

5. DIALOGUE LANGUAGE QUERIES EXAMPLES

Several query examples to sample DB are considered here. DB is assumed to include the following relations:

Q (part, organization - supplier, supply date, cost of the part);

P (part, project, the number of part in the project);

R (organization, address);

S (organization -designer, project).

In query examples variables are named by following identifiers:

c - address,

u - cost of the part

v - supply date

t - the number of the part in the project

x - part,

y - project,

z - organization

Query examples:

1. Get all suppliers which supplied only parts 1 on the 6.th of October 1972.

GET z: $\forall x (\exists v (Q(x,v,z) \& v = 6.10.72) \rightarrow x = 1)$

2. Get addresses of organizations which supply only those parts which are used in all projects

GET c: $\exists z (R(z,c) \& \forall x (Q(x,z) \rightarrow \forall y (P(x,y)))$

3. Get projects all parts which are supplied only by organizations-suppliers, having address A.

GET y: $\forall x (P(x,y) \rightarrow \forall z (Q(x,z) \rightarrow \exists c (R(z,c) \& C = A)))$

4. Get projects all parts of which had cost $\geqslant 5$ till 5.5.71.

GET y: $\forall x (P(x,y) \rightarrow \forall u (\exists v (Q(x,v,u) \& v < 5.5.71) \rightarrow u \geqslant 5))$

5. Get suppliers which supplied on the 2 -nd of March 1971 parts with total cost $\geq$ 50.

GET z: $TOTAL(\exists v (Q(z,v,u) \& v = 2.3.71), u) \geqslant 50$

6.CONCLUSION

High level DB access language implementation approach considered in this paper in future is planned to apply to data base management systems belonging to the class described in /1,2/. In this case dialogue language selective feature should provide construction of entity selection criterion by set of entity attributes and by set of entity relations. Because of much more complicated DB logical structure it may be not possible to express such criterion by means of dialogue language based on the first order predicate calculus.

Besides that in this case data base access language of system level
should be close to the language of DML kind defined in /1/.
Nevertheless, research of dialogue language implementation methods
described in this paper will contribute to the design of high
level DB access language used in network DB structure
environment.

Note: This paper was not presented, only published, because
      the author was unable to come, so no discussion took place.

Data Base Management, J. W. Klimbie and K. L. Koffeman, (eds.)
© *North-Holland Publishing Company (1974)*

A MULTILEVEL RELATIONAL MODEL FOR

DATA BASE MANAGEMENT SYSTEMS

G. BRACCHI, A. FEDELI, P. PAOLINI

Istituto di Elettrotecnica ed Elettronica
Politecnico di Milano, Italy

Abstract : In this paper the features of a multilevel relational model for a
data independent information management system are illustrated.
Five logical levels are individuated in the proposed model; binary relations are utilized for describing the totality of information in the data
base, while hierarchical relations are available to the user and any kind
of storage structure is allowed for the physical files. The data independence, flexibility, and optimization features of the model are illustrated. Problems concerning the operational behavior are finally discussed.

I - Introduction

In past data base management system technology application programs were
dependent, for their successful execution, on a particular data base organization, and were forced to respect preexisting and fixed logical structures of
data (Codasyl 1971, Codd 1969, Codd 1970).

Logical and physical data independence is now being recognized as a primary goal in designing a generalized data base management system (Astrahan 1972,
CODASYL 1971, Collmeyer 1972, Date 1971). In such a system users (application
programs) can utilize the logical data structures that are more suitable for
their specific problems, and they are not concerned with physical storage structures that may change with time.

The relational approach to data base management is potentially capable of
providing such an independence (Bracchi 1972, Codd 1969, Codd 1970, Codd 1971,
Lorie 1970, Strnad 1971).

In the relational model the data items are viewed as linked in one-level
relations (normalized relations), which are structured, regarding in same way
semantic features of data, to minimize the number of occurences of the same data
item (third normal form)(Codd 1971).In this way there are no preferential paths
and all data are accessible in a uniform way.

To obtain data independence, a logical data structure, organized as normalized relations, can be utilized as an intermediate representation level between
user and physical storage structure (Bracchi 1972).

Moreover, the relational approach provides theoretical tools to develop
powerful high level languages based on first order applied predicate calculus
(Bracchi 1972, Codd 1971).

However, efforts to design systems based on the relational approach (Brac
chi 1972, Goldstein 1970, Jervis 1972, Notley 1972) have showed some failures
that we briefly summarize :

1) In the relational approach logical problems are not clearly distinguished
from physical ones; normalized relations indeed are often considered both
a logical tool to describe the data base and a proposal for the structure of
physical files.

2) If every normalized relation corresponds to a separate physical file, it should pointed out that in this way an arbitrary prefixed structure is given disregarding particular real access needs to the data base.

3) The structure of an n-ary normalized relation can make transparent some information which are needed to obtain an efficient data base management, so that a deeper examination of the correlations between data items becomes necessary in operating on the relation (Codd 1971, Jervis 1972).

4) The normalized relational structure makes very complex (and sometimes impossible) logical restructuring of the data base for meeting particular user's problems. For example, it's very heavy to build on hierarchical relations utilizing normalized relations.

Hence, the need to provide a logical tool which gives a semantic view of real correlations among the data should be recognized. A semantic definition of data indeed would be a non-arbitrary way of describing information belonging to the data base, completely independent on one hand from user's logical structures, and on the other hand from physical file structure; any change in logical or physical structures (the change, of course, should not modify the set of information stored in the data base) will not affect this semantic description.

In the following section we will first illustrate some auxiliary concepts; we will then make a proposal for this semantic description of data utilizing binary relations. We will show that such a solution provides an interesting way of achieving a complete logical and physical data independence, and that it makes possible an automatic optimization of access to the physical files, whose structure is completely transparent to the user.

II - General Concepts

In this section we will recall some accepted definitions (CODASYL 1971) and will illustrate some new concepts in order to introduce an unambiguous terminology; we will then propose a new structure for an information management system, utilizing those concepts.

1) A Data item is the name assigned to a kind of data.

2) An Occurence of a data item is a representation of a value.

3) A Domain is a set of occurrences of a data item, and it is identified by its own name (generally different from the data item).

4) A Descriptor is a named collection of one or more data items and zero, or one, or more Descriptors. In the usual terminology, logical record has the same meaning as Descriptor.

5) A User Logical File (ULF) is a set of occurrences of a Descriptor. The term "Logical File" can be justified thinking of these occurrences as existing in the user's view. An example of ULF is illustrated in Fig. 1.

(Data items)

(Descriptor)	EMPLOYEE	"Name"	"Tax"	"Birthyear"
(User Logical File)		Cox	1.000	1936
		Christie	3.000	1907

Fig. 1 - Example of a Descriptor and the corresponding User Logical File.

6) A System Physical File (SPF) is a set of occurrences of a Descriptor that are physically stored in the data base. An SPF is not necessarely corresponding to a ULF, neither viceversa.

7) A Schema is a description of the logical correlations among the various data items whose occurrences are stored in the SPF's . We outline that there are no occurrences of the Schema; we could rather say that it can be also built by breaking down the Descriptors of the ULF's and reassembling them in a different way.

8) A User Subschema is the Descriptor of a User Logical File.

9) A Logical Mapping Model (LMM) is the description, expressed in terms of elements of the Schema, of the logical correlations among the Data Items of a User Subschema.

10) In a Schema File Subset (SFS) the elements of the Schema which are stored in the same System Physical File are indicated.

11) A Physical Mapping Model (PMM) is the description of the physical organization of the storage structure of a System Physical File, and of the storage representation of the elements of a Schema File Subset.

The above concepts suggest the architecture of a data base management system, which is illustrated in Fig. 2.

This architecture can appear, at first sight, cumbersome and unnecessary; it can be, instead, very helpful in solving some of today's problems in data base management.
First of all, we can see that real data (i.e., occurrences) are present only at the ULF and SPF levels; all other levels include only the description of relationships between data.

Moreover, physical and logical independences are obtained. In fact, all the operations concerning updating of the data base, (like deletion of an occurrence, or insertion of a new one, etc.), affect only the SPF ' s (and the ULF's, of course!). Any change is a User Subschema (i.e. in the Descriptor of a ULF) is instead reflected on the corresponding LMM only, without involving the Schema or the SPF's. In the same way, any internal modification of the storage structure of a System Physical File requires a modification in the corresponding Physical Mapping Model only; a reorganization of a set of System Physical Files (and of Physical Mapping Models) instead, will concern the Schema File Subsets without affecting the Schema. The LMM and the PMM then act as interfaces between ULF and Schema, and Schema and SPF, respectively, so that any action on the files will let unchanged the Schema.

III - The schema

We will now discuss the feasibility of the use of binary relations in the schema; more precisely, the schema we will propose is a set of descriptors of binary relations.

Note that this choice is not an arbitrary one, since in the real world too the smallest meaningful unit of information is an element of a binary relation: in fact a value is significant if we associate it with another value (Bell 1966, Levien 1967).

A careful exploitation of a binary relational model for the schema can provide the following advantages :

1) No external arbitrary logical structures are imposed on the information in the data base.

2) Nor preferential paths among the data nor limitations on the access to them are introduced.

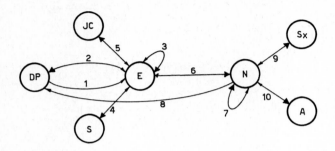

SCHEMA DATA ITEMS

E   = employee code number
DP   = department
S   = salary
JC   = job code
N   = name
Sx   = sex
A   = age

Binary relations describing association between :

 1 : department and code number of the employees belonging to it
 2 : code number of the managers and their departments
 3 : a code number of an employee and the codenumber of his superior
 4 : a code number of an employee and his salary
 5 : a code number of an employee and his job code
 6 : a code number of an employee and his name
 7 : a name of an employee and the names of his sons
 8 : a name of an employee and his department
 9 : a name of a son of an employee and his sex
10 : a name of a son of an employee and his age

Fig. 3 - A sample schema composed of binary relations.

3) High flexibility is obtained: an elementary modification in the set of data in the data base causes only an elementary modification in the schema; in fact, addition or deletion of a binary relation do   not modify other relations.

4) Since the totality of information is broken down into atomic units, constructing complex logical structures (particularly hyerarchical relations), by using binary relations as building blocks, is an easy task.

5) A multilevel privacy control is possible, forbidding access, or retrieval, or use of binary relations, or of their occurrences, or of their domains.

On the other hand, the need of describing a large information set as binary relations can make the schema very cumbersome; to reduce its size and complexity all the names of domains corresponding to the same data item can be grouped in the Schema, and they are identified by the name of that data item: we will call this name Schema Data Item (SDI).
Binary relations are thus defined on these SDI's, (e.g., the domains which contain person-names will refer to a single SDI) so that a better compactness to the schema is provided.

A further consideration is that a binary relation defined on A and B can join A to B and/or B to A; hence, we must distinguish two kinds of binary relations: the simple relations and the complete relations. We call simple binary relation a directed one (from A to B, for example) so that no possibility exists to visit it in the inverted direction (from B to A). In a complete binary relation it's instead possible to visit the relation in both directions.

In Fig. 3 an example of a Schema represented as an oriented graph is illustrated.

In Fig. 3 the simple arrows ($\longrightarrow$) correspond to the simple binary relations and the notation $(A)\longrightarrow\!\!\!\!\times\!(B)$ means that it is possible to associate to every value of A the corresponding value(s) of B.

Double arrows correspond to the complete binary relations and the notation $(A)\times\!\!\!\longleftarrow\!\!\!\!\longrightarrow\!\!\!\times\!(B)$ establish a direction from A to B, that we arbitrary define positive, while we define negative the direction from B to A.

Definitions of Fig. 3 correspond to the positive directions: thus the binary relation 3 in the positive direction connects an employee code number to the code number of his superior, and viceversa in the negative direction.

We will write: 2^+ to point out the binary relation 2 in the positive direction (i.e., connecting E to DP), and 2^- to indicate the binary relation 2 in the negative direction (i.e., connecting DP to E). We will also write: 1^+ (assigning a positive direction to a simple binary relation) to obtain a uniform notation.

An oriented binary relation connecting A to B, is said to be negatively incident to A and positively incident to B.

By b_i we denote the generic i^{th} binary relation with no definite sign, while by b_i^s we indicate the generic i^{th} oriented binary relation (i.e., with a specified sign).

We will define now, using graph terminology, the concept of progression. A progression of length n is a sequence of (not necessarily distinct) oriented binary relations b^{s_1} , b^{s_2} ,..., b^{s_n}, such that for an appropriate sequence of n+1 SDI's, SDI_0, SDI_1,..., SDI_n, we have that b^{s_i} connects SDI_{i-1} with SDI_i for i=1,2,...,n. If $SDI_0 \neq SDI_n$ we say that the progression leads from SDI_0 to SDI_n. For example, referring to Figure 3, progressions 8^+, 1^+, 4^+, and 6^-, 4^{+n} and 6^-, 3^+, 4^+, lead from N to S.

Two other types of information are necessary in order to complete the semantic description of the schema.

1) Information that make recognizable equivalence, in a semantic sense, between progressions.

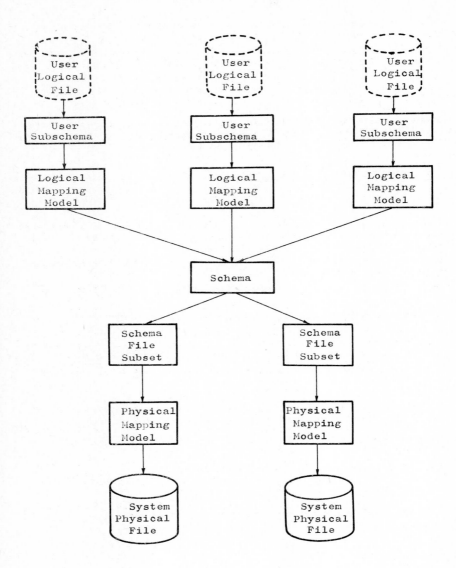

Fig. 2 - Organization of a Data Independent Information Management System.

2) Information concerning the types of the binary relations (i.e.: one to one, many to one, one to many, many to many).

Knowledge of the types of the relations has resulted very useful in verifying correctness of some operations on the data (Jervis 1972).

Finally note that at first sight it could appear impossible introducing in the Schema the relation : (region, year, population) in which a value of "population" depends on a couple of values (region, year). However, that difficulty may be overcomed by considering the following binary relation:((region, year), population) in which the first domain is, on its turn, a binary relation. It is quite easy to see that such a binary relation can be managed, with some care, as all other binary relations in the Schema.

IV – User Subschema and Logical Mapping Model

This section will deal with the definitions of Logical Mapping Model and User Subschema.

There are no intrinsic limitations on the choice of the subschema structures; however, in most real situations hierarchical relations seem to be able to satisfy user requirements (Eracchi 1972).

We will therefore assume, for the sake of simplicity, that user subschemas are structured as hierarchical relations.

In defining subschemas, and corresponding LMM's, two main problems arise :

1) An intrinsic problem, i.e., binding in an unambiguous way the elements of the subschema with the corresponding elements of the schema (LMM).

2) A user facility problem, i.e. allowing definition of the appropriate logical mapping model without any need for the user of knowing the whole structure of the schema, which in the real situations may be vary large and complex.

We will first illustrate, be means of same examples, a possible solution to the former problem; we will then give some suggestions on feasible solutions to the latter problem.

Let us show an example that illustrates the definition of a user relation and the corresponding logical mapping, referring to the schema of fig. 3.

department is ($\neq$ department = DP; number = E : 1^+; job = JC : 1^+, 5^+; salary = S : 1^+, 4^+);

This definition corresponds to the subschema shown in fig. 4.

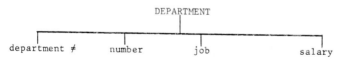

Fig. 4 – A sample User Subschema

From the above definition we may derive the following considerations :

1) for every domain of the user relations we must indicate the corresponding SDI in the schema.

2) One (or more then one) domain is a key (it is denoted by the symbol "$\neq$ ").

3) For every domain which is not a key it's necessary to indicate a progression of oriented binary relations leading from the SDI corresponding to the key to the SDI corresponding to it.

4) Every value of the key domain(s) corresponds to one occurrence of the relation (Codd 1969, Codd 1970).

5) The key has only a logical meaning, in order to establish the structure of the n-tuples; it could be possible to have a key not actually represented in the relation. For example, if we want to make statistical searches about jobs and salaries, it is unconvenient defining the relation :

$$\text{job is } (\neq \text{ job } = JC; \text{ salary } = S : 5^-, 4^+);$$

because in that way we could associate with every "job" the corresponding salaries, but we couldn't know, for example, how many employees with a specified job have a specified salary. Instead, if we define the relation :

$$\text{job is } (\neq E; \text{ job } = JC : 5^+; \text{ salary } = S : 4^+) ;$$

it's possible to reply to such an interrogation; in fact the n-tuples of this relation have the same composition of the n-tuples of the previous relation, but there is one n-tuple for every employee, while in the previous relation there was one n-tuple for every job.

We will now show the definition of a hierarchical relation :

employee is ($\neq$ name = N; his department = DP : 8^+; his superior = N: 6^-, 3^+, 6^+; his manager = N : 8^+, 2^-, 6^+; his job = JC : 6^-, 5^+; son that is ($\neq$ name of son = N; sex of son = Sx :9^+; age of son = A : 10^+) : 7^+);

The structure of the relation employee is represented in fig. 5. Note the following features :

1) At any level in the hierarchy the progression leading from a key to every domain of the same level is specified;

2) The progression leading from the key of the ith level to the key(s) of $(i+1)^{th}$ level is also specified.
In the above example the progression 7^+ leads from the first level key to the second level key.

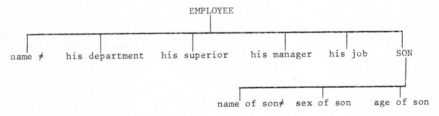

Fig. 5 - A hierarchical User Subschema

Let us now briefly discuss same problems that arise in defining subschemas and logical mapping models.

As we showed in previous examples, a complete freedom is provided for restructuring information in user subschemas; the method that has been illustrated to define logical structures provides a powerful and flexible tool for defining and accessing the data base.

On the other hand, it should be noted that starting from a very large and complex schema could make a serious task the recognition of the appropriate logical mapping model for particular subschemas.

However, if two SDI's are correlated in a very large number of user subschemas, it will be useful having the binary relation linking them inserted in the Schema (and obviously stored in an SPF). Then a frequent use of a too long pro-

gression generally denotes an inaccurate schema definition; hence, a reorganization of the schema is desirable in order to substitute such a progression with
a shorter one (e.g., just a binary relation).

Moreover, using a proper interactive strategy, the system could be enabled
to instruct the user, step by step, in defining the logical mapping model corresponding to his subschema.

V - Schema File Subset, Physical Mapping Model and System Physical File.

In the present section we will discuss the problems arising in the choice
of the storage structures.
Different kinds of physical storage structures (sequential, list, inverted, etc.)
should be available in the data base (Bracchi 1972); however, some considerations
must be beared in mind in choosing them :

1) only unidirectional queries are easily answered when simple relations are involved;

2) the storage strategy of complete relations should allow queries in both directions;

3) a careful choice must be operated on what relations to store in a same SPF;

4) an interface (the PMM) is necessary between a Schema File Subset and an SPF.

If the binary relation to be stored is a simple one (See Section III), the
structure to be chosen should allow an intelligent search on the first domain
of the relation (i.e., the domain to which the relation is negatively incident)
only; nothing similar is required on the second domain. Thus every query that
implies a search starting from the first domain can be answered; on the other
hand, a query which requires to go back to the first domain from the second one,
can be answered only by an exhaustive search.

If the number of occurrences of the relation is quite large, such a search
will be time-consuming; different solutions could be possible in a real system
for this problem : the exhaustive search could be forbidden, so that some queries are not allowed; or the system can ask the permission of the Data Base Administrator, before executing the search; or else the system can ask the user
if a reorganization of the direction of the relation and of the storage structure
is needed.

If the binary relation is a complete one, two fundamental ways of storing it
are available. The storage structure can be organized so as to allow queries star
ting from the first or the second domain indifferently, or the storage structure
can be unidirectional; in the latter case the stored relation must be duplicated
to allow queries in both directions.

Another problem concerning the storage structure is related to what relations are to be stored in the same file, i.e; how to choose a Schema File Subset. If all relations would have the same probability to be accessed, a casual
distribution of the relations into system physical files could be accepted. In
real situations, however, there will generally be some preferential progressions
of binary relations, and it will be desirable that all those relations are stored in the same file. It can also happen that some binary relations (not logically
linked) are to be contemporaneously retrieved at a high frequency; it can again
be convenient storing them in the same file. A computer algorithm for choosing
both the type of storage structure and the distribution of relations in the files
is highly desirable in implementing an information management system.

Then, whatever the choice of a Schema File Subset will be, its elements
(i.e., binary relations) must be physically represented (i.e. stored) in a Sy-

stem Physical File. This implies creation of a Physical Mapping Model, in which
two kinds of information are collected: 1) characteristics of the SPF (kind of
storage structure, physical location of the SPF, etc.) 2) mapping of the elements
of the SFS into the SPF.

Let us illustrate the above concepts with an example. The following SFS

$$(4^+, 6^+, 6^-) \longleftrightarrow SPF \quad 1$$

indicates that binary relations 4^+ (only the positive direction) and 6 (both directions) are stored in the SPF 1. The corresponding PMM will contain, for example,
the indication that relation 6^+ is stored starting from location 201, relation 6^-
starting from location 307, and relation 4^+ starting from location 201 too.

If the occurrences which must be stored are the following :

	E	N		E	S
	2936	ABRAMS		2936	10.000
rel. 6	3052	GATE	rel. 4	3052	8.000
	4036	COX		4036	18.000

a possible trivial physical structure for the SPF 1 is :

ADDRESS	E	S	pointers
201	2936	10.000	307
202	3052	8.000	309
203	4036	18.000	308

ADDRESS	N	pointers
307	ABRAMS	201
308	COX	203
309	GATE	202

Moreover it can be seen that every query concerning salaries (given an
employee code number), or names (given an employee code number), or employee code
numbers (given a name) can be immediately answered; on the other hand, a query con
cerning code numbers, given a salary, will require an exhaustive search on domain
S to be answered.

If a binary relation is deleted, or another one is added, or a simple relation is modified to a complete one (or viceversa), and the new oriented occurrences
are stored in the file, both the SFS and the PMM must be modified; if in the Schema a new direction is added in a relation but the new oriented occurrences are
not stored in the SPF, both the SFS and the PMM are left unchanged.

VI - Operating strategies

In this section we will discuss same features of an operating strategy which
could allow exploitation of the capabilities offered by the proposed multilevel
relational model.

It's not the aim of this paper to present a complete discussion; advantages
and problems arising from the proposed solutions will instead be outlined.

As illustrated in section IV, in a LMM at any level of a hierarchical relation a progression of oriented binary relations is specified leading from the key
to every domain of the same level and to every key of the inner level.

These progressions can be translated, utilizing information contained in
the PMM's and SFS's, into progressions of domains of the SPF's. This translation
can be operated having as a goal the optimization of the resulting progression.
In particular, two (not exclusive) techniques can be followed :

1) The whole (or a subset of the) progression indicated in the LMM can be substituted by equivalent progressions (see section III).

2) If an oriented binary relation is stored in more than one SPF, the most suitable SPF must be chosen.

Using the above strategies, the progression minimizing the number of SPF 's to be accessed can be found (e.g., by applying particular shortest path algorithms). We remark that the resulting progression can be quite different from the progression that was indicated by the user in defining his LMM.

The second step of the operating strategy consists of building the inverted progressions, i.e., progressions leading from every domain to the corresponding key and from every key to the key of the upper level. This task can be accomplished by changing order and sign of the oriented binary relations in the progressions specified in the LMM's. Obviously it can happen that one (or more) of the oriented binary relations so obtained is not actually existing (for example, relation 8^- does not exist, that is obtained by inverting progression 8^+ corresponding to the domain "his department" of the subschema "employee", defined in sec-tion III); in this case the system can look for equivalent progressions (in the previous example the oriented binary relation 8^- can be substituted by the progression 1^+, 6^+). Note that it can happen that for one (ore more) of the domains of the subschema it's not possible to find a progression leading from it to the corresponding key; we will discuss such a case later on.

The inverted progressions that are so obtained will then be transformed into progressions of domains of the SPF's by utilizing the same techniques illustrated above.

We will now illustrate the general characteristics of the procedures involved in the execution of a query statement, referring to the subschema "employee" which was defined in section III. We will utilize the COLARD query language (Bracchi 1972), which is a self contained language, operating on hierarchical relations, and specified by a context-free grammar. The query statements of COLARD include a conditional part which is structured as a well formed formula of first order applied predicate calculus.

Let us consider the following query :

If there is employee such that (his department = 3 and his superior = 'Abrams' and (his job = 3032 or his job = 2939) and for every son (sex of son = 'male' only if age of son < 18)) then write name, his manager, his job;

As a first execution step, it's convenient reducing, by utilizing the techniques illustrated in (Bracchi 1972), the conditional part of the query to a combination of atomic conditions (such as 'his job = 2939'), which are connected by 'and' and 'or' operators. It's then possibile, starting from the bottom level of the hierarchical relation, to select the values satisfying atomic conditions, and, by utilizing inverted progressions and operations indicated by logical connectives, to find the corresponding values for the keys; hence, the procedure is repeated for the upper level, by utilizing also the values of the lower level key. Finally, we find the desired values for the first level key, and from these values, by utilizing directed progressions, the desired values of the specified domains will be found.

The above procedure fails if it does not exist a progression leading from a domain, involved in an atomic condition, to the corresponding key. This means that atomic conditions are forbidden on the domains for which the system cannot find an inverted progression; however, it will be possible to state queries having values of these domains as results, because in this case directed progressions only are utilized.

Remark that appropriate progressions can be built at the subschema definition time (they can be automatically updated when a change is operated in the PMM's and the SFS's);overhead in the retrieval time is so avoided.

Problems arising in updating operations will be finally discussed. It's clear that a subschema can involve a large number of binary relations; then an apparently limited updetingcan actually involve a large number of operations. Moreover 'side effects' are also relevant; for example, deletion of an employee name will cause deletion of all the data correlated to it. These difficulties can be overcomed by utilizing different techniques, such as inferential procedures for deciding appropriate side effects, advices to the user on consequences of updating and eventually request of more detailed information, restriction of the updating facilities to a limited class of users.

VII - Conclusions

In this paper the features of a multilevel relational model for data base management systems have been illustrated. Five logical levels are individuated in the proposed model : the Schema; the User Subschema; the Logical Mapping Model, which represents the interface between the User and the Schema; the Schema File Subset, which represents the portion of the Schema which is stored in a single physical file; and the Physical Mapping Model, which is the interface between the physical storage and the Schema.

Binary relations are proposed as elements of the Schema, while hierarchical n-ary relations are allowed in User Subschemas. The features of the Logical and of the Physical Mapping Models has been discussed, and the file storing strategy has been examined. The physical and logical data independence, the flexibility, and the optimization features that the proposed model is offering have been discussed.

General characteristics of the operating strategies of the system have been finally illustrated.

References

- Astrahan M.M., Altman E.B., Felder P.L., Senko M.E. (1972) "Concepts of Data Independent Accessing Model". Proc. ACM - Sigfidet Workshop

- Bell C.J. (1966) "A Relational Model for Information Retrieval and the Processing of Linguistic Data". IBM Research Report RC 1705.

- Bracchi G., Fedeli A., Paolini P. (1972) "A Relational Data Base Management System" Proc. ACM 25th Annual Conference

- .... (1972) "The Architecture of an Online Information Management System". Proc. ONLINE-72 International Conference,Brunel University, Uxbridge, England.

- .... (1972) "A Language for a Relational Data Base Management System". Proc. Sixth Annual Princeton Conference.

- CODASYL (1971) Data Base Task Group Report

- Codd E.F. (1969) "Derivability, Redundancy and Consistency of Relations Stored in Large Data Banks". IBM Research Report RJ 599.

- .... (1970) "A Relational Model of Data for Large Shared Data Banks" Comm. ACM. 13, 377.

- .... (1971) "Further Normalization of the Data Base Relational Model" Courant Computer Science Symposia, Prentice Hall. 6 .

- .... (1971) "Relational Completness of Data Base Sublanguages" Courant Computer Science Symposia, Prentice Hall. 6

- Codd E.F. (1971) 'A Data Base Sublanguage Founded on the Relational Calculus" Proc. ACM - Sigfidet   Workshop.

- Collmeyer A.J. (1972) "Implications of Data Independence on the Architecture of Data Base Management Systems". Proc. ACM- Sigfidet Workshop

- Datè C.J., Hopewell P. (1971) "File Definition and Logical Data Independence" Proc. ACM - Sigfidet Workshop.

- Goldstein R.C., Strnad A.L. (1970) "The Mac AIMS Data Management System" Proc. ACM-Sigfidet Workshop.

- Jervis B., Parker J.L. (1972) "An Approach for a Working Relational Data System" Proc. ACM - Sigfidet Workshop.

- Levien R.E., Maron M.E. (1967) "A Computer System for Interence Execution and Data Retrieval" Comm. ACM 10, 715.

- Lorie R.A., Symonds A.J. (1970) "A Schema for Describing a Relational Data Base" Proc. ACM-Sigfidet Workshop

- Notley M.G. (1972) "The Peterlee IS/1 System" UKSC-0018 IBM United Kingdom Limited

- Strnad A.L. (1971) "The Relational Approach to the Management of the Data Base" Proc. IFIP Congress.

DISCUSSION

Titman :   What do you mean when you refer to a "uniform access time" ?

Bracchi :   I mean that the system presupposes no preferential path from one schema data item to another. In other words, any graph is definable in the schema, including the completely connected graph.

Titman :   It seems that the specification of preferential paths is an important part of the design process. One generally would not want completely connected graphs among the schema data items.

Bracchi :   True, but the system is flexible and does not force any a priori set of access paths on the designer.

Langefors : I have several comments. First, it is important to realize that an elementary unit of information need not always take the form of the binary relation. The unit could be ternary, as in Sundgren's model. Rather, the important point to remember is that the elementary unit or concept should be small and easy for the user to understand. Second, when separating infological from datalogical design, it is useful to use different terminology. In this way, the two levels will not become intermixed and confused.
Finally, I question the use of the word "optimal".
Information processing systems are complex enough so that the word optimal can never be used in the strict sense.
Rather, one should think of the design being sufficient for the requirements and reasonably efficient.

Abrial :   Why did you distinguish between simple and complete relations. This is only an implementation distinction. The users view is that of complete relations.

Bracchi : I agree that the users view is often complete relations, but in constructing a model, we may want to simplify this in certain situations. Thus the designer has this additional tool at his disposal.

Data Base Management, J. W. Klimbie and K. L. Koffeman, (eds.)
© *North-Holland Publishing Company (1974)*

A Descriptive Methodology suitable for multiple views
of an Information Processing System.

J.R. Lucking (International Computers Limited, Systems Programming
Division, Kidsgrove, Stoke-on-Trent, ENGLAND)

1. Introduction and Summary

This paper describes some alternative, and mutually orthogonal, views of
the architecture of an Information Processing System (IPS) incorporating
one or more shared data bases. Certain commonalities in the descriptions
of these views are noted and the paper suggests that a declarative
language based upon the fundamental concepts of Codasyl's Data Base Task
Group could be used for encoding these descriptions.

The views, of an IPS, described in this paper are that of the system's
users and that of the data base management software (DBMS) system's
implementors, the latter description being hierarchically structured.
Other views have been presented in the literature.

2. The users of an Information Processing System (IPS)

2.1   There are various classes of user at any IPS. Four classes are indicated
on Figure 1 and the following paragraphs are commentary upon this figure.

2.1.1   One class of users contains the system's 'end-users' or customers. These
users use the system routinely whilst performing their job which itself
exists independently of the system. Examples of such users are air-line
ticket staff, hospital administrators, stores clerks etc :-. Such users
will normally use some approximation to a natural language in their
interactions with the system and they need possess no computer expertise.

2.1.2   The second class of users contains the installation's application design
and programming staff. Such users write programs which transform
'English-like' requests from end-users into a series of accesses and
manipulations of the systems data bases and files. Such users will
normally use a, but not necessarily only one, standard high level programming language (e.g. COBOL) or some application package and besides
being competent programmers they also need to possess knowledge of the
operations of the organisation using the IPS.

2.1.3   The third class of users contains the installation's operating and
maintenance staff and also the data administrative staff responsible
for the design and content of the system's data bases. Such users are
responsible for ensuring that the application program's requests for data,
and other resources, are met. Such users will normally use a standard
high level programming language plus some language independent data,
and other resource, description facility but they may also use specia-
lised software implementation languages. Naturally such users require
considerable computer expertise and some of them, in particular the data
administrators, need detailed knowledge of the operations of the
organisation using the IPS.

2.1.4   The last class of users are the system programmers who wrote the operating system, the language compilers and the general purpose DBMS for
the computer or computers upon which the information processing system
is based.

2.2   Hence one may view the users of an IPS as a nest of symbiotic parasites –
        end-users depending upon application programmers who in turn depend
        upon installation staff who in turn depend upon system programmers.
        Some readers may doubt the validity of considering the latter classes
        of users as users of the IPS. But the development of an IPS is seldom,
        if ever, complete as new application programs are continually being
        added and the performance, resilience and controllability of the system
        is continually being enhanced. In order to make the enhancements these
        users must be able to determine the state of the IPS itself and this
        need for accurate and timely information about a complex situation is
        the basic reason for **originally implementing an IPS**   . Hence
        an IPS besides modelling some real world system, that is that of the
        organisation which installed the IPS, also models itself.

2.3   As an extension of the arguments above it is clear also that the IPS,
        or rather parts of it, is itself a user. For example operating systems
        often need to interrogate device and storage catalogues and certain
        application programs may select between alternative methods of
        accessing a data base after consulting similar catalogues.

3.   Mappings within an Information Processing System.

3.1   An alternative way of characterising the structure of an IPS is to
        analyse the transformations which a typical end-user's query undergoes
        within the system whilst it is being answered.
        One such query could be

        "What is the average height of men resident in Edinburgh?"

3.2.   The first transformation, which either an application program or
        programmer performs is to transform this query into

        "Calculate the arithmetic mean of item height of all person entries
        where sex item equals male and date-of-birth item is less than 560401
        and city item of address group-item equals Edinburgh".

        In other words the query is restated in a form related directly to the
        data-structure of the data base being interrogated. This transformation
        may itself be restated as a sequence of accesses, for individual entries,
        to the data base.

3.3   The next transformation is to convert the query into terms meaningful
        to the storage structure of the data base. For the purposes of this
        example the basic unit of storage structure will be termed a page and
        the query may be transformed into one of the following forms –

        (a)   What pages contain person entries where sex item is made and
                date-of-birth item is less than 560401.

        (b)   What pages contain person entries where city item of address
                item equals Edinburgh.

3.4   Further transformations are then applied to interrogate volume, device
        and,possibly archival storage catalogues to determine where the appro-
        priate pages are located and whether any devices need re-loading etc:-

3.5   Note also that there are some essential differences in the form and
        meaning of the answers to the query and its transformation.
        For example the following may be acceptable answers

(a) To the query in para. 3.1 ------ '5 feet 9 inches'
(b) To the statement in para. 3.2 --- 17539
(c) To the queries in para. 3.3 ----- lists of integers = page numbers
(d) To the queries in para. 3.4 ----- list of volume labels &
                                       device identifiers.

(Note - 17539 is the millemetric equivalent of 5 feet 9 inches).

3.6   Thus there are at least four 'semantic-levels' at which a query is
       processed. At the highest (end-user's) level the query is posed in terms
       of 'intelligible data' or information, and then in terms of 'data' and
       'storage', and finally in terms of media or 'devices'. These levels
       exhibit the same type of symbiotic and parasitic interrelation as the
       classes of user described in paragraph 2 ; a diagram similar to figure 1
       may be used to illustrate this interrelation.

3.7   Structures

       At each of the levels indicated above the IPS exhibits a structure to
       its users. At the intelligible data or information level this structure
       is essentially that of the real world, or at least of the real world as
       viewed from within the (IPS-using) organisation's ambit - as such it is
       conveniently described in terms of entities, their attributes and their
       inter-relationships.
       At the data level the structure is essentially that of the data
       processing procedures used by the organisation and it is conveniently
       described in terms of entries (or records), items and inter-record rela-
       tionships. At the storage level the structure is essentially the view
       provided by the operating system of the storage capability at the
       installation - as such it is conveniently described in terms of pages
       (blocks), bytes (or words) and relationships between pages.
       At the media device this structure describes essentially the physical
       characteristics of the storage media and their handlers.

4.   One of the main reasons for an organisation installing an IPS incor-
       porating a data base is to foster the sharing, by the organisation's
       various parts, of the system. Such sharing takes place at each of the
       semantic levels described above for just as end-users share the use
       of intelligible-data (information) so also do application programs,
       access routines and the constituent modules of the general purpose DBMS
       and operatin system share the data, storage and media volumes/devices.
       Some mechanisms are necessary in order to control this sharing of an
       IPS's information, data, storage and media resources. By analogy with
       many real world systems (for examole commodity markets) concerned with
       the control and allocation of resources and also by analogy with resource
       allocation algorithms used within currently available operating systems
       such mechanisms are based upon the availability of two types of quanti-
       tative and qualitative descriptions. The first type describes the
       totality of the resource which is available for allocation and the
       second describes the requirement, per user, for a resource.
       Figure 2 demonstrates these two types of description for the semantic
       levels and queries described in paragraphs 3.1 to 3.4.

       In the Codasyl specifications, which apply to the semantic level called
       data, the two types of description are termed schema and subschema.
       At this level there is an additional reason for explicitly differen-
       tiating between the two types of description as the languages used to
       encode a description of a data requirement may be designed to be compa-
       tible with the various high level languages used for writing application
       programs.

The existence of these two types of resource description also provides
the user, that is the user of a requirement description, with independence from other users of that resource and also, at least conceptually, with independence from the actual availability of that resource.
At the data-level this need for data-independence is an often recurring
theme in the literature ; though the literature is also remarkable in
its lack of definitive mechanisms for achieving such data-independence,
particularly dynamically, without severe performance degradation.

5.   A hierarchically structured view of an IPS.

5.1   Hierarchically structured modelling of software systems.

Within the last few years various papers advocating a methodical
approach to the design of a software system involving a gradual elabo-
ration of the system's description have been published. The methodo-
logies normally involve the division of the software system into a
tree-like structure of 'sub-systems' comprised of 'sub-subsystems' or
'components' with certain constraints on intercommunication between
the components and the level of a component being controlled by the
fineness with which the component is specified.

5.2   The major sub-systems of an IPS.

Figure 3 depicts the first two levels of the structure of an IPS.
The top row shows the IPS as a 'black-box'
which receives requests for information or other services and provides
either that information or that service. The previous sections of this
paper describe some functional aspects of this black-box.

The second row of the diagram indicates that the IPS has to possess
knowledge of the system's users, data or information, of its own facilities and of the computers facilities in order to service the user
requests. Further as more than one user may simultaneously request some
service from the system then the system must also possess knowledge
of all the services it is providing. Conceptually the action of these
five subsystems are synchronised by a single job description record
whose creation (and final erasure on completion of the job) is performed
by the JOB subsystem. The USER subsystem is responsible, for example,
for checking that the user requesting the service described by the
job description record is allowed to do so, the DATA subsystem is
responsible for providing the information, data, storage and media
resources required, the CODE subsystem administers the programs etc: -
necessary to service the job and the MACHINE subsystem administers the
computer and its hardware and firmware.

At this level of detail the number of parameters in the job description
record is rather small, for example in COBOL notation it could be

```
01, JOB DESCRIPTION,
      02, USER-NAME, PIC IS X(20),
      02, TERMINAL-ID, PIC IS 9 (6),
      02, FILE-NAME, PIC IS X(10),
      02, PROGRAM-NAME, PIC IS X (20),
      02, JOB-NUMBER, PIC IS 9 (10),
      02, REQUEST-CODE, PIC IS X,
      02, TIME-STAMP,
            03, DATE, PIC IS 9 (6),
            03, TIME, PIC IS 9 (4),
      02, JOB-STATUS, PIC IS 9 (5),
```

Each subsystem is here pictured as a black box wich performs some service as specified in the job description record. Naturally each system contains files of data necessary for their internal working and each has an internal structure, that for the DATA subsystem is shown in figure 4.

5.3   The DATA subsystems structure.

Figure 4 illustrates four further levels of the structure of an IPS. At the top level the DATA subsystem is exhibited as three components, one processing (data etc.) declarative statements, one processing (data etc.) manipulative statements and the last administering the control of the data system. Successive levels are then exhibited in which these components' constituents are analysed further.

Only one branch of this tree is considered below, this is that which is effectively a description of the run-time system involved in a general purpose DBMS of the host-language-type, in other words it describes the software which obeys DML commands. This branch is shown in figure 5 using double lines. The basic functions of the various components in this branch of the tree are as follows.

5.3.1   The Mapping Specification processor determines whether the stated mapping requires processing. The mapping itself is defined by two descriptions each describing either a requirement for a resource or the availability of a resource at the same or adjacent semantic levels (as defined in para.3). To do so this processor needs at least three further data items in the job description record and the FILE-NAME item of this record may well be expanded to :

        02, FILE-NAME,
            03, NAME, PIC IS X (20)
            03, REQUIREMENT DESCRIPTION NAME, PIC IS X (20)
            03, SOURCE DESCRIPTION NAME, PIC IS X (20)
            03, MAP-NAME, PIC IS X (20),
            03, MAP-STATUS, PIC IS 1,

On the basis of this additional data and also using a catalogue of processed maps the processor may determine whether the map needs processing and which of the map-processors is required. Note MAP-STATUS is set to 1 when the mapping specification has been processed.

5.3.2   The Data-to-Storage map processor's function is primarily to control the interaction between its constituent components, all of which are fairly major blocks of code. The first two of these blocks, Map Analysis and DML-Generation, are applicable only if the Map is not specified as a program incorporating DML commands - in other words if the map is specified via mechanisms involving name matching within the two resource descriptions or some specially designed DML macro facility. The Map Analysis process is itself shown further divided into blocks which analyse both the storage structure and any statistics, either specified by a data administrator or gathered during routine system operation, on the frequency of access to the data and storage ; a further module determines an optimal access strategy. The DML-generation block expands any DML macros or generates any necessary DML (plus high level language code) necessary to provide the optimal access methods. The DML compilation and Storage (Structure) Manipulation Language blocks together complete the processing of this data to storage mapping specification by generating the necessary assembler language (or other implementation language) code augmented by commands to manipulate the data-storage resources of the system ; this code is inserted into a system library and is available for use as required.

To control the operation of these lower-level subsystems the job-description record needs to be specified in much more detail and in practice the complexity involved is sufficient to require that it be specified as a set of records particularly as the same fields are available for access by components of the other major subsystems (i.e. JOB, USERS etc: -) of the system.

6.   Language implications.

The last paragraph has demonstrated that even a highly constrained model of the software comprising an IPS exhibits much structural complexity. If the dynamic and static relationships between the elements of this structure, for example, relationships between subsystems like 'called-by', 'shares data with', 'callable by' are added then this structure becomes a network rather than a tree. The description of such a model requires the use of a declarative language just as the speci-fication of any application program involves the use of such a language.

Previous paragraphs of this paper have argued that a data description language is in fact a special case of a more general declarative language namely one which describes the media, and storage used to store data and also describes the information content of the data.

Such a language has to provide certain facilities along the lines suggested below.

6.1   The language has to contain facilities for declaring various types of object and for describing the components which constitute an occurence of an object-type. At the four semantic levels defined in para.4 these objects and components are often named respectively entities and attri-butes, entries (records) and items, pages (blocks) and words, tracks and bits.

6.2   The language has to contain facilities for declaring the relationships which may or must exist between objects. Two types of relationship are normally considered important.

One is used to specify some convenient subdivision of the population of objects being described normally for some physical or historical rather than logical reason. At the four semantic levels of paragraph 4 these subdivisions are often termed clusters, areas (or realms), cylinders (or extents or physical files) and volumes though at the intelligible data level the concept is only rarely used. Essentially such relationships are recognised only as a convenient way of naming a subdivision of objects for allocation purposes.

The second type of relationship is used to specify some logical connec-tion between two or more objects. Many occurrences of such relationships may exist and any object may participate in more than one relationship occurence. Such relationships are seldom considered at the lowest semantic level (media) of paragraph 4 but at the other levels they are often termed relationships, sets and files.

6.3   A procedural (or object-manipulation) language is required so that operations upon the objects may be performed. Its requirements will not be analysed in great depth in this paper though there are obvious simi-larities between the types of functions performed by procedural languages operating at the four semantic levels described in paragraph 3 and also upon the model of the software system described in paragraph 5.

7.   Conclusions

The conclusion of this paper is that it is technically feasible to
develop from the basic constructs of the Codasyl Schema Data Description
Language a declarative and directive language suitable for use by all
the users of an Information Processing System. The term user is used
above in its most widest sense and includes the implementors of the
basic software needed to support an IPS, the implementors of the IPS
itself, the development and operating staff of the IPS, and those
'end-users' who use the IPS routinely as a part of their job-function
which itself is independent of the existence of the IPS.

The paper has shown that all such users interact with the IPS in terms
of some naturally and conveniently occurring group — this group being
termed a module of code, a record, an object, a block etc. Each such
group may be subdivided, for example into instructions, or data-items,
or measurable attributes, or word etc., but, more importantly, defines
a context within which occurrences of groups may be named or identified.
The totality of occurrences of such groups may for reasons of convenience
be sub-divided and any group-occurrence may be related to other group-
occurrences, such relations being maintained by the IPS. Hence the
Schema DDL of Codasyl allows for the declaration and description of
records, data-items, areas and sets. The Schema DDL also contains
directive statements to indicate to the IPS how to process occurrences
of these declared constructs.

Certain logistic arguments which have not been expounded in this paper
exist for developing a declarative language suitable for use by all an
IPS's users. For example, widespread use of such a language should
narrow the currently widening gulf between IPS implementors and IPS
users thus permitting a freer exchange of ideas and reducing the cost
of training IPS specialists.

8.   Acknowledgements

The author is grateful to his employers, International Computers Limited,
for permission to publish this paper and for supporting his Codasyl
activities; he is also grateful for the many discussions with colleagues
and fellow members of Codasyl's committees which have contributed to
the content of this paper.

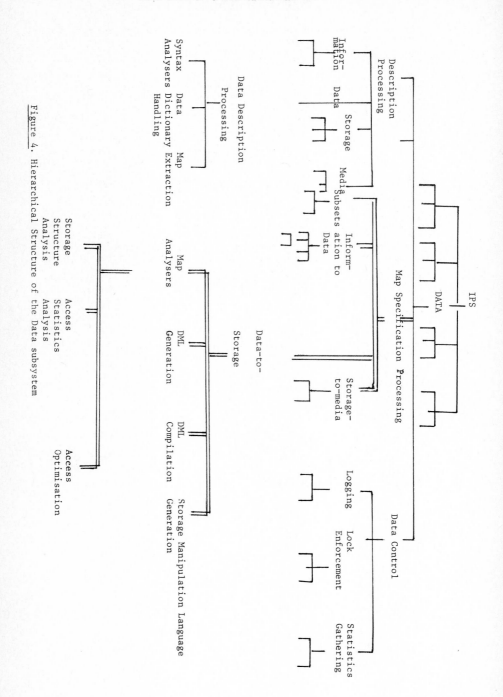

Figure 4. Hierarchical Structure of the Data subsystem

SEMANTIC LEVEL	DESCRIPTION OF REQUIREMENT FOR RESOURCE	DESCRIPTION OF AVAILABLE RESOURCE
INTELLIGIBLE DATA (INFORMATION)	Information about the height of men living in Edinburgh.	Information about people residing in Scotland, the houses they live in, their incomes, hobbies, etc: –
DATA	Occurrences of PEOPLE record-types whose contents obeys a particular constraint.	Occurrences of records of types PERSON, HOUSE, SCHOOL, CLUBS, EMPLOYMENT, etc:–...
STORAGE	The pages (blocks)containing particular record occurrences	The complete storage capacity of the media at the installation.
MEDIA / DEVICES	Those media volumes and devices containing particular pages.	All the media volumes and devices available at the installation.

Figure 2. Table exhibiting the four semantic levels provided
by an Information Processing System and the sharing
at each level.

J.R. Lucking

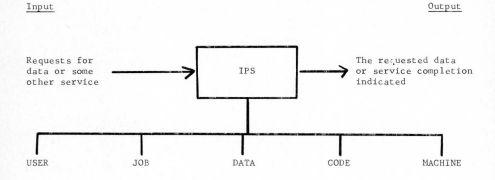

Input   Output

Requests for   The requested data
data or some   IPS   or service completion
other service   indicated

USER   JOB   DATA   CODE   MACHINE

Privacy   Scheduling   Description handling   Compilers   Interrupt
Security   Specification   Data(etc)scheduling   Loaders   handlers
Priority   JCL processing   Map handling   Library   Virtual
Check Point   System Model   Storage

Figure 3.   Major Subsystems of an Information Processing System.

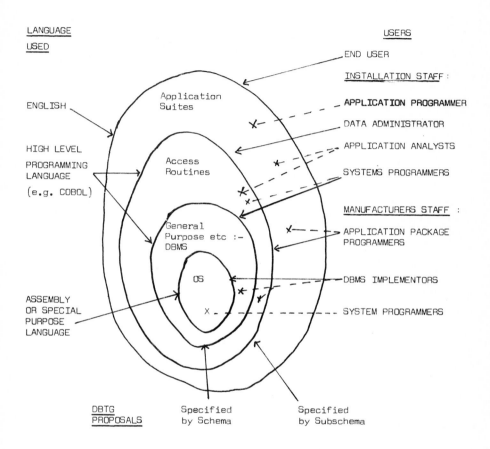

Figure 1   Users of an Information Processing System

Legend (a)   On the right hand side, dotted-lines imply 'provides',
                  solid lines imply 'use'.

  (b)   The ring labelled General Purpose DBMS also contains the
                  standard language compilers for the IPS.

  (c)   The ring labelled 'Access Routines' also contains precompilers
                  for enforcing implementation standards upon application pro-
                  grammers, data-base-procedures as defined by DBTG and other
                  programmer support packages.

Bibliography and references

Data Base Aspects

1.   The Data Base Task Group Report to the Codasyl Programming Language
        Committee — April, 1971

        Available in Europe from both the British Computers Society
        (29, Portalnd Place, LONDON) or from the IFIPS Administrative Group
        (IAG) in Amsterdam. In USA as National Bureau of Standards Handbook 113.

2.
        The Codasyl Journal of Data Description Language Development Available
        in Europe from IAG and BCS (1 3.00).

3.   The Codasyl Systems Committee reports

        (a)   Survey of Generalised Data Base Management Systems May, 69
        (b)   Feature Analysis of G1 DBMS May, 71

        Both these were available from the ACM and IAG.

4.
        Guide-Share-Requirements for Data Base Systems.

5.   Suggested approach to Disc File Labelling Standards.
        A white cover document available from ECMA.

Structural Modelling

6.   A Modular Approach to File System Design — by S. Madnick &
        J.W. Alsop II — IAG Journal Vol. 2 No. 3 (also 1969 SJCC).

7.   A Software Engineering Approach within ICL. D.J. Pearson
                  Computer Weekly July 26, Aug. 2, 9. 1973.

8.   Software Engineering Reports of NATO sponsored Conferences
                  January '69 and April, 1970. (Available from NATO in
                  Brussels).

DISCUSSION

 Steel   : Network structures are certainly useful in certain contexts,
but they are not always useful. Users should have the opportunity of choosing
structural representations which fit their needs and increase productivity.

Lucking   : I agree

Tsichritzis : Along the same line, one must be very hesitent in using words
like "natural". Each data management system today promotes its own view of
data as the "natural" one, yet each is different, and of course none arise
in nature.

Nijssen   : The relational view "versus" the network view is a non-issue.
The real issue is the users' ability to define collections of data and functions over those collections.

Bayer   : I sense that there has been a lot of controversy at this conference regarding issues which I will categorize as issues in optimization.
While the means whereby a structure is realized may be transparent to a user,
the performance of that structure will not be transparent.
There are at least two kinds of optimization to be kept in mind. On the one
hand, there are the local improvements which can be gained by having control
of certain access paths. This kind of control yields modest performance improvements and can probably be automated, as has taken place in the field of
compilers. On the other hand, there is a second kind of optimization. Namely,
that which deals with simplifying the complexity of algorithms.
What I have in mind is that sometimes by using a completely different structure and algorithm, one can realize fantastic speed-ups in appropriate
situations. This kind of optimization does not seem so amenable to automation.
For example, when dealing with binary relations, where one may have to compute
the transitive closure, one can store the transitive closure or derive it
when needed.

Since the fastest algorithm for computing the transitive closure is of order n^3, one can see the differences in performance that a user may see. One of the hard jobs for a data administrator will be to choose at this second level of optimization.

Data Base Management, J. W. Klimbie and K. L. Koffeman, (eds.)
© *North-Holland Publishing Company (1974)*

CONCURRENT UPDATE CONTROL and DATABASE INTEGRITY

by

Gordon C. Everest

Assistant Professor
Graduate School of Business Administration
Management Information Systems Research Center
UNIVERSITY OF MINNESOTA
U. S. A.   55455

CONCURRENT UPDATE CONTROL AND DATABASE INTEGRITY

1. INTRODUCTION

The uncontrolled operation of concurrent processes can have an
adverse affect on the integrity of a database. This paper explores
the problem of concurrent processes, how concurrency can affect database
integrity and process integrity, and evaluates several suggested solutions
to the problem in the light of database integrity.

A straightforward solution to the concurrency problem involves some
form of exclusive use of resources. However, mutual exclusion leads to
the possibility of deadlock. Preventing deadlock is the real problem of
concurrent operation, a problem for which a desirable solution has not
yet been found. Aspects of a desirable solution are discussed later in
this paper.

The problems of concurrent update and deadlock prevention are here
addressed exclusively from the standpoint of maintaining database integrity.
The problem and approaches to its solution are discussed from the viewpoint of the database management system rather than the job management
system (the operating system responsible for scheduling and controlling
the execution of processes). Considerable literature in recent years
has focused on the problem of concurrency and deadlock with the objective
of scheduling the execution of processes (tasks) and the allocation of
resources (including data resources) to the processes.

An examination of concurrency from the standpoint of integrity of
shared data leads to some interesting observations and conclusions. Data
as a shared resource exhibits some unique characteristics not possessed
by other resources within a computer system. Concurrent sharing of data
demands a re-examination of some suggested lockout mechanisms and approaches to deadlock prevention.

2. THE INTEGRITY OF SHARED DATA

Moving toward the concept of a shared corporate database, an organization finds it increasingly important to maintain the integrity of shared data resources. Users who previously held exclusive administrative control over the data they used, will be reluctant to delegate the responsibility for maintaining database integrity to a database administrator without assurances that adequate mechanisms and procedures are set up to maintain database integrity.

The willingness of users and managers to release control of needed data resources, trust someone else to look after the data, and have confidence in using the data, depends upon the establishment of formal procedures for the maintenance of database integrity.

In the broadest sense, database integrity implies the completeness, soundness, purity, veracity, and confidentiality of data. Database integrity involves:
- protecting the _existence_ of the database through physical security, and backup and recovery measures.
- maintaining the _quality_ of the database through input validation, diagnostic routines to ensure that the data always conforms to its definition (a definition which includes validation criteria on the stored data), and controlling processes which update the database.
- maintaining the _privacy_ of the stored data through isolation, access regulation, encryption, and monitoring.

Control of concurrent update processes contributes to database quality maintenance. Proper control of concurrent update processes is a necessary condition (though not a sufficient condition) to sharing common data resources at the same time.

At an elementary level, two or more users (or processes) can share the same data resource by taking turns. In other words, the users use

the resource sequentially rather than concurrently. Such an approach
poses no threat to database integrity and is often used as an administrative solution to the problem of concurrent update. The ultimate in
sharing is achieved when multiple processes are permitted to operate on
the database simultaneously. This can result in some rather peculiar
situations which threaten database integrity. The next section briefly
describes the problem of concurrent update processes.

3. THE PROBLEM OF CONCURRENT UPDATE

When a process updates a database concurrently with another update
process, the integrity of the database is threatened. Similarly, the
integrity of a reading process is threatened by a concurrent update process.
Loss of process integrity can give the appearance of database integrity
loss. Use of a lockout mechanism is the obvious solution but that can
lead to deadlock. Several approaches to handling deadlock have been suggested. This section expands on these ideas from the unique perspective
of data resources.

3.1 Concurrent Updates Threaten Database Integrity

Suppose that two concurrent processes, P and Q , desire to update
the same record, A , at the same time. Since all requests to access the
database are funnelled through a single process or function (the Database
Manager) such requests are ultimately handled in a sequential fashion.
Suppose further that the following sequence of events takes place (refer
to Figure 1):
1. Process P requests and receives a copy of record A in its buffer
    (see Figure la).
2. Process Q also requests and receives a copy of record A in its
    buffer (see Figure lb).
3. Process P modifies record A (see Figure lb) and requests that
    it be written back into the database (see Figure lc).
4. Process Q then modifies its copy of record A (see Figure lc)
    and requests that it be written back into the database (see
    Figure ld).

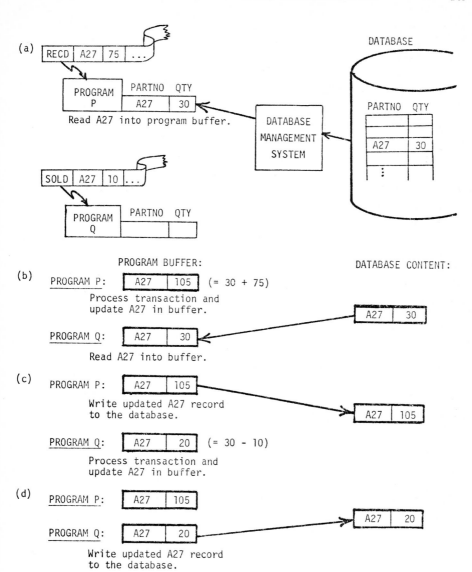

Figure 1.   Concurrent Update Destroys Database Integrity.

As a result of Q's action, the update of A performed by P is lost
forever. This example demonstrates the problem of concurrent processes
and the need to control their interaction to protect database integrity
and insure the validity of the actions of the users of those resources.[1]

3.2 An Obvious Solution: Lockout

The general solution to this problem seems rather obvious--process
Q must not be permitted to acquire resource A until process P is
finished using it. That is, when one process is updating part of a database,
another process must not be permitted to intervene by updating the same
data. We say "seems rather obvious," but the solution gives rise to a
whole new set of complex problems. Lockout provides a solution to the
above breach of integrity by reserving a part of the database (or resource)
for exclusive use by a single process. Lockout is a process of mutual
exclusion in which the object data of the multiple update actions is
assigned exclusively to at most one update process at any one time. The
reason for this reservation is to protect the state or integrity of the
data.

> RULE 1: If data is to be altered by a process, then the
>   entire sequence of events essential to the
>   alteration must be protected from any inter-
>   ference which would affect the proper completion
>   of the change.

If a lockout mechanism is not used to control concurrent updates,
the integrity of the database can be lost and never detected. For example,

---

[1] A most understandable and more detailed discussion of the problems
of simultaneous access and simultaneous update is found in Edward Yourdon,
Design of On-Line Computer Systems, Englewood Cliffs, NJ: Prentice-Hall,
1972, Chapter L.

simultaneous posting of improperly recorded receipts and withdrawals from inventory may be improperly recorded and the resulting discrepancy might be attributed to theft (if the book inventory level exceeds the actual inventory count and assuming the auditors do not discover the incorrect posting). From the standpoint of database integrity a mechanism of mutual exclusion or lockout is needed to control concurrent update processes.

3.3 Process Integrity Loss: The Appearance of Database Integrity Loss

Another situation calls for a somewhat weaker level of control. Rule 2 is primarily intended to protect the integrity of a process.

> RULE 2: If a process is reading data but not changing
> it, then that process requires protection against
> any changes in the data which would affect the
> validity of the whole set of data the process
> receives.

It is popular to refer to rule 1 as "exclusive control" and rule 2 as "shared control". When a process gains exclusive control over a part of the database, no other process is allowed to look at it or change it. When a process is given shared control over data, concurrent processes are permitted only to look at it but not change it. As will be argued later, this popular interpretation is misleading. It reflects a concern for resource allocation rather than for database integrity.

To illustrate the need for shared control, consider a process designed to produce an accounting trial balance. It operates by successively printing the current balance of each account in the code of accounts. If a concurrent process is allowed to post transactions to the accounts while the trial balance is being prepared, it is possible that the debit of a transaction is posted in time to be included in the trial balance while the corresponding credit of that transaction is not posted in time to be included. The resulting trial balance would be out of balance.

The integrity of the process was destroyed and, although the integrity
of the database was actually maintained, it will appear to have been
lost.

3.4 Lockout Leads to Deadlock

The use of a lockout mechanism to control the interaction of concurrent processes can lead to an even more difficult problem. Suppose
that two process, P and Q , are contending for the use of two resources,
A and B , and that the following sequence of events ensue:
1. Process P requests and acquires exclusive control of resource A .
2. Process Q requests and acquires exclusive control of resource B .
3. Process P requests resource B but must wait until process Q
    releases it.
4. Process Q requests resource A but must similarly wait until
    process P releases it.
At this point in time both processes are waiting for each other and will
wait indefinitely. Such a situation has been called deadlock, interlock,
or deadly embrace. At step 4 the system would be able to detect the existence of a deadlock.

Deadlock results when a set of resources are exclusively assigned
to a set of processes and each process cannot continue unless it is
assigned a resource which another process is using. Deadlock is a
logical problem which arises when concurrent processes can hold resources while requesting additional resources. In the simplest case,
process P holds resource A and requests B , while process Q holds
resource B and requests A . Neither can continue. All such processes
are permanently blocked from further processing.

3.5 Approaches to Handling Deadlock

If update processes are allowed to run concurrently, some form of
lockout mechanism is required to protect the integrity of the database,
and, if a lockout mechanism is used, the possibility of deadlock exists.

Three possible strategies for handling deadlock are ignorance, detection, and prevention.

3.5.1 <u>Ignoring Deadlock</u>. If a lockout mechanism is used and explicit provisions are not built into the system to detect deadlock, it can only be discovered by external means -- an astute machine operator, a programmer waiting to get his job back, a user waiting for an answer, or when the system is shut down and active (but blocked) processes are discovered.

For most computer installations, deadlock has not been a problem of major practical importance, but the factors which increase the possibility of deadlock are on the rise in newer installations. These factors include greater cost of the total pool of shared system re- sources, a larger number of online users demanding realtime response, and more significantly, the trend toward large, online, shared databases.

3.5.2 <u>Detecting Deadlock</u>. If the sequence of events described above is allowed to occur, a deadlock situation can be detected at step 4. A deadlock situation does not exist prior to step 4, for if process Q does not request resource A , both processes can continue processing. Several authors have presented methods for detecting a deadlock situation.[1]

The only solution to a detected deadlock situation is to release some resources by terminating one (or more) of the blocked processes and letting the remaining processes continue. While detecting deadlocks may itself be a difficult task, the real problem from a data viewpoint, is getting out of a deadlock situation gracefully while maintaining the integrity of the resources (the database). Consider the problem of trying to undo a large amount of update activity performed between steps 2 and 3 above.

---

[1]See, for example, Peter J. Denning. "Third Generation Computer Systems," <u>Computing Surveys</u> (3:4), 1971 December, pages 197ff; and E. G. Coffman, Jr., M. J. Elphick and A. Shoshani, "System Deadlocks," <u>Computing Surveys</u> (3:2), 1971 June, pages 73ff.

3.5.3 <u>Preventing Deadlock</u>. Since backing out can be practically impossible, it is most desirable to prevent deadlocks from arising in the
first place. Therein lies the central difficulty. So far, all database-
viable proposals for the prevention of deadlocks have required the process
to state *a priori* in some form all the resources needed (memory blocks,
communication lines, input-output devices, data channels, processors,
data) before it begins processing. For a generalized process which
is highly data driven, such a requirement may be nearly impossible to
meet.

In writing processes it is increasingly necessary for the process
to perceive its resource needs as early as possible, to establish its
pattern of processing, and to explicitly communicate this to the system.

3.6 <u>Search for a Solution</u>

In summary, when lockout mechanisms are used to control concurrent
update processes and protect database integrity, adequate mechanisms are
needed to prevent, or at least detect, the more general problem of deadlock. It is a more general problem because it relates to the demands of
processes for exclusive use of <u>any</u> system resource -- data, communication
channels, programs, disk space, tape drives, main memory, or a central
processing unit. Therefore, the discussion of lockout and deadlock
problems and approaches to their solution cannot assume only data resources. Discussion must proceed from interacting concurrent processes
and the synchronization or control of their interactions.

The subject of controlling concurrent processes and preventing
deadlocks has been treated in some detail in the literature. The
wealth of literature in the last few years is evidence that many people
are seeking, proposing, and analyzing various approaches to this
exceedingly difficult problem.

When reviewing the literature on concurrent process interaction, one can detect some rather subtle differences in objectives, for example, synchronize interactions with respect to data, synchronize interaction with respect to communication between processes, allocate system resources (a prerequisite to scheduling the processes), schedule process execution, prevent deadlock, or detect and recover from deadlock. All of these objectives are interrelated in various ways. The focus here is on synchronizing interactions with respect to data.

From the standpoint of database resources, no viable technical solutions have yet been found. The threat to database integrity resulting from the concurrent execution of processes has so far been handled using gross internal measures, such as lockout on the basis of a whole file, or handled by external administrative procedures, such as controlling the scheduling of jobs. Jobs which access the same part of a database are run in sequence rather than concurrently. While these solutions may be acceptable for batch operations, they are quite unsatisfactory for online systems when several people and processes should be able to manipulate the database on demand, even at the same time.

Where an author has not considered the uniqueness of data as a resource but treated a file as the single data entity or as the unit of resource allocation, his statement of the problem and suggested solutions must be re-examined with a primary focus on maintaining data integrity. First, the unique problems of data need exploration. Then aspects of coordination with other resources under control of the job manager need to be examined in achieving the goals of mutual exclusion and the prevention of deadlock. The latter has not yet been seriously attempted (see section 9.).

4. DESIRABLE CRITERIA FOR CONTROLLING CONCURRENT UPDATE PROCESSES

The following list of criteria are put forth as being desirable
in the design of a mechanism for controlling concurrent update processes.
No prior implication is intended that these criteria are all attainable.
In fact, as will be shown, some of them are mutually exclusive.

- keep it simple for the programmers who write process specifications;
  place a minimum of restrictions and demand a minimum of discipline
  on the programmer; ideally, he should not be concerned with what
  else is going on when his program is in execution, he should be
  able to assume he is alone in the world making simple declarations
  that are meaningful to him in order to protect the integrity
  of the process.

- allow a process to request any number of resources as needed and
  release them when no longer needed.

- permit a reasonable level of resolution in the data when the process
  specifies its use of resources in the database -- at least at the
  level of record or entry instances.

- allow a process to continue execution after being denied exclusive
  control of data in the database.

- avoid permanent block, a condition where the scheduler consistently
  bypasses a process requesting exclusive use of a resource because
  of a continuous stream of allocations which could lead to deadlock
  if the request were granted.

- prevent deadlock and avoid the necessity of backout; do not assume
  that a programmer knows what to do to backout of a deadlock
  situation.

- protect the integrity of the database in spite of the actions of the
  process; do not place the burden of database integrity on the
  programmer, he should not be responsible for data integrity when
  it is threatened by the interaction of concurrent update processes;
  do not assume the programmer knows what he is doing.

- do not depend upon external administrative procedures for sequencing
  the running of processes so as to avoid conflict and thereby
  maintain database integrity; such a dependence is intolerable
  in an online, realtime database environment.

5. DATA AS THE OBJECT OF RESOURCE ALLOCATION TO CONCURRENT PROCESSES

In attempting to characterize data as the object of resource
allocation to concurrent processes, it will be useful to classify all
types of resources.

5.1 Consumable Resources

The first distinction is made between consumable and reusable resources. Once a consumable resource is assigned to a process, it is
consumed and no longer available for reallocation. This would include
card images from a card reader, and messages and signals such as "ready-
to-send," "ready-to-receive," and "receipt acknowledged" transmitted in
interprocess communication.

5.2 Reusable, Conserved Resources

A reusable resource can be reassigned to another process when released
by a using process. Reusable resources are further divided into those that
follow the law of conservation and those that do not because they can be
reused an unlimited number of times. A conserved resource is usually a
physical resource which inherently can have only one owner at any point
in time. For a conserved resource, lockout is inherent in its allocation
to a process. For example, it is physically impossible for a printer to
print two lines of output simultaneously. Similarly, a clocking mechanism
is used to resolve conflicting references to main memory, using read-
followed-by-write as an indivisible operation. Undesirable interaction
of processes cannot destroy the integrity of a conserved resource because
simultaneous use is impossible. Alternatively, if the internal state of
the reusable resource can be modified during use, it is a conserved reusable resource only if it can be initialized upon assignment to another
task.

5.3 Data: A Reusable, Unconserved Resource

Stored data is an unconserved resource and differs in some fundamental respects from conserved resources. Lockout is not inherent in

the allocation of data to a process. (Lockout is inherent with respect
to the physical access mechanism but not the data being accessed.) The
same stored data can be accessed over and over again. If lockout is not
imposed when the process intends to update the data, the integrity of
the database may be threatened.

Unlike processes which use conserved resources, processes which
use an unconserved resource must be distinguished by what they intend
to do with the resource. It is absolutely necessary for a process to
declare its intention to either read only or modify the data resource.
If it intends to modify, all other processes which intend to modify that
same object data must be locked out until the first process is finished
with the object data.

If a process only intends to read the object data, it must still
have the option of locking out all other processes which intend to modify
the data it is reading. A process which only wants to read some object
data, always has the option of reading, whether or not the object data is
locked by some other process. Furthermore, it is impossible for a concurrent update process to make the lockout decision (exclusive versus shared
control) for the reading process. Data can be read concurrently by any
number of processes but can only be modified by one process at a time.
These ideas are sometimes obscured when authors discuss the control of
concurrent access to data.

Whereas pre-emption may be an option with conserved resources, it
is never a viable option with data undergoing modification by a process.
Pre-emption means that a previously allocated resource can be taken away
from a process before the process voluntarily releases it. In other words,
a process must be prepared to release on demand a previously allocated
resource. Such a resource is called a pre-emptive resource.

Generally, when the responsibility for concurrency control rests
with the operating system, the operating system allocates data resources
to concurrent update processes at the file level. In some cases, a process can only request lockout on one file at a time with the result that
database integrity is threatened when the process must update more than

one file simultaneously. If the operating system permits a process to
separately issue exclusive requests on multiple files in succession the
possibility for deadlock exists.

In most environments sharing a large database, lockout control at
the file level is unacceptable. It must be possible for the process to
request lockout on a smaller subset of the database. The general method
of identifying data in interrogation requests can be used to identify
data which is to be the object of lockout. The identification is given
in terms of named data items in named group, record, or entry types, satisfying a Boolean selection expression.

In the design of a database management system, the unit of data in
terms of which the object data is identified, can be at the file level
for coarse resolution or at the item instance (value) level for the finest
degree of resolution. With respect to lockout and concurrency control,
there are arguments for selecting each extreme in this spectrum of levels
of data identification. Resolution at the file level, makes it easier
to prevent deadlock because the small number of resource units makes it
easier for a process to *a priori* declare its set of needed resources.
Resolution at the item level represents the ultimate in sharing but results in more bookkeeping overhead. Since lockout is placed on smaller
pieces the possibility of deadlock is reduced but it also makes it practically impossible for a process to specify its set of needed resources
a priori.

6. LOCKOUT OF CONCURRENT UPDATE PROCESSES

A necessary condition for controlling concurrent update processes
is that each process declare to the system that other update processes
be locked out from operating on identified object data. Such a lockout
request is manadatory if the requesting process intends to update the
identified object data. Notice the distinction here -- the process is
not requesting that a particular data resource be allocated or attached
to the process, rather a request is made to lockout all attempts by
concurrent processes to update the object data while it is being used.

If the requesting process only intends to read the object data, it has the option of requesting that concurrent update processes be locked out or not. Since the integrity of a reading process can be threatened when concurrent update is allowed, the reading process must be allowed to have a request enforced that certain identified object data will not undergo any modification until the process is finished reading. To the system, lockout requests from reading and modifying processes are the same -- they want concurrent updates locked out. They are not requesting full exclusive control of the object data, only <u>exclusive</u> <u>control</u> <u>with</u> <u>respect</u> <u>to</u> <u>update</u> <u>actions</u>.

In terms of maintaining database integrity, the above discussion indicates that the request to make data available to a process need not be coupled with the request to lockout concurrent update processes. In some systems, the lock and unlock requests are implicit in the open and close statements. Such a procedure puts an unnecessary burden on the system in attempting to protect data integrity from concurrent update processes.

In 1966, Dennis and Van Horn proposed a locking mechanism to control concurrent updates. Since then, several variations and improvements have been suggested in the literature.[1] Within a process desiring lockout of concurrent updates, the following could be written:

```
LOCK        identified-object-data
    .        ⎫  section of code from which concurrent
    .        ⎬  update is to be locked out
    .        ⎭
UNLOCK   [identified-object-data]
```

LOCK instructs the system to test for a lock on the object data which was set by a concurrent process. If the lock is set, the system can

---

[1] Jack B. Dennis and Earl C. Van Horn, "Programming Semantics for Multiprogrammed Computations," <u>Communications of the ACM</u> (9:3), 1966 March, page 147; for a discussion of and references to several variations of lockout, see J. L. Baer, "A Survey of Some Theoretical Aspects of Multiprocessing," <u>Computing Surveys</u> (5:1), March, pages 35-36.

put the requesting process into a wait state and keep testing the lock until it is unset. In addition, the system could queue the requests for each resource to ensure a first-in-first-out or a priority allocation to requesting processes. Alternatively, the system could return control to the requesting process indicating that the lock was set, a "busy signal", and to try again later. The alternative approach gives the process an opportunity to do some other processing in the interim instead of waiting idle.

If none of the identified object data is locked by another process, the LOCK statement would set a lock on the object data and return control to the requesting process. The test and set functions of the LOCK instructions must be indivisible, that is, the system must not initiate execution of another LOCK instruction from a concurrent process before it completes the test and set sequence for the requesting process. To do so would destroy the integrity of the lock -- a problem of concurrent update processes again!

If the LOCK matching the UNLOCK is unambiguous, the object data need not be identified with the UNLOCK statement.

If the database is divided up into mutually exclusive units of data a single bit lock can be associated with each unit of data. However, if the identified object data is allowed to overlap with other identified object data (the more general case), the maintenance and testing of locks on object data is more complex. Each identification of object data would have to be kept in a current lock table and the table would be checked upon receipt of each new LOCK instruction. The process of checking, testing, and setting any locks on the object data must not be interrupted by another process of checking, testing, and setting locks.

Another problem arises if a reading process has set a lockout of updates against the object data and another reading process is requesting that updates be locked out. To avoid the second reading process from being unnecessarily denied access, two types of LOCK instructions are needed. LOCKR could be issued by a process intending to read the object

data and desiring to have concurrent updates locked out. In this case,
any number of processes issuing a LOCKR would be permitted to access
the object data. A LOCKU command would be issued by a process intending
to update the object data. Alternatively, the system can note any prior
mode declaration of retrieval or update.

While Yourdon has an easily understood discussion of the problem
of concurrent access to a database, his conclusion concerning lockout
must be rejected. He says that use of a locking mechanism in an online
system is fraught with problems such as vulnerability to deadlock, vulnerability to extended lockout by a long process, and overhead expense.
While this is true, he concludes that locking "is not a useful concept
if all of the users are sharing a common database, where an extended
delay in their ability to access or update the database is an intolerable
nuisance. In short, then, the concept of locking is useful in a scientific or university time-sharing environment, but is not useful in a
centralized information retrieval system, or in most other forms of
'dedicated' systems."[1] Unfortunately he does not have an alternative.
Would he impose serial execution of update processes? If concurrent
updates are allowed, and if the integrity of the database is to be maintained, then some form of exclusion must be implemented, whatever the
cost and whatever the nuisance.

7.   APPROACHES TO THE PREVENTION OF DEADLOCK

At the outset, it is important to distinguish between detection
and prevention of deadlock. Detection of deadlock requires that the
system maintain some form of state graph showing the resources allocated to each process at any point in time. The graph is updated each
time a resource is allocated to or released by a process. Whenever
a process requests a nonpre-emptive resource, a routine checks for cycles
which would result in the state graph if the request were granted.

If a cycle would result, and the requesting process already has
exclusive control of resources, then one or more of the processes in

---

[1] Yourdon, page 327.

the cycle must be backed out. The processes are backed out in some
sequence (inspection of the graph may reveal the least disruptive
sequence) until sufficient resources become available to remove deadlocks in the remaining set of processes.

To avoid the necessity of backing out a process in execution, deadlocks must be more than simply detected, they must be _prevented._

7.1 Conditions Under Which Deadlock Can Occur

To discover the conditions under which deadlock can be prevented it
is helpful to examine the set of conditions under which deadlock can
occur. Deadlock can only arise when all five of the following conditions
are true.[1]

CONDITIONS FOR DEADLOCK	SOLUTION STRATEGY
• lockout: a process can obtain exclusive control of needed resources (that is, exclusive with respect to update processes).	(none)
• concurrency: two or more (update) processes concurrently compete for exclusive control of two or more resources.	Presequence
• additional request: a process can request exclusive control of additional resources while holding exclusive control of other resources.	Preclaim
• no pre-emption: a process cannot be forced to release an exclusively controlled resource before it is finished with it, that is, a resource cannot be pre-empted.	Pre-empt
• circular wait: a circular chain of processes exists such that each process holds a resource being requested by the next process in the chain.	Preorder

---

[1]adapted from four conditions as stated in Coffman, _et al_., page 70.

Deadlock can be prevented by relaxing any one of these conditions independently. In the preceding section it was argued that some form of mutual exclusion or lockout was necessary to protect data integrity. Therefore, the first condition cannot be relaxed. Relaxing each of the remaining four conditions imposes a particular discipline on the use or operation of the system, called presequence, preclaim, pre-empt, and preorder, respectively. Each of these four strategies for preventing deadlock are discussed.

7.2 Presequence the Processes

For those processes which potentially compete for exclusive control of the same object data, deadlock can be prevented if their execution is presequenced by external administrative procedures. In other words, when a process is updating a file, no other conflicting processes are allowed to run concurrently. A conflicting process is either one that also updates the file, or one that only reads the file but cannot permit another process to update the same file concurrently. This solution may be acceptable in a batch processing environment where all jobs are normally run in some sequence. It is not acceptable in an online, multiprograming, shared-database environment. Nevertheless, even in a dynamic processing environment, presequencing, or at least sequencing according to strict time limits, may be the only possible solution. For example, all of the accounting transactions for the month must be processed before the books of account are closed. Similarly, all of the deposits and withdrawals for a given period have to be posted to savings accounts before earned interest is calculated.

7.3 Pre-empt Exclusively Controlled Resources

Under a pre-emption strategy, deadlock can be prevented if a process can be required to release all exclusively controlled resources when a subsequent request is denied because of a possible deadlock. This is the

solution suggested by Murphy.[1] Unfortunately data resources cannot
reasonably be considered pre-emptible when they are undergoing modification.

7.4 Preorder All System Resources

The third strategy for the prevention of deadlock requires establishing an arbitrary preordering on all system resources which are nonpre-
emptible and used under exclusive control. All resource requests from
each process must be issued according to the preordering, that is, assuming
that resources are requested from a high to low preordering, the next
resource a process requests must be lower in the preordering than the
resources currently held. This solution is due to Havender.[2] The linear
preordering of all system resources ensures that a circular chain of
processes both holding and requesting resources is impossible. When considering all of the different ways of dividing up a database into resource
units, the preordering strategy for preventing deadlock is practically
infeasible. Even considering resource allocation at the file level, it
may be impossible to establish a preordering on each of the files in the
database such that all processes could operate properly by requesting the
files according to the preordering. In any case, it would impose a
severe, and perhaps unnecessary, discipline on the programmer.

7.5 Preclaim Needed Resources

The fourth strategy for preventing deadlock requires each process to
preclaim or declare and receive exclusive control of all needed resources
before using any of them. In this way, a process can never request
resources while holding others. In one variation, the process must state

---

[1] James E. Murphy, "Resource Allocation with Interlock Detection in
a Multi-Task System," Proceedings of the AFIPS Fall Joint Computer Conference (vol. 33), 1968, pages 1169-1176.

[2] J. W. Havender, "Avoiding Deadlock in Multitasking Systems,"
IBM Systems Journal (7:2), 1968, pages 74-84.

a priori the maximum set of resources needed for the entire process.
A less restrictive alternative is possible if the process can be partitioned into a series of steps such that all resources can be released
or unlocked between steps. Again, throughout the process, no resources
are held or locked when the process makes its next resource request.
This solution strategy has been explored rather completely by Habermann
in the context of general system resources.[1]

Under a preclaim strategy the system in effect assumes that the
process needs all declared resources simultaneously. By using a stronger
condition for the exclusive control of resources, false deadlock threats
may arise which can lead to degraded resource utilization. On the other
hand, such a more inclusive declaration of resource needs leads to more
efficient algorithms to test for 'safe' resource allocations in scheduling
processes. In any case, the maximum resource needs do not generally
occur simultaneously and continuously throughout the execution of the
process.

A process requiring the exclusion of concurrent updates can issue
a succession of locks against object data until it has exclusive control
of all the data objects, say records, that will be affected by the intended update or retrieval. If the process cannot obtain exclusive control
of all the needed records, it releases control of the records already held.
It would be helpful if the system could indicate to the process which
record is being requested by another process and, therefore, potentially
causing deadlock. The important point is that no resources will be locked
by a process until all resources needed by the process are available for
its exclusive control.

Under a preclaim strategy, a process may ask indefinitely for exclusive control of a particular combination of records. Such a permanent
block situation can be solved by the system adding one to a counter on
each bypass. When the counter reaches some threshold, no other processes

---

[1]A. Nico Habermann, "Prevention of System Deadlocks," _Communications of the ACM_ (12:7), 1969 July, pages 373-377, 385.

would be given exclusive control of the resources needed by the requesting process. In effect, all needed resources would be held in reserve until they were all unlocked and available for the exclusive control of the requesting process.

Effectiveness of the preclaim strategy with respect to data requires that reasonably fine resolution be possible in identifying data to allocate exclusively to processes. That would imply identifying object data at least at the level of record or entry instances.

Two excellent and detailed presentations of the preclaim strategy as it applies specifically to data resources are given by Frailey and by King and Collmeyer.[1] In fact, these are the only viable solutions presented in the literature so far which focus on data resources and consider all four possible strategies for preventing deadlock. The conclusion to be drawn is that if processes are to run concurrently, if data is a dominant resource, and if deadlock is to be avoided, then all processes must state their resource needs *a priori*. To relax the requirement for an *a priori* statement of resource needs means that either competing processes cannot be run concurrently or that the possibility of deadlock and consequent backout must be accepted.

7.6 Required Process-System Communication

Even though the solutions presented by Frailey and by King and Collmeyer are the most viable to date, they still do not meet all the desirable criteria stated earlier. They do place a discipline on the programmer and they do not allow a process to request any number of resources as needed and release them when no longer needed. With no

---

[1]Dennis J. Frailey, "A Practical Approach to Managing Resources and Avoiding Deadlocks," Communications of the ACM (16:5), 1973 May, pages 323-329; and Paul F. King and Arthur J Collmeyer, "Database Sharing -- An Efficient Mechanism for Supporting Concurrent Processes," AFIPS National Computer Conference Proceedings, 1973, pages 271-275.

formal, required communication between the database manager and the
process, the system is unable to protect the integrity of the database
from the interaction of concurrent updates and is unable to prevent
deadlock. The required communication is in terms of *a priori* statements
of needed resources and requests to lock and unlock resources.

8. THE CODASYL DATA BASE TASK GROUP APPROACH

In the April 1971 DBTG Report,[1] two elements of the language related
to the question of controlling concurrent processes -- the OPEN declaration and the KEEP/FREE mechanism. Upon opening an area of the database,
the process declares the usage mode to be exclusive or protected, and
retrieval or update. If a concurrent process had already opened the area,
the diagram at the top[2] of Figure 2 would determine whether or not the
requesting process was permitted to open the area.

Seven usage modes are unnecessary to accomplish the intended purpose
of prohibiting two processes to open the same data area in conflicting
usage modes. An update process must request lockout of concurrent update
processes so the (none, update) option must not be made available to him.
Another process opening in the same mode would threaten the integrity of
the database. If an update process requests lockout of concurrent updates
it makes no difference whether it is protected or exclusive, a distinction
that permits or does not permit concurrent reading. Whether or not reading is permitted is up to the reading process to decide. Similarly, a
reading process either requires concurrent updates to be locked out or

---

[1] CODASYL Programming Language Committee, Data Base Task Group Report,
New York: Association for Computing Machinery, 1971 April, 273 pages,
(in Europe: British Computer Society, London, or IFIP Administrative
Data Processing Group, Amsterdam).

[2] adapted from CODASYL Systems Committee, Feature Analysis of
Generalized Data Base Management Systems, New York: Association for
Computing Machinery, 1971 May, page 394, (in Europe: British Computer
Society, London, or IFIP Administrative Data Processing Group, Amsterdam).

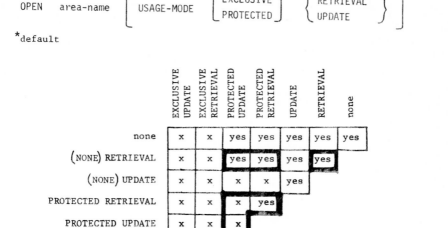

*default

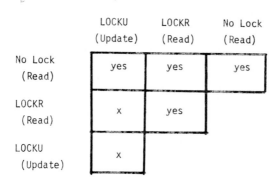

Figure 2.   Concurrency Control in DBTG.

not and the distinction between exclusive and protected is meaningless.
There is never a conflict between two reading processes so there is no
reason to not always permit such usage. In short, both exclusive and
protected modes are not required. Finally, no usage declaration is the
same as (none, retrieval) so a distinction need not be made in determining conflicting usage modes.

The net result is that the seven usage modes in the upper diagram
in Figure 2 reduce to three in the lower diagram. Such a result is
consistent with the previous discussion on lockout mechanisms.

The second language element relating to concurrency control is the
KEEP/FREE pair of statements. Through the use of a KEEP statement, a
process requests that the system monitor an object record for any modifications performed on it by a concurrent process. If an intervening
update occurs, a subsequent attempt by the requesting process to modify
the object record will not be performed. The system will return an
exception condition indicating what changes had been made by any intervening concurrent processes. At this point, the requesting process can
decide to modify the record anyway or reaccess the revised copy of the
record and repeat the modification.[1] Although the KEEP is only intended
to be advisory to the system, such a "modify anyway" option can destroy
database integrity. Such unilateral actions on the part of processes
must never be permitted. As said before, the system must maintain the
integrity of the database in spite of the actions of programmers and
processes. Unfortunately, the revised proposal of the CODASYL Data Base
Language Task Group[2] is silent on this "modify anyway" option.

---

[1] ibid., page 29.

[2] COBOL Data Base Facility Proposal, Ottawa, Canada: Government
Department of Supply and Services, 1973 March, 140 pages.

9. COOPERATION BETWEEN THE DATABASE MANAGER AND JOB MANAGER

Preventing deadlock is a job management responsibility and maintaining database integrity is a database management responsibility. Since
simultaneous update, locking, and deadlock are interrelated, the actions
of the job manager and the database manager must be coordinated. A full
understanding of the relationships among concurrency control, deadlock
prevention, and integrity maintenance depends on an understanding of
processes, processors, and their interaction. In general, a single locus
of control must ultimately be responsible for the allocation of all resources -- data, processors, and processes. Not only must the database
manager and the job manager cooperate, they must be subordinate to a higher
controlling authority. More study and research is still needed in this
critical area.

10. SUMMARY

Several lockout and deadlock prevention strategies have been explored
from the perspective of data resources. Data is an unconserved, reusable
resource. It can be "allocated" concurrently to requesting processes an
unlimited number of times. However, if one of the processes intends to
update the data, all other update processes must be locked out and all
read processes have the option of reading or not.

The maintenance of data integrity requires some form of lockout or
mutual exclusion between concurrent update processes. Lockout leads to the
possibility of deadlock. Deadlock can be handled by presequencing the
processes, by pre-empting exclusively held resources when deadlock threatens
(and then attempting to backout the process gracefully), by preordering all
system resources, or by requiring each process to preclaim all resources
need for a complete unit of processing. Only the last strategy is viable
in an online, realtime environment dominated by a large, shared database.

In communicating with the system, a process must identify the data
(and all other resources) it wishes to access, whether it intends to read
or update the data so identified and, if read only, whether it desires
concurrent updates to be excluded.

REFERENCES

BAER, J. L., "A Survey of Some Theoretical Aspects of Multiprocessing,"
    Computing Surveys (5:1), 1973 March, pages 31-80.

CODASYL Data Base Language Task Group, COBOL Data Base Facility Proposal,
    Ottawa, Canada: Government Department of Supply and Services,
    1973 March, 140 pages.

CODASYL Programming Language Committee, Data Base Task Group Report, New
    York: Association for Computing Machinery, 1971 April, 273 pages,
    (in Europe: British Computer Society, London, England, or IFIP
    Administrative Data Processing Group, Amsterdam, Netherlands).

CODASYL Systems Committee, Feature Analysis of Generalized Data Base
    Management Systems, New York: Association for Computing Machinery,
    1971 May, 520 pages, (in Europe: British Computer Society, London,
    England, or IFIP Administrative Data Processing Group, Amsterdam,
    Netherlands).

COFFMAN, E. G., Jr., M. J. Elphick and A. Shoshani, "System Deadlocks,"
    Computing Surveys (3:2), 1971 June, pages 67-78.

DENNING, Peter J., "Third Generation Computer Systems,"
    Computing Surveys (3:4), 1971 December, pages 175-216.

DENNIS, Jack B. and Earl C. Van Horn, "Programming Semantics for Multi-
    programmed Computations," Communications of the ACM (9:3), 1966
    March, pages 143-155.

FRAILEY, Dennis J., "A Practical Approach to Managing Resources and
    Avoiding Deadlocks," Communications of the ACM (16:5), 1973 May,
    pages 323-329.

HABERMANN, A. Nico, "Prevention of System Deadlocks,"
    Communications of the ACM (12:7), 1969 July, pages 373-377, 385.

HAVENDER, J. W., "Avoiding Deadlock in Multitasking Systems,"
    IBM Systems Journal (7:2), 1968, pages 74-84.

KING, Paul F. and Arthur J. Collmeyer, "Database Sharing -- An Efficient
    Mechanism for Supporting Concurrent Processes,"
    AFIPS National Computer Conference Proceedings, 1973, pages 271-275.

MURPHY, James E., "Resource Allocation With Interlock Detection in a
    Multi-task System," AFIPS Fall Joint Computer Conference Proceedings
    (volume 33), 1968, pages 1169-1176.

YOURDON, Edward, "The Problem of Simultaneous Access to the Data Base,"
    Design of On-Line Computer Systems, Englewood Cliffs, NJ: Prentice-
    Hall, 1972, Chapter L, pages 310-339.

269

DISCUSSION

Tsichritzis : I have a few comments on Everest's paper.

First, I mentioned that when the level of locking is high (e.g. locking at
the file level) then the probability of deadlock is high. Would it not be
better to say that the probability of interference is high.
For instance, if the complete data base is locked, the probability of deadlock
is zero, although the probability of interference is high.
Second, I fail to see why Everest makes a distinction between "conserved"
and "unconserved" reusable resources. From the point of view of concurrency
and locking, there is not difference between physical and logical resources.
Third, Everest failed to mention the heaviest burden on the application
programmer. If the lock request fails, he has to have logic in his program
to handle this situation.

Everest   : I agree on Tsichritzis' comments, Ideally, we would like to
have no impact on the programmer, that is, keep concurrency hidden from him.
However, a central point I am making is that this is impossible.
We should try to minimize the effort required of the programmer, although
further investigation is needed to understand the problem.

Lucking   : I believe Everest's assessment of DBTG's "integrity" facilities
is unfair. The facilities specified by the DML "OPEN AREA" command can be
modified by use of the "PRIVACY LOCK" clauses in the schema DDL, and hence
the seven by seven array may be reduced, by a data administrator, to correspond to the three by three array Everest suggests. I agree, however, that
further work by the various CODASYL Committees is required to improve the
concurrency-handling and data-integrity handling specifications.

<u>King</u>   : If record instances can be locked by value e.g : set of all
employees with salary = X), then the integrity problems Everest mentioned
become much more difficult. In addition, the above example illustrates an
important difference between concurrency control in data bases and operating
systems i.e. that the identified resource can change in data base systems
(by modification of data values) whereas in operating systems this does not
happen.

<u>Neuhold</u> : It should be pointed out that resources are locked at a given
point in time. What ever happens (such as the addition of new data to the
set) will not effect or become part of the locked set of data.

<u>King</u>   : Everest's proposal for solving the deadlock problem by preclaiming
all resources has drastic implications for existing block structured programming languages in that all data requests will have to be migrated to the
outer block. I think this will be unacceptable.

<u>Everest</u> : Certainly additional discipline will be required on the part of
the programmer, we need to explore further the full impact and try to minimize
it. From a data viewpoint, preclaiming resources seems to be the most viable
strategy, though not perfect and costly.

Data Base Management, J. W. Klimbie and K. L. Koffeman, (eds.)
© *North-Holland Publishing Company (1974)*

DATA BASE INTEGRITY
AS PROVIDED FOR BY A PARTICULAR DATA BASE MANAGEMENT SYSTEM

BARBARA M. FOSSUM
Data Processing Consultant, Sperry Univac
San Antonio, Texas

INTRODUCTION

One of the greatest advantages associated with the use of a data base is that
multiple applications share data which may be structured in a variety of manners
such that data redundancy is avoided. However, sharing of data by multiple
applications also poses one of the greatest problems to the effective administration of data in a data base environment. The problem referred to is the
preservation of the integrity of the data in a data base.

Preservation of the integrity of data in a data base is protection against
inconsistent and unreasonable data. (Security is protection against unauthorized
access of data in the data base, and is not the subject of this paper.)
Inconsistent and unreasonable data may result from access of the data base by
concurrent (simultaneously functioning) run units and/or from hardware, software,
or operational errors.

This paper presents the methods for preserving integrity provided for by a data
base management system[1], titled DMS in this paper, which is based conceptually
on the work of the CODASYL Data Base Task Group (DBTG).[2] Although the DMS is
based conceptually on the specifications of the DBTG, the method of the DMS
for providing for integrity in a concurrent run unit environment differs somewhat
from the method suggested by the DBTG. The methods of the DMS for protecting
against unreasonable and inconsistent data which may result from hardware,
software, or operational errors are extensions to the specifications of the DBTG.

The reader should become familiar with the following definitions and diagrams,
and with the list of definitions attached to this paper.

DDL: The data description language, DDL, is a stand alone language which
is used by the data administrator to describe the data base. The
description which is input to the DDL translator is in terms of
definitions of data items, data aggregates, records, sets and areas.
The DDL translator translates the syntax used to describe the data
base into a series of tables, the schema, which is maintained in
a mass storage file.

DML: The data manipulation language, DML, is the procedural language used
by the programmer to access the data base. The DML requires the
presence of a host language for processing the data when the data
is accessed. DML commands are embedded in the COBOL syntax. The
data manipulation language preprocessor, DMLP, accepts the syntax
of a COBOL/DML program, converts all DML commands to a COBOL compatible
format, adds DDL record descriptions, and produces the required DMR
communication area. The altered source program is input to the
COBOL compiler.

DMR: The data management routine, DMR, is a collection of reentrant on-line
routines which maintains, and preserves the integrity of, the data base.

Note: This paper was presented by Gordon C.Everest because
Barbara Fossum was unable to come.

SCHEMA: A schema is a complete description of the data base, as opposed
         to the data base itself. The DDL is used to develop a schema.

DDL TRANSLATION PROCESS

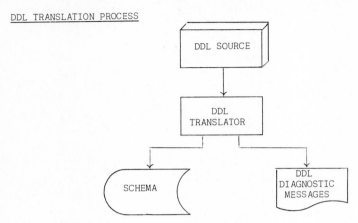

DML COMPILATION PROCESS

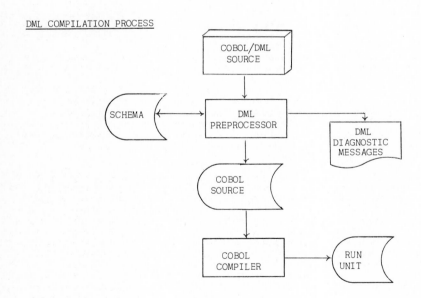

RUN UNIT EXECUTION

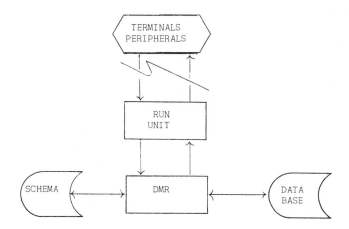

The DMS uses a system of reentrant on-line processor control, deadlock detection, queues, locks, rollback, recovery, and utility routines to preserve the integrity of the data base. Each of these facilities is discussed in the following sections.

REENTRANT, ON-LINE, PROCESSOR CONTROL

The reentrant, on-line, processor control (REP) consists of two interfaces, the user interface and the systems interface.

The required interface between the user run unit and the data management routine (DMR) REP is made by a DMS program called the Linker. The Linker is collected with each run unit. The data manipulation language preprocessor (DMLP) generates a call to the Linker for each data manipulation language (DML) command in a COBOL/DML program. The Linker, upon entry from a command, saves COBOL registers, makes a command parameter packet available to the DMR, performs validity checks on the command, and checks for, and if necessary, establishes a valid run unit identity. The types of command validity checks made by the Linker are the following. If the call to the Linker originated from a DML IMPART command, the Linker must verify that the program had not previously issued an IMPART, or that if the program had previously issued an IMPART, it had also issued a DEPART prior to its next IMPART. If the DML command from which the call to the Linker originates is not an IMPART or DEPART, the Linker must verify that an IMPART was previously initiated. When an IMPART is issued by a program, the Linker registers a contingency address with the system.

The Linker calls the DMR, and return from the DMR to the user program is made through the Linker. A normal return causes the Linker to return control in line to the main program, i.e., the COBOL program's next statement. Abnormal return is caused by errors or contingencies. If the DMR detects an error during the execution of a DML command, special error registers are initialized.

The error registers are checked by the Linker when control is returned to the Linker by the DMR. If an error has occurred, the Linker returns control to the user specified error paragraph for the particular DML command. If no error paragraph is specified by the user program for the command, the Linker returns control to the next statement in the main program.

If a contingency occurs, the system transfers control to the contingency routine registered with the system by the Linker when an IMPART command was issued by the main program. The type of contingency and subsequent action to be taken are determined by this contingency routine. If the contingency was caused by a key-in at the operator console, the DMR performs a DEPART WITH ROLLBACK, and return is made to the rollback paragraph in the main program. (Rollback reverses the effects that a run unit had on the data base. Rollback is discussed in a following section.) If the contingency occurred within the DMR, i.e., a DMR internal error occurred, run unit rollback is performed and return is made to the rollback paragraph in the main program.

If a contingency occurred within the user program, control may be passed to the COBOL contingency routine, or to a user specified contingency routine. Divide overflow and floating point overflow, for example, cause COBOL contingencies. If the contingency is not a COBOL contingency, and the user has not specified a contingency routine, a DEPART WITH ROLLBACK is performed and return is made to the rollback paragraph in the main program. If the user has registered a contingency routine, control is passed to the contingency routine before a DEPART WITH ROLLBACK is performed, and return in made to the rollback paragraph in the main program.

The DMR interfaces with the system. Transfer of user and recovery information to the audit trail (discussed in a following section) by multiple run units is performed by the DMR. The DMR also maintains the system file, which contains information necessary for recovery after a system failure (power failure, irresolvable I/O error, etc.), and times out run units on the basis of a system's generation parameter.

DEADLOCK DETECTION AND QUEUES

In a concurrent run unit environment several facilities, such as main storage, buffers, data pages, control tables, etc., must be shared by several run units. In some instances, one run unit may have a facility which another run unit needs and without which cannot proceed. The DMR recognizes the latter condition and queues the run unit, that is, it stops execution of the run unit while the facility is unavailable to the run unit. When the facility becomes available, the DMR removes the run unit from the queue and the run unit continues.

An outgrowth of the capability of recognizing conflicting requests for facilities and consequently queuing run units is "deadlock". Deadlock is defined as a situation in which two or more run units are queued and each holds a

facility required by another run unit. In the latter situation none of the
queued run units may continue until another releases a facility; but since
none of the queued run units is active, no facility is released.

The DMR recognizes a deadlock condition and takes action to break it to allow
the run units to continue. A run unit is selected by the DMR and rolled back.
Selection, unless overridden by a user specified parameter, is based on the
number of alterations made to the data base by each run unit. The run unit
having made the least number of alterations is selected for rollback.

A user may specify a parameter which will affect a run unit's priority for
rollback selection. The parameter is established in the main program by a
PRIORITY statement, or by a COBOL MOVE into the PRIORITY word prior to the
program's issuing a DML command. Since no run unit knows its priority relative
to other existing run units, it is envisioned that the basis for the rollback
priority scheme would be established by the data administrator and could be
the number of external messages involved, or a value arrived at by an algorithm,
etc. If a run unit's rollback priority is user specified, a system's generation
parameter must have been set to indicate that the DMR selection process is not
to be used to resolve deadlock.

LOCKS

Locks are applied for a run unit at two levels, the area and the page.

Page locks are required for an economical run unit rollback capability. When
a run unit alters a page, a lock is applied to the page, and the lock remains
in effect until the run unit terminates or issues a DML FREE command. No
other run unit can access the page while the lock is in effect. Because of
the types of data structures supported by the DMS, situations exist in which
a record on one page may be related, through pointers, to records on other
pages. A premise of the DMS locking facility is that a pointer change within
a record constitutes a page change. Therefore, any of the following DML
commands cause page alteration, and consequently page usage locks: STORE,
DELETE, MODIFY, INSERT, and REMOVE. For example, assume that records of
types A, B, and C are located in the data base on page 1, 2, and 3 as illustrated
in Figure 1. If record B is removed, via execution of a DML REMOVE command,
from the ring, the pointer in record A must be changed to point to record C.
Thus, both pages 1 and 2 are locked.

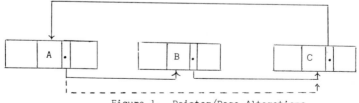

Figure 1. Pointer/Page Alterations

A DML FIND command causes a temporary lock to be applied to the page on which the current record of run unit is located. The lock is released, however, when a subsequent FIND, or STORE, command is issued. The two DML commands which uniquely involve page locks are the KEEP and the FREE. The KEEP command causes a lock to be placed on the page which contains the current record of the run unit, even though no alteration has been made to the page. Assume, for example, that a run unit accesses a record of type DEPARTMENT through a DML FETCH DEPARTMENT command, inspects the record, and then wants to access a record of type PERSONNEL to compare an item within the PERSONNEL record with an item within the DEPARTMENT record. If the run unit next issues a FETCH PERSONNEL command, the page on which the DEPARTMENT record is located would be unlocked and subject to alteration by another run unit. To prevent another run unit from intervening, the run unit would issue a KEEP DEPARTMENT command before the FETCH PERSONNEL command. A FREE command releases all page locks and quick before looks. (Looks are discussed in a following section.)

Locks applied for a run unit at the area level facilitate either exclusive or protected use of an area or areas by the run unit. Specification of the locks to be applied to an area for a run unit is made in the COBOL/DML program when the run unit issues a DML OPEN command. Exclusive use of an area by a run unit means that no other run unit can access the area. Protected use of an area by a run unit means that records in the area may be retrieved by concurrently processing run units but the area may not be updated by concurrently processing run units. While one run unit has exclusive use of an area, any other run units attempting to access the area will be queued. Use of the DML KEEP command for records in an area is not necessary if a run unit has either exclusive or protected use of that area.

ROLLBACK AND RECOVERY

The rollback/recovery mechanism provided by the DMS is an extension to the specifications of CODASYL. The vehicle the DMS uses to provide for rollback and recovery is the "look". A look is a copy of a data base page which is written to a file for use at a later point in time if the contents of the data base must be reestablished. The types of looks are:

> before look - a look taken prior to the alteration of a page and
>   and written to a sequential tape file, the audit trail.

> quick before look - a look taken prior to the alteration of a page and
>   written to a random access mass storage device, the quick look file.

> after look - a look taken after alteration of a page and written to the
>   audit trail.

If the rollback/recovery mechanism is to be used, the data administrator specifies in the schema data description language (DDL) which types of looks are to be written by the DMS. The actual writing of looks by the DMR is invisible to the run unit.

Before looks and quick before looks are used by the DMS to move backward in time to remove the effects of an error on the data base. When the run unit prepares to alter a page for the first time, the DMS will take a before look and/or quick before look. After looks are used by the DMR to move forward

in time to reestablish the data base to a stable state. An after look for a
page is written whenever a modified page is returned to the data base. (If a
page is not altered, it is not written back to the data base.) A page is
written back to the data base only when it has been modified and one of the
following conditions exist:

    * The page must be swapped from core to provide room for another page.

    * The run unit terminates.

    * The run unit issues a FREE command.

The DMR appends control information to each look before the look is written
to a file. The type of information used for control is run unit identity, time
stamp, area identifier, etc. Quick before looks are used for rollback and
quick recovery. Before and after looks are used for long recovery. Selective
recovery uses after looks.

Rollback

Rollback is the procedure which reverses the effects of a run unit, or a command
of a run unit, on the data base and on the internal tables of the DMR. The DMR
applies the quick before looks from the quick look files to the data base,
releases buffer space which had been acquired by the run unit, or command of a
run unit, and reestablishes all DMR internal tables which were altered by the
run unit's processing. While rollback is being performed on a run unit, other
run units may access the data base through the DMR.

Run unit rollback is the mechanism which reverses the effect that a run unit
had on the data base and the DMR internal tables since the run unit's IMPART
or last FREE command. A rollback paragraph is required in all COBOL/DML programs. Control is returned to this paragraph after run unit rollback has been
performed. When control reaches the rollback paragraph, a DEPART has taken
place internal to the DMR as far as the user program is concerned. The returned
error status will indicate the reason run unit rollback was performed.

Run unit rollback could be performed for three reasons:

    (1) An error was detected in a command after alteration had occurred
         and the run unit has not specified that command quick before looks
         be taken. (Command rollback is discussed in subsequent paragraphs.)

    (2) The run unit was selected for rollback to resolve a facility dead-
         lock with another run unit.

    (3) The operator elected to remove the run unit from the DMS via a
         console key-in. (Such action may be prompted by a run unit time-out
         message from the DMR to the operator console.)

Command rollback is the mechanism which reverses the effects that a run unit
had on the data base and the DMR internal tables since the issuance of the
current command which was found in error. Command rollback for a particular
run unit does not impair the access to the data base by other run units. After
command rollback is performed, control is returned to the run unit at the
error paragraph specified for the particular command, or if no error paragraph
is specified for the command, to the general error paragraph. If no

error paragraph is specified, control is returned in-line in the main program. The returned error status will indicate why command rollback was performed. When the user program obtains control after command rollback has occurred, the program may issue another DML command. The latter situation differs from the situation after run unit rollback is performed since run unit rollback causes an internal DEPART to be performed for the run unit before the program regains control.

The quick before looks necessary for run unit rollback require that one copy of each altered page be made prior to the first alteration of the page by the run unit. No other copy of that page will be taken even though the page may be altered several times by subsequent commands in the run unit unless the run unit issued a FREE command. Following a FREE command, one copy of each altered page is made prior to the alteration of the page by the run unit. The quick before looks necessary for command rollback require that one copy of each altered page be made prior to the first alteration of the page by each command of a particular run unit.

Quick Recovery

Quick recovery is the procedure used to restore the data base to the state which existed prior to the operations of all run units which were active when a DMR internal error occurred (e.g., the DMR detected an irresolvable I/O error), or when a system failure was encountered. The quick recovery procedure applies the quick before looks taken for these run units to the data base. Only the copy of each altered page made prior to its first alteration by any run unit is applied to the data base. As the data base is restored to a stable state, the restored pages are written to the audit trail as after looks. The DMR is reloaded from mass storage.

Quick recovery may be initiated external to the DMR. If an internal DMR error occurs, for example, a message is given to the operator directing him to initiate quick recovery. If a system failure occurs, the first run unit to issue an IMPART command after the system has been rebooted causes the DMR to detect, from inspection of the system file, that run units were active at the time the failure occurred, and quick recovery is initiated automatically.

Long Recovery

Long recovery is the procedure which reestablishes a data base, from a prior dump of the data base, up to a specified point in time. Long recovery may be used to restore a data base after one or more files (areas) have been lost due to hardware, software, or operational failure, or may be used to reestablish one or more areas which have been improperly modified by a run unit. Long recovery requires a previously taken dump of the data base, and an audit trail which contains after looks, before looks, and recovery points, or after looks and checkpoints. (Recovery points and checkpoints are described in following paragraphs.)

The entire data base or selected areas may be dumped. The data base dump must be taken when no run units are accessing the data base. Two DMS utility routines insure that no run units are accessing the data base while a dump is in progress, and, after the dump has been made, make the DMR available once again to run units. When the first of these routines is executed, the DMR is informed that a data base dump is to be taken. The DMR allows all active run units to continue processing, but will return an error status to any new run unit attempting to IMPART. When all the run units which were active have completed, the DMR updates the system file and returns control to the utility routine.

The utility routine obtains a new audit trail tape reel number and records it in the system file. An end of reel block is written to the audit trail tape reel, in the audit trail, which corresponds to the previous data base dump. All additional information pertaining to the audit trail tape is recorded in the system file before the utility routine terminates. A system processor then moves the requested areas from random access mass storage to tape. The system file must also be dumped since it contains information, acquired by the first utility routine, necessary for long recovery. Following the dump, the second utility routine informs the DMR that new run units may be accepted.

An audit trail tape is a cataloged tape file. The initial cataloging is performed by a system file initialization routine if the system's generation parameters specify that an audit trail tape is to be used. Thereafter responsibility for an audit trail tape is assigned to the DMR. The DMR directs the writing, to the audit trail tape, of before looks, after looks, recovery points, checkpoints, and start and end of run unit sentinels. However, nothing is written to the audit trail by the DMR for a run unit unless the run unit alters the data base. Additionally, the FREE command causes a special block to be written to the audit trail tape. The special block is, effectively, an end of run unit sentinel followed by a start of run unit sentinel.

A recovery point is a point in time to which the DMS can return during the long recovery operation. A recovery point may be generated by a run unit via the DML LOG command, or may be generated automatically by the DMR. In the latter case the data administrator must have specified, in the schema data description language (DDL), recovery point frequency in terms of the number of blocks written to the audit trail between successive recovery points. Run units accessing the data base are active when recovery points are written to the audit trail.

A checkpoint is similar to the recovery point with the exception that a checkpoint is written to the audit trail when no run units are active. Long recovery may recover to a checkpoint in the same manner as to a recovery point. When the long recovery procedure reaches a recovery point, it uses before looks to "back out" run units which were active when the recovery point was written. Since no run units are active when checkpoints are written, use of before looks is unnecessary after the long recovery procedure reaches a checkpoint. A DMS program, Checkpoint, writes checkpoints to the audit trail. When Checkpoint is executed, it interfaces with the DMR such that all active run units are allowed to process to completion, but new run units are queued if they attempt to IMPART. When the last active run unit terminates, a checkpoint sentinel is written to the audit trail, and all run units which were queued are removed from the queue.

Long recovery is initiated external to the DMR. The DMR is informed that long recovery is to be performed. All runs which are active at this time are given an error status with control being returned to their rollback paragraphs. Any run unit attempting to IMPART while long recovery is in progress will likewise be given an error status and control will be returned to its rollback paragraph.

The loading, from tape(s) to random access mass storage, of the data base and system file dump is performed by a system processor. The long recovery procedure

obtains the reel numbers of the required audit trail tapes from the system file
and assigns the tapes. The long recovery procedure applies after looks from the
audit trail tape(s) to the data base, or areas of the data base, loaded from the
dump until the specified recovery point or checkpoint is reached. If a recovery
point is specified, the procedure then does a backward read of the audit trail
tape(s) to apply before looks to the data base, or areas of the data base, such
that the effects on the data base by run units, active when the recovery point
was taken, are removed, i.e., the run units are backed out. The run units are
backed up to their start of run unit sentinels. The run unit identity of each
run unit backed out is displayed on the operator console. (If a checkpoint is
specified, the "backout" procedure is not necessary.)

As each recovery point or checkpoint is written to the audit trail, the time at
which it was written and the sequence number relative to the last data base dump
are displayed on the operator console. Thus the recovery point or checkpoint to
be used by long recovery may be specified, in a system run stream or from the
operator console, in terms of time or sequence number. The time directive
includes month, day, year, hour, minute, and second. The sequence directive
includes the sequence number, relative to the last data base dump, of the
required recovery point or checkpoint, and the number of dumps to be bypassed
before the long recovery procedure becomes sensitive to recovery points or
checkpoints.

After the completion of a long recovery procedure it is not necessary that a
dump of the restored data base be made. When a recovery point is specified
for long recovery, the long recovery procedure, during back out, writes all
before looks to a new audit trail tape reel as after looks. An end-of-reel
mark is written to the old audit trail tape reel following the recovery
point used by long recovery. After the completion of long recovery, all run
units which were active when the specified recovery point was written, and/or
all run units initiated after the time associated with the specified recovery
point must be reinitialized.

Selective Recovery

Selective recovery is the procedure which reestablishes a selected area, or
areas, of the data base from a prior dump of the area or areas, up to the
current point in time. During selective recovery, the remainder of the areas
in the data base may be accessed by other run units. The latter is a
significant distinction between selective recovery and long recovery.
Selective recovery would be especially useful, for example, in the situation
in which a bad spot is encountered on a device, or the whole device is down,
and the remainder of the data base is not affected by the failure.

Selective recovery requires a previously taken dump of the areas to be
recovered, and an audit trail tape which contains after looks. Selective
recovery also requires that the areas to be recovered are "downed", i.e.,
made unavailable to concurrently processing run units. Areas are downed via
the utility processor (described in a following section) and may be downed
with or without an IMMEDIATE option. If the areas have been downed without
the option, the DMR allows run units which are accessing the areas to
terminate normally; however, the DMR will give any run unit attempting to
gain access to one of the areas an error return indicating that the area is
down. If the areas have been downed with the IMMEDIATE option, any run unit
accessing one of the areas, or queued waiting to access one of the areas, will
be given an error return indicating that the area is down. Subsequently, the

areas are made available for processing by all run units, after the areas have
been recovered, via the utility processor.

The selective recovery procedure, when initiated, causes a checkpoint
corresponding to the current time to be written to the audit trail. An end
of reel block is written on the current audit trail tape reel, and a new tape
reel is assigned to the audit trail such that the DMR may continue to record
recovery data on the audit trail for concurrently processing run units.

The selective recovery procedure determines the reel number(s) of the required
audit trail tape(s), from the utility command which initiated selective
recovery, and assigns the tapes.   (Thus the system file is not dumped with
the areas dumped prior to selective recovery.) The selective recovery
procedure applies after looks from the audit trail tape(s) to the areas
loaded from the dump until the checkpoint, written when selective recovery was
initiated, is reached.

Data Administrator Considerations

The type of rollback/recovery protection to be utilized by the DMS must be
determined by the data administrator. The options available range from no
protection of the data base to complete protection through the use of all
available DMS routines.

If the data administrator uses rollback protection, he must insure that the
following steps are taken:

(1) Quick before looks must be specified, in the schema data description
     language (DDL), for all areas which may be altered. Additionally,
     if a set spans areas, quick before looks must be specified for each
     of the areas spanned by the set. An unstable data base will result
     from rollback if the latter action is not taken.

(2) Specification of either command or run unit quick before looks must
     be made in the COBOL/DML program.

(3) The quick look files must be defined during system generation,
     cataloged, and assigned to the run unit involved.

Since quick recovery uses quick before looks and quick look files, the above
steps must be taken if the DMS is to provide the quick recovery facility.

If the data administrator selects to use long recovery, he is responsible for
determining the policy to be followed in dumping the data base. He may decide
to dump the entire data base at periodic intervals, or to dump the entire
data base at long intervals and the highly active areas at shorter intervals.
Maintaining the tapes containing dumps and a record of which areas were
dumped, and when they were dumped, is the responsibility of the data
administrator. Since long recovery may be used to reestablish one or more
areas which were improperly modified by a run unit, the data administrator
must consider the impact which the bad data may have had on run units
processed after the improper modification.

The data administrator must determine whether recovery points or checkpoints
are to be used by long recovery. The decision is dependent upon the impact
of temporarily stopping access to the data base while a checkpoint is written

versus the impact of writing before looks to the audit trail for back out
when a recovery point is reached.

If recovery points are to be used, the data administrator may specify the
frequency of recovery points in the schema DDL, which causes the
DMR to write recovery points automatically, or the application programmer
may use the DML LOG command within a run unit to write each recovery point.
Additionally, before looks and after looks must be specified in the schema DDL
for all areas which may be altered. If a set spans areas, the looks must be
specified for all areas spanned by the set.

If checkpoints are to be used, after looks must be specified in the schema
DDL for all areas which may be altered. If a set spans areas, the after looks
must be specified for all areas spanned by the set. If a checkpoint is used
for long recovery, and the time directive is specified, the time must match the
time associated with a checkpoint on the audit trail tape.

If the data administrator selects to use selective recovery, his responsibilities
associated with dumping areas of the data base are the same as those required
for the use of long recovery. Additionally, after looks must be specified in
the schema DDL for all areas which may be altered. If a set spans areas, the
looks must be specified for all areas spanned by the set.

For the use of either long recovery or selective recovery, the use of an audit
trail must be specified during system generation. (The required audit trail
tapes are cataloged automatically.)

UTILITY ROUTINES

The routines within the utility processor are designed to interface with the
DMR to ensure proper data locking and recovery. This interface essentially
consists of establishing the collection of utility routines as a DMR run unit.
This run unit is capable of performing the utility functions as "special"
commands. The routines directly affecting preservation of the integrity of
the data base and not previously referenced, are discussed in the following
paragraphs.

A patch utility provides the data administrator with the ability to modify any
word (system information or user data) in any page of a data base. The data
administrator specifies where the word which is to be modified is located, and
its current desired value. To prevent an incorrect modification, the patch
routine verifies that the actual value of the object word is the same as the
data administrator's specification of the current value.

A set verification utility routine provides a means of verifying set
relationships within a data base. The utility performs this function
by traversing records of a set and examining their set types and their
pointers. The set verification utility may be requested to vary its domain
of examination from a single set occurrence, to all occurrences of a
specified set, to all sets of a data base. For each set being examined, the
following types of error conditions may be detected: a pointer points to an
undefined area or page number; a pointer points to a deleted or non-existent
record; a pointer points to a record of a type not possible within the set;
an owner record is encountered which is not the owner record at which the check
started; a specified member record is encountered twice in a set occurrence.

The set verification routine never attempts to correct an error it detects and reports. Correction is left to the data administrator. (The patch utility may be used, as may long recovery or selective recovery.)

The set verification routine provides, optionally, the following statistics for a single set occurrence, all occurrences of a specified set, or all sets of the data base: the data base key of the owner of an occurrence; the data base keys of all members in the occurrence, and therefore the number of and physical location of members in the occurrence; the sort key(s), if any, of member occurrences; the number of I/O's required to traverse the set occurrence; the average number of I/O's required to access each member from the owner of the occurrence; the number of records in the occurrence which are located on data pages and the number of records in the occurrence which are located on overflow pages. Additionally, respective totals and averages may be obtained for all occurrences of a set type.

The DMS implementation of the calculation (CALC) location mode links records, whose values produce identical results as output from the calculation routine, via a chaining mechanism termed a calc chain. A calc chain verify routine of the utility processor provides for the verification of calc chain integrity. The routine allows for checking of all existing calc chains in the data base, or in a specific area, or on a specific page within the area. Additionally, any specific calc chain may be verified. Checks are performed for chain completeness (i.e., the chain can be traversed to its end without encountering undefined or illegal records) in both forward and backward directions. The routine does not attempt to correct an error it detects and reports. Correction is left to the data administrator.

The calc chain verify routine provides, optionally, the following statistics for any or all calc chains: the calc key(s) for each record in the chain; the data base keys of all records in the chain, and therefore the number of and physical location of records in the chain; the number of I/O's required to traverse the chain; the average number of I/O's required to access any record in the chain from the beginning of the chain; the number of records in the chain which are located on the prime data page (the result of the calc procedure) and the number of records in the chain which are located on non-prime data pages and overflow pages. Additionally, respective totals and averages may be obtained for all calc chains in a given area, or areas, or for the entire data base.

DEFINITIONS

area: An area is a named subdivision of the data base. An area is mapped
            by the DMS to a system file. Each area in a data base is divided
            into pages. Records may be assigned to areas independently of their
            set associations. An area may contain occurrences of one or more
            record types, and a record type may have occurrences in more than
            one area.

CALC location mode: Location mode is the specification by which the data
            administrator controls record placement by the DMS. CALC location
            mode requires a user defined or system defined data base procedure,
            and identifiers within the record and an area name as input to the
            data base procedure. The output from the data base procedure is a
            page number. Records whose input identifiers produce identical
            results as output from the data base procedure are linked on that
            page.

CLOSE: CLOSE is the DML command DMS execution of which terminates access
            to an area.

current record of run unit: The current record of run unit is the record most
            recently accessed by the run unit. The DMS retains the data base key
            of the current record of run unit. The DMS also retains the data
            base keys of the records which are current of each area, current of
            each record type, and current of each set type. The run unit may use
            a current record as a positional reference, for example, by requesting
            the next record of an area, the prior record of a set, or by using
            a DML command which assumes the object record of the command is the
            current record of run unit. Currency data base keys are, in effect,
            DMS "place markers" within the data base.

data aggregate: A data aggregate is an occurrence of a named collection of
            data items within a record. There are two types of data aggregates
            -- vectors and repeating groups. A vector is a one dimensional
            sequence of data items, all of which have identical characteristics.
            A repeating group is a collection of data (data items, vectors, and
            repeating groups) which occurs a number of times within a record
            occurrence.

data item: A data item is an occurrence of the smallest unit of named data;
            it is represented in the data base by a value.

DELETE: DELETE is the DML command, DMS execution of which removes, logically,
            the current record of the run unit from the data base. The data base
            key and assigned space for the record are freed for reuse. The
            record is also removed from all sets in which it is a member.

DEPART: DEPART is the DML command, DMS execution of which terminates the run
            unit. Execution of a DEPART WITH ROLLBACK cancels any updates to the
            data base made by the run unit, i.e., the data base is returned to
            the state existing prior to the execution of the run unit's IMPART
            or most recent FREE command.

FETCH: FETCH is a combination of the DML FIND and GET commands.

FIND: FIND is the DML command, DMS execution of which causes the DMS to
            locate and determine the availability of a record. A FIND may take
            place in several different manners, allowing a record to be located
            directly via its data base key, through its position relative to
            a current record, through a calc procedure, or through its membership
            in a set relationship.

FREE: FREE is the DML command, DMS execution of which causes the release
            of all page locks and quick before looks effected by the run unit.
            Execution of the FREE command causes an effective end of run unit
            sentinel and start of run unit sentinel to be placed on the audit
            trail.

GET: GET is the DML command, DMS execution of which causes the transfer
            of the contents of the current record of run unit from the data base
            to the record delivery area for the record type in the main program.

IMPART: IMPART is the DML command, DMS execution of which registers the run
            unit with the DMS.

INSERT: INSERT is the DML command, DMS execution of which links the current
            record of the run unit into the proper occurrence of the set types(s)
            named in the command. The record type must have been defined, via
            the schema DDL, as a manual member of the named set type(s).

KEEP: KEEP is the DML command, DMS execution of which places a lock on the
            page which contains the current record of the run unit.

LOG: LOG is the DML command which directs the DMS to write non-DMS data
            and, optionally, to write recovery points on the audit trail.

MODIFY: MODIFY is the DML command, DMS execution of which replaces the values
            of the data items of the object record in the data base with the
            values of the data items of the object record in the record delivery
            area for the record type in the main program. The MODIFY may be
            used to alter the record's membership in an occurrence of a set
            type, or it's intraset position.

OPEN: OPEN is the DML command which directs the DMS to make an area or
            areas available for access by the run unit, and indicates to the
            DMS the usage mode of the area or areas. Usage may be initial load,
            or exclusive or protected update or retrieval. Exclusive and
            protected uses of an area are defined in the LOCKS section of the
            paper.

page: A page is a subdivision of an area and is the basic unit of DMS I/O.
            A page may contain from zero to n records, depending upon the page
            size which is defined, in words, in a schema DDL area entry.

program: A program is a set or group of instructions.

record: A record is an occurrence of a named collection of zero, one, or
            more data items or data aggregates.

REMOVE: REMOVE is the DML command, DMS execution of which cancels the member-
            ship of the current record of the run unit in the occurrence of the

set type(s) named in the command. The record type must have been
defined, via the schema DDL, as a manual member of the named set
type(s).

run unit: A run unit is the execution of one or more programs. The life of a
run unit known to the DMS is that part between IMPART and respective
DEPART commands.

set: A set is an occurrence of a named collection of records. A set
type is a logical relationship among record types and thus provides
the mechanism for representing data structures.

STORE: STORE is the DML command, DMS execution of which places a new record
in the data base in accordance with the location logic specified in
the schema DDL record description for the record type. The record
is chained into the proper occurrence of those set types in which
the record type is defined, via the schema DDL, as an automatic
member.

system's generation parameters: System's generation parameters are constants
which the data administrator may change to alter operational or
structural characteristics of the DMS.

utility processor: The DMS utility processor is a collection of routines
which performs, as directed by the data administrator, a variety of
functions on the data base. The data administrator specifies, via
the utility language, the functions to be performed and the portion
of the data base to be operated upon. The utility processor interfaces
with the DMR.

REFERENCES

1. Univac 1100 Series Data Management System (DMS 1100) Operator Reference
   UP-7971 Rev. 1, Schema Definition UP-7907 Rev. 1, American National
   Standard COBOL (ASCII) Data Manipulation Language UP-7992, and System
   Support Functions UP-7909 Rev. 1.

2. CODASYL Data Base Task Group October 1969 Report. (Currently out of
   print.)

   CODASYL Data Base Task Group April 1971 Report. (Available for $6.00
   prepaid from ACM, Order Department, 1133 Avenue of the Americas, New
   York, N. Y. 10026. Available in Europe from the British Computer
   Society, 29 Portland Place, London W1N 4AP, England or IFIP Administrative
   Data Processing Group, 6 Stadhouderskade, Amsterdam 1013, Netherlands.)

   CODASYL Data Description Language Journal of Development June 1973.
   (Available for $1.70 prepaid from the National Bureau of Standards, Depart-
   ment of Commerce, Washington D. C. 20234. Reference NBS Handbook 113.)

DISCUSSION

Abrial : It seems that the addition of software to provide a backup and
rollback mechanism is a very costly way of solving the problem of deadlock.
It is costly in terms of all the testing and overhead required.

Everest : The backup and rollback mechanism is perhaps costly, but it is
required for purposes other than deadlock detection and correction. For
example, if an update process goes wild and makes incorrect changes, it is
necessary to stop it and undo all the changes it made incorrectly.

Data Base Management, J. W. Klimbie and K. L. Koffeman, (eds.)
© *North-Holland Publishing Company (1974)*

Data definition spectrum and procedurality spectrum

in data base management systems

T. WILLIAM OLLE

Independent Consultant

27 Blackwood Close, West Byfleet, Surrey

KT14 6PP, ENGLAND.

Abstract : This paper describes two spectrums - the phys-log
spectrum along which all data definition languages
must lie and the procedurality spectrum along which
all languages to act on a computerized data base
must lie. A proposal for a multi-stage data definition
process supported by different user interfaces is
outlined.

1. Introduction

It is useful at the outset to suggest the following taxonomy of DBMS
interests. First we have the practitioners, whom I break down in the
following way : specifiers, implementers, marketeers, and users. Among
users, we have data administrators, programmers, non-programmers, and
parametric users. Some people use the term "end-users", which refers
to both the non-programmer and the parametric user. Next, we have
educators, analytic researches, experimenters, and theoreticians, and
I like to think of myself as an analytic researches although I know perfectly well that if I were talking to an audience of people in the user
class, they would claim that the talk I am about to give was theoretical.

There is an important difference between conceptualization, technical
feasibility, and commercial viability. The British and French governments,
when considering the Concorde project know this only to well.

Conceptualization is step often all too easy. It may be difficult
to achieve technical feasibility, but the step that really hurts is the
one from there to commercial viability. There must be a lesson to be
learned here, in our data base management world.

2. Physical-logical spectrum

The physical-logical spectrum, or phys-log spectrum is a spectrum
along which every data definition process must lie. Each "data structure
class" lies somewhere on this spectrum.

A lot has been said at this meeting about the relational model which
Bill McGee referred to as the FDSC (flat data structure class), and that
is at one extreme end. Most of the theoretical studies heard at this
conference tend to deal with some aspect of this end of the spectrum.

This particular end is not necessarily everybody's ideal. It might be
somebody's ideal, but it is not necessarily that which is pleasing to
all the people all of the time.

3. Procedurality Spectrum

We have been in some ways rather like mankind coming out of the cave and realizing there is a difference between night and day, and were happy to identify the difference between procedural and non-procedural.

These two terms are now essentially undefinable, in the sense that they are two undefinable points on the procedurality spectrum.

We should talk rather about more procedural or less procedural, but not about a binary on/off kind a situation.

Procedurality is a property of a statement class as well as a property of a collection of st tements (which we will define for the purpose of this paper as a language). One can, for example, look at the DBTG STORE statement and say that is "non-procedural". The programmer includes a single statement in his program and as any implementor or user knows, a lot of things happen. One can look at some other statement classes and say that they are more procedural.

My definition of "less procedural" implies ease of writing, whereas "more procedural" implies more user writing to specify some process.

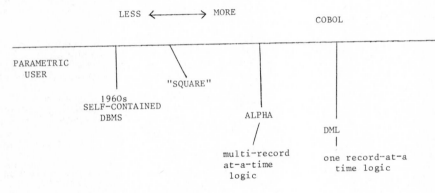

Figure 1. Procedurality spectrum

The end points on the spectrum are not necessarily ideals, and one end point on the procedurality spectrum can be regarded as the interface between the man and the machine as exercised by the parametric user.

My parametric user, as some of you know, is the bank clerk or the airline clerk or the inventory control clerk, and I am going to say a bit more about this parametric user in a minute.

In Figure 1, at the least procedural end, we have the parametric users: interface and next to it we have the 1960's self-contained DBMS.

The essential difference between ALPHA and DML, is the fact that the DML is quite clearly one record-at-a-time logic, whereas ALPHA allows multi-record at-a-time logic. There is a very important difference between those two.

The parametric user level represents the Data Independence Mecca because it is very easy to do all kinds of things behind the parametric user's interface without having to revise his particular interface with the database when the data base is restructured. The more procedural levels, such as the DML level, the ALPHA level, the SQUARE level, and the self-contained DBMS level, are needed to specify the transaction types which are later invoked by the parametric user.

The language which is at present specifically used to set things up for the parametric user is very much the DML. The other procedural levels could be used in the future without any significant problems being incurred.

4. Factors affecting procedurality

The factors affecting procedurality are the following :
Firstly comes knowledge of and ability to use Boolean connectors. The parametric user does not need to understand Boolean algebra, and I do not think we should expect this. On the other hand, the SQUARE user and the 1960s self-contained user needs to understand Boolean algebra.

Next comes knowledge of logical structure. The parametric user, does not need to understand the logical structure while the other levels do.

Thirdly, we have use of working space. The ALPHA user and the DML user need to have a clear awareness of working space. They are controlling data flow between the data base and primary storage, and they move data from the data base into working regions.

The semantic implications of a statement class affect the procedurality level. Consider the DML FIND statements, some of which are more procedural than others. Format 1 is in itself a simple effectively non procedural statement but, if used, implies the program is quite procedural.

Another factor affecting procedurality is knowledge of logical to physical mapping. If the user of an interface needs to have knowledge of the logical to physical mapping, then it is fair to assert that this makes the procedurality level more.

5. Factors influencing the Phys-Log spectrum.

The chief factor here is the degree of logical to physical mapping in the DDL, such as LOCATION MODE, the WITHIN clause, SET MODE, and other clauses influencing the logical to physical mapping. There have been examples of implementers taking out some of these clauses and the DDLC took out the SET MODE clause in their recently published Journal of Development.

In a given DBMS, the Data Definition process could become a multi-stage process. The concept of a compatible multi-stage data definition process is basically not new. The DBTG 1971 proposal provides for a two-stage data definition process. I do not mean the Schema DDL and the Subschema DDL, but the Schema DDL and the Device Media Control Language. These are two separate but compatible stages in an overall data definition process. The sub-schema is in effect a selection mechanism which at least for the DBTS's DML is at same point on the phys-log spectrum as is the Schema DDL. The DBTG included in the DMCL everything that DML programmer did not need to know in order to write a program to process the data base. This two stage definition is a valuable concept, and we can take it a bit further and think in terms of a multi-stage definition process, where the data definitions are at different points on the phys-log spectrum.

6. The Nijssen Principle.

This states that the user population should be allowed a choice of points on the procedurality spectrum. In order to support this, one must identify corresponding points on the phys-log spectrum, because one cannot have a procedurality level (at one end of one spectrum) which operates as a DDL at the other end of the other spectrum. These points, in fact the whole of each spectrum have a relationship or effectively a correlation one with the other. This is what Nijssen was saying.

The choice between ALPHA level procedurality and DML level procedurality should be made by the user (that is the customer) and not by the implementer. Maybe it is the customer's data administrator who makes the choice, but it should be his choice. It should not be a choice forced on the customer by a group of people such as the DDLC, by a manufacturer.

7. Commercial Viability.

The DML procedural level has attained commercial viability, and it is not something which is attained because of the DBTG proposal, but is a little older than that. There is some difference between IDS and DBTG but not on this all important question of the procedurality level.

The DML is commercially viable and it would be rather an exciting project, at the ALPHA level to seek commercial viability in the COBOL speaking world, which is one way to refer to the world of data processing practioners.

One has to try to communicate with people in the language to which they are accustomed. From a study of the concepts in relation of databases and in the ALPHA paper, these capabilities (as defined) seem eminently translatable. The time is appropriate for them to be put to the commercial viability test, and I sincerely hope that they succeed.

The customer would then have a choice ; he can buy up his DBMS from vendor X or vendor Y, and then he can choose how he uses it. This concept of a multi-facetted DBMS with a finite number of different user procedurality levels, should be a powerful one. This whole idea depends on the multi-stage data definition process.

8. Proposed syntax outline for Primary Data Definition.

Figure 2.

MULTI - STAGE DATA DEFINITION

SCHEMA NAME IS schema-name 1

DEFINITION STAGE IS PRIMARY

RECORD NAME IS record-name

LOCATION MODE IS CALC (db-proc)

USING db-id-1 (, db-id-2).....

DUPLICATES ARE NOT ALLOWED

(ON Clause)...
(PRIVACY clause).....

```
Data Sub-entry skeleton
N.B. exclude   OCCURS   clause
               RESULT   clause
               SOURCE   clause
               ENCODING clause
```

In Figure 2 is given a proposed outline for a Schema DDL subset which could be used to define a relational level DDL. For each record type, it would be necessary to define a LOCATION MODE OF CALC. It seems to be a basic premise in the relational approach that each record type (or relation) in fact has a key. One purpose of the LOCATION MODE IS CALC to specify that there exists an application oriented key which enables a DML programmer to access an occurrence of this record type using that key.

The other two location modes do not imply this is possible. LOCATION MODE CALC means one is able to make what I call an "out of the blue" access to the data base. More importantly a way of defining a unique identifier for the record type seems to be a basic premise of the relation approach. CALC does not necessarily mean hashing. It could well imply some other technique depending on the system.

The DUPLICATES ARE NOT ALLOWED clause is reputed to ensure that the key is unique. The OCCURS clause must clearly be excluded and we will also exclude the RESULT clause, the SOURCE clause, and the ENCODING clause.

At the secondary stage of the data definition, one has the set entry skeleton where one defines the set types, and they introduce what Bracchi called the "preferential paths". Finally one gets down to the DMCL, which might depend on how many stages one wants.

This is the way we should try to go. The most significant proposal here, is that someone should try to translate the ALPHA capabilities into COBOL speaking world. It would be very interesting to see how a capability of this kind would stand the test of commercial viability.

This presentation was not followed by a discussion due to lack of time.

Data Base Management, J. W. Klimbie and K. L. Koffeman, (eds.)
© *North-Holland Publishing Company (1974)*

ON THE DEVELOPMENT OF DATA BASE EDITIONS

Robert W. Taylor and David W. Stemple
Department of Computer and Information Science
University of Massachusetts, Amherst, Massachusetts

1. INTRODUCTION

A recognized fact of life when dealing with data bases is that they evolve over time. This evolution takes place on a number of levels of data structure. The first of these, and the level with which most existing systems deal well, is the level of data occurrences. That is, new occurrences of data are inserted, and existing occurrences are changed or deleted. But through all of this, the data base structure--the schema*--remains unchanged. New item, record and set types are never added to or deleted from the data base schema, nor are the definitions of which occurrences of records are linked to which other occurrences of records, e.g. the SET OCCURRENCE SELECTION clause of the set member sub-entry, ever changed.

The static nature of the data base schema has a number of implications for the run-time modules of the data management system. Generally, it means that the storage format of records is bound at compile time for any program accessing the data base. That is, if two records A and B are related by set S, then whatever method is used for representing occurrences of this set--say chaining--there is no question concerning "where in an occurrence of record A is the pointer for following set S". The answer is always the same for record occurrences of type A. A similar argument holds for items and groups within occurrences of record type A. This is not to say that the run time modules of the data management system may not have to search through the stored version of the schema to discover the position--it is merely to say that there is a binding between record type and storage format, which may indeed be defined by the stored schema.

Because of the fixed nature of data base schemas, usually the only way to allow a data base to evolve is to dump the data base under one schema and reload it under a different one. The introduction of new record types, so long as they are not heavily linked to existing record types, is an exception to this. But the fact remains that not much flexibility beyond the introduction of new record types is allowed.

In addition to the dumping and reloading of at least a part of the data base, there is the concurrent problem of recompiling any programs which deal with the changed record or set types. The user working areas, used for communication with the data base manager, will have been given a specific storage layout by the compiler. A re-compilation and possibly a change to the program's data division may be necessary depending on the sophistication of the sub-schema facility provided by the data management system.

---

*For purposes of the exposition, we use the terminology of the DBTG report [1]. The issues discussed here are independent of any particular data management system, however.

This paper explores techniques which will allow data base schemas to evolve over time without the necessity of dumping and reloading or of re-compiling application programs. In particular, we explore the problem of allowing data base "editions"--an edition of a data base is defined as follows:

The original schema is the edition O schema. This schema (compiled into schema tables), together with data occurrences conforming to it, comprise an edition O data base. An edition n + 1 schema is created from an edition n schema by one or more of the following:

1. The addition and/or deletion of one or more items within one or more record types.

2. The addition and/or deletion of one or more record types.

3. The addition and/or deletion of one or more set types.

4. Changes in set occurrence selection or virtual/actual result specifications.

Further, an edition n schema specifies the mapping, if needed, of all editions j (j < n) data occurrences into forms suitable for presentation to edition n programs, i.e. programs compiled with an edition n schema*.

An edition n data base is an edition n schema (compiled into schema tables) together with data occurrences conforming to editions O through n of the schema.

We further assume that an edition n program wishes to access data occurrences from both prior and later editions. We focus our discussion on the design issues which arise from such an environment, namely:

1. What features of a data base management system are necessary to support editions?

2. How can one edition differ from another and still be processed by programs compiled later or earlier?

3. What attributes of the data base are still resolvable at program compile time, implying little loss in run time efficiency? When is a re-interpretation necessary?

2. NECESSARY FEATURES TO SUPPORT EDITIONS

Consider the case where items are added to a given record type in a new data base edition. For example, record type R, edition O (R.O) may contain items A,

---

*Strictly speaking, it is only necessary to specify mappings from edition n-1 to edition n, but we allow the more general case for efficiency.

B, and C whereas record type R, edition 1 (R.1) contains items A, B, C, and D. If we wish to allow edition O programs to access edition 1 records, there is clearly no problem, since record type R to edition O programs contains only items A, B, and C. Thus the system need only deliver items A, B, and C in the formats they had at data base edition O, and the program will execute properly (we explore the problem of storing new data occurrences in later paragraphs).

Retrieval of edition O record occurrences (of type R) by edition 1 programs is somewhat more complicated. Clearly a value must be provided for item D. We thus arrive at a following necessary condition in a data definition language which allows for data base editions:

If in a later edition, an item is added to a record type, the definition in the later edition must provide a way of defining the value for accessing records of a previous edition. A data base procedure incorporated into a VIRTUAL RESULT specification will suffice for this task.

It should be clear that as soon as a generalized virtual result facility is available, the deletion of items in new editions becomes possible. In this case, when an edition O program accesses an edition 1 record, the virtual result will have to be computed since the item will be included in edition O of the record, but not in edition 1. If an item is deleted from a record type in a subsequent edition, then the edition definition must provide a means for computing the value when the record is accessed by programs compiled under a previous edition. Again, a generalized VIRTUAL RESULT mechanism will suffice.

The case of accessing set definitions which may or may not be present with respect to a particular edition of a data base is similar to item addition and deletion. However, allowing set types to be added/deleted across editions imposes some limitations on the structure of the records participating in the sets. For example, suppose that an edition O record occurrence is the current one of a particular run unit, and suppose also that in edition 1 of the data base, this record type is the owner record in a set type S that did not exist in edition O (see figure 1). Assume further that the run unit is an edition 1 program and wishes to traverse members of set S. The set occurrence can be traversed so long as in edition 1 there is a proper "set occurrence selection" clause for the new set. This set occurrence selection clause must be phrased in terms of values existing in both editions. It must specify criteria whereby a record occurrence can be implicitly associated with a particular set occurrence by virtue of the value of certain items existing within the record itself. Furthermore, the data management system must have an independent access path to record occurrences specified in the "set occurrence selection" clause.

Consider the example of Figure 1. As shown, in edition O of the data base, record types A and B exist, but are not explicitly related via a set. In edition 1, the two record types are related by set S. Further, the conditions for an occurrence of record B to be considered related to an occurrence of record A (i.e., a member of set S) is that they have matching key values. This is stated in the revised syntax of the forthcoming DDLC Journal of Development [2]. If an edition 1 run unit issued the DML command

FIND NEXT MEMBER OF S SET

and the "current" record of set S was an occurrence of record type A, edition O, the data base system would locate (by some means) those occurrences of record type B whose designated item values matched those in the record A occurrence. The record occurrence presented to the run unit would be that occurrence which satisfied the edition 1 SET OCCURRENCE SELECTION clause and was first under any set ordering defined in edition 1 for set S. We can thus draw the following conclusions:

So long as the determination of set occurrence selection is based on data values existing in the participating records (as opposed, say, to currency), and the data management system has an independent access path to the participating records, new set types can be incorporated across editions.

EDITION 0   EDITION 1

Sample Set Occurrence Selection Clause in Edition 1 of the Data Base.

SET OCCURRENCE SELECTION IS THRU S OWNER
IDENTIFIED BY CALC-KEY OF A EQUAL TO KEY
IN RECORD-B.

FIGURE 1

ACCESSING IMPLICIT SETS ACROSS DATA BASE EDITIONS

We now consider how this "independent access path" might be specified. The most obvious method is to make each record type a member of a singular set (i.e. one owned by the SYSTEM). This will always provide an exhaustive access path, but it also forces the data management software through a lengthy search in a large data base. A more sophisticated mechanism makes use of data base procedure mechanisms, often associated with location mode CALC. Given certain data values in the occurrence of record type A of our example, the data management system could use the appropriate values as inputs to a data base procedure which was much more than a CALC routine. Rather, this data base procedure could be a whole access method, as long as it eventually returns a data base key. Thus, by giving record type B a CALC location mode, a whole range of possible set traversal mechanisms is possible.

The most important point, however, is that the evolution of sets across data base editions requires a "matching value" philosophy when using the set occurrence selection clause. This reflects an approach similar to the match condition definition facility in the L-string of the DIAM model [3].

There remains the question of when to introduce a new record type as opposed to a new edition of an existing record type. A moment's reflection should convince the reader that the following outline should guide a data base administrator when making this decision:

A new edition is justified if:

1. An edition O program need ever access data values in a record stored by an edition 1 program

2. An edition 1 program needs to access an edition O record as if it were the augmented (or diminished) record under consideration.

If neither of the above conditions obtain, then introduction of a new record type (possibly containing as VIRTUAL RESULTS items from record types defined under the old edition) is a proper evolution of the data base. This will guarantee that the old program can never make reference to the new record type, since its name is not in the edition O program's name space.

The question of whether to create a new record type or new edition of an existing record type can also be approached using the concepts of the Entity Set Model and DIAM [3].

We first view a record type in the DBTG sense to be an A-string corresponding to an entity description (in DIAM terminology). If a data administrator is creating a new A-string (record type) corresponding to a new entity description, then the new edition of the schema should contain a new record type. The old program should be unaffected since it deals with entity descriptions which have not been revised; the old program need have no knowledge of the new entity description. If, on the other hand, the data administrator is augmenting or otherwise changing an existing entity description, then the new edition should contain a revised definition of the existing A-string, reflecting the fact that the entity level model is changed, but in a different sense.

For storing records, we adopt the guideline that creation of new record occurrences or modification of existing ones will be made using the current edition. This has several advantages. Primarily, it means that the run time modules of the data management system do not have to search back through the stored version of the several schemas in order to discover the proper storage format. They always use the most recent one, which is accessed frequently anyway and is apt to be in main storage. They do have to use the old schema in order to decode the data occurrences, but as will be seen in section 3, this does not imply a heavy overhead. In addition, the purpose of editions is to allow the data base to evolve. By always writing under the current edition, the data base occurrences will tend to be brought up to date as they are accessed. Only those records which are truly archival in the sense that they are read and never modified will remain under the old storage format.

There are some difficulties with this approach, however. In particular, when writing a record occurrence where an item or set type which existed in edition 0 does not exist (explicitly) in edition 1, information may be lost. This loss results from the fact that the set was explicitly represented in edition 0. There is no guarantee that the data values which implicitly represent set membership are present in the new edition (after all, the set is presumably no longer of interest). This loss, however, is due to a choice made by the data administrator and should therefore be a loss of little consequence. As a practical matter, it is our experience that additional set and item types are more frequent by far than the deletion of item and set types across editions. Thus, bringing the record occurrences "up to date" will usually not imply an information loss from previous editions.

3.   IMPLICATIONS OF EDITIONS ON RUN-TIME EFFICIENCY

The run-time inefficiencies of data management systems are well known. These inefficiencies are generally the result of a large amount of interpretation by the run-time modules of the data management system; they can generally be justified by savings in other areas--increased data independence, reduced program development time, etc. On the other hand, one would hope that inefficiencies would be avoided wherever possible. By this we mean that when a decision can be bound without loss of data independence it will be bound. This approach is preferable to total interpretation by the run time modules, especially if data management systems are to service applications which need a fast response.

There are several cases where a binding is possible, if desired, when dealing with data base editions.

Consider the case where an edition n program wishes to access edition m records, n > m. Most data management systems require that the run unit must first "register" its existence with the run-time modules of the data management system. That is, the operating system job scheduler will start execution of a run-unit, but this run-unit must still inform the data management system of its

existence in order to establish communications areas in storage and to allow the
data management system to resolve concurrent requests for data resources, free
deadlock conditions, etc. During this "registration", the run unit could provide
all information pertaining to the mechanism for transforming data occurrences from
prior editions into edition n format. This is true because at program compile time
all editions of the stored data base schema were (presumably) available to the
compiler. Each of these editions specified how to transform earlier editions into
later editions. Thus this information can be carried with the compiled version of
the program and "registered" with the data management system. There is no
necessity for the data management system during data access to also access the
stored schema in order to find out "how can I transform edition i to edition j".
That question is resolvable at compile time for all data base editions less than or
equal to the program edition.

If the data base record is of a later edition than the program edition, there
is, of course, no way the program can tell the system how to do the transformation.
When the system discovers an edition number in the accessed record which is greater
than the edition number of the accessing program, it will have to search for the
appropriate version of the stored schema. Thus the stored schema is interpreted
only when absolutely necessary.

4. CONCLUSION

This paper has introduced the concept of a data base edition and explored
ways in which it could be used to allow data bases to evolve over time without
the necessity of dumping and reloading. Of course, periodic dumping and reloading
to bring all data occurrences up to the present edition, as well as recompilation
of frequently used programs, may be desirable for the sake of efficiency. However,
with the ability to define editions, the decision of when to bring the data base up
to date can be made using a cost/benefit analysis in the same way that periodic
"garbage collections" of a data base can be justified on an operations research
basis [4].

For completeness, we note that there is a third kind of data base evolution,
more complex than creation/deletion of data occurrences and less complex than
full schema editions. This intermediate level deals with changing storage structures
for a fixed data base schema. An example would be a change in set implementation
specification from a mode of CHAIN to one of POINTER ARRAY with no other
change to the schema edition. Another would be a change in item representation
from binary to decimal.

It is felt that the techniques developed in this paper will aid in allowing this
intermediate level of editions--indeed, the concept of a sub-schema already incorporates many of these flexibilities.

In summary, if we accept the evolution of data base structures--both logical
and physical--as a way of life, it follows that the data base administrator must be
allowed to accommodate this evolution without dumping and reloading for every
change. The concept of a data base edition gives much of the machinery to let
this happen without massive recompilations. It is also possible under a data base

management system with editions to try some experiments which improve efficiency. As with so many programming systems, analytical and simulation techniques can often only suggest possibilities.   To see if a change will really help, the only way may be to try it.   If it works out, then a more complete restructuring can be undertaken; if not, then the occurrences will eventually be removed by reversing the effect of the experiment in the next edition.

REFERENCES

1. CODASYL Data Base Task Group, April, 1971, Report, Available from ACM.

2. CODASYL Data Definition Language Committee, Journal of Development, in press.

3. Senko, M. E., E. B. Altman, M. M. Astrahan, P. L. Fehder, Data Structures and accessing in data base systems, IBM Systems Journal, 12:1, 1973.

4. Schneiderman, B., Optimum Data Base Reorganization Points, Communications of ACM, 16:6, June, 1973.

DISCUSSION

Everest : Some of the differences between editions that you mention seem
to me to be very similar to the kinds of difference which may exist between
schema and sub-schema. For example, System 2000 will allow a sub-schema
record to differ from the corresponding schema record in the omission of a
data-item. When a program stores an occurrence of this record using this
sub-schema the system simply sets the omitted item to null.

Taylor : What you say is true ; but I think the difference between the
editions concept and the schema/sub-schema concept is that a new edition
may introduce new data (e.g. new data-items), whereas a sub-schema may not.

Nijssen : The real problem which cannot be handled by the edition concept
is the problem of what Codd calls attribute migration. For example, the
correspondence between products and warehouses may change from N:1 to N:M.
A program based on the N:1 assumption will no longer work.

Taylor : I agree. We are not claiming that editions will solve everything –
only the types of problem discussed in the paper.

Bayer : I would like to emphasize that the edition concept is important and
useful. For example, in a real-time situation, it may not be possible to
perform a static restructuring of the database (unloading it according to
the old schema and reloading it according to the new one). In such a situation it is essential to allow occurrences of a given record type created
under different editions to coexist in the database.

Data Base Management, J. W. Klimbie and K. L. Koffeman, (eds.)
© *North-Holland Publishing Company (1974)*

THE INTERFACE BETWEEN A DATABASE AND ITS HOST LANGUAGES

G.M. STACEY
Edinburgh Regional Computing Centre

Abstract

A description of database data from a program frame of reference may be divided into a part concerned with host language data unit representation and a part concerned with relationships between those data units. This concept is developed in an examination of the interfaces between a database and its host languages in which emphasis is placed on the search for commonality among different host language interfaces. Reference is made to the CODASYL DBTG proposals and to the relational model of data.

Introduction

The interfaces between a database and its users take the form of languages whose characteristics depend on the type of usage involved. In this paper we address that class of languages known as procedural which are intended for application programming. Examples are ALGOL, COBOL, FORTRAN and PL/1.

Procedural languages are usually conceived of interfacing with a database by means of the "host language concept". That is the language is extended by permitting it to host a set of commands (commonly known collectively as a data manipulation language (DML)) which provides the capability of storing and retrieving database data. Associated with a particular host language and database are a number of data description languages (DDL). Each DDL describes the structure of the data from a given frame of reference. Typical frames of reference are that of the centralized database and of the program. These DDL are utilised by the DML statements in the execution of their functions.

Before considering the details of interfacing a number of host languages to a database it is first necessary to justify the position that more than one host language is necessary. It should be remembered that a database is intended to serve a variety of types of application. There may for instance be administrative and scientific programmers sharing data but with quite different processing requirements.

The current state of program usage is such that a number of major languages do exist. A very common occurrence in an organisation is likely to be the use of COBOL in administrative applications and FORTRAN in scientific applications. It is therefore postulated that a database must be capable of interfacing to a number of host languages.

Analysis of the interface between a database and a host language

If we accept the postulate that a number of host languages must be interfaced with a database, an important consideration is how the different interfaces for different host languages may be related.

In the interests of standardisation and co-ordination there is much merit in providing as great a degree of overlap of host language interfaces as possible.

To determine what may be common to all host languages, it is necessary to analyse the complete interface between a database and a host language to see how the database functions relate to the database and host language structures. This analysis is developed in this section round the model of the interface illustrated in Fig. 1 and using the CODASYL DBTG (1971) proposals as a point of reference.

Fig. 1   The interface between a database and a host language

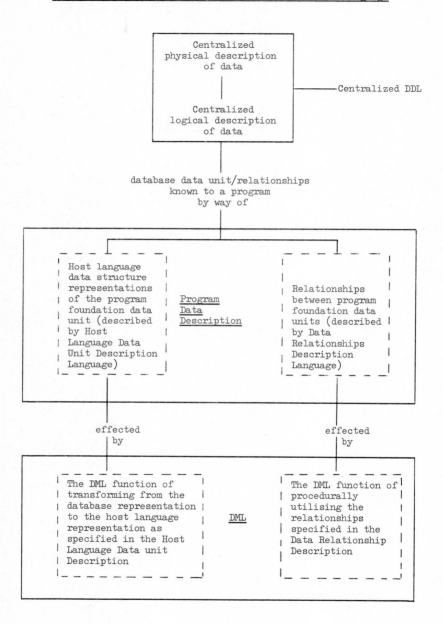

In considering the interfacing of host languages to the database we start from the description of the database itself. Some form of centralized co-ordination of data is generally considered necessary. In Fig. 1 is shown a centralized description of the database composed of two parts, a logical part and a physical part. These are shown coupled together. The extent to which they may be separated is a matter of debate at present. However, this is not a central issue in this paper and so is not discussed here. The <u>Centralized DDL</u> corresponds in Codasyl DBTG terms to the Schema DDL.

The next consideration is how a database data description is made known to a host language program. We conceive a <u>program data description language</u> which describes the database data in a form appropriate for a given host language and which is utilised by DML commands within a host language program. These correspond to the CODASYL sub-schema DDL and DML.

<u>A data description may be considered in general to consist of data descriptions in terms of a chosen data unit plus descriptions of relationships between realisations of that data unit.</u> For example the CODASYL DDL are basically descriptions in terms of the record data unit with relationships between records represented as sets. We shall call this special data unit the <u>foundation data unit</u> of a data description. This division has a correspondence in the way the DML presents the database data structure to a program. Firstly the DML functions explicitly utilise in a procedural manner relationships between foundation data units, as described in the program DDL, to select occurrences of foundation data units. Secondly the DML transforms the selected occurrences of foundation data units into host language data structure representation as described in the program DDL. The program data description is related to the database by the use in it of the database data names that appear in the database data description.

Thus the program data description naturally divides into two parts which we shall call the <u>host language data unit description</u> and the <u>data relationship description</u>. This is shown in Fig. 1.

It is assumed here that the centralized database description has the record as its foundation data unit. This does not imply that the program data description foundation data unit should also be the record. It is worth considering the options in this respect.

The argument against using higher data units (such as the CODASYL set) as the program foundation data unit is that at present major programming languages do not possess an appropriate unit. Rather than develop such units (or a relational expression of them) for each host language, it seems preferable that they are developed as part of the general database structures and are expressed (as are sets in CODASYL) via the DML.

Going to data units smaller than the record, it seems sensible to eliminate the group data item from consideration. Groups are usually conceived only as part of a record and cannot stand alone. For this reason they are not suitable as a foundation data unit.

The final possibility is to go to the data item as the program foundation data unit. The problem here is that on its own a data item is often (but not always) meaningless, in the sense that it is without context. The structuring of data items into a record is a way of providing context. All the data item instances in a record typically relate to one entity. One (or more) of the data items identify the entity thus providing the context for all the data items in the record. Grouping within a record is a means of further defining context. The relational approach to data as typified by the "third normal form" is simply a way of organising data item context. Associated with this approach is the fact that in some cases programs are not interested in context or are only interested in partial context. This is typical of many statistical programs where a natural way of looking at data is as collections consisting of instances of a single data item.

An example of a program data description with a data item foundation data unit is the relational system described in Strnad (1972), where data is represented as sets of data elements and sets of relations among them.

From the above we are left with the record and the data item as possible program foundation data units. An important point is that choice of a program foundation data unit does not imply choice of a host language. This is fundamentally a result of the fact that a program data description provides firstly a particular way of looking at data and only secondly a way of representing that view in host language terms. For example a CODASYL type data description founded on records and a relational-type data description (as suggested by Codd (1970)) founded on data items could exist for the same host language.

A major question at this point is whether the two cases must be treated as completely separately or whether some overlap is possible from the point of view of data description.

Data items can in all cases be formed into records. Two examples are worth presenting. Firstly a record could consist of instances of a single data item. Then a host language view of sets of data items would access data items one by one in the DML. The option could exist of making the record data unit transparent to the host language program. Secondly, even where languages do not recognise records, a record may still be considered as the foundation data unit. This may be achieved by associating independent host language data items to a record unit in the host language data unit description. The host language program then processes the data items independently but the DML commands manipulate them collectively as a record. This technique is utilized in an interface to the DBTG proposals as specified in Stacey (1974).

It would therefore seem that a data item foundation representation could always be arranged via a record foundation interface. Whether this would always be desirable is difficult to predict.

Within the context of the current CODASYL proposals such an arrangement does seem advantageous. In references Stacey (1972, 1974) a common CODASYL sub-schema framework for all host languages is proposed which is in essence a communal record interface.

For the remainder of this section it is assumed that all data foundation representations do operate via a record foundation interface in such a way that the data relationship description between data items may be emulated by a data relationship description between records and a data relationship description between data items within records. This is illustrated in Fig. 2.

Fig. 2 A possible organisation of program data relationship
descriptions based on records and those based on data items

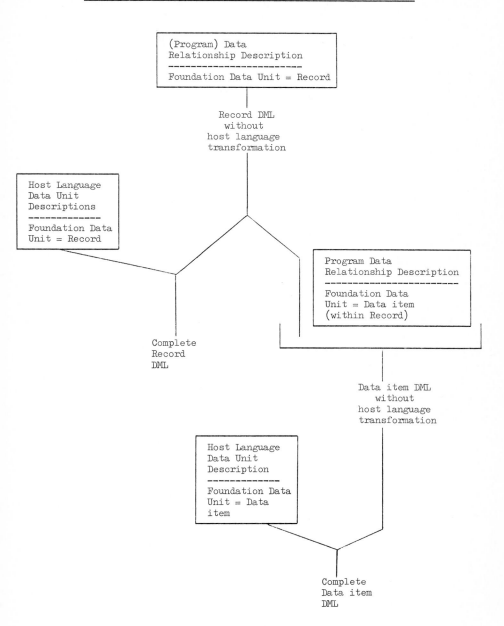

It is now possible to inspect the program interface to the database to determine which parts must be host language dependent and which parts may be communal to all host languages. The data relationship description of the program data description are independent of host language representation. This is opposite to the case of the host language data unit description which by definition is host language dependent. The DML is functionally independent of the host language in that all dependence on the host language representation is handled through the host language data unit description. There may be syntactic reasons for providing the DML in a form oriented to the particular host language involved. There may also be ancilliary reasons concerning the interaction of the DML with host language or machine specific facilities such as error handling. It would seem desirable however to keep these to the absolute minimum.

The communal data relationship description at the record level is an important part of the database-host language interface. In some sense it can be described as a partial view of the database. It describes relationships between records; and the record is the foundation unit for the database. It does not describe the database representation of the records. It may correspond to a subset of the database data simply by the exclusion of database names (which appear in the centralized data description). It is also possible to exclude from it reference to those parts of the centralized data description which are concerned purely with centralized control of the database.

It does, however, also relate to the host language interface. It was implied earlier that the record descriptions of the communal record interface (describing a subset of the database data) are related to the choice of host language interface and associated program foundation data unit. For example the description of a record as a collection of instances of a single data item is orthogonal to that of a record as a single instance of each of a collection of different data items. Yet in a database, both views may have to be supported simultaneously. This implies that although the communal data relationship description is specified in terms of records and relationships between them, these records may differ from those described in the centralized data description. For example, if we relate this to the CODASYL DBTG proposals, the centralized description would be in terms of records and sets as would be the communal data relationship description but the actual record and set types would be different.

The existence of orthogonal modes of usage of data in a database causes considerable efficiency problems. The choice of an "optimal form" of data structures as implied by a centralized data description may be difficult or even impossible to determine where no single mode is dominant. Just as the group data item forms an intermediary level between the data item and record so a centralized description effectively based on groups, by describing a large number of small simple record types with more (set type) relationships between them, may be a suitable form of compromise. On the other hand it may be necessary to return to the use of data duplication (with automated or semi-automated co-ordination) to achieve satisfactory efficiency. Considerable flexibility is thus required in the mappings allowed from the centralized data description to the communal data relationship description. The possibilities should exist for central records to become groups of larger program interface records and for program interface records to be composed of instances (more than one) of a single data item of a central record.

Summary

This paper represents an exploration of the way in which a number of host languages may be interfaced to a database. A central concept presented is the structuring of the program data description into a part concerned with host language data unit representation and a part concerned with data relationships. Of particular significance is the role of the program data relationship description. The fact that this relationship description is independent of host language data structure representations raises the possibility of it being communal to all host languages. However preliminary investigation suggests that a number of different program "views" of data relationships are necessary, although each view may itself be host language independent. The fact that the program data relationship description may be also independent from the database data representation means that a database may be capable of supporting several quite different program views of the data relationships. Hence a CODASYL type sub-schema data description and a relational data description (as suggested by Codd (1970)) may both be supportable for one database. Given a particular program view of a database, the program data relationship description may be communal to all host languages. The extent to which a communal program data relationship description may be defined for all program views is difficult to assess. The suggestion in this paper of a communal record interface is a possibility but further study is required in this area.

References

CODASYL DBTG (1971), Data Base Task Group Report, April 1971.

Codd, E.F. (1970), "A Relational Model of Data for Large Shared Data Banks", Comm. ACM, 13, p 377.

Stacey, G.M. (1974), "A FORTRAN Interface to the CODASYL Data Base Task Group Specifications", Computer Journal, scheduled for 17, (Feb. 1974).

Stacey, G.M. (1972), "A Common Sub-schema Framework for all host languages", CODASYL DDLC Proposal UKM-72001, August 1972.

Strnad, A.J. (1972), "The Relational Approach to the Management of Data Bases", Information Processing 71, p 801.

DISCUSSION

<u>Codd</u> : If I have understood you correctly you are opposed to the (mathematical) set as the unit of retrieval in a programming language. However, the non-programmer needs to be able to retrieve sets ; and once we have implemented such a facility for the non-programmer, why should we not make it available to the programmer too ?

<u>Stacey</u> : What I am saying is that the set should be a unit for the DML — possibly — but not for the host language. I do not want to add new data constructs to procedural languages such as Fortran.

<u>Douque</u> : You have shown that a given collection of data can be expressed at the schema level in a variety of ways — netword, relational and so on. Since you claim that all users access the data via a sub-schema, it is your conclusion that the structure is irrelevant at the schema level ?

<u>Stacey</u> : No. I'm not quite sure what I do want at the schema level — but I want a structure which will be fairly stable, one which is simple and easy to manage, one for which the mapping to storage can be reasonably straightforward. The DBTG structure is probably too complex. Maybe I am arguing in favor of a flat structure. Let me repeat, however, that there will be multiple user views available at the sub-schema level.

<u>Olle</u> : If you have owner-coupled sets at the sub-schema level but not at the schema level, what do you do about the 'preferential paths' that these sets represent ?

<u>Stacey</u> : I didn't say you wouldn't have sets at the schema level. In fact I think you must — but not quite as DBTG does it.

Data Base Management, J. W. Klimbie and K. L. Koffeman, (eds.)
© *North-Holland Publishing Company (1974)*

S T A F

STANDARD AUTOMATION FUNDAMENTS

a model for automatic information processing

by F. Grotenhuis

Department of Information
Systems and Automation

Philips Industries,
Eindhoven

With acknowledgements to: J. van den Broek, P. van der Ham and M. Huits
of the same department

CONTENTS

1. INTRODUCTION

When people start talking about automatic information processing there
is a good chance that they end in a perfect babel of tongues, especially
when the "real" world is confronted with the world of the machine.

In the real world of business information processing there exists a large
amount of information, relatively simple processing, an everlasting
growth, many changes and very strong requirements for reliability.

Most of the time the problems of describing the information or the
processing needed can be solved. It is getting worse when such a
description is presented to the machine. This machine then appears to
be unfamiliar with a number of concepts used in the description:
- a simple request for data is translated into get and put-facilities,
  chains, data-management etc.;
- dependencies of certain operations have to be expressed in a job control
  language or in supervisor calls;
- most of the time the machine remains unaware of the real intentions;
  the user knows the totality of data he needs, the machine only receives
  requests for pieces of data;
- Besides that the machine is not able to recognize the structure of the
  processing, so it cannot give a helping hand in building or correcting
  the processing system.

The result is that the world of information processing has to adapt itself
to the world of the machine and has to introduce concepts which are not
relevant for their world.

It is easy to blame the machine. But from the world of the machine the
question may rise: "Which are the concepts from the information processing
I should understand?". The answer will be: "We do not know.... what do
you understand?". This project is an attempt to break through this vicious
circle.

TARGETS OF STAF

The first target will be to present a model of automatic information
processing, including the concepts needed for the description of
information and which are recognized by the machine. These concepts must
be general and independent of implementation possibilities and specific
hardware. Later on a language can be developed, based on the above
mentioned concepts, to enable the system-designer to define information
processing systems.

PROCEDURE

First a picture of the world of information processing is given,
introducing an information-model and the requirements for information
processing based on that model. After that the world of the machine is
described, giving some requirements and some basic concepts.

In the third part it is tried to illustrate, in a bottom to top approach,
a model for information processing based on the requirements and
possibilities of both worlds.

As most of the concepts mentioned in the first two parts are wellknown,
the emphasis will lie on the third part.

2. THE WORLD OF INFORMATION

INFORMATION MODEL

A model is made with a specific goal in mind. So one will make, with information processing in mind, a model of (parts of) a firm. In that model the important data for information processing of an <u>object</u> (e.g. employee X, machine Y, product Z) or a <u>class of objects</u> (e.g. personnel, machinery, products) have to be expressed.

So the system designer draws a model of the firm. This model with the occurring objects forms the real world for information processing. The information itself can be regarded as values attributed to the model.

REPRESENTATION IN SPACE

Data, belonging to an object, are called <u>components</u> and can be represented in space

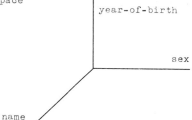

When a value is given to each of the components, a point in space will be the result.

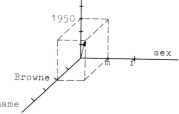

This point or <u>vector</u> represents the model of employee Browne. "Browne" is the value of the name-component of the vector (Browne, 1950, m). More vectors can be added to the space, as for instance:

$$
\begin{array}{lll}
(\text{Andersen}, & 1945, & \text{m}) \\
(\text{Browne} & , 1950, & \text{m}) \\
(\text{Layman} & , 1930, & \text{f}) \\
(\text{Phillips}, & 1940, & \text{m})
\end{array}
$$

Together these employees form the <u>vector-set</u> "Employees of the Bookkeeping Department".

TERMINOLOGY

In the preceding paragraph some terms are mentioned in connection with
actual objects. Besides that a formal description is necessary. So the
formal description of the vector (Browne, 1950, m) is (name,
year-of-birth, sex) and is called a <u>vector-description</u>. This vector-
description refers to the <u>vector-component-description</u>, e.g. "year-of-
birth". The values given to the components depend on the model chosen for
the class of objects. The values to be attached to the component "year-
of-birth", called the <u>domain</u> of this component, may be all numbers of
4 digits.

All components mentioned in the vector-description with their domains
define the theoretically needed space, called <u>descriptive space</u>
(cartesian product). In practice there will always be restrictions and
then remains the <u>definition space</u>. All vectors, and hence vector-sets
too, have to remain within the definition space.

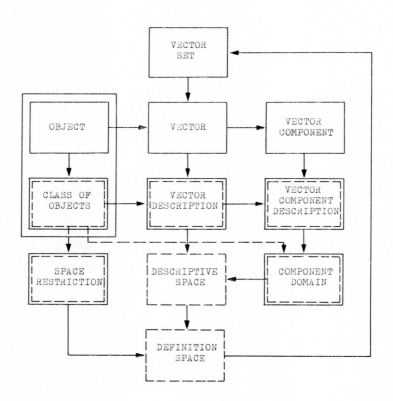

SPACE RESTRICTIONS

When two vectors have the same values for all components there is no difference between them and so they refer to one object only. Hence it follows that the whole of component-values must differ for each vector. This means that at least one component of a vector must be different from the same component in the other vectors. Such components are called identifying components. The space, formed by them, is called the identifying space. Projections of vectors from a vector-set on the identifying space may not result in coinciding points.

Another restriction may be expressed by a function, e.g. given the vector-description (a,b) the descriptive space may be restricted by the function $(a + b) < 6$, resulting in the definition space.

NIL VALUE

Components which do not belong to the identifying space need not have a value for each object. If that value for a certain object is not relevant or unknown, the value "nil" will be taken to enable a vector-representation. The consequences are that the domains of not-identifying components must include the value "nil".

INFORMATION PROCESSING

Generally speaking information is time dependent: information is changed
and new information is added. Besides there is a need for presenting
information in an understandable form and to create new information
derived from the existing information.

So one can distinguish registration, processing and presentation of
information. With reference to the concepts already introduced it will
be tried to describe information processing in terms of operating with
vectors.

REGISTRATION

When information changes a new version of the information is created.
Usually that change of information will influence a set of related
vectors, so the information is not consistent as long as the change is
not completed. The new version of the information must be available
as soon as the change is completed. In the meantime the old version
remains available. This concept introduces the fact that several versions
of the information exist at a given time. The old versions have to be
kept until they are not longer needed or till they pass a defined
expiration date.

Adding a new object results in adding a new vector. After the addition
of a vector or a group of related vectors a new version of the vector-
set exists.

Changing the values of one or more components also results in creating
and adding a new vector. So completion of the operation on one vector
or a group of vectors also creates a new version of the vector-set.

PROCESSING

Processing can be seen as:
- selecting and adding vectors;
- transformation of individual vectors;
- dialogue between user and processor.

About the first item much has been said already in the literature.
Actions like join, composition and union have to do with adding vectors.
For selective actions one will find operations like projection, intersec-
tion, division etc.

A transformation creates a new vector based on one or more existing
vectors, according to the definition that states the relation between
the components of the new vector and the components of the existing
vector.

In many cases processes are related. A dialogue is a model of the relation
between processes. The message that asks something from another process
is called a "stimulus" the answer is called "response". It is possible
that a process does not get enough information to give a response; in
that case it can start a (sub)dialogue with the questioner or another
process to gather the necessary information and thereafter continue the
original dialogue. The dialogues may include dialogues.

3. THE WORLD OF THE MACHINE

Information can be processed automatically by means of information processing machines. These machines consist of more or less independent components and must be able to process large amounts of information, according to rules defined by a user. Aims, requirements and restrictions of information processing machines are:

Aims: - to store information;
      - to process already stored or available information;
      - to present information to a user in an understandable form.

Requirements: - the working of a machine has to be surveyable and
                understandable, i.e. transparent;
              - to achieve this a building block concept will be necessary;
              - the concepts of the machine must be near to the concepts
                of the user;
              - the machine must be reliable, no information may be lost
                because of machine errors;
              - the machine must allow that information can be handled
                by several users simultaneously;
              - the machine must be able to attach priority to certain
                activities;
              - the machine must work efficient.

Restrictions: - a machine can handle only a limited amount of information
                simultaneously;
              - the processing has a finite speed;
              - a machine can make errors.

CONCEPTS

Information processing is always initiated by means of **commands** given by the user. A command must refer to:
- the information to be processed;
- the action to be taken.

Often a number of related commands are given, which are to be worked out successively. The working of a command depends on the result of the preceeding commands. The activities due to one or more related commands are called a **process**.

Between commands information has to be kept. To do this the concept of **dossier** is introduced. A dossier is coupled to a process and is created at the moment a process is started. When the process is terminated, the dossier disappears. A dossier gives the status of the process and contains all information of the preceeding part of the process that might be of interest for the following part of the process. A command for a process must always be seen in the context of the situation of the process as it appears in the dossier.

WORKING OF THE MACHINE

A machine consists of one or more submachines which can work simultaneously. Such a submachine is called a <u>processor</u>. A processor can handle a
limited amount of information only, so it will not always be possible to
have the complete set of vectors needed available for the processor.
Hence it follows that the processing has to be split up in smaller steps,
therefore a vector is taken as the unit of information to be processed.
To process a vector the following steps have to be taken:
- locate the vector in the available set;
- transform the vector into a new vector;
- add the new vector to the new set.

Deriving a new vector from an available vector is called a <u>transformation.</u>
The available vector is called Transformation Input Vector (TIV) and the
new vector is called Transformation Output Vector (TOV).
A transformation generates from each TIV one TOV.

A set of vectors can be processed by transforming the vectors one by
one.
If one TOV depends on one TIV only, the processing can be done by transforming all TIV's independently.
If one TOV depends on a fixed number of inputvectors, the collection of
these vectors is used as TIV.
If one TOV depends on a variable number of inputvectors, the transformation
can be done by transforming these vectors one by one as TIV's, but now
it has to be taken into account that each transformation needs the results
of the preceeding transformations. That history-information is kept in the
dossier of the process, as defined before.

So a TIV can consist of two parts. One part is the original inputvector
or message and is called Message Input Vector (MIV). The other part is
derived from the dossier of the process and is called Dossier Input
Vector (DIV). In the same way can be explained that a TOV may consist of
a MOV and a DOV.

As stated before, the inputvectors have to be located and made available to the transformation and also the outputvectors must be added to the new space. It is assumed that these vectors reside outside the processor, either as stored information together with other types of information, or as information generated by a user-process or presented to a user.

Work-instructions for the process are derived from the process-definition of the user and can be read by the processor.

As conclusion it is clear that, when a process has to be realized, the processor must be able to:

- handle vectors;
- transform available inputvectors to outputvectors;
- accomplish a transformation according to a work-instruction triggered by commands;
- keep necessary status and history-information in a dossier.

PROCESSOR

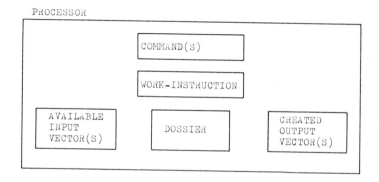

4. STRUCTURE OF THE MACHINE

On the following pages some already mentioned concepts will be worked
out and some new concepts will be added to give an overview of the
structure of an information processing machine.
The approach will be:
- definition of the building blocks transformation and selection;
- description of the join of building blocks, resulting in chips;
- some remarks about the associated dossier;
- definition of the communication channels between chips;
- description of the structure of processes;
- definition of the communication between processes;

TRANSFORMATION

A processor executes transformations.
In a transformation the actual values of the components of a vector are
used. The formal description of a transformation is called a <u>function</u>.

A function defines for each possible vector in the input-space R_I one
vector in the outputspace R_O. So one can refer to this definition by:

$$R_I \qquad F \qquad R_O$$

As R_I and R_O are defined by their vector-descriptions

$$R_I : (I_1, I_2, \ldots I_n)$$

$$R_O : (0_1, 0_2, \ldots 0_m)$$

one can refer to a function as

$$(I_1, I_2, \ldots I_n) \qquad F \qquad (0_1, 0_2, \ldots 0_m)$$

The function itself has to be defined too. This can be done by defining
each vector-component of R_O by the functional relation with a vector in
R_I for all vectors in the definition-space of R_I.

$$F : \quad 0_1 = f_1(I_1, I_2, \ldots I_n)$$

$$0_2 = f_2(I_1, I_2, \ldots I_n)$$

$$\vdots$$

$$0_m = f_m(I_1, I_2, \ldots I_n)$$

SELECTION

As a control mechanism one can think of a building block called <u>selector.</u>
A selector determines from an inputvector the next step of the process,
thereby it has a fixed number of choices, from which only one is chosen.
The inputvector is constructed out of a MIV and / or a DIV, and will be
called a Selector Input Vector (SIV).

Reference to a selector can be made by

$$(I_1, I_2, \ldots \ldots I_n) \qquad S \qquad (C_1, C_2, \ldots \ldots C_m)$$

$(C_1, C_2 \ldots \ldots C_m)$ are the possible choices of which one is selected depending on the SIV $(I_1, I_2, \ldots \ldots I_n)$. The SIV itself is not changed by the selector.

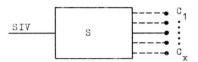

$(C_1, C_2, . C_m)$ are called <u>triggers</u>.

PROCESS-STEP

After each transformation or selection, the process is in a stable or well defined state, therefore a transformation or selection is called a <u>process-step</u>.

COMPOSITION OF FUNCTIONS

A function may be composed out of functions. These functions may be combined sequentially or in parallel. An example of a sequential combination is:

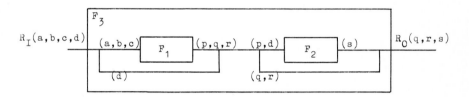

This can be expressed as follows:

$$(a, b, c. d) \qquad F_3 \qquad (q, r, s)$$

$$F_3 \quad \overset{DEF}{=} \quad F_1, F_2$$

$$(a, b, c) \qquad F_1 \qquad (p, q, r)$$

$$(p, d) \qquad F_2 \qquad (s)$$

An example of functions in parallel, where the functions F_1 and F_2 can be processed simultaneously:

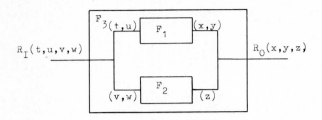

$$(t,\ u,\ v,\ w)\qquad F_3\qquad (x,\ y,\ z)$$
$$F_3\qquad \underset{=}{DEF}\qquad F_1,\ F_2$$
$$(t,\ u)\qquad F_1\qquad (x,\ y)$$
$$(v,\ w)\qquad F_2\qquad (z)$$

An example of the use of a selector in combination with two functions is given below:

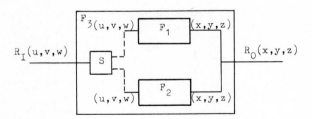

The function $(u,\ v,\ w)\qquad F_3\qquad (x,\ y,\ z)$

$$F_3 = C_1F_1,\ C_2F_2$$
$$(u,\ v,\ w)\qquad S\qquad (C_1,\ C_2)$$
$$(u,\ v,\ w)\qquad F_1\qquad (x,\ y,\ z)$$
$$(u,\ v,\ w)\qquad F_2\qquad (x,\ y,\ z)$$

Since the output of S is only one trigger, either C_1 or C_2, F_1 or F_2 is chosen respectively.

THE DOSSIER

The execution of combined functions produces intermediate results i.e.
after each process-step the status of the process changes. This status
can be indicated by a vector (dossiervector) which has as components
the components of the outputvectors of the individual transformations
and the component giving the status of the process itself.

With each process-step a vector is created giving the new status of
the process. In the long run a stack of vectors is created of which
only the last one is relevant. The other ones serve a possible restart
only.

A part of the available information, the inputvector, remains unchanged.
Together with the dossier there is at any time sufficient information
to proceed with the process. The outputvector is taken from the dossiervector and eventually the inputvector.

For some functions a recursive definition must be used. Important for
such a type of definition is a criterium that indicates the end of the
recursion.

A transformation according to a recursive function can be constructed
with a simple transformation and a selector which can detect the end
of the recursion. The figure below gives an example where also the important
role of the dossier is given.

EXAMPLE: N!

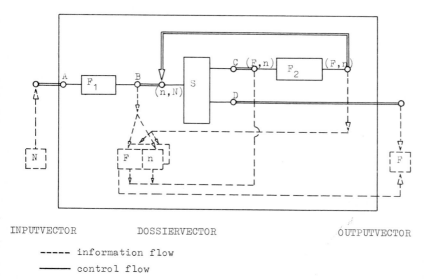

INPUTVECTOR   DOSSIERVECTOR   OUTPUTVECTOR

        ----- information flow
        ——— control flow

Where F_0 $F := 1$
              $n := 0$

      F_1 $n := n + 1 \quad (n_{new} := n_{old} + 1)$
              $F := F * n$

      S   If $n < N$ then C else D

STATUS	F	n
A	NIL	NIL
B	1	0
C	1	0
B	1	1
C	1	1
B	2	2
D	2	2

The dossiervectors
generated for N = 2.

THE CHIP

In the hitherto mentioned combinations it was always taken for granted
that there was an inputvector available and an outputvector could be
left. Now a chip is defined as a unit, build from transformations and
selectors, to which vectors can be given and from which vectors can
be derived. The chip can carry out a command of a process. The supply
and removal of vectors is accomplished via vector-channels.

VECTOR-CHANNEL

A vector-channel serves as communication-channel between processes.
It also adjusts for the differences in speed between the processes.

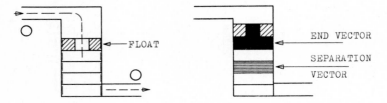

A vector-channel has a fixed capacity and contains only vectors of
one definition type. A vector producing process is coupled to the entry
and a vector consuming one to the exit; the working is "first in, first
out".

As said before the vector-channel contains one type of vectors only,
but in addition there are 2 special vectors:
- an end-vector which is brought in by the producing process as soon
  as there are no more vectors;
- a separation-vector that can divide the vectors into groups.

Furthermore a vector-channel is equipped with some control-mechanisms:
- a float, which indicates the number of vectors in the vector-channel;
- wait-indicators at the entry and exit of the vector-channel.

VECTOR-CHANNEL OPERATIONS

The stream of vectors through a vector-channel is controlled by a
channel-process. It is necessary that commands can be given to this
process. These commands are:

Read to get one vector out of the vector-channel.
The Read results in 3 possible triggers: - N Normal   , a normal
                                                          vector has
                                                          been produced;
                                         - E End   , an end-vector
                                                          has been
                                                          produced;
                                         - S Separator, a separator-
                                                          vector has
                                                          been produced.

Write to put one vector into the vector-channel.
The Write knows 3 possible entries: - N Normal   to put a normal vector;
                                    - E End   to put an end-vector;
                                    - S Separator to put a separator-
                                                      vector.

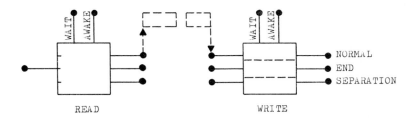

            READ   WRITE

The read and write can introduce a wait if the vector-channel is empty
or full respectively. It also can cause the process at the other end
of the channel to be awakened if this is waiting (indicated by the
wait-indicator).

The chip contains a connection for each input vector-channel and for
each output vector-channel. This connection will be presented by the
symbols:

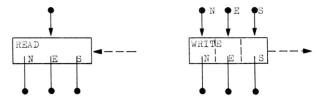

With the mechanisms now available the processing of a variable number
of inputvectors is illustrated.

a) One outputvector depends on one inputvector, (a,b) T_1 (p,q).
   At the end of the inputvector-set, an end-vector is generated in
   the outputvector-set.

   All vectors (a,b) in the inputvector-channel are transformed one
   by one to vectors (p,q) and stored in the outputvector-channel.

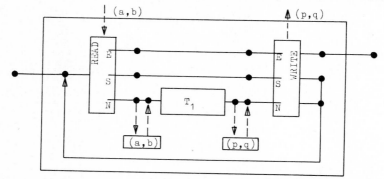

b) One outputvector depends on more than one inputvector,
   $$T_1 \qquad s := 0$$
   $$T_2 \qquad s := s + a \quad (S_{new} := S_{old} + a)$$

   The inputvector-set (a) has been divided into groups by separation-
   vectors. Each time a separation-vector is read in the intputvector-
   set, a vector (s) is put into the outputvector-set and the dossier
   is reset by T_1.

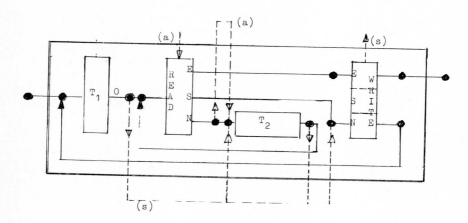

EXTENSION OF CHIP CONSTRUCTIONS

If a chip consists of a sequence of transformations, outputvectors
may under certain conditions be available at different points in the
chip. In this case more outputvector-channels are connected to a chip.

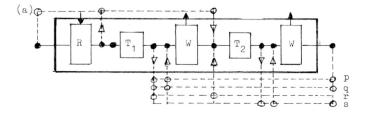

Also more inputvector-channels can be connected to a chip:

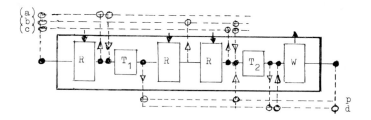

(Note: the vector-channel mechanism guarantees a correct synchronization
      between coupled processes).

The preceeding examples have in common that the number and type of
chip-exits are fixed. It is possible to describe a construction in
which the type of output is not predefined but depends on input and
the result of the processing.

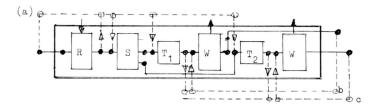

To summarize, a chip has one entry-control and one exit-control point
and several inputvector-channels and outputvector-channels.

VECTOR CABLE

The complete set of vector-channels, serving as input or as output for a
chip is called a <u>vector-cable</u>. So a vector-cable may connect two chips or
may be split to connect more than two chips.

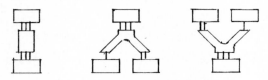

A chip can handle one inputvector-cable and one outputvector-cable at a
time. The inputvector is of a predefined type, but the outputvector-
cable may be a choice of the possible outputcables for that chip.
Furthermore a chip may communicate with chips to which parallel processing is delegated. For this purpose another inputvector- and outputvector-cable may be involved.

The connection of inputchannels and outputchannels to a chip may vary,
depending on the way the input is arranged or the output has to be
offered. If for instance an inputvector (a,b,c,d,e) is expected at a certain point of the chip, this could be achieved by means of one vector-
channel containing the complete vector (a,b,c,d,e) or by means of two
vector-channels, originating from different sources, containing the vectors (a,b) and (c,d,e) respectively. In case that more cables end in one
point of the chip a 'read' has to be provided for each cable. Processing
can go on only if all the vector-channels contain at least one vector.

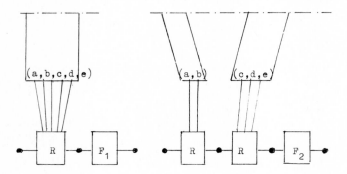

Vector-channels, combined to vector-cables, form a communication path
between processes, regardless where these processes may reside (either in
the same processor or in separate processors). The communication process
will take care that the appropriate paths are selected. The function of
the vector-channels and -cables always remain the same.

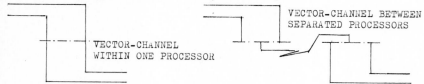

5. STRUCTURE OF THE PROCESSING

A chip describes a complete process or part of a process and can be interpreted by the processor allocated to the chip.

A process has a unique identifier, the <u>process-key</u>, which is attached to the process when it is started. Because a process refers to a dossier, the process-key also serves to identify the dossier.

A process may communicate with other processes. The transportation of vectors between the processes is realized by the vector-channels. Besides that control information has to be passed. This information can be described with the following vector-description with the vector-name <u>message</u> :

(type, sender, receiver, commandcode, sendingcable, returncable, urgency)

- type: may be S for Stimulus or R for Response;
- sender: the process-key of the sending process;
- receiver: the process-key of the receiving process;
- commandcode: gives further specifications of the action to be taken
                 by the receiving process;
- sendingcable: the cable ends of the inputvector-channels;
- returncable: the cable ends which will receive the outputvectors;
- urgency: an indication of the urgency with which this message
                 has to be handled.

The message-vectors are send via a special vector-channel called <u>message-channel</u>.

COMMUNICATION BETWEEN PROCESSES

A process is started on request of another process. This request is forwarded to a service-process which is performing the following actions:

- a processing location is selected;
- a dossier is created for that process;
- a process-key is attached to that process and its dossier;
- a message-channel is connected between the requesting and the new
  process.

The new process then starts. After the requesting process has received the acknowledgement of the service-process, it sends a message via the message-channel containing the above mantioned components. When the new process reads this message it can connect the vector-channels to the appropriate points on the chip and start processing the input.

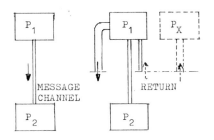
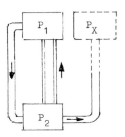

If the outputvectors are routed to another process, the returncable to
the requesting process contains a return message-channel. This channel
is used to send back the following messages:
- A response that the action has been completed;
- In case that, depending on the input, different types of output could
  be produced, a response is send back referring to the selected output;
- If the process received incomplete information it sends back a stimulus
  to the requesting process; in the meantime it starts a process to
  handle a possible return (A). The stimulated process may react by starting also a new process to obtain the necessary information (B). The
  two new processes take over the action until the missing information
  has been produced and the original processes can resume their
  activities.

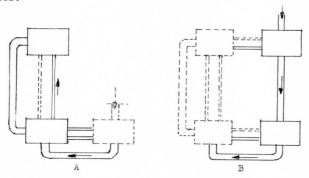

A   B

When a process has finished a command described in the message, it reads
again its inputmessage-channel. If this read results in an end-vector,
the process is closed.

General processes deal with information shared by several processes, for
instance database processes. The inputmessage-channel of a general process may be filled by more than one process. Each time that this channel
is read the most urgent message must be selected. A start-request for a
general process results in a process that is connected to the general
process that can handle the common resources.

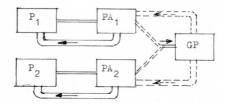

MAPPING

A chip may be mapped on one processor or on more processors. The maximum
number of processors involved is equal to the number of building blocks
on that chip. Each part of the chip, when residing in a separate processor, forms again a chip and describes a (sub)process.
The service-process which handles the start will also select the appropriate vector-cables to connect the separate chips.

The picture below demonstrates the possibilities to allocate a chip on
one, two or three processors.

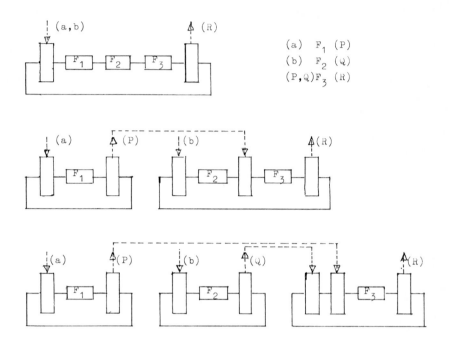

(a) F_1 (P)
(b) F_2 (Q)
(P,Q)F_3 (R)

If more processing power is needed for input coming via a vector-channel,
this can be achieved by distributing the vectors over several vector-
channels, each connected to a separate chip in a separate processor.
At the outputside the separate outputvector-channels are collected to
one channel.

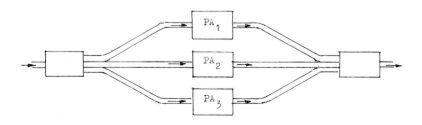

6. SUMMARY

A data-model has been introduced which is convenient for the system-
designer to specify his general requirements for information processing.
It has been shown how an information processing machine could be
modelled with this data-model.

Processing is divided in discrete steps for which the concepts transformation and selection are introduced. They are described by functions.

The assembly of these functions on chips, together with the associated
vector-channels, represents the "instruction sheet" for a processor which
has to execute a process.
The dossier, associated with a process, reflects the status of the
process after each process-step.

The machine-model is independent of hardware configurations and can
be mapped on a mono-processor machine as well as on a poly-processor
network.

DISCUSSION

Sundgren : Your formalism includes operations to add and change vectors but not vector components (attributes). Do you see any difficulty in providing such operations ?

Grotenhuis : We did not consider such operations — but no, I do not see any difficulties at the moment.

Data Base Management, J.W.Klimbie and K. L. Koffeman (eds.)
© *North-Holland Publishing Company (1974)*

A SELF-ORGANISING DATA BASE MANAGEMENT SYSTEM

P.M. Stocker and P.A. Dearnley

School of Computing Studies, University of East Anglia,
Norwich, England

Abstract: This paper sets out the mechanisms used in a self organising data base management system and describes the experience gained from the operation of a limited pilot system.

1.0   The motivation for the work described here is the growth of data bases within computer networks.

At the present time this area is one of rapid development, but current-ly both base and network are almost always restricted to a single user organisation (Aschim, 1974), for example, in seat reservation. Our initial interest was, however, directed towards a more general network, loosely organised for the collection and interrogation of information in a particular sphere of interest.

The work described here is concerned only with one particular aspect of this problem, that is, the management of the storage, amendment and interro-gation of data which is known to exist. The data is assumed to be divided into major units, which in some sense are named. This talk is concerned with the processing of these units by content, and also with the construction of connections between the units by content. It is in no way concerned with the problems of the network itself, nor with the problems in information retrie-val of determining the names of the units which contain the information which is sought. No attempt has been made to provide an interface language for the ordinary user because the data management scheme is intended to be driven by other user oriented systems. The work is concerned solely with the manage-ment of the data, and even the question of a system interface has received little of our attention so far.

It is important at the outset to stress a difference in philosophy between the system upon which we are working and many current systems, or, put in another way, to indicate that we are considering a different kind of usage. Systems intended for military use or, say, air-line seat reservation have necessarily placed an emphasis on response time; the emphasis here is on the cost to the user for the particular task he has in hand, with the assump-tion that the whole system cost will be passed back to the users as a body.

This emphasis does not appear unreasonable for the class of system under investigation.[†] To encourage enough users to make it viable it must be cheap. If a user requires instant service he must pay for it, and the sys-tem may be designed to provide such service, but it should not be obligatory. The consequence of this approach is to shift emphasis away from the problem of the single enquiry or amendment towards that of batched enquiries. It is interesting to note that some authors (Aschim, 1974) regard as a problem simultaneous access to a particular piece of data in a network, whereas it is precisely this situation which we hope to encourage.

2.0   The cost of data processing in the base will depend greatly upon the data structures and access techniques which are used. It will depend equally upon the type of use which is made of the data. Since frequently used items are likely to be processed more cheaply, the individual user will see not only the effect of his own activity but also that of all other users.

[†]I would like an international system which will furnish me with references on a particular topic. I am unlikely to read even one of these in the next hour, few in the next month, many not at all, so what's the hurry?

Thus the situation will be highly interactive between system management and users, moreover, cost minimisation must be attempted over a large range of parameters.

2.1   It is assumed that:

(i)   Users will be independent in the sense that their principal interaction will be only through the data and its use;

(ii) That the data to be entered into the system cannot be foreseen;

(iii) That the form of its use cannot be predicted a priori;

(iv) That the data management system must be capable of communication independent of the language, manufacturer and code of the ultimate user;

(v)   That the user must not be concerned with the internal structures of the system.

2.2   In response to these assumptions this data management system has the following design criteria.

(i)   The data structures used and the access methods adopted are determined by the system itself as constructions from a number of basic modules provided within it; that is, the system is self-organising;

(ii) Appropriate structures can only be chosen by observation of the usage, and the system may dynamically revise its structures to maintain cost minimisation in response to changes in user activity;

(iii) Interrogation and amendment are by data content and the system is fully opaque to the user as regards the internal structure of data;

(iv) Because usage is uncertain, structuring must lag a little behind the requirement for it (apart from the advance bid mechanism discussed later); hence most of the structuring will occur during operation, not in advance of it.

3.0   The previous paragraphs are intended to indicate the flavour of the type of data management system which we are studying. It must be obvious that the construction of a self-organising data management system (SODMS) is an appreciable task and so far our work has consisted of preliminary studies of particular aspects together with the production of a rudimentary pilot system. The object of the pilot system was to help us to rid ourselves of the worst of our ideas and to highlight the points which had been overlooked in our basic thinking. The remainder of the talk is principally concerned with the self-organisation mechanism and with some results obtained in using the pilot system.

At this point it is best to specify simplifying restrictions which have applied to this initial work.

(a)   It has been assumed that data will be transferred to and from backing storage in fixed size units called pages. The cost of any process is taken to be the number of page transfers involved, all mill processing is free.

(b)   All data in the base is regarded by the user as composed of relations (Codd, 1974). That is, the user sees the data as made up of files of records, each record broken into fields. Each interrogation (or amendment) is achieved by specifying values (or a range of values) for certain fields, key values, and requesting that the values of one or more other fields associated with the key values be returned. More complex interrogations are achieved by associating in some way fields in records in different files.

4.0   It is possible to gain some appreciation of the problem of automatic
data structuring by considering the simplest possible case, which is the following. Access is required to a file with a simple record structure with a
number of attributes (fields) a_1, a_2, ..., a_n. The key value supplied for
the access is always a_1.

Let us first consider certain extreme cases:

(i)   The file is frequently added to but never used; in this instance a
       serial structure is most economic.[+]

(ii)   The file is frequently used and in content is entirely static.

       In this instance we distinguish again.

       (a) The interrogation is by specified key values; a random key-to-
            address mechanism is better than index-sequential, though not
            overwhelmingly so;

       (b) The interrogation is by value range: index sequential (or some
            other ordered key to address mechanism) is very much better than
            a random mechanism;

(iii) Only one attribute, say, a_2, is requested in response to the key.

       The question of whether to use a file of sub-records containing a_1 and
       a_2 together with a pointer to the remaining attributes now arises. If
       the file is assumed to be serial initially then

       (a) the search cost is greatly reduced by using the sub-records,

       (b) the construction cost of an index-sequential version is reduced,

       (c) for index-sequential or random the probability of multiple 'hits'
            on one page is increased.

     In general, usage will not reach these extremes and may well vary with
time. Thus in a SODMS routines must be provided which optimise performance
in even this simple instance. For instance in (iii) suppose a third attribute, a_3, is required occasionally. Should it be included in the sub-record
or not? Is the pointer referred to in (iii) more economic than the duplication of a_1 and a_2 in the main file?

     It is clear that the following parameters are involved:

     frequency of simple key value access

     frequency and average batch size of multiple key value access

     frequency and average batch size of range of key value access

     frequency and average batch size of additions

     frequency and average batch size of amendments;

and if real refinement is sought one might consider distributions specifying
frequency as a function of batch size.

     The range of possibilities for the single key file is not yet exhausted.
It may be that only particular key values are used. In this instance a pro-
motional type of structure (called self-organising by Knuth) depending upon
access frequency may be more appropriate, or a combined promotional-content
determined one.

[+] It might be argued that this case is too extreme, but if the base is used
as an archive it is quite likely.

Again (apart from response-time considerations) there is no point in applying amendments to a file in advance of an interrogation.[†] Even then it may be optimum to apply them only when they exceed a critical number in total, and this number will depend upon the parameters listed earlier.

Thus a simple file in a SODMS may be represented by an assortment of files of sub-records, sub-files of sub-records, files of amendments, direct-ories pointing to these and so on. We have found it confusing to refer to the whole and the parts by the same word 'file' and the whole may only exist as a user concept. Hereafter we distinguish it by calling it the folio.

In the case of a single access key there is at any instant, with para-meters 'frozen' at their current value, an optimum structure, but in practice the system has an historical memory. Anarchy appears to be avoided by the cost of constant restructuring, so that, as elsewhere, one must live with one's mistakes (see later example).

We have devoted some study to this simple problem (as have many others) and we hope the results will appear elsewhere in due course.

5.0   When more than one attribute is used as a key for access then the poten-tial complexity of the folio increases in much the same way as physical pro-blems do when the number of dimensions increases.

There are now reasons for producing files of sub-records connected with access by different keys. For example, consider a static data folio which is accessed in only two ways,

given attribute a_1 find values of a_3,

given attribute a_2 find values of a_4.

The optimum solution is two files. One ordered on a_1, containing only a_3 in addition, the other ordered on a_2 and containing a_4.

Our analysis of the multi-key problem is less complete than the simple-key one. It should be noted, however, that a multi-key folio is largely composed of single key files, which are open to the preceding analysis.

It will be easiest to understand our current multi-key search procedure if a folio of given structure is considered. Suppose for definiteness that the key values given are a_1, a_2 and a_3, and that associated values of a_7 are being sought. Almost every file accessing procedure must terminate in a file which contains all the attributes, in this instance, a_1, a_2, a_3 and a_7. This we shall call a target file. The only exception is where the values of two attributes are unique and in exact 1-1 correspondence, in which case they are interchangeable.

The routine which determines the strategy for access to a folio which contains files organised on more than one key is called the route finder. The objective of the route finder is to derive a complex procedure which, when obeyed, will extract from the target file a set of records which contains all those matching the original specified key values, but which will usually contain additional non-matching records which are then discarded. The access to the target file will be by means of the key upon which it is ordered, and so the procedure must derive a set of values for this key from the data key values. To obtain this set of values other sets of values of intermediate keys may be required.

[†] This is not absolutely true if, for instance, system time has different values at different times of day.

A graph is constructed in which the nodes represent attributes. An arc represents a file search which will result in obtaining the set of all values of the terminal attribute which arise from a set of values for the incident attribute. The arc will be directed except for serial files. A backward tree with root at the target file, which contains at least one of a_1, a_2 and a_3 is a feasible solution to the search problem. It is desirable to find the feasible solution which results in the minimum cost. This is impossible to predict because the cost of traversing an arc can only be found by carrying out the operation which it represents, but it can often be estimated. If the arc represents an ordered file then the number of distinct values of the ordering key can be determined during the ordering process. If in a file of n records an attribute takes d distinct values then the ratio d/n is termed its uniqueness factor. If the uniqueness factors for the attributes at each end of an arc are known then an estimate of the ratio of input keys/output keys can be made.

An upper bound for the minimum cost tree is the cost of a serial search on the terminal file. By using this fact to limit the search an algorithm may be constructed on these principles, though arbitrary decisions may arise where basic data is not available, for example, an unknown uniqueness factor.

A constructed example may make the process clearer. Consider a folio based upon a relation with attributes a_1 through a_8 and containing the files shown in Table 1. The underlined attribute in a file indicates ordering on that attribute value.

File Number	Attributes contained
2	$\underline{a_1}$, a_6
3	$\underline{a_2}$, a_6
4	$\underline{a_6}$, a_4, a_5
5	a_3, a_5
6	$\underline{a_4}$, a_8
7	$\underline{a_5}$, a_8
1	a_1, a_2, a_3, a_4, a_5, a_6, a_7, a_8
8	a_1, a_2, a_3, a_7, $\underline{a_8}$

Table 1

Suppose we have a single set of key values a_1, a_2, a_3, with all associated values of a_7 as objective. The target files must be file 1 and file 8. File 1 is unordered and has longer records than file 8. File 8 is the better target and the cost of a serial search through this file provides an upper limit on cost. The algorithm now searches for a backward tree, containing one or all of a_1, a_2, a_3. A graph of feasible routes is shown in Figure 1.

Starting from a_1 we estimate, using the uniqueness factor for a_1 and a_6, the number of values of a_6 which may be obtained. Similarly starting from a_2 the number of values of a_6. At node a_6 the first divergence arises. We may use a_1, or a_2, or both. If we use both we may reduce the number of values of a_6 carried forward (since only values which arise from both paths are valid) but at extra cost. The node a_5 is reached from a_3 and from a_6, and again divergence of possibilities arises, and so on. The minimum cost tree of those generated in this way is the result required. It is this minimum cost tree which is evaluated by the route finder.

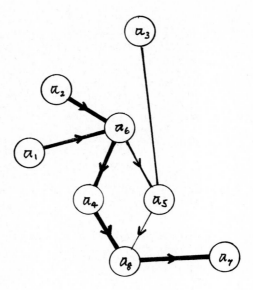

Figure 1

As an example, the final result indicated by the heavier arcs in Fig. 1 would arise if the following held true:

The uniqueness of attributes a_1 and a_2 are low enough to make the use of both, followed by a data reduction at node a_6 economic.

The high cost of serial processing file 5, together with a low uniqueness factor for a_5, makes the route $a_6 \rightarrow a_4 \rightarrow a_8$ more economic than one involving a_5. It should be noted also in this case that the uniqueness factor of attribute a_3 is unknown, since it has not been used for ordering.

The cost of the overall path so obtained turns out to be lower than the serial search on file 8, because the use of the ordered attribute a_8 reduces the cost of searching this file to an extent which more than compensates for the cost of obtaining a set of values for a_8.

6.0   The overall operation of the pilot system is described generally in Stocker and Dearnley (1973) and Dearnley (1974). A brief description is included here for completeness.

The file structuring in the system is based on the folio concept just described, and incorporates some but not all of the mechanisms for file construction and search which have been described.

No mention has yet been made of how decisions are taken to add new files to a folio. In the pilot model the algorithms used are primitive and await further effort in this area. At present new files arise in two ways. First, in response to a search request. The initial action by the system is to employ the route-finder. When a minimum cost tree using existing files has been found, the SODMS calculates the cost of constructing a new file by restructuring, specifically for this request. If this is cheaper than the route-finder solution then construction takes place. This mechanism is only likely to be activated when the batch size of the search request is large.

The second way in which new files are generated is as follows. A history of previous searches, recorded in terms of batch size, key and reply attributes is maintained, and from time to time the SODMS reviews these. Briefly the first stage is to find tentative proposals for new files, those which would have had a high activity in the past had they existed. The second stage is to call the route finder to recost past activity over a period on the assumption that a tentative file had existed; the cost saving is estimated and compared with the cost of constructing and storing the new file. If the comparison is favourable a statistical routine is called to determine estimated future activity and the cost comparison is again made. If this is favourable the new file is constructed. In the present model the only external parameter used in prediction is 'folio life'. In an operational system more sophisticated user estimates or 'bids' would be used.

The update and amendment control mechanisms in the pilot model are minimal and for this reason we have little to say at present concerning file destruction. This usually means not that a file is destroyed but that it ceases to be maintained. There is provision in the SODMS for 'bargain offers' of incomplete information.

7.0   The pilot model system operates on an ICL 1905E, it was constructed by Dr. Dearnley under difficult conditions. The ICL 1905E is the central university processor and in order to obtain a reasonable turnaround during daytime it was necessary to write the system to conform to the conditions enforced on such program runs. These are not more than 32K of 24-bit core store and only one personal 4 million character disc drive. Also, although the interface was directed towards interactive use, the program was normally developed and used in batch mode. Much of the code is written in FORTRAN with some sections in assembly language and some system routines were used. These factors have had a strong influence on the pilot model.

To conclude we now describe one of the examples which has been run on the pilot system and describe the behaviour which resulted.

The example is based on the file used by universities to keep track of student applications. The file is created and maintained by a central authority and copies are sent to the universities at regular intervals through the year. The usage of the file changes as offers of places are made to students, as student react to the offers, and when examination results are published and so on.

The actual file used consists of one record per student containing his personal and school details with a repeating group embedded in the record containing an entry for each application made for a place at university, with an upper limit of five. The record length is 240 characters and the records are held in a sequential file keyed on a centrally allocated reference number. The file builds up very rapidly in the first two months, then it is used for amendments (e.g. offers made, refusals etc.) and interrogation (e.g. reply to offers). The vast majority of amendments are to the application repeating group entries; the personal and schooling details remaining largely unchanged.

For the test a reduced number of records and fields were used and the record structure was normalised. It was also assumed that updates were sent to the universities in place of a new master file. Folio 1 was used to hold the relationship between student reference number and personal/schooling details. Folio 2 was used to hold the relationship between student reference number and a single application. Table 2 gives the folio definitions used.

Whilst the original file is designed to provide information about students it can also be used to get information about types of offers made by other universities and for reviewing the offers made for particular courses.

Table 2. Folios used in Example.

Folio 1 - Students

Field	Type
Reference Number	Numeric
Name	Alphabetic
Address	Alphabetic
Sex	Alphabetic
School Code	Numeric
School Type	Numeric
Age	Numeric

Folio 2 - Applications

Field	Type	Notes
Reference Number	Numeric	
Reference Rating	Numeric	Indicates the candidate's order of preference for applications
University Reference Number	Numeric	
Course Code	Numeric	
University Decision	Alphabetic	
Conditions on offer	Alphabetic	Indicates the examination grades required of the student by the university
Conditions expressed in"points"	Numeric	As above but expressed numerically with each grade given a weighting
Candidate Reply	Alphabetic	

The various types of enquiries made are given in table 3. The communication enquiries are used when writing to candidates to offer interviews, to offer places, to confirm offers etc. The interview enquiries are used prior to selection interviews to give information about the current states of other applications. Strategy and position enquiry types allow departments to choose a competitive offer strategy and to observe the results of offers. Clearing is used after examination results are published to try to allocate unplaced students to vacant places. The general school and personal profiles of candidates applying for particular universities and courses are given by review type enquiries. The frequency of the various enquiry types is given in figures 2 and 3. The cumulative costs of performing enquiries, creating new versions and occupying further disc storage were recorded. The approximate cost of answering the same enquiry pattern with a conventional system from one file, sorted and indexed on student reference number was calculated for each time period. Similarly the costs with a conventional system and two files (one of reference number with personal/school details, the other with reference number with application details) were calculated. The comparisons are given in figure 4.

Table 3. Enquiry types for Example.

Enquiry Type	Specification
Communication	Given student reference number get name and address.
Interview	Given student reference number get all application details.
Offer Strategy	a) Given university number and course number get university decision and conditions. b) Given course number get university number, decision and conditions. c) Given university number and course number get preference rating.
Recruitment Position	Given university number, course number and decision get candidate's reply.
Review	Given university number and course number get reference number. Then from reference number a) Get school areas b) Get school types c) Get sex distribution d) Get age distribution.
Clearing	Given course number and university decision = "reject" get reference number.

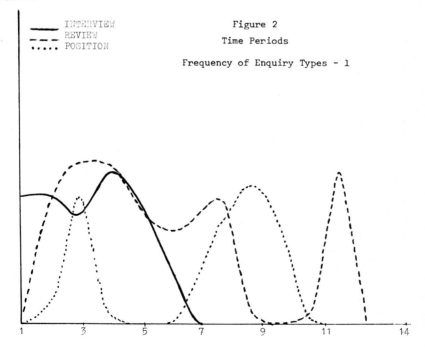

FREQUENCY

INTERVIEW
REVIEW
POSITION

Figure 2

Time Periods

Frequency of Enquiry Types - 1

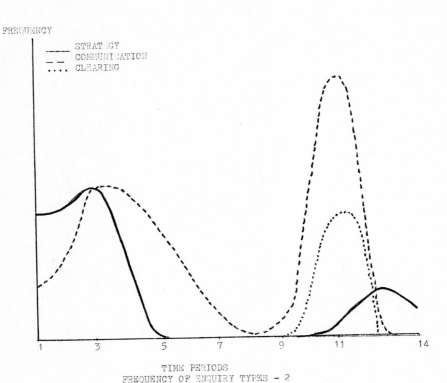

TIME PERIODS
FREQUENCY OF ENQUIRY TYPES - 2

Figure 3

The SODMS was initialised to the same state as the two file conventional system. During time periods 2 through 11 it constructed three additional files, underlining denotes the ordering attribute,

(i)   Course number, University number, University decision, conditions (Period 1).

(ii) Course number, University number, University decision, student reply (Period 2).

(iii) Course number, University number, Student reference number (Period 3).

These files illustrate a weakness of the pilot model which was not provided with a mechanism which would add a field to an existing file.

It seems possible that if a mechanism which permitted advance notice of future usage were included then the system would have constructed a composite file at the end of period 1, but the later addition of field when required may be more economic.

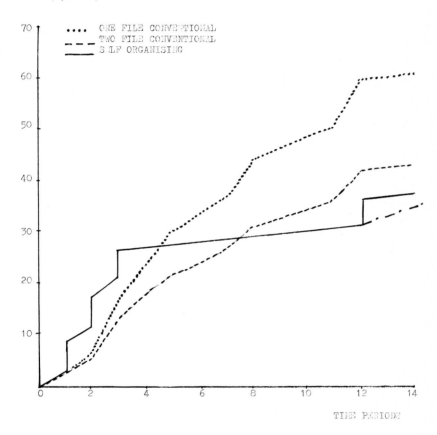

COST COMPARISONS

Figure 4

At the end of period 11 the SODMS constructed a file containing

Course code, <u>University Decision</u>, Student Reference Number.

It is produced in response to 'clearing' type interrogations for computing students who have been rejected by their first choice university on the
basis of their examination result. It highlights a number of points. First,
because no mechanism exists in the pilot scheme for producing sub-files of
sub-records (only files of sub-records) it produces a sorted file of which it
uses only one area. Second, because no sub-sort mechanism is included the
pilot scheme cannot extract both rejects and computing course code. Finally
the file is not economic as it stands since 'clearing' ends in period 12, but
the SODMS anticipated it continuing until period 14. The effect of not producing this file is shown in chain-dot in figure 4. Despite all these mistakes the system appears to operate economically.

References

Aschim, F. (1974). Data base networks - an overview, Management Informatics, <u>3</u>,
          13.

Codd, E.F. (1971). Further normalisation of the Data Base Relational Model,
          Courant Computer Science Symposia, <u>6</u> "Data Base Systems", Prentice Hall,
          New York.

Dearnley, P.A. (1973). A Model of a Self-organising Data Management System, Comp.
          Journal, <u>16</u>, No. 4.

Stocker, P.M. and Dearnley, P.A. (1973). Self-organising Data Management Systems,
          Computer Journal, <u>16</u>, No. 2, 100.

DISCUSSION

Sundgren : I have a question about the problem of <u>presearch statistics</u>. You have taken the approach of calculating and saving certain averages concerning the distribution of attributes among the objects in the data base. This approach works provided that the attributes are "evenly distributed". When this condition is not satisfied (very common in practice) I would suggest an alternative, the "<u>mini-base approach</u>". A mini-base is a Random <u>sample</u> from the data base proper (which is assumed to be large). Before you access the data base proper in order to reply to a query, you submit the query to the mini-base, which will then produce cost and time estimates by simulation perhaps. In addition it may very well produce an <u>approximate answer</u> to the user's query. On many occasions this answer may even be sufficiently precise to make it superfluous to access the data base proper. Thus for users wanting information of a statistical kind from a large data base the mini-base approach may imply significant cost reductions. Would you care to comment ?

Stocker : I have great sympathy with the spirit of the question. The idea of producing a mechanism which offers the user a cheaper but less exact answer is also present in the system in another form. If a slightly obsolete file exists which is well structured to answer a query, then the system will offer the user the cheaper incomplete answer from this file as an alternative to the full one. Your scheme is another way of producing 'bargain offers'. I think pre-costing and cheap alternatives are likely to be an important feature of such systems.

Bayer : You talk about adding relations to a folio to lower user costs of access, but do you ever delete or destroy relations ?

Stocker : No, relations are not destroyed. If a relation is not used, it is moved to archival storage, where it is still known to the system.

Data Base Management, J. W. Klimbie and K. L. Koffeman, (eds.)
© *North-Holland Publishing Company (1974)*

AN EXPERIMENTAL DATA BASE SYSTEM USING BINARY RELATIONS

P J TITMAN

IBM United Kingdom Laboratories Limited

Introduction

This paper describes an experimental data base system to evaluate a particular conceptual approach to data representation and manipulation. The concept, which has been frequently adapted in one form or another for systems requiring complex data structures, is that any collection of data can be represented in terms of sets of values, and of binary relations. The purpose of the evaluation was to determine whether a data base using a binary relational structure could be implemented in a way which compared favourably in cost performance terms with conventional systems, while providing the flexibility of a relational structure. The paper contains a general description of the experimental system, some measurements of space and retrieval performance, and some observations about recovery, integrity and security.

Why Binary Relations?

The main reason for choosing a binary relation as the primitive unit of data in the system is that it is the simplest unit which can be used to construct arbitrarily complex models. A binary relation is a set of ordered pairs. The first component of the pair identifies an element in the domain set and the second an element in the range set. Since a binary relation is itself a set either the domain or range sets may be relations; thus relations may be connected to relations to form more elaborate structures.

Fig 1 shows a simple bill of materials structure expressed in terms of binary relations. PARTS is a set of part numbers, and BM is a relation with PARTS as domain and range. The relation BMQ represents the number of each component used in each assembly. The domain of BMQ is the relation BM, and the range a set of integers contained in the set QTY. Fig 1 shows in addition the set NAME and the relation PARTNAME. Notice that the representation used applies equally well to 1 : n, n : 1, or n : n relations.

This structure can be extended without requiring any changes to existing data, or transactions. Suppose we wish to extend the model of Fig 1 to include engineering change information. We need a new value set EC, a relation PARTEC which identifies the engineering change (or changes) associated with the part, and possibly another relation BMEC which identifies the change which added the part to the bill of materials. These sets are shown in Fig 2, the identifiers in the PART and BM domains are the sequence numbers assigned in Fig 1. These additions can be physically quite separate from the original data, so that performance is not directly affected by the extension.

Because all the data is held in a uniform representation the operations on the data are few and simple and easily defined. This leads one to expect a reliable system, and also offers the potential of an economic hardware or microcode implementation.

Representation

All communication with the data base is in terms of sets of values where each element is a character string. Each set is sorted (to simplify searching), and value sets are front compressed. Sets are partitioned into fixed length blocks and indexed in order to avoid the need for a complete scan. All blocks in the system are 600 bytes long, including a standard 8 byte header.

An element of a set is identified by the block in which it occurs, and the sequence number of the element within the block.   An element of a relation consists of a pair of these identifiers. In non compressed form an identifier is represented by a two byte block number and a two byte sequence number.   An element of a relation therefore requires 8 bytes.   This can be reduced by encoding.

Binary relations in real life data bases tend to be highly clustered.   The coding scheme is designed to take advantage of this without requiring prior knowledge of the statistics of the data base.   The coding is illustrated in Fig 3.

At creation, or after re-organisation, the data base is entirely in ordered compressed form. The provision made for accommodating change is to store separate add and delete sets for each set in the data base.   (Some add and delete sets may be null.)   This technique has the advantage that changes are separable from base data, so the base sets can be made read only. Data is never removed, except at re-organisation, and then only after checking.   Thus recovery is simplified.

It is desirable that identifiers should not change when insertions and deletions are made, in order to avoid propagating changes to all elements referencing the changed set.   The problem is overcome by holding add sets in two forms: a chronological add set in which members are always added to the end of the set, and an ordered set in which new elements are inserted in correct collating sequence (additions may require existing blocks to be split).   All references to add elements are to the unchanging identifiers of the chronological add set.   Delete set entries are kept only in ordered form since they are never pointed at.

Operations

A retrieval transaction uses input values to select a subset of the data base, and then organises this subset into a form suitable for a report.   The principal operation used in doing this is COLLATE.

This operation matches two ordered sets, element by element.   Each operation may generate up to three result sets, one or two from those elements which match, and one set from those elements which do not match.   The result elements are formed by selecting one or two components from the input elements.   For instance, the composition of a relation R1 with domains (A, B) and a relation R2 with domains (A, C) is obtained by matching for equality on A and selecting the right hand sides of R1 and R2 to give a new relation with domains (B, C).

Functions are normally performed on ordered sets, so a SORT operation is provided.   VALIN matches input with value sets to obtain IDs.   It has modifiers to allow selection of partial matches and values in a range.   VALOUT obtains character strings corresponding to given IDs. Other operations are union, intersection and set difference, and a function is provided to produce readable reports.   A single element may be selected from a set, and there is a conditional branch (rarely used) which tests for a null set.

System Organisation

Users write sequences of operations which define a transaction.   This list is then stored and is invoked by name.   When the system reads a transaction name, it loads the appropriate list of operations, scans the input to load argument sets, and then interprets the list of operations. The experimental system is designed for ease of implementation and measurement, so there is no overlap of I/O and processing.

The interpreter selects the next operation and invokes the I/O scheduler. This is designed to read in all the required blocks for that step with minimum seek time and rotational delay, and then return. The interpreter then invokes the appropriate function for that step. Each phase is timed and a timing trace can be produced.

Space

The original data was a subset of a sequential hierarchical file used in engineering and manufacturing.

The structure and record formats are shown in Fig 4. The binary relational structure corresponding to this file and the space required for each set and relation is shown in Fig 5. The original data required approximately 5M characters, not including record type prefixes. The binary relational form required approximately 1.5M characters including indices.

The reduction in space was due to the following factors:

    a.   Some fields in the original records were blank.

    b.   Some field values had a highly skewed distribution.

    c.   Some relations were small subsets of the cross product of their domains.

One interesting aspect of the results is the small proportion of the space required for the value sets, even though the compression used for values was very simple.

Performance

It is evident from the structure shown in Fig 5, that access to all the fields corresponding to a single record in the original data base is a very indirect process. Most transactions are concerned with extracting a subset of fields from a group of related records. All transactions in the system are defined with sets as input arguments, so a single transaction may access more than 1 bill of material, for example Fig 6 shows the time taken to extract bills of materials for a range of sizes of result sets. The requests were taken from an actual week's transactions on the operational system, so they reflect the clustering which occurs in practice. The data base was held on 2 x 2311 disk packs, one for the change sets, and one for the base sets. The CPU used was a System 360 Model 65, which would at first seem somewhat surprising for the input output configuration. One of the assumptions which influenced the selection of the method was that processing power for simple functions such as those involved in decoding and string comparison would eventually become a cheap resource.

Certain types of retrieval are particularly suited to the relational structure. One such example is a request for a list of all parts in an assembly which are used in that assembly and no other. Such a request might be required when an assembly is made obsolete for example.

This type of retrieval requires considerable work in a conventional system, but in the relational system could be answered in less than two seconds. The reason for the fast response is that only the BM and WU domains are accessed for most of the retrieval, and that these lie within a few cylinders.

The overall conclusion was that the experimental system did provide acceptable performance for the mix of activity encountered in this application.

Reliability and Recovery

There is no direct experimental evidence of reliability since the use of the system was limited. There are some general considerations which would lead one to expect a reliable production system should one ever be constructed. The first reason for expecting a reliable system is its simplicity. The sorting and matching operations are easily defined and tested, and are independent of each other.

The second factor contributing to reliability is the separation of base and change sets. The bulk of the data is held in the base sets, which can be on a separate device which is never written on except during reorganisation. A copy of the base sets is created on tape during reorganisation and can be used for restoring the base sets in case of physical damage. Normal checkpointing is carried out by saving the current contents of the change sets. Since these are small they can be dumped frequently and if necessary restored in seconds. A log tape contains copies of each updated block written to the data base. Each block contains a sequence number which identifies the transaction which last updated it so that the data base can be quickly restored in a given transaction following a checkpoint.

Each user has a pointer to a directory which identifies the sets he can access and the operations he can perform using those sets. Included in the directory is a pointer to each change set. This makes it possible to have users associated with different change sets. This is useful in testing because tests can be performed using copies of the change sets together with real base sets, thus providing a realistic testing environment without endangering live data.

Security and Integrity

The directory is used to check that a user is authorised to access and change data, and to check that attempted changes obey the constraints of the model. One of the features that simplifies checking is that the specifications of the domain and range of a relation are distinct from the relation itself.

Two users may have access to the same transaction, which let us say updates a bill of materials. If one user is allocated a directory which does not permit the set PARTS to be updated, then he can only add previously defined parts to an assembly. The second user however may be permitted to update PARTS, in which case he can add previously unknown parts to an assembly.

As the structure increases in complexity so the checking can become more detailed. In the structure illustrated in Fig 5 the domains B.C.D and E each contain a one byte code. Of the 256^4 combinations which can be physically represented, only 91 are actually permitted. The codes are checked in the original system by a mixture of tables and logic contained in the programs which update the files. The same checking can be defined in the data base by prohibiting normal transactions from updating the sets B.C.D and E, and the relations RC, RD and RE.

This has the advantage of concentrating the responsibility for checking into one place rather then relying on a number of different programmers. Changes to the checking rules are easily enforced by changing the contents of the sets given the appropriate authority.

Multi dimensional constraints such as the ones above are often difficult to define in words, and are not always uniformly and accurately reflected in programs. A relational structure helps to define such constraints as well as to implement them.

Acknowledgments

I would like to thank R N Cuff, I J Heath and P Hopewell who were responsible for most of the work described in this paper.

Fig. I   <u>Sets and relations for a bill of materials</u>

PART	
ID	Value
I	0099
2	0129
3	3172
4	3174

NAME	
ID	Value
1	BOX
2	CARD
3	SCREW

QUANTITY	
ID	Value
1	1
2	2
3	4
4	6

BM		
ID	PART ID	PART ID
	(Assembly)	(Component)
I	3	1
2	3	2
3	4	1
4	4	2
5	4	3

BM QTY		
ID	BM ID	QTY ID
1	1	3
2	2	4
3	3	1
4	4	1
5	5	1

PART NAME		
ID	PART ID	NAME ID
1	1	3
2	2	3
3	3	1
4	4	2

Fig. 2   Adding engineering changes

EC #	
ID	Value
I	197A
2	199A
3	201B

PART EC		
ID	PART ID	EC ID
1	1	1
2	2	1
3	3	1
4	4	2

BMEC		
ID	BM ID	EC ID
1	1	2
2	2	2
3	3	2
4	4	3
5	5	3

Fig. 3   Coded representation of BM Relation

Control byte coding (procedes each entry)

Bit	Value	
0-1	00	same LHS as previous element
	01	next sequential ID for LHS
	10	only last byte of LHS given, previous 3 bytes same
	11	4 byte full length representation
2-3	--	same as above, applied to RHS
4-7	0-15	number of repetitions of this form

BM relation in Fig. I

byte 1	'F0' x	LHS and RHS full length, one occurence
bytes 2-9	'0000000300000001' x	8 byte first element
byte 10	'10' x	LHS same, RHS next
byte 11	'60' x	LHS next, RHS I byte
byte 12	'01' x	new RHS low order byte
byte 13	'11' x	LHS same, RHS next, repeated once

Fig. 4   Original data base subset

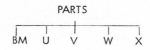

Record type	Fields	Field length	Rec'd length	occurrences	bytes
PARTS	PART	7			
	A	10			
	B	1			
	C	1			
	D	1			
	E	1			
	F	7	28	22928	641984
U	J	7			
	K	1	8	24200	193600
V	L	2			
	M	1	3	58004	174012
W	G	22	22	18525	407550
X	PART	7	7	1562	10934
BM	PART	7			
	H	14			
	I	5			
	J	7			
	B	1			
	C	1			
	A	10	45	78332	3524940

TOTAL: 4,953,020

Fig. 5   Binary relational representation

Set name	cardinality	data blocks	index blocks	domain	range
PART	22928	103	2		
A	8605	79	2		
B	8	1			
C	6	1			
D	4	1			
E	9	1			
F	132	2	1		
G	8357	220	10		
H	7285	90	3		
I	321	2	1		
J	5371	37	1		
K	10	1			
L	43	1			
M	6	1			
BM	78332	330	5	PART	PART
WU	78332	388	6	PART	PART
RA	22928	93	2	PART	A
RB	18779	26	1	PART	F
RC	48	1		B	C
RD	36	1		D	E
RE	91	1		RC	RD
RF	22928	24	1	PART	RE
RG	18525	156	3	PART	G
RH	126	1		L	M
RJ	80932	217	3	PART	RH
RK	78332	83	2	BM	I
RL	48000	223	3	BM	H
RM	78332	91	2	BM	RC
RN	1578	5	1	BM	J
RO	24200	102	2	PART	J
RP	24199	22	1	RO	K
RQ	1562	9	1	PART	PART

2312   53

Total # of blocks = 2365
Total # of bytes = 1,419,000

P J TITMAN

FIG 6 - RETRIEVAL TIME FOR BILL OF MATERIAL LINES

(10 fields per assembly, 6 fields per component)

Assemblies	Lines	I/O (msec)	Process (msec)	Lines/second (no overlap)
1	0	1870	90	0
1	7	3150	220	2.1
1	49	3310	620	12.5
5	146	4250	2030	23.2
9	263	5040	3880	29.4

DISCUSSION

Stacey : Your paper was interesting but I still don't have a feel for the various factors involved. For example, you did two things in the data structure -- compaction and a changed data view. What proportion of the reduction in storage space from 5 million to 1.4 million bytes was attributable to each.

Titman : The effect of the compaction and the data view are intervelated. Some of the clustering, which contributes to the compaction is directly due to the data view chosen. For example one of the relations which connects four one byte fields, has a cardinality of 91, and is therefore highly clustered.

Stacey : You have reported actual timings. Can you give any comparison with existing systems, such as this one before it was redesigned.

Titman : Yes, but the comparison of performance is complex, because of the number of factors involved, and I do not want to make an over simplified comparison which might be used for propaganda. The performance we obtained was satisfactory.

Bracchi : Your structure is good if the data base is stable but what kind of structure would you have for a volatile database ?

Titman : First, adding new relations is easy. Regarding deletion, I have been surprised at how little change there actually is in the real world. The more you fragment the database into elementary pieces, the less the affect of a change on the database structure, because only a few of the relations will change much.

Data Base Management, J. W. Klimbie and K. L. Koffeman, (eds.)
© *North-Holland Publishing Company (1974)*

DATA STRUCTURING IN THE DDL AND RELATIONAL MODEL

G.M. NIJSSEN

Control Data Europe

Brussels

Foreword

During the conference, there was organized a discussion on the topic "DDL and Relational Data Model". After one section of the discussion it became clear that a short presentation on the main data structuring elements of DDL could greatly contribute to the quality of the next part of the discussion on the same topic during the conference. The Program Committee then charged its chairman with the task to present this in a quarter of an hour. It is with this limitation in mind that one has to understand that the concepts are somewhat losely defined. Nevertheless it was decided after the presentation that an edited transcript should be included in the proceedings in order to contribute to the debate on the DDL and Relational Data Model.

Summary

In this paper the main data structuring elements of the CODASYL DDL and Relational Data Model are compared. The comparison is illustrated with an example and some data descriptions. The main conclusion is that a common DDL could be specified, encompassing the main aspects of the CODASYL DDL and Relational Data Model. An instant guideline for DDL users and some DDL modifications are also shortly described.

Contents

6. Instant guideline for a DBA using DDL (73)

7. Some DDL modifications

8. Laws of Cargese

9. Invitation

1 Environment of the DDL

In a database system, one may consider several levels of
data description. A database contains data of a certain
part of the reality (see figure 1.a). The end user point
of view of the data is called the information structure.
The point of view of the DML programmer (1) the ALPHA
programmer (2) or the database administrator is called
data structure. The collection of data as stored in the
computer is called storage structure. In this paper we
consider the DDL as a language to describe a data structure.
The information structure and storage structure should be
described in separate languages, which are not discussed
in this presentation.

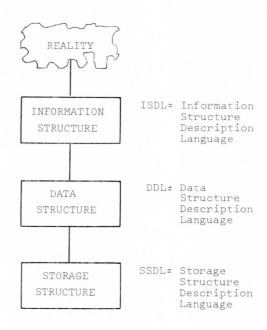

Figure 1.a

2 Four assertions

Before going to the heart of the presentation, let us make four assertions:

1. A DDL should serve several classes of users or levels of data sublanguages, such as:
   - DML (1)
   - ALPHA (2)
   - casual user language

   If this is the case then a DDL may be considered as a common data description language, giving the freedom to groups of people to use their preferred language.
   This is essential because a database may be defined as a collection of data, used by m a n y individuals and which is associated with a model.

2. The CODASYL DDL as specified in the DDLC (3) Journal of Development, June 1973, contains some deficiencies, which in our opinion can be rectified. From here on we mean by DDL the DDL as specified in the CODASYL DDL Journal of Development, June 1973.

3. The CODASYL DDL needs more mathematical foundation.

4. Modifications in the CODASYL DDL will result in a DML with the same power, yet much less complex and more data independent.

The assertions 2, 3 and 4 will be discussed at great length in a future paper.

3 Data structure elements

There are four elements which can fruitfully be used in a comparison of data structure aspects in different systems, such as the DDL and the Relational Data Model, namely:

- entity
- attribute
- function
- access path

An attribute is a single-valued characteristic of someone or something; e.g. the birthdate of a person, the salary of an employee.

An entity is a collection of one or more attribute values, such that at least one subset of the collection, called identifier, identifies the entity within an entity set, while all other attribute values in the collection are functionally dependent on the identifier; e.g. the entity person consists of the attributes name, address, birthdate, social security number. An entity set is a collection of entities with the same attributes.

A function is a rule which assigns to each entity of a given
entity set exactly one entity of some other entity set; e.g.
suppose there are two entity sets, employees and departments
and each employee has one attribute that he is employed by
exactly one department, then we may say that there exists a
function, name it "assigned", which assigns to each employee
of the employee entity set exactly one department of the
department entity set.

There exists for one or more attributes of an entity set an
access path, if it requires considerably less effort, than
scanning all entities, to retrieve an entity from the entity
set, if the constituent attribute values of the access path
are known; e.g. suppose the entity employee has the attributes
"department" and "birthdate", and for "department" there exists
no access path, but for "birthdate" there exists an access path,
then it takes considerably less effort to retrieve the employees
with a given birthdate than with a given department.

4 Comparison table DDL and relational data model

The four elements for data structuring as introduced in the
previous section will be used as columns in a table to compare data structuring aspects of the DDL and the Relational
(4) Data Model. (see figure 4.a). The table will be illustrated with an example to be discussed in section 5.

data structure element system	attribute	entity	function	access path
DDL	yes	yes	yes	yes
Relational Data Model	yes	yes	yes (but)	no

Figure 4.a

The attribute concept is known in the DDL as a data item,
and the domain-role is the equivalent concept in the relational data model.

The entity concept is known in the DDL as a record occurrence
which is the equivalent of the tuple concept in the relational data model.

The function concept is known in the DDL as a record owned
CODASYL set type. (This akward terminology is needed because
the CODASYL set concept is the equivalent of a function in
set theory). One may however distinguish two different aspects in the CODASYL set type.

A declaration of a CODASYL set type (record owned) results at
least in three navigational routes, one from each owner record
occurrence to the associated member record occurrences, one
from member record occurrences to other member record occurrences belonging to the same owner record occurrence and one
from member record occurrences to the associated owner record
occurrence, while it may also serve as a semantic rule indicating that an element in the domain (member record) cannot
exist without the corresponding element in the range (owner
record).
In the relational data model, there exists an equivalent for
the semantic rule, called integrity constraint by E.F. Codd
on page 46 of reference 2. The relational data model does not
encompass the concept of predefined navigational routes.
Either one may say that there exist no predefined navigational
routes in the relational data model, or that all possible routes
are dynamically materialized.

The access path concept corresponds to the ownerless or system
owned set type in CODASYL. The relational model does not encompass the concept of a predefined access path.

5 An illustrative example

In this section we will describe an example and several
pieces of data description. Once again, because of the time
limit, the example is very simple in order to be able to get
the diagrams ready in time.

5.1 The problem

We will now describe an example, which will be used to
illustrate the comparison of some aspects of the DDL and
Relational Data Model. The example describes a part of a
wholesale trade company and the scope of the example includes some aspects of suppliers, products and the deli-
very time of a product by a given supplier. To be more
precise, there are three classes of entities, (see figure
5.1.a), SUPPLIER, PRODUCT and SUPPLY; the supplier has the
attributes supplier-number, supplier-name, supplier-location,
and turnover; the product has the attributes product-number,
product-name, product-location and price; the supply has
as attributes supplier-number, product-number and delivery-
time. (To avoid any misunderstanding, we add to the description that a supplier is located in exactly one location,
and a product will be stored in our wholesale trade company
in exactly one location). A supplier is identified by his
number, a product by its number, and a supply by the concatenation of the supplier number and product number.

SUPPLIER

S#	SN	LOC	TURNOVER

PRODUCT

P#	PN	LOC	SALES PRICE

S#	P#	DELIVERY TIME

SUPPLY

Figure 5.1.a

A sample database, which will be used in the diagrams in the next section is given in figure 5.1.b.

SUPPLIER

S1	ABC	NEW YORK	12
S2	DEF	MINNEAPOLIS	41
S3	XYZ	MINNEAPOLIS	76

PRODUCT

P1	WHEAT	CHICAGO	50
P2	CORN	NEW YORK	62

SUPPLY

S1	P1	4
S1	P2	7
S2	P1	4
S2	P2	6
S3	P2	8

Figure 5.1.b

Our wholesale trade company has its warehouse for wheat in Chicago and for corn in New York. And our company can get corn from supplier ABC in 7 weeks, from DEF in 6 weeks and from XYZ in 8 weeks.

5.2 Illustrative diagrams

In this section we will describe several diagrams with
the aim to illustrate the problem.

5.2.1 Data structure (schema) diagram

The example as introduced in section 5.1 will be represented in a data structure (schema) diagram as presented
in figure 5.2.1.a. Data structure diagrams were introduced by C. Bachman (5). A data structure (schema)
diagram represents entity sets and the inverse of functions
as defined in section 3.

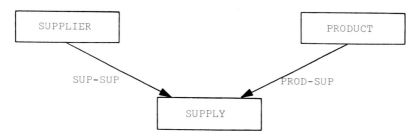

Figure 5.2.1.a

5.2.2 Set theory (schema) diagram

Several people would prefer a schema diagram with symbols which are in general use in mathematical set theory.
A diagram, describing our example in these symbols, is
presented in figure 5.2.2.a.

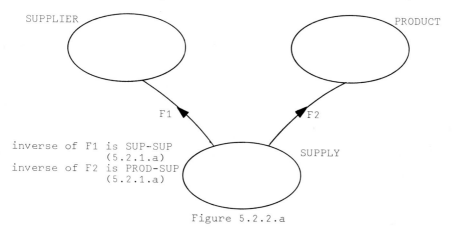

Figure 5.2.2.a

In figure 5.2.2.a, the arrows represent a functional mapping.
E.g. function F1 assigns to each element of the set SUPPLY
one element of the set SUPPLIER.

Note: Arrows in data structure (schema) diagrams and set
        theory diagrams point in opposite directions.

5.2.3. Set theory (element) diagram

        Diagrams at the schema or class level are useful, but
        for improving the understanding it is desirable to add
        diagrams at the occurrence, instance or element level.
        A set theory element diagram for our example, with 3
        suppliers, 2 products and 5 supplies is presented in
        figure 5.2.3.a.

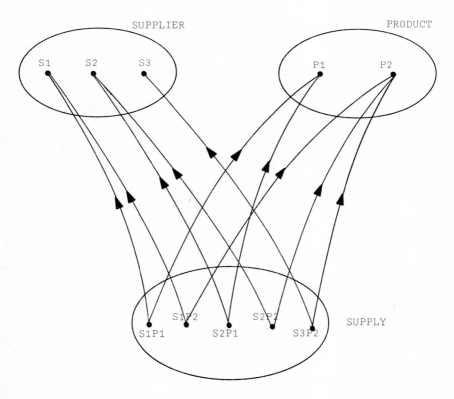

Figure 5.2.3.a

5.2.4 Data structure instance diagram

A programmer who wants to navigate thru a database prefers another kind of element diagram, which we will call
data structure instance diagram. In such a diagram each
record occurrence or tuple is presented, together with
the main navigational routes. Figure 5.2.4.a contains
the data structure instance diagram for our example.
One can navigate from S1 to S1P1, from S1P1 to S1P2,
or from S1P1 to P1 etc. A circle with a cross indicates that the record occurrence serves as owner of the
CODASYL set, (or is an element of the range of the
function), while a circle without anything in it indicates
that the record occurrence serves as member in the
CODASYL set (or is an element of the domain of the
function).

The preceeding four types of diagrams have proven their
usefulness, especially in database education.

G.M. NIJSSEN

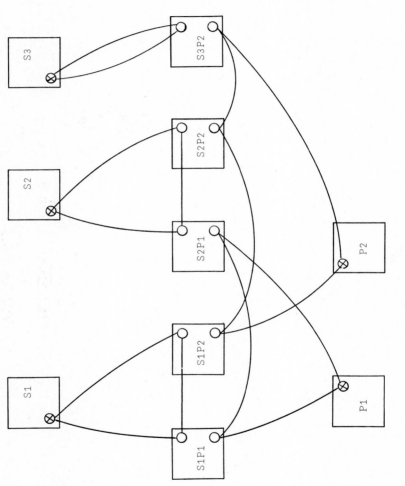

Figure 5.2.4.a

5.3 Data description

In this section we will describe the several "facets" of
a data structure description to illustrate the similarity
between a modified DDL and the Relational Data Model.
The syntax used in these examples is a derivate from the
DDL.

5.3.1 Record description

To describe the three record classes or record types
of our example, one could use the following description:

```
RECORD NAME IS SUPPLIER
    SNUMBER             TYPE IS CHARACTER 2.
    SNAME               TYPE IS CHARACTER 30.
    LOCATION            TYPE IS CHARACTER 20.
    TURNOVER            TYPE IS DECIMAL 2.


RECORD NAME IS PRODUCT
    PNUMBER             TYPE IS CHARACTER 2.
    PNAME               TYPE IS CHARACTER 30.
    LOCATION            TYPE IS CHARACTER 20.
    SALESPRICE          TYPE IS DECIMAL 5,2.


RECORD NAME IS SUPPLY
    SNUMBER             TYPE IS CHARACTER 2.
    PNUMBER             TYPE IS DECIMAL 2.
    DELIVERY-TIME       TYPE IS DECIMAL 2.
```

In the Relational Data Model the information contained
in the description of the three records will be conveyed to the system as partial descriptions of relations.
In the terminology used in section 3 we have now described
the structure of the entities and attributes.

5.3.2 Function or record owned set description

The three classes of entities, suppliers, products and
supplies are associated in such a way that each supply
is related to exactly one supplier and exactly one
product, while a supplier may be related to many supplies
and a product to many supplies.

The two functions can be described as follows,
(see also figure 5.2.1.a)

```
FUNCTION-SET NAME IS SUP-SUP
    OWNER IS SUPPLIER
    MEMBER IS SUPPLY
    SNUMBER IN SUPPLY
        IS EQUAL TO
    SNUMBER IN SUPPLIER


FUNCTION-SET NAME IS PROD-SUP
    OWNER IS PRODUCT
    MEMBER IS SUPPLY
    PNUMBER IN SUPPLY
        IS EQUAL TO
    PNUMBER IN PRODUCT
```

In the Relational Data Model the same information is conveyed to the system. In analogy with reference 2, page 46, Codd would have written:

The relation SUPPLY satisfies the following integrity constraints:

1. The set of supplier numbers appearing in the SUPPLY relation is a subset of the set of supplier numbers appearing in the SUPPLIER relation.

2. A similar constraint applies to product numbers relative to the PRODUCT relation.

Note: It is clear that the word OWNER and MEMBER could be fruitfully exchanged to RANGE and DOMAIN respectively.

A CODASYL set declaration serves two aims:

1. to declare that there is an integrity constraint or semantic rule

2. to declare that access paths or navigational routes need to be maintained by the system.

The semantic rule is available in both the DDL and Relational Data Model; the predefined access paths are only available in the DDL, because the Relational Data Model does not (yet?) include the concept of a predefined access path.

The combination of semantic rule and predefined access path
in the CODASYL set type has been criticized by respected
Relational Data Model supporters. We would like to remark
to this criticism that, if one declares a semantic rule such
as the ones in this section, one also knows at declaration
time that update operations will result in accesses via certain attributes to owner (range) or member (domain) records.
In other words, why not using this information to lower
the access costs?

5.3.3 Access path or ownerless set description

> It could happen that many questions to our sample data-
> base involve both the location of the supplier as well
> as the location of the product. In such a case, it would
> be advantageous to declare to the system that two access
> paths need to be maintained. These access paths give
> a fast access if the value of the location is provided.
> In other words this is an access from outside the data-
> base into a specific record occurrence, and one could
> call this absolute access paths, while the navigational
> routes as described in section 5.3.2 could be named
> relative access paths. Figure 5.3.3.a represents the
> data structure schema diagram extended with the two
> access paths to LOCATION.

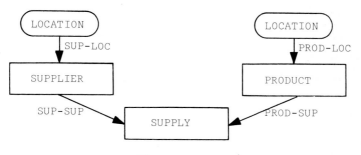

Figure 5.3.3.a

The two access paths can be described as follows:

ACCESS PATH NAME IS SUP-LOC
    TARGET IS SUPPLIER
    SEARCH KEY IS LOCATION

ACCESS PATH NAME IS PROD-LOC
    TARGET IS PRODUCT
    SEARCH KEY IS LOCATION

For one of the access paths, say SUP-LOC, we will give the
description according to the DDL as specified in the JOD-1973
(3):

SET NAME IS SUP-LOC;

    OWNER IS SYSTEM;

    ORDER IS PERMANENT INSERTION IS IMMATERIAL.

    MEMBER IS SUPPLIER

        MANDATORY AUTOMATIC;

    SEARCH KEY IS LOCATION OF SUPPLIER

        DUPLICATES ARE ALLOWED;

    SET SELECTION FOR SUP-LOC IS

        THRU SUP-LOC OWNER IDENTIFIED BY

        SYSTEM.

The only real difference between this description and our
ACCESS PATH description is the clause DUPLICATES ARE ALLOWED;
this semantic rule could easily be added to the ACCESS PATH
description.

6 Instant guidelines for a DBA using DDL (73)

If a database administrator (DBA), who is using the DDL 1973
to describe data bases, has the intention to let use in the
near future the more productive languages like ALPHA in his
organization, while at the same time going on with running
the well-tested DML programs, and he also places some priority
on data independence, then he should follow the following
guidelines:

    1 do not mix set types and data aggregates in one schema

    2 do not exchange a databasekey for an attribute

    3 use the option "ORDER IS PERMANENT, INSERTION IS
      IMMATERIAL"

    4 do not use search key in record owned set

    5 use only one search key in system owned set

    6 declare all "absolute" access paths via ownerless sets
      (system owned sets)

    7 use the option LOCATION MODE IS SYSTEM

    8 use the option MANDATORY AUTOMATIC

    9 declare a record identifier

   10 for record owned sets, use the option in the set selection
      "THRU...BY SYSTEM...THEN THRU...WHERE...EQUAL TO..."

The guidelines are not all independent. If a database administrator follows these guidelines or applies this discipline,
he has the additional advantage to be able to select a subset
of the DML to be used by the application programmers, which
is much simpler than the "full" DML, however with the same
functional capabilities.

7 Some DDL modifications

In this section we will briefly list some of the modifications
that in our opinion could improve the DDL.

1. The four kinds of set type membership, AUTOMATIC,
   MANUAL, MANDATORY and OPTIONAL should be dropped.
   MANDATORY and OPTIONAL could be replaced by a
   semantic rule; AUTOMATIC and MANUAL could be described
   in the storage structure description language, if
   efficiency was the argument to use them. Dropping
   the four kinds of set type membership results in
   dropping the INSERT and REMOVE statements and 3
   options of the DELETE statement from the DML.

2. A set type can have more than one record type as
   member. This is a feature which is not of interest
   for data structuring, and it should therefore be
   dropped.

3. Drop the LOCATION MODE from DDL and introduce in the
   storage structure description language a declaration
   to describe a more elaborate placement optimization.

4. Simplify set selection (as used in 5.3.2), assuming
   that tuples or record occurrences possess always
   an application oriented identifier.

5. Drop the restriction that a function cannot have the
   same set (in mathematical sense) as both domain and
   range, or in CODASYL terminology, drop the restriction
   that a record type cannot be owner and member in the
   same set type.

6. Drop the ORDER clause.

7. Drop the search key from record owned set.

A database declared in a DDL modified as suggested above, can
be accessed by several classes of languages, namely:

- DML (simplified, yet same power)
- ALPHA type
- casual user

8   Laws of Cargese

It is quite possible to have "relational" and "CODASYL"
databases and languages working together, after some
modifications to both approaches. We therefore like to
list the following "laws":

First Law of Cargese:

      Peaceful coexistence is possible for the Relational
      Data Model and the DDL.

Second Law of Cargese:

      DDL + discipline = Relational + access paths

Third Law of Cargese:

      DDL + modifications = Relational + access paths

9   Invitation

The author will welcome any paper or letter that can contribute to the debate on the Relational Data Model and DDL.
Please address such comments to:

                  G.M. NIJSSEN

                  53, Boslaan

                  1900   OVERIJSE

                  (BELGIUM)

References

1   CODASYL DBTG

          Data Base Task Group report 1971.
          Available from ACM, New York.

2   CODD E.F.

          A data base sublanguage founded on the relational
          calculus.
          Proceedings of 1971 ACM SIGFIDET Workshop on
          Data Description, Access and Control.

3   CODASYL DDLC

          Data Description Language, 1973, Journal of
          Development.
          Available from ACM, New York, 1973.

4   CODD E.F.

          Further Normalization of the Data Base Relational
          Model.
          In: Data Base Systems, edited by R. Rustin,
          Prentice-Hall, Inc., Englewood Cliffs, New Yersey,
                                                        1972.

5   BACHMAN C.W.

          Data structure diagrams
          In: Data Base, volume 1, number 2, 1969, pp. 4-10,
          Quarterly Newsletter of ACM SIGBDP.

DISCUSSION

Lehot: I would like to take the issue with the suggestion that the programmer wants to "navigate". When Christopher Columbus crossed the Atlantic, he had to do a lot of navigation.
When I cross the Atlantic, I sit in an armchair in a 747. I know which I prefer.

Nijssen: In my point of view, it is essential that a common DDL serves both navigational programmers as well as others. This means that a c o m m o n data model should not take away the freedom from any large group of programmers or users. In other words, a true common data model should leave the selection of the data sublanguage open to the programmers or users.

Codd: I am definitely with Mr. Nijssen in the spirit of his presentation. If we can find a common ground and I think there is a good deal of common ground, so much the better.

With regard to navigation, I would suggest a careful investigation of about four aspects of the owner coupled set construct. One is on the user side and the other three are on the architectural side and they have to do incidentally with database administration.

On the architectural side, I think that one could investigate the impact on concurrency control of introducing the owner coupled set.

The second thing is the impact on authorization control. In that area even though the owner coupled set may bear information inessentially, nevertheless it is bearing information and there is the possibility that users can extract information from the structure somewhat independent of the data itself.
But let me give you a simpler example on the owner coupled set, and that is the following: if you have something ordered on salary values, but you do'nt permit the user to see salary. At least you can get from the ordering which is a structural thing, whether Smith earns more than Jones. So I think there could be some implications on complexity of authorization control in having the owner coupled set.

DISCUSSION

And the third area is the impact on mapping, from logical to the physical. I eluded rather superficially earlier in the week to the problem of N logical data types (= data structure) having to be mapped into M physical data types, and I said rather carelessly that you would have N times M mappings, now that is only so if you want to keep the structuring at the logical level free from implications as to the physical structures to be supported. These are the three architectural questions on which I think we could have some good papers.

Then there is on the user side the navigation question. I think it is worth investigating to see under what circumstances, what kinds of applications, one can get more efficient exploitation of the essential information in the database thru having this particular tracking capability. And at the same time investigate whether you get this increase in efficiency as a result of the owner coupled set being visible. That is absolutely important. In other words, is there the possibility of having it below the application programmer's level and still getting the efficiency that it undoubtedly gives in some circumstances.

Nijssen: Regarding the navigational aspect, I would like to say that in the IFIP IAG Database Workshop, held last week in Brussels, a few examples were discussed for which it was not easy to write the ALPHA program. Your (Codd) answer was to introduce a function (or subroutine). If we someday have enough functions or subroutines such that we can program in an ALPHA type language, extended with functions (subroutines), all the problems we program in the DML, then the DML will very probably die automatically and not by force.

Regarding the other three points: - concurrency, authorization, mapping N data structures into M storage structures, I would like to say that these points are the same in the DDL and Relational Data Model if the discipline is applied in using the DDL (as earlier described) or some modifications are made in the DDL.

Codd: With the imposition of the discipline as you (Nijssen) are suggesting, I believe that it would be possible to support an ALPHA type language (via a common DDL). I think that part of that

discipline probably has to be the avoidance of owner coupled sets
carrying information essentially.
And if you do that, and don't have the repeating groups (= data
aggregates), one data interface can serve both a DML level language
and a higher set oriented level language.

Olle: Just one point on this business of navigating, it seems to be
a central issue, so I think that we have to discuss it.
If we analyze and present the FIND options in the DML, I break them
down into two classes:
One class I call an "out of the blue" access, you come from nowhere
into the database and you get a single record occurrence. Now there
are two ways of doing an "out of the blue" access. The first one is
if it happens to be a CALC record and the second one is using a
databasekey. Like Codd and Nijssen say, I think we should quietly
forget that second one.
Now the navigational aids that come from the set type. If you require that every record type has a key, then you are essentially
saying in other words that it has a location mode of CALC and you
can do an "out of the blue" access.
Now the issue then would be, with navigational aids or without
navigational aids. With navigational aids, set types or owner
coupled sets, whatever they are called this week and you come
"out of the blue" into the database and then you move around inside
the database. If you do not have navigational aids, every access to
the database is an "out of the blue" access and it seems to me that,
you know, this is sort of where the action is. The set type is put
in to minimize, essentially, the number of "out of the blue"
accesses that one needs to make in a given processing program.

Nijssen: You are saying that a record identifier or key has to be
described using the LOCATION MODE IS CALC. I think this is not entirely correct. Namely a tuple or record may have more than one
identifier, but one may only describe one LOCATION MODE for a
record type.
Record or tuple identifiers may be declared in the DDL using
either LOCATION MODE IS CALC or using an ownerless or system owned
set with duplicates are not allowed. In my opinion the LOCATION
MODE does nothing else, than assigning in a special way a data base

key to a record. So I would say, if you want to support tuple or
record identifiers, then always describe this with an ownerless or
system owned set, because then you have the freedom to declare
alternates without changing any program and that is still a good
aim to have this aspect data independence.

Date: I would like to make two comments. First of all I think that
in the discussion we ought to try very hard to avoid idiosyncrasies
of the CODASYL proposal as such, and as Mr. Nijssen has very
clearly shown, we can drop a lot of the things, LOCATION MODE is
a good example.

We are still left with the basic network structure and the argument
should be about the network structure and relational structure.
I think that is usually accepted, but in the heat of the argument, it sometimes is forgotten.

Referring to what Bill Olle said just now, he said that there are
two types of FIND, and that is true. There is the "out of the blue"
FIND and the navigational FIND.
But an unspoken assumption behind that is that what you really
want is single record access and I think that this is something
that we should consider. Why should we restrict programs to access
one record at a time? Isn't it important to think in terms of
mathematical sets as opposed to CODASYL sets?

Olle: I am lucky you (Date) made that opening for me, because there
is a significant difference between one-record-at-a-time logic and
a multiple-record-at-a-time logic. It has been pointed out earlier
that peaceful co-existence of the single-record-at-a-time logic
and the multiple-record-at-a-time logic can be achieved during the
course of the years. I think we should strive towards that. But I
think that the thing we have to be very careful about is wrap-
ping what is still to be proven, multiple-record-at-a-time logic,
down the industry throat and depriving them of the essentially
proven efficiencies of single-record-at-a-time logic.
That is it.

Date: I do not agree with that.

<u>Nijssen</u>: I would like to comment on the question regarding the
network versus relational. Date is saying that the real issue is
relational versus network. I object very heavily to the name network, because there is nothing that supports in the whole DDL
language, in the semantic rules and the syntax rules, the concept
that the network is very essential.
What I want to stress is that you have in the CODASYL DDL a structuring facility to describe one or more functions associating one
set with another set, and this has no bias for a network. Several
structures, like trees and networks and many more, can be described
with the DDL structuring facilities of the owner coupled set.

<u>Date</u>: Well I am simply trying to categorize and what I mean by the
word network is that you have owner coupled sets and navigation.

<u>Olle</u>: Date has said that he has identified the issue as relational
versus network and I agree with Mr. Nijssen here that this is not a
clear and useful identification of the issue. In order to argue
intelligently, I think that we have to identify the issues we are
arguing about. I think the issue is predefined preferential paths
versus figured out at execution time, if you like, paths. And that
is how I would like to identify it.

<u>Durchholz</u>: The remark I would like to make is a bit out of line, it
is a general remark and I was hesitant to give it here for this
reason. But I think that the statement that DDL needs mathematical
foundation, should not go without challenge.
What is really needed is a clarification of the conceptual foundation. Too much maths may give rise to two dangers, namely, many
people will not understand en will give up, and incorrect reasoning
may be concealed under cloak of formalization.

Data Base Management, J. W. Klimbie and K. L. Koffeman, (eds.)
© North-Holland Publishing Company (1974)

ON THE SELECTION OF ACCESS PATHS IN

A DATA BASE SYSTEM

H. WEDEKIND

Department of Informatics, Technical University of
Darmstadt, Darmstadt, West-Germany

Abstract: Data-base design can at least be separated into three
design levels. The first level is the user's logical
level. We assume in this paper that the data model
on this level is a relational one. The second level
is the system logical level, which is not visible for
the user. On this level access paths have to be
provided by using some performance criterion. A B-tree,
which was proposed by Bayer and McCreight (Bayer 1972)
is introduced as a standard access path to overcome the
difficulty of too many eligible path structures. Besides
high performance B-trees have the advantage that only
one parameter representing the page size is linking the
system logical level and the physical device level, the
third level to be considered in a complete data-base
design. A selection procedure is outlined in which
B-trees are tested against ordered and unordered
sequential access paths and hashing.

1. Introduction

A relational data model is a table-oriented representation of
the data of an application world (mini world). It is required that
all attribute domains within a relation are simple, i.e. no domain
subsets are allowed. For example:

$$DEP(D\#,DD) \quad EMP(E\#,D\#,ENAME)$$

are two relations for departments and employees of a relational
data model. $D\#$ = Department No, DD = Department Description,
$E\#$ = Employee No., ENAME = Employee Name. The identifying keys
are underlined. An instance or a line item of a simple relation
is called a tuple. Hierarchical relations with domain subsets
could be represented in the following way:

$$DEP(D\#,EMP,DD)$$

$$EMP(E\#,ENAME)$$

Codd (Codd 1970,1971) has provided a theory to cluster data in a
standardized form known as the third normal form of simple
relations. He starts from a hierarchical relation and transforms
this relation stepwise via a first and second normal forms into
the third normal form. Meanwhile the advantage of this data
representation on the user's logical level are widely recognized.
Another approach to come to normalized relations was taken by
Wang and Wedekind (Wang 1974). In this paper we are concerned
with the system logical level. The input for this level are the
relations of a user community, typ, and frequency of queries and
parameters for batch and transaction processing. As a framework
of our discussion we choose a special access path typ, called
B-tree for standardization. Standardized access path structures

are needed to simplify the design work and to improve portability
of systems. Standardization has always a dogmatic component, because possible solutions are ruled out a priori. If, however, a
broad class of applications is covered, there can be no argument
against standardization. Codd's relational model can be looked
at as a standardized data model from the user's logical view.

The three design levels are overviewed in the following
set-up:

$$
\text{performance} \atop \text{dependent}
\left\{
\begin{array}{l}
\text{User's logical level} \\
\text{(relational level)} \\
\hline
\text{System logical level} \\
\text{(access path level)} \\
\uparrow k \\
\hline
\text{Physical device level}
\end{array}
\right.
$$

From a methodological and technical point of view it is
recommendable to provide a minimal number of links between the
design levels. The relational level is fully independent on the
deeper levels. Logical considerations have nothing to do with
performance aspects. When using B-trees the access path level
and the physical device level are just linked by one parameter,
i.e. the parameter k, which represents a page (block, bucket)
size. A page is a transportation unit between two levels of
storage and is a device and performance dependent concept.

Normalized relations can equally well be used to define access
path structures. Consider two data elements a and b.

$$
\underset{a}{\bullet} \longrightarrow \underset{b}{}
$$

We say that a direct path (a path of length 1) exists between
a and b, if b is accessible from a. We refer to a as the HEAD
element and to b as the TAIL element. Let $a_i \in A$ and $b_i \in B$
we write an access path relation in form

$$P(\text{HEAD}/A, \text{HEAD}/\text{POINTER}, \text{TAIL}/B)$$

a_1	p_{11}	b_1
a_2	p_{12} ·	b_1
⋮		
a_m	p_{mn}	b_n

HEAD and TAIL are role names and are separated by a slash from
the primary domain name. p is an instance of a POINTER domain.
If p > 0 we speak about a pointer access path. If p = 0 a
contiguity path is given. In a valid path relation p must be
defined. p may be calculated by a procedure or may be tabulated.
Data elements are tuples of the user's relation augmented by
pointers and addresses or tuples of control data relations, e.g.
indexes.

The following is the format of a general access path relation:

P {restrictions} (HEAD/dom. names,...,HEAD/POINTER,

TAIL/dom. names,...)

Restrictions are conditions with respect to elements of HEAD and TAIL domains in the parenthesis.

2. B-trees and B*-trees

Most of the access path structures described in the literature are assuming a one level storage structure. Many kinds of complicated tree structures and multilink list structures were developped within the field of systems programming. Recently Bayer and McCreight (Bayer 1972) suggested a tree typ called a B-tree, which is very suitable for a basis in the access path design of formatted data-bases, because

-   a two level storage is considered
-   the dependence on the physical device level is confined to only one parameter
-   a high performance in all four basic operations, i.e. retrieval, modifying,insertion and deletion in the batch and single transaction mode of processing
-   a flexibility to provide a scheme for secondary indexes with respect to non key domains
-   a fairly good storage occupancy.

A B-tree is defined as follows:

-   Each path from the root to any leaf has the same length   h.
-   Each node except for the root and the leaves has at least k+1 sons. The root is a leaf or has at least two sons.
-   Each node has at most 2k+1 sons.

Two parameters, determine a B-tree, i.e. h, the height of the tree and 2k, the total number of elements (tuples) in a node. The node is like a page, bucket or block a transportation unit between two levels of storage.

The format of a node is given below:

$$\boxed{P_0 \mid K_1 \mid D_1 \mid \ldots\ldots\ldots\ldots \mid K_{2k} \mid D_{2k} \mid P_{2k}}$$

P = pointer

K_i, D_i = tuple of the user's relation

A node has to be filled at least by 50 %, i.e. k tuples, or when a variable tuple size is given by 50 % of the bytes provided per node (extension of the B-tree concept). Experiments by Bayer (Bayer 1972) and the author show that the node occupancy in a practical case is much higher than the lower bound. All operations mentioned before perform proportionally to $\log_k I$ where I is the total number of tuples to be stored.

A B-tree with k=1, h=3 is shown below. The natural numbers represent the keys. The data part is omitted.

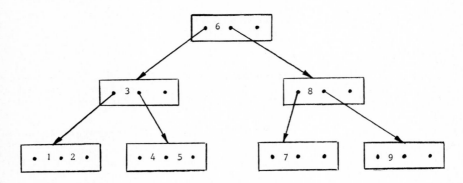

The functionally unnecessary pointers in the leaf nodes are introduced to provide one common format for all nodes. Note that the ordering in the tree is in the postorder fashion.
The performance of B-trees is so high, because in all operations only a very small subtree is used in general.

A slight variation of the described B-tree is a tree, where all data are stored in leaf nodes. The non leaf nodes contain only pointers and keys. We call this tree typ a B^*-tree.

Non leaf node of a B^*-tree:

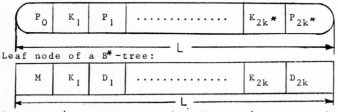

Leaf node of a B^*-tree:

P_j are pointers to son nodes. K_i are instances of the key domain and D_i are instances of the data domain. M is a mark to distinguish leaf nodes from non leaf nodes. B^*-trees are described by three parameters k, k^* and h. An example of a B^*-tree with k=1, k^*=2 and h=2 is given below.

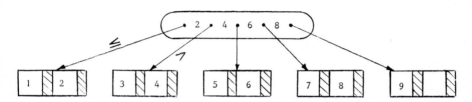

The left pointer in a B*-tree denotes $\leq$. The right pointer stands for $>$.

Both node formats in a B*-tree have the same capacity L in bytes.

$$L = (\lambda_K + \lambda_D)2k + \lambda_M = 2k^*(\lambda_K + \lambda_P) + \lambda_P \qquad (1)$$

where

λ_K = length of the key field

λ_D = length of the data field

λ_M = length of the mark

λ_P = length of a pointer field.

We want to show that B*-trees are dominant in performance with regard to B-trees. For this purpose λ_P comes into play. λ_P, the length of a pointer field, is a device dependent parameter. λ_P is not a parameter on the system logical level. It has just been introduced to compare B*-trees with B-trees. To simplify the calculations below, we assume that λ_P is very small and can be neglected. The same holds for λ_M. Eq (1) becomes

$$a = \frac{\lambda_K + \lambda_D}{\lambda_K} = \frac{k^*}{k} \qquad (2)$$

a is a parameter comparing the total tuple length with the key length.

Bayer and McCreight in their paper showed that the height h of a B-tree is a variable on which the performance of the four operations mentioned above depends. h of a B-tree is given by

$$\log_{2k+1} (I+1) \leq h \leq 1 + \log_{k+1} (\frac{I+1}{2}) \; ; \quad h \geq 1 \qquad (3)$$

where I is the total number of tuples stored.

For a B^*-tree the height is bounded by

$$\log_{2k^*+1} \left(\frac{I}{2k}\right) \leq h^* \leq 2+\log_{k^*+1} \left(\frac{I}{2k}\right) \ , \quad h^* \geq 2 \qquad (4)$$

To compare the performance of B-trees and B^*-trees, we choose the upper bounds h_{max} and h^*_{max} under the assumptions that I is equal in both trees and that eq (2) holds.

It can be shown by using the mean value theorem of differential calculus that

$$\Delta h_{max} = h_{max} - h^*_{max} \geq 0$$

if

$$a > 1 + \frac{k+1}{k} \ \ln \left(\frac{1+\frac{1}{k}}{1+\frac{1}{I}}\right) \cdot \frac{1}{\log_{k+1} \left(\frac{I+1}{2}\right)-1} \quad ; \ I \geq k \quad (5)$$

This is an approximate lower bound for a.

Since the second term on the right hand side is almost equal to zero one can state that B^*-tree are dominant, if there are only small data parts. In case of a=1 Δh_{max} is slightly negative.

$$\Delta h_{max} = \log_{k+1} \left(\frac{1+\frac{1}{I}}{1+\frac{1}{k}}\right) \ ; \quad a=1, \ I \geq k \qquad (6)$$

Since the case a=1 is very seldom in real data-base systems one can infer from (5) and (6) that B^*-trees are preferable from the performance point of view.

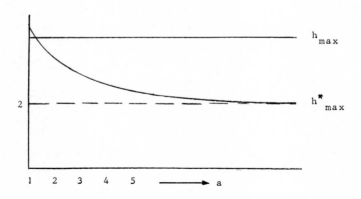

The illustration above shows qualitatively h_{max} and h^*_{max} as a function of a.

We take B^*-trees within our selection of path structures. In order to provide good batch processing capabilities the leaf nodes are linked by pointers.

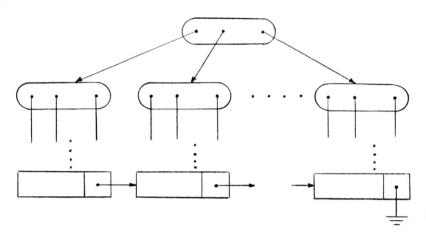

In the selection of access path structures we dinstinguish two classes:

A) Main class, i.e. B^*-tree.
   case 1) $h^* \geq 2$

   This class covers in particular the "famous" index-sequential path structure, i.e. $h^* = 3$ (one level for the cylinder index, the second level for the track index and the third level for the data). Binary trees are covered, if $k=1$ and $I=I_{min}$ for a particular h^*.

B) Marginal class, i.e. a sequence of B^*-trees, where only the roots of trees are provided.
   case 2) $h^* = 1$, sequential-ordered

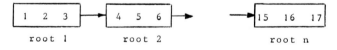

   root 1   root 2   root n

   case 3) $h^* = 1$, sequential-unordered

   case 4) $h^* = 1$, hashing, i.e. key-to-address transformation.

Let $t = 0,1,2,3,...,T$ be an index and replace h^* by $h^*_t = h^*+t$. h^*_t is the maximal path length. The four cases can be described as follows:

case 1)

$$h^*_t \quad \begin{cases} h^* & \geq & 2 \\ t & = & 0 \end{cases}$$

case 2) and 3)

$$h^*_t \quad \begin{cases} h^* & = & 1 \\ t & = & T \end{cases}$$

case 4)

$$h^*_t \quad \begin{cases} h^* & = & 1 + \zeta \quad ; \quad \zeta = \text{random variable} \\ t & = & 0 \end{cases}$$

Not covered by B^*-trees are multilink list structures, digital trees, threaded trees etc. It is worth to mention at this point that the first relational data-bases implemented by IBM and others are using multilink list structures. We refer to BOMP (Bill of Material Processor) and the extention to this called PICS (Production Information Control System). Both systems are fairly restrictive. BOMP, e.g. can handle only two normalized relations, i.e. the part master relation and the part structure relation. Because of the multilink list structure the system is unexpandable to handle more than two relations. Hierarchical relations on the other hand can not handle bill of material typs of data structures adequately.

B^*-trees can also be used for secondary indexes with respect to non key attribute domains. This will be explained by an example. Suppose the following relation on cars is given.

	CAR (OC#	,	C	,	M	,	B	)
	MCA1		green		Förd		1971	
	KA35		blue		Ford		1972	
	DVA8		blue		GM		1970	
	HRS4		white		GM		1970	
j	= 4		3		2		3	
N_{max}	= 1		2		2		2	
$\bar{N}$	= 1		4/3		2		4/3	

OC# = car number (key)

C   = color

M   = manufacturer

B   = date when built

The parameters j, N_{max} and $\bar{N}$ for each domain are defined in the parameter list of the next paragraph. In a list below the direct file is shown above the line. Below the line the full inverted file is listed. Here the numbers of the data part refer to the ordinal numbers. The keys are underlined. The total list is ordered lexicographically with respect to domain name.key instance.

1.	OC# .	DVA8	blue	GM	1970
2.	OC# .	HRS4	white	GM	1970
3.	OC# .	KA35	blue	Ford	1972
4.	OC# .	MCA1	green	Ford	1971
				•	

5.	B.	1970	1	2
6.	B.	1971	4	
7.	B.	1972	3	
8.	C.	blue	1	3
9.	C.	green	4	
10.	C.	white	2	
11.	M.	Ford	3	4
12.	M.	GM	1	2

If we take the ordinal numbers as keys and if we omit the data
in the leaf nodes the following illustration depicts an access
path for the relation CAR with a secondary index for every domain.

catalog as a supernode

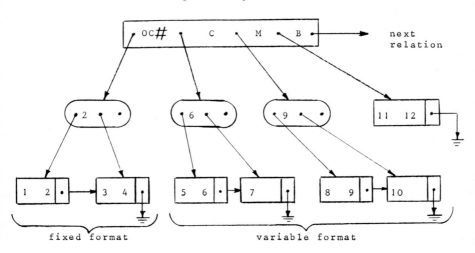

In the leaves of the secondary indexes inverted tuples of
variable length may be stored. In this case k and 2k are interpreted
as lower and upper bounds for filling a page with bytes.

3. Design procedure with B*-trees

Performance costs are the selection criterion for the four
cases described above. Cost unit is a page fetched or written.
We assume that fetching a page and writing a page requires the
same effort. If f and w are the number of pages fetched or written,
respectively, then the total cost for a particular operation with
respect to a particular domain is

$$c(k) = p(f+w), \qquad\qquad\qquad (7)$$

where p is the frequency with which the particular operation
occurs. c is only a function of k even in the case of hashing, if
the key-to-address-transformation algorithm, the method of
collision handling and the load factor are fixed. In a pratical
case we have to evaluate many formulas of the typ (7) for every
domain and operation. The costs are added up for every case. The
total costs of an access path as a function of k are compared for
every case. The case with the minimal costs is picked. The cost
functions are monotonously decreasing functions with k. Intersection points of the cost functions determine critical k values.
At a critical k value one case with minimal performance costs is
swapping into another one. If the devices are given k can be
determined in a way shown by Bayer (Bayer 1972), e.g.. The selection
of an access path can then be completed.

The illustration below shows the general approach of evaluation.

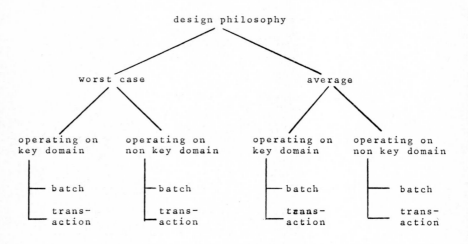

On the top of the tree we have a dichotomy. Either we are following
the worst case philosophy of design for a subset or the whole set
of path structures or we are satisfied by an average performance
design. In general worst case designs are more costly than systems
based on an average performance. It can be seen from a particular
query whether an operating on a key domain or a non key domain or
both is required. By operating we mean retrieval, modifying,
insertion or deletion. The frequency telling, how often these

operatings take place within a time span must be captured from
the application environment. By batch a serial processing according
to an order criterion is meant. In an transaction typ of processing
only single tuples are subject to retrieval, modification, insertion or deletion.

Since it is too cumbersome here to list all the formulas for
every design philosophy,every selection case, every operation on
key and non key domain in batch and transaction mode, we confine
ourselves to a list of important parameters used in the formulas.
As far as explicit formulas and the underlying search models are
concerned we refer to Knuth (Knuth 1973) and Bayer and McCreight
(1972).

List of parameters:

I	=	number of tuples in a relation
$2k$	=	maximal number of fixed length tuples in a page or number of bytes in a page, when variable length tuples are stored
$\alpha, \beta, \gamma, \sigma$	=	captured frequency for retrieval, modifying, insertion and deletion, respectively
n	=	batch size for retrieval, modifying, insertion or deletion
j	=	number of distinct values in a domain ($j = I$ for a key domain). j replaces I, if a non key domain is considered.
N_p	=	number of instances of the pth value inna domain, $1 \le p \le j$.
$N_{max} = MaxN_p$	=	maximal number of instances in a domain. The parameter determines the maximal filling of a leaf page of a non key domain. The parameter is used in the worst case calculation to determine the accesses to the direct files.
$\bar{N} = \Sigma N_p / j$	=	average number of instances of a particular value. This parameter is used instead of N_{max} in the average calculation. Note that $\Sigma N_p = I$. $\bar{N}$ is called resolution (Wang 1973).
ρ	=	load factor in hashing
u	=	average percentage of leaf page occupancy
s_i	=	space required for a B^*-tree index. s_i is a function of k and h^*.

It is worth to point out that hashing is no solution in a worst
case design. Hashing models are confined to the average case.

Let $c_1(k)$, $c_2(k)$, $c_3(k)$, and $c_4(k)$ be the total cost of an
access path for a B^*-tree access, a sequential ordered access, a
sequential-unordered access and hashing, respectively. A design
calculation may yield to the following curves, if a key domain
is considered.

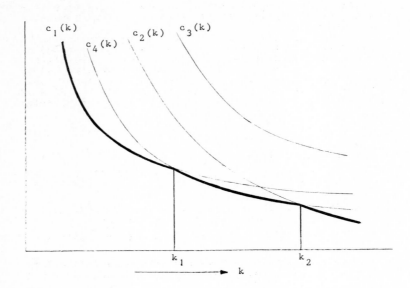

The path selection is then done in the following way, if the device dependent k is given.

if $k \leq k_1$ choose B^*-tree

if $k_1 < k \leq k_2$ choose hashing

if $k > k_2$ choose a sequential-ordered access path.

In the case of a non key domain we are only concerned whether and what typ of secondary index should be selected. We have to compare the following costs:

$c_1(k)$ =   total cost if a B^*-tree with $h^* \geqq 2$ is provided

$c_2(k)$ =   total cost if a simple index (ordered-sequential) $h^* = 1$ is provided

$c_3(k)$ =   total cost if a simple index (unordered-sequential) $h^* = 1$ is provided

$c_4(k)$ =   total cost if no index is provided, i.e. full search of the direct file.

The intersections of these functions determine the critical values k_1, k_2, k_3, if they exist.

The selection of an index has to be done subject to space restrictions. With the procedure outlined above we only designate domains and candidates for an index. The problem of selecting an index subject to space restrictions can be stated as follows:

T = total data base space (secondary storage capacity)

B = $z.T$ = provided index space, $0 \le z < 1$

s_i = space required for index number i

p_i = priority assigned to s_i. This parameter may be derived from response time requirements

x_i = $\begin{cases} 1 & \text{if space is provided} \\ 0 & \text{if space is not provided.} \end{cases}$

The problem is now:

$$\text{Maximize } \Sigma p_i x_i$$

$$\text{subject to } \Sigma s_i x_i \le B. \quad \text{(knapsack problem)}$$

If x_i = 0 select a case with next higher costs and put s_i = 0.

References:

1) Bayer, R. and McCreight. (1972). Organization and maintenance of large ordered indexes. Acta Informatica. Vol. 1, p. 173.

2) Codd, E.F. (1970). A relational model of data for large data banks. CACM, Vol. 13, p.377.

3) Codd, E.F. (1971). Further normalization of the data base relational model. Courant Computer Science Symposium No. 6, "Data Base Systems", New York, Prentice Hall.

4) Knuth, D.E. (1973). The art of computer programming. Vol. 3, Sorting and Searching, Addison-Wesley.

5) Senko, M.E., Altman, E.B., Astrahan, M.M., and Fehder, P.L. (1973). Data structures and accessing in data base systems, IBM Systems Journal, Vol. 12, p. 30.

6) Wang, C.P. (1973). Parametrization of information system application. IBM Research, Report, RJ 1199.

7) Wang, C.P., and Wedekind, H. (1974). An approach for segment synthesis in data base design. IBM Research Report, submitted for acceptance to IFIP Congress 1974 in Stockholm.

Note: This paper was not presented, only published, because author was unable to come, so no discussion took place.

Data Base Management, J. W. Klimbie and K. L. Koffeman, (eds.)
© *North-Holland Publishing Company (1974)*

IMPLEMENTATIONAL ASPECTS OF THE CODASYL DBTG PROPOSAL

by

Hans Schenk

Project leader of the DBMS Development Team
System Software Programming Department
PHILIPS ELECTROLOGICA B.V.
THE NETHERLANDS

1. THE POSITION OF THE DBMS IN RELATION TO THE APPLICATION PROGRAM(S)
    AND THE OPERATING SYSTEM

2. THE REALIZATION OF THE SEVERAL DATA AREAS

2.1   The UWA
2.2   System Buffers
2.3   The Data Base itself
2.4   Object Schema and Sub-schema

INTRODUCTION

Although the CODASYL DBTG specifications can be considered to be rather
complete, they still leave the implementor of a DBMS, based on these
specifications, with quite some questions to be answered. Apparently,
it has not been the objective of the task group to be complete, reading
the following statement:

'This Journal is not a complete specification for a DBMS. However, it
may be helpful to an understanding of the DDL to conceptualize a
complete system. The system presented is for pedagogic purposes only and
is illustrated by Diagram 1.'

In this presentation diagram 1 will be used to discuss some of the
problem-areas with which the implementor is confrontated.
These areas are:

- The position of the DBMS in relation to the application program(s) and
  the operating system.

- The realization of the several data areas as there are:
  . User Working Area
  . System Buffers
  . Data Base
  . Object Schema and Subschemas.

This list is in no way complete, e.g. the areas of privacy, recovery
and concurrent-use are not included, which does not imply that they
are considering as being less important.

CONCEPTUAL DATA BASE MANAGEMENT SYSTEM

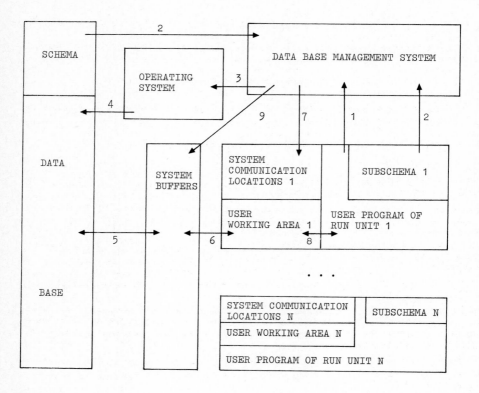

Diagram 1

1 THE POSITION OF THE DBMS IN RELATION TO THE APPLICATION PROGRAM(S) AND THE OPERATING SYSTEM

The main purpose of diagram 1 is to illustrate the flow through the DBMS, however it can be easily used to define the position of the DBMS in relation to the applications and the Operating System.
A clear definition, however is only possible when the meaning of the boxes is determined. What do they represent, tasks, programs? And how do they cooperate?
As far as the position of the DBMS is concerned, there are three possibilities, each with their own advantages and disadvantages:

1. The DBMS is an integrated part of the application (linked).

2. The DBMS is an independent job under the Operating System.

3. The DBMS is an integrated part of the Operating System.

Possibility 1 has some advantages, especially in a 'mono-use' environment, e.g. a very direct way of transferring control between application and DBMS. But, also in a multi-use environment this concept can be employed. First of all in the situation where the application, to which the DBMS is linked, is an asynchronous process (multi-tasking). In this way, a real time application with a number of terminals, can be conceived.
A requirement is that the host-language in some way supports multi-tasking- and data-communication facilities.
Furthermore one could think of a situation where the employed multi programming operating system supports the shared segment (code) feature. Now a number of applications might run simultaneously each having linked in their own DBMS logically, where actually the DBMS is present only once.
In both cases the DBMS should be reentrant.
The last case however causes some distinct problems in the area of concurrent use, because the logical available DBMS's at a certain moment are not aware of each other's presence and so can not take the necessary precautions else than through the facilities offered by the operating system. Now a days this means at most exclusive access facilities at file level.

Possibility 2 makes it possible to solve the concurrent use problems. In fact with this concept all problems can be handled, assuming that the employed operating system allows for transferring data between programs in main memory.
The disadvantage of this concept is the rather inefficient way of trans- ferring control through the operating system (how inefficient is highly depending on the way the operating system works).
In this respect one should keep in mind the reason for multi-use, being a technique to use the CPU wait time, caused by accesses to relatively slow secondary storage devices, in order to reduce the overall through-put time. Multi-use however implies extra control, and in this situation control is maintained at three possible levels:

- OS controls the programs running under it.

- DBMS controls the applications running under it.

- Application controls possible tasks if the asynchronous processing technique is employed.

It is a fair question whether the total amount of 'overhead' caused by the control functions, at the several levels, operating more or less independent, leaves sufficient time to do anything useful. One can imagine the extreme situation where nearly all of the available CPU-time is used to protect the different processes against each other.

   Possibility 3 could be the solution to all problems. In this case the
operating system should take care of all concurrent use problems including
the multi tasking within programs. In fact this is an area which is already
known to OS's for a long time and is called resource allocation.
The difference is that the processing- and data-units to be controlled
become smaller and the fact that these units can be structured in some way.
The fact that practically no operating system in use, covers these requirements satisfactorily, is a good indication for the size and complexity of
these problems. The new developments in this area (e.g. firmware) increase
the feasibility of this concept.

   What does this mean? That we all have to wait till our computer
supplier offers this 4th generation operating system? May be a very few
people have to say yes, however in a time were a great deal of users have
hardly overcome the difficulties of an indexed-sequential file, the majority
will be satisfied by one of the two first possibilities.
The fact however that there is a range of users, starting from the tape
oriented, towards the very small class of 4th generation is important, and
means that a generalized DBMS should be conceived in such a way that each
user must be able to use a version of the system which is adepted to his
level without the burden of more sofisticated functions.

2 THE REALIZATION OF THE SEVERAL DATA AREAS

The first section was dealing with processes. In this section the several data areas as indicated in diagram 1 are subject of discussion. These areas are:

- User Working Area (UWA), being the loading and unloading zone between the DBMS and an application.
- System Buffers, being the loading and unloading zone between the DBMS and the Operating System.
- Data Base itself, which need no further comment at this place.
- Object Schema and Sub-Schema, containing the description of the data base (storage - and data structure) and the way the user sees it.

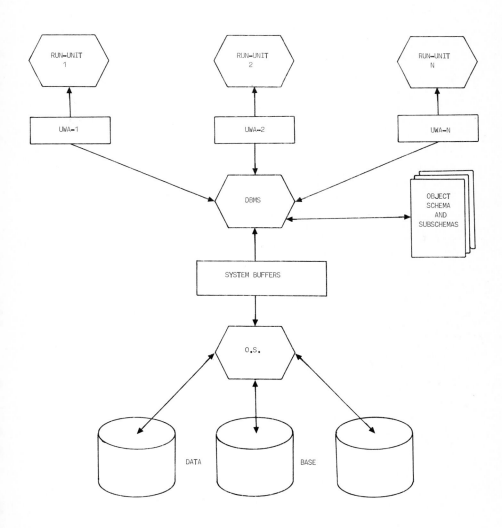

2.1 The UWA

The function of this area is clear; the way to define this area is an
open question. In principle there are two approaches namely the static
approach where the layout of this area is completely determined at sub-
schema compile-time and the dynamic approach where the layout is determined
at run-time.

In the static approach it is assumed that the displacements of the
items within a record-type are fixed and that the position of record-areas
within the UWA are also fixed. Within these constraints there are still
several possibilities.

- one record-area per record-type or more than one record-area per record-
  type.
- record-areas of different record-types in overlay or not.

Actually the current COBOL DML and Sub-Schema DDL offer no facilities
to distinguish between different record-areas for the same record-type or
to specify any explicit overlay requirement for record-areas of different
record-types. However, it is possible to define a default situation where
by record-areas of record-types stored in the same AREA are allocated in
overlay.
The disadvantages of the static approach are:

- Possible loss of core space since not all record-areas associated with a
  certain sub-schema are always required.
- Loss of data-independency since changes in the sub-schema will make
  recompilation and/or relinking necessary.

The advantage of the static approach is that at run-time no allocation and
interpretation is required.

In the dynamic approach it is assumed that the position of the record-
area within the UWA is part of the interface. So, the address where a
record, or part of it, has to be delivered or obtained by the DBMS is one of
the parameters passed to the DBMS.
In this approach there are two possibilities:

- the space allocation for the UWA is a DBMS responsibility.
- the space allocation for the UWA is a user responsibility.

In the first possibility the allocation could be done at READY-time by the
DBMS and remain unchanged till the associated FINISH statement is
performed.
In the second possibility it is the responsibility of the user (program)
that the addresses of the record-areas in the UWA are correct. This last
feature is very strongly related to the capabilities of the host language.

Within COBOL this dynamic allocation is probably rather difficult to
handle, however, with PL/1 it is very well possible.

2.2 System Buffers

The concept of system buffers serves two purposes. In the first place there has to be an area in which the data of the database can be read. It is clear that this cannot be the UWA. Secondly, the number of physical I/O events can be reduced by keeping frequently used parts of the database in memory. Especially this last aspect can have a great influence on the performance of the system.

The portions of data at this level are physical blocks or pages and the DBMS should try to keep in memory those pages which will be used again. Therefore some kind of algorithm must be used. A good algorithm is the so called "Least Recently Used" algorithm, which is based on the idea that the chance that a page will be used again decreases in time.

There are two requirements for the administration of the system-buffers.

- A particular page within the system-buffers must be allocatable in a fast way.

- The buffer in which a new page should be read in must be determined in a fast way.

The best results are obtained in the situation where each buffer can contain exactly one page and all pages are of the same size.

In case the number of buffers is relatively small it may be feasible that the search for a particular page is performed by sequentially inspecting all buffers. In general a more efficient approach is required such as a randomizing or binary-search technique.

System-buffer management is one of the control functions which are found in a multi-use environment. As indicated in the first section, these functions should be part of the operating system. If this is not possible, the implementor has to be very careful when designing these functions. In case a database with fixed length pages e.g. is not acceptable, buffer-management becomes less efficient and may not be worthwhile to implement at all.

A side-effect of the concept of buffer management is the fact that a page after it has been updated is not immediately re-written to the database. This has the advantage that several modifications can be made with only one physical write-event. However, this has some consequences for the integrity of the data-base, especially in case of a break down of the system. For this reason it could be necessary that the modified pages in the system buffers have to be re-written at specific points in time (check-points).

2.3 The Data Base itself

This is the most important and also most difficult problem area. Within
this area several aspects can be distinguished:

- Realms
- Records
- Sets

These will be discussed in the following subsections.

Realms:

The easiest way for an implementor to realize realms is to use the
existing file (dataset) concept of the standard software. It is probably
also the best way when realizing the purpose of the realm concept. In fact
there are a number of reasons for realms:

- the on/off line problem.

A database can be quite large, which makes it possible that the database
can not completely be on line. Therefore some kind of sub-division is
required by which it is possible to define which portions are to be on
line and which are not.

- the multi use problem.

Within a multi use environment it is necessary to offer some kind of
exclusive access mechanism. Exclusive access rights are always related to
a portion of data. It is clear that for performance reasons it is not
acceptable that such a portion consists of the whole database. Therefore
a subdivision is required.

- the recovery problem.

For recovery purposes it is necessary to make back up copies of the data
base. The frequency is depending on the update rate, which is not the same
for all parts of the database. Therefore a sub-division is required.

- the privacy problem.

For security reasons it could be necessary to use some kind of protection-
mechanism. However the level and kind of protection will not be the same
for all information in the database. Therefore a sub-division is required.

For all these reasons realms should be logical- as well as physical-
non overlapping storage-containers.

Since a realm in general will be too large to read in or to store as a
whole, it has to be divided in a number of physical blocks (or pages).
Still two problems remain to be solved, how to organize these pages and how
to map the database information into these realms.
The first problem can be solved in a simple and efficient way by using the
direct organization (relative recording mode) with fixed length pages.
The second problem will be discussed in the Record and Set subsections.

Records:

Although the record concept in the DBTG proposal is rather clear, there
is one problem associated with it, namely the DATABASE-KEY. The
specifications say that the database-key is the unique identifier of a
record within the database which will remain unchanged during the time the
record exists in the database.

The last part of the definition makes it practically impossible to use the physical address of the record in the database as the database key. This would imply that a record cannot be physically moved in the database, what in general will be a not acceptable restriction.

The alternative is some kind of symbolic value from which the physical address can be derived. A solution for this particular problem could be the following concept.

The database key is a symbolic value consisting of two parts; one being the identification of the record type of the record associated with the database key and the other a number sequentially assigned by the DBMS per record type. The DBMS maintains a table per record type in the database, where each table contains as many entries as there can be occurrences of the associated record type at a certain moment (the table should be extendible). Each entry is related to the database key with the record number equal to the entry number in the table. In case a database key is assigned to a record to be stored in the database the associated entry in the pertaining table is filled with the physical address of this record. In case of a deletion of a record this address is nulled.

This method serves two purposes, it realizes the transformation from symbolic value to physical address and it realizes an administration of those symbolic values which are in use and those which are free for use.

In fact these tables can be used for other purposes too, which will be discussed in the Set-subsection.

Within the Schema the user defines in what way a record has to be stored. Actually there are two possibilities; the record has to be stored somewhere in an realm or the record has to be stored at a specific place within a realm. In both cases the DBMS should maintain some kind of free space administration in order to know in which page a record can be stored. In the first situation the DBMS will use some algorithm to locate a suitable page. An obvious method is to inspect the pages, which are in the system buffer already, first. The second situation can be split in two cases, namely the case where the specific place is determined by hashing a user key (CALC-KEY) and the case where the specific place is determined by the position of records which are already stored in the database.

In the first case the DBMS has to solve the problems of duplicate user keys and duplicate hash-keys (results of the hashing). Herefore an adequate page-overflow mechanism has to be available.

The problems of the second case will be discussed in the Set-subsection.

Besides the fact that records have to be stored, they also have to be retrieved. This is done either sequentially using the set or realm concept or direct using a primary or secondary key. In all these cases use is made of the internal referencing scheme in which the database key is used for identification purposes. The database key as defined in this presentation has a distinct disadvantage namely the indirection of the 'transformation tables', which doubles the number of logical accesses to the database.

To increase the performance the internal referencing scheme should be changed in such a way that to each database key in this scheme is added the physical address of the associated record. The physical address consists of a realm identification and a page-number.

In case the physical position of a record is changed it is not necessary to update the complete referencing scheme. It is sufficient to update the associate table entry. When the DBMS is using the referencing scheme after such a modification it will not find the record at the indicated place. Now the DBMS should use the correct table entry to update the pertaining part of the referencing scheme. Also a special utility can be run to check the internal referencing scheme and eventually update it.

The solutions indicated in this section are not the only ones. It is possible e.g. to store the records themselves into the transformation table-entry, instead of their physical addresses. The table should be mapped into the realms in such a way that not-occupied entries do not take any real space. Here also some form of indirection appears. Besides it is practically impossible to support a real physical-sequential organization, as is required in maintaining index tables and list-processing.

Sets:

The set concept is one of the corner stones of the Codasyl DBTG proposal. Before discussing the implementational aspects it is necessary to define what a set is. Very often a set is defined as the definition of a relationship among records. Although this is true this definition is not complete. A better definition is:

'A set is the definition of an access-path through a number of related records'.

There may be a great number of relations between records in the database for which the user does not want to specify an access-path. The creation and maintenance of an access path is a rather costly affair, therefore such access-paths should only be declared for the frequently used relationships. Basicly a set can be implemented in two ways which are usually called:

- pointer sequential and

- physical sequential.

Each of these methods can be further divided in two sub-methods, where the difference is that in one method the data associated with a record is stored at the referenced point and in the other the data is stored at a different place and the referenced point contains only a pointer to the data. The following picture shows these four different methods.

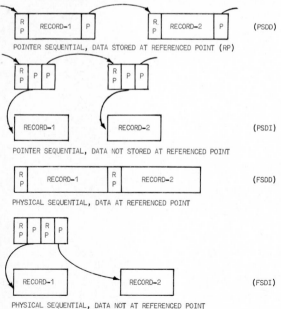

POINTER SEQUENTIAL, DATA STORED AT REFERENCED POINT (RP)   (PSDD)

POINTER SEQUENTIAL, DATA NOT STORED AT REFERENCED POINT   (PSDI)

PHYSICAL SEQUENTIAL, DATA AT REFERENCED POINT   (FSDD)

PHYSICAL SEQUENTIAL, DATA NOT AT REFERENCED POINT   (FSDI)

Method 1 is usually known as the chaining technique.
Method 2 is in fact only a theoretical possibility which is only used in
an environment where a strict separation of user- and system data is
required.
Method 3 is generally known as the list technique and is most useful in case
records are frequently processed in a sequential way. This technique could
also be employed to replace the OCCURS (DEPENDING ON) facility in record
descriptions.
Method 4 is often called the pointer array technique.

These four methods should be seen as the basic methods to which
refinements can be made such as:

- bidirectional chains

- linked to owner option

- attached to owner for lists and pointer-arrays.

From these four methods it appears that besides records also tables
have to be stored into the database.
Examples of tables to be stored are

- pointer-arrays

- index-tables for searchkeys

- record lists.

The difficulty with these types of tables is that first of all the number
of entries is not fixed and second that a new entry has to be inserted in
between already existing entries. Since the type of tables is identical
the implementor will develop one table handling concept. A possible solution
is the so called dynamic-levelled-index-table concept. In this concept
a table starts with zero entries and grows when entries are inserted till
the boundary of a page is reached. At this point in time an additional page
is required to contain the table at the main-level. In addition a level is
added to the table containing two entries pointing to the two pages at the
main level. For each page added to the table at the main level an entry is
inserted at the first index level. This process continues till the first
index-level hits the page boundaries. Now at this level a page is to be
added and a new index-level is added to the table, etc. For adding a page
at a certain level some kind of split-technique is required. A method could
be the technique where contents of the page which appears to be full is
split in two parts and divided over the original and the new page. This
method, although rather easy to implement has the disadvantage that after
some time a rather bad filling rate is obtained (something like 55%), which
not only cost a lot of extra storage space, but also results in more
physical I/O events.
Actually this method is a specific case of a much more general concept
where the search for space for an entry to be inserted is not restricted
to one page but is extended to n pages (around the page where the insertion
point is situated). If no space can be found a page is added and the
contents of the n pages is now divided over n+1 pages.
For n=1 the first method is obtained. It will be clear that the amount of
work to be done by the DBMS increases with the increase of n. It is also
obviously that the filling rate becomes better if n increases. This method,
in fact, is a dynamic reorganization tool which makes it unnecessary to
reorganize off-line. If n is a user parameter the user can make the trade
off between loss at update time and gain at retrieve time.

Finally, in the Record subsection it was stated that the
'transformation-tables' could also serve other purposes. Two will be
mentioned here.
In case a record is defined as owner in one or more sets there is a
possibility that there are a number of tables associated with this record,
e.g. pointer-arrays and index-tables for search-keys. These tables must be
allocatable via the owner record. Normally the pointers to these tables will
be attached to the owner record as system-data, just as next- and prior-
pointers in a chain. However, it is very well possible to attach these
pointers to the associated entry in the transformation-table. In this way
a clear separation of user- and system data is possible.
The second purpose for which the 'transformation-table' could be used is to
implement a special type of set.
In the last two years quite some attention has been paid to the relational
approach of Mr. Codd and others.
The main difference between the relational approach and the DBTG proposal
is the fact that within the relational approach access-paths should not be
predefined (static) but in a much more flexible way at run-time. Herefore
a number of functions are required called the alpha-language. Within the
relational approach one basic type of set could be distinguished, namely
for each record-type there is a singular set (OWNER IS SYSTEM) with the
ORDER IS IMMATERIAL and the MEMBER IS MANDATORY AUTOMATIC options. If
necessary SEARCH KEY clauses can be added.
The member records should be in third normal form. The earlier mentioned
'transformation-tables' can be used to realize these types of sets.
A database structured in such a way could very well be the basis for a
relational database management system. Even more, apparently it is possible
to combine the two approaches into one DBMS.

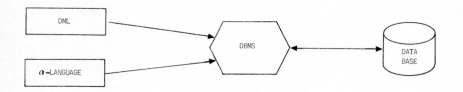

All what has to be done is to define and implement an alpha-language
interpretor and to extend the DBMS function which the typical set operation
function. The two concepts do not hurt each other or cause any
inconsistencies if applied carefully.

2.4 Object Schema and Sub-schema

Within a DBMS which is designed to offer a maximum of data independency, it is of vital importance that the information, which describe the user-, data- and storage-structure aspects of the data base, is available and accessible at run time in a very efficient way.
This information has to be interpreted at run time and may be 50% of the total amount of required CPU time is used for this purpose.
It is possible to keep this information in core using the standard buffer management concept. However, this will still cost some extra time consuming indirection. Therefore a construction is required where this information is directly available to the DBMS. The information could be read in at run-unit initialization time, unless some other run-unit has already made the required information available. The information remains available till the run-unit is terminated, unless it is still required by other active run-units.
The situation in diagram 1 represents a different view. It is not explained why it is done in this way, and what the reason was for the only actual change in diagram 1 of the '71 to the '73 report.

DISCUSSION

Abrial: 1) When you re-use a data-base key of a deleted record don't you get a lot of problems with cleaning all the pointers associated with the earlier records?

2) You didn't talk about memory management problem?

Schenk: We do not delay the deletion of the pointers but do it immediately. The block index (which we have in each page) and the pointers are updated at once. The table concept could very well be used as a mechanism for delayed updating.

Taylor: Have you done any experiments with page size?

Schenk: Yes. Page size is the same for the whole data-base. This size can be controlled by means of a parameter setting. The efficient size depends on such things as the number of logical records. Size of logical records etc.. We tried to develop a formula over these variable, to compute the optimum size but this turned out not to be suitable. We usually recommend from 2000 to 3000 characters. This will be 2 or 3 pages per disc trade.

LIST OF PARTICIPANTS

ABRIAL, Jean-Raymond
        Université Scientifique et Médicale de Grenoble
        Laboratoire d'Informatique
        B.P. 53 Centre de Tri
        38041 Grenoble Cedex
        France

BAYER, Rudolf
        Technische Universität München
        Mathematisches Institut
        Barer Strasse 23
        8000 München 2
        Germany

BOUSSARD, Jean-Claude
        Université de Nice
        Laboratoire d'Informatique
        06034 Nice Cedex
        France

BRACCHI, Giampio
        Politecnico di Milano
        Istituto Di Elettrotecnica Ed Elettronica
        Piazza L. Da Vinci 32
        20133 Milano
        Italy

BUXTON, John
        Warwick University
        School of Computer Science
        Coventry CV4 7AL
        Warwickshire
        England

CODD, Edgar
   I.B.M.
   Monterey & Cottle Roads
   K 51/282
   San Jose CA 95193
   U.S.A.

DATE, Christopher
   I.B.M.
   Hursley House
   Hursley Park
   Winchester Hampshire
   England

DEARNLY, Peter
   University of East Anglia
   School of Computing Studies
   Norwich
   England

DELOBEL, Claude
   Université de Grenoble
   Département Mathématiques - Informatique
   B.P. 53 Centre de Tri
   38041 Grenoble Cedex
   France

DÖMÖLKI, Balink
   Infelor Systems Engineering Institut
   H-1281, P.O. Box 10
   Budapest
   Hungary

DOUQUÉ, Bodo
   Philips Electrologica B.V.
   Post Box 245
   Apeldoorn
   Netherlands

DURCHHOLZ, Reiner
      Gesellschaft für Mathematik und Datenverarbeitung m.b.H.
      Bonn (GMD)
      Schloss Birlinghoven
      Postfach 1240
      5205 St. Augustin 1
      Germany

EVEREST, Gordon C.
      University of Minnesota
      Graduate School of Business Administration
      Management Information Systems Research Center
      Minneapolis Minnesota 55455
      U.S.A.

FALKENBERG, Eckhard
      Universität Stuttgart
      Herdweg 51
      7 Stuttgart 1
      Germany

GAUTHIER-VILLARS, Gilles
      C.I.I.
      68, Route de Versailles
      78430 Louveciennes
      France

GROTENHUIS, Frans
      Philips N.V.
      Dept. ISA-AS
      Boschdijk - Building VN3
      Eindhoven
      Netherlands

HAGERTH, Steven
      Firemans' Fund American
      3333 California Street
      San Francisco California 94119
      U.S.A.

HUTT, Andrew
          University of Southampton
          Dept. of Mathematics
          The University Highfields
          Southampton
          England

JACOLIN, Michel
          I.B.M. France
          B.P. 247 Centre de Tri
          38043 Grenoble
          France

JARDINE, Don
          Queen's University
          Dept. of Computing & Information Services
          Goodwin Hall
          Kingston Ontario
          Canada

KING, Frank
          I.B.M. Research
          Monterey & Cottle Roads
          San Jose CA 95114
          U.S.A.

KIRSHENBAUM, Frank
          The Equitable Life Assurance Society
          1285 Avenue of Americas (9-J)
          New York NY 10019
          U.S.A.

KLIMBIE, Jan
          Philips Nederland B.V.
          Building VBe
          Eindhoven
          Netherlands

KOFFEMAN, Klaas
        Philips N.V.
        ISA-DSA Boschdijk
        Building VN5
        Eindhoven
        Netherlands

LANGEFORS, Börje
        University of Stockholm
        Dept. Adm. Information Processing
        Fack
        S-10405 Stockholm
        Sweden

LEHOT, Philippe
        University of California-Berkeley F.F.A.
        976 Longridge Road
        Oakland CA 94610
        U.S.A.

LUCKING, James
        International Computers Limited
        West Avenue Kidsgrove
        Stoke-on-Trent
        ST 7 1 TL
        England

MAMAN, Prosper
        C.N.R.O.
        Parc St. Véran
        06803 Cagnes/Mer
        France

MARX, Gary
        I.B.M.
        1501 California Ave.
        Palo Alto California 94304
        U.S.A.

McGEE, William
          I.B.M.
          1501 California Ave.
          Palo Alto California 94304
          U.S.A.

NEUHOLD, Erich
          Universität Stuttgart
          Institut für Informatik
          Herdweg 51
          7 Stuttgart 1
          Germany

NIJSSEN, Sjir
          Control Data Europe
          46 Avenue des Arts
          Bruxelles
          Belgium

NORDLING, Jan
          Swedisch Cellulose Company
          85188 Sundsvall
          Sweden

OLLE, T. William
          27 Blackwood Close
          West Byfleet, Surrey
          KT14 6PP
          England

PAIR, Claude
          Université de Nancy
          I.U.C.A.
          Château Du Montet
          Avenue Général Leclerc
          54500 Vandoeuvre-Les-Nancy
          France

PAOLINI, Paolo
          Politecnico Di Milano
          Istituto Di Elettrotecnica ed
          Elettronica Di Milano
          Piazza L. Da Vinci 32
          20133 Milano
          Italy

PECK, John E.L.
          University of British Columbia
          Dept. of Computer Science
          Vancouver 8, B.C.
          Canada

PETEUL, Bernard
          I.B.M.
          Service 2452
          Tour Septentrion Cedex no. 9
          92081 Paris La Défense
          France

PRUTCH, Shirley (Mrs.)
          Martin Marietta Data Systems
          400 Continental National Bank Building
          Englewood Colorado 80110
          U.S.A.

RAMEBACK, Jan
          Saab-Scania
          Sturegatan 1
          Linköping
          Sweden

REMMEN, Frans
          Technological University
          Mathematics department
          Computing Service Group
          Eindhoven
          Netherlands

RETHFELD, Ulrich
        Siemens AG
        Hoffman Strasse 51
        München
        Germany

RICHTER, Gernot
        Gesellschaft für Mathematik und Datenverarbeitung m.b.H.
        Bonn (GMD)
        Schloss Birlinghoven
        Postfach 1240
        5205 St. Augustin 1
        Germany

SCHENK, Johan
        Philips Electrologica B.V.
        Postbus 245
        Apeldoorn
        Netherlands

SCHNEIDER, Hans Jochen
        University of Stuttgart
        Institut für Informatik
        Herdweg 51
        7 Stuttgart 1
        Germany

SCHUSTER, Stewart
        University of Toronto
        Department of Computer Science
        Toronto M5 S 1 A7
        Canada

SÖDERSTRÖM, Peter
        Statskonsult
        Box 4040
        17104 - Solna
        Sweden

STACEY, Geoff
Edinburgh Regional Computing Centre
King's Buildings
Mayfield Rd.
Edinburgh
Scotland

STEMPLE, David
University of Massachusetts
University Computing Center
Amherst
Massachusetts 01002
U.S.A.

STEEL, Thomas
The Equitable Life Assurance Society
1285 Avenue of Americas (9-J)
New York NY 10019
U.S.A.

STOCKER, Peter
University of East Anglia
School of Computing Studies
Norwich
England

SUNDGREN, Bo
Statistiska Centralbyrån (SCB)
Fack
10250 Stockholm
Sweden

TAYLOR, Robert
University of Massachusetts
Computer Science Dept.
Graduate Research Center
Amherst
Massachusetts 01002
U.S.A.

TITMAN, Peter
         I.B.M.
         United Kingdom Laboratories Ltd.
         Hursley Park
         Winchester Hampshire SO21 2 JN
         England

TSICHRITZIS, Dennis
         University of Toronto
         Dept. of Computer Science
         Toronto M5 S 1 A7
         Canada

WALK, Kurt
         I.B.M. Laboratory Vienna
         Parkring 10
         A 1010, Vienna
         Austria

WATSON, Harry
         Shell Internationale Petroleum MIJ. B.V.
         Afdeling ICH/2
         Carel van Bylandlaan 30, Postbus 162
         The Hague
         Netherlands

WIEDERHOLD, Gio
         University of California, San Francisco
         155 Marine Road
         Woodside California
         U.S.A.

WODON, Pierre
         M.B.L.E.
         Avenue Van Becelaere 2
         1170 Bruxelles
         Belgium

ZONDERLAND, Theo
        I.B.M. Nederland
        P.O. Box 9999
        Amsterdam
        Netherlands

GUEST

GENUYS, François
        Chairman AFCET
        France